Communication

FIFTH EDITION
Communication

Larry L. Barker
AUBURN UNIVERSITY

Prentice Hall, Englewood Cliffs, New Jersey 07632

Library of Congress Cataloging-in-Publication Data

Barker, Larry Lee
    Communication / Larry L. Barker. -- 5th ed.
        p.   cm.
    Includes bibliographical references.
    ISBN 0-13-168535-X
    1. Communication.   I. Title.
P90.B296 1990
302.2--dc20   89-37807
                                                      CIP

Editorial/production supervision: Joe Scordato
Interior design: Christine Gehring-Wolf
Cover design: Bruce Kenselaar
Cover art: *On the Promenade*, August Macke (1887–1914). German
                Photography from Super Stock
Photo research: Kay Dellosa
Photo editor: Lori Morris-Nantz
Manufacturing buyer: Ed O'Dougherty

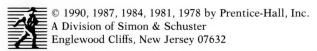

© 1990, 1987, 1984, 1981, 1978 by Prentice-Hall, Inc.
A Division of Simon & Schuster
Englewood Cliffs, New Jersey 07632

Printed in the United States of America
10 9 8 7 6 5 4 3 2 1

ISBN 0-13-168535-X

Prentice-Hall International (UK) Limited, *London*
Prentice-Hall of Australia Pty. Limited, *Sydney*
Prentice-Hall Canada Inc., *Toronto*
Prentice-Hall Hispanoamericana, S.A., *Mexico*
Prentice-Hall of India Private Limited, *New Delhi*
Prentice-Hall of Japan, Inc., *Tokyo*
Simon & Schuster Asia Pte. Ltd., *Singapore*
Editora Prentice-Hall do Brasil, Ltda., *Rio de Janeiro*

Contents

PART 3   PUBLIC COMMUNICATION

Preface

The word "communication" literally means "to share." This text focuses on the sharing of ideas, feelings and concepts across different levels of human interactions. Beginning with internal or intrapersonal communication, the communication process is discussed through increasingly complex communication levels involving dyads, groups, organizations, large audiences and mass media. Research and personal experience demonstrate that communication can be improved at all levels through increased effort, knowledge, practice and understanding.

Communication, 5th edition, provides information, examples and exercises that can make you more effective as a communicator. The text, in conjunction with a course in speech or communication, provides a basis for substantial improvement of basic communication skills. The book focuses on the total range of communication settings we may be involved in on a daily basis—from formal to informal, and from public to private.

Previous editions of **Communication** contained several features that appealed to a substantial number of its users. These included: (1) a complete "minitext" in public speaking within the larger comprehensive text; (2) an extensive chapter on intrapersonal communication; (3) a major emphasis on nonverbal communication throughout the text, accompanied by a fully developed chapter on nonverbal behaviors; (4) emphasis on receiver-oriented communication reflected by a complete chapter on listening; (5) an integrated set of chapters focused on interpersonal and relational communication; and (6) an emphasis on applied communication represented by a complete chapter on organizational communication. All these features have been retained in the 5th edition, and several new features have been added. These include:

1. An extensive revision of Chapter 6, *Interpersonal Communication*. The expanded chapter includes several new sections with increased emphasis on relational communication.

2. An expansion and revision of Chapter 7, *Small Group Communication*, including practical examples of small group communication in "action."

3. Substantial revision and updating of other chapters in this edition, including Chapter 1, *A Look at Human Communication*, Chapter 3, *Listening and Feedback*, Chapter 9, *Ethics, Intentions, and the Speaker-Audience Relationship*, and Chapter 13, *Communication Through the Mass Media*.

4. An updated *Bibliography* of all references, placed at the end of the text.

5. An expanded and revised *Glossary of Terms*, coded to boldface type within each chapter in the text.

6. New Chapter opening examples and illustrations in each chapter.

7. A completely revised instructors' manual. The new manual contains numerous instructional aids as well as class tested item-analyzed examination questions to help instructors prepare tests and quizzes on the text material.

In addition to the new features noted above, the 5th edition also includes: (1) numerous visual examples and illustrations, including new photographs, cartoons and drawings; (2) a new text design for reading ease and increased student interest; (3) key concepts and terms at the beginning of chapters to help students identify the most important concepts covered; and (4) complete summaries, activities, discussion questions and exercises at the end of each chapter.

ACKNOWLEDGMENTS

By the time a book has gone through five editions, the number of people who have contributed to its success are many. Any attempt to acknowledge all those contributors completely and appropriately is bound to be incomplete. However, I do want to express my sincere thanks and appreciation to all those at Prentice Hall who contributed to the development, creation, and refinement of this and previous editions. Special thanks go to Steve Dalphin and Joe Scordato for their contributions to the 5th edition.

I owe a debt of gratitude to two individuals who contributed significantly to the content and revision of this and previous editions. Kittie Watson screened and carefully worked with the entire manuscript for the 2nd edition of **Communication.** In addition, she wrote original drafts for earlier versions of *A Look at Human Communication* and *Organizational Communication.* Deborah Barker served as editoral assistant and contributor to the 3rd, 4th, and 5th editions of this text. She tirelessly combed the manuscript to update research, provide relevant examples, and make the text more readable and accurate. The time, energy, and dedication of both these friends and colleagues is greatly appreciated.

In addition, several of my friends and students (not mutually exclusive categories) helped with research and development of individual chapters in previous editions. Special thanks to Renee Edwards, Loretta Malandro, Janice Lumpkin, Frances Sayers, Ginger Tubbs, Debbie Smith, Cheryl Fisher, Karen Harris, and Sondi Feldmaier. Bob Kibler, Wini Vallely, John Stone, John Garrison, Charles Roberts, Karl Krayer, Kathy Wahlers, and Mary Helen Brown also provided special assistance on the project. Mary Etta Cook of Belmont College, Mary Helen Brown of Auburn University, and Charles Roberts of McNeese State University served as reviewers for this 5th edition. Teachers who used previous editions of the text also were especially helpful in providing feedback from their classes.

Special thanks go to Frank E. X. Dance for his unique contributions to this text, particularly in the first edition. Frank was inadvertently omitted from the acknowledgments in the first edition, and to add insult to injury, his name was misspelled in the second. Thanks also to my students during the past two years who were patient with me while I worked on this revision, and to students over the past 21 years who helped provide examples and insights.

I hope that this 5th edition of **Communication** will continue to serve the needs of previous users, and grow to serve the needs of those teachers who have not used previous editions. I welcome letters, cards, or calls concerning specific items in the text that you like or dislike, as well as suggestions for improvement in future editions.

L. L. B., Professor
Department of Communication
Auburn University, AL 36849

1

A Look at Human Communication

KEY CONCEPTS AND TERMS

Communication
Verbal communication
Language
Nonverbal communication
Oral communication
Written communication
Formal communication
Informal communication
Intentional communication
Unintentional communication
Source
Encode
Message
Symbol

Channel
Receiver
Decode
Feedback
Negative feedback
Positive feedback
Ambiguous feedback
Barriers
Intrapersonal communication
Interpersonal communication
Small group communication
Public communication
Organizational communication
Mass communication

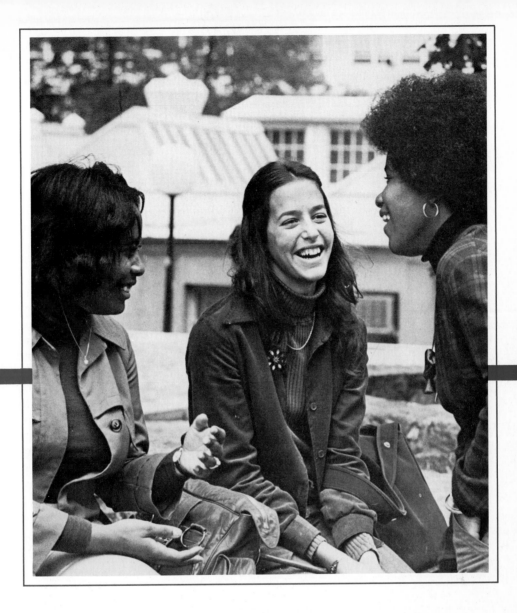

WHY STUDY HUMAN COMMUNICATION?

Recently over 2,000 executives from top American companies and businesses were surveyed regarding the dimensions of corporate success. Out of that study, one very startling finding emerged. On the average, two-thirds of these executives agreed that 70 percent of graduates from colleges and universities today are unable to communicate adequately—including MBAs from some of the finest institutions in the country. Specifically, the majority of these executives agreed that:

1

- 60 to 70 percent of students who graduate from American institutions of higher learning are unable to write well-constructed sentences;
- close to 80 or 90 percent of graduates from these schools need instruction on how to write a simple business report; and
- less than 20 percent are capable of presenting a concise, clear oral report.

In fact, several top executives reported that the problem has become so far-reaching that their respective companies have set up remedial communication courses for their up-and-coming executives (Molloy, 1985). Others are spending millions of dollars each year on communication training for their executives and managers and are sending their engineers and technicians back to college to improve their communications skills.

Although these statistics, indeed, are frightening, the fact that you are reading this book and are probably enrolled in a speech communication course right now suggests that you are aware of the importance of maximizing your communication skills. It is hoped that the previously quoted statistics will underscore the importance of these skills and serve as a reminder of their salience throughout your readings.

To help you achieve your fullest potential as a communicator, this text is designed to provide you with the most current information on human communication theory and research available. Additionally, we will present a number of basic communication principles in each chapter to aid you in mastering a variety of social settings and interactions. By increasing your knowledge and understanding of basic communication principles, we hope to accomplish our primary aim: to help you become a more effective and *successful* communicator.

So before you close this book and reenter the fast-paced, ever-changing world of compact discs, satellites, and high-speed computers, take some time to acquaint yourself with the study of human communication. By doing so, you may avoid becoming "just another statistic."

Communication Inventory

Before reading further, take a few minutes to complete the Communication Inventory on the next page. Use each question to assess your current level of satisfaction regarding your communication behavior.

If you are honest with yourself in answering these questions, you can begin to determine more fully how well you communicate. In addition, by establishing specific communication goals—both here and throughout your readings—you can gauge your progress in these areas along the way. Examples of specific goals that you might have identified include: "I want to be able to organize an oral presentation more effectively" or "I want to be able to express my feelings more completely to my loved ones." Having completed this preliminary assessment, we are now ready to embark on your "pursuit of excellence." Let's first begin with a working definition of communication.

Communication Inventory

1. Circle the response that best represents the degree to which you are comfortable in the following communication settings:

C = Comfortable
SC = Somewhat Comfortable
N = Neutral
SU = Somewhat Uncomfortable
U = Uncomfortable

	C	SC	N	SU	U
a. Asking someone for a lunch date	5	4	3	2	1
b. Facilitating a group discussion	5	4	3	2	1
c. Preparing a written report	5	4	3	2	1
d. Discussing a problem with your boss	5	4	3	2	1
e. Giving an oral presentation	5	4	3	2	1
f. Listening to difficult material	5	4	3	2	1

2. How would you rate your *effectiveness* in each of the following communication settings?

E = Effective
SE = Somewhat Effective
DK = Don't Know
SI = Somewhat Ineffective
I = Ineffective

	E	SE	DK	SI	I
a. Leading a discussion	5	4	3	2	1
b. Promoting yourself to others	5	4	3	2	1
c. Managing difficult people	5	4	3	2	1
d. Creating small talk	5	4	3	2	1
e. Interpreting others' nonverbal behavior	5	4	3	2	1
f. Group problem solving	5	4	3	2	1

3. In which of the following areas do you feel that you could improve? (Place an X beside each response that is appropriate.)

_____ Developing satisfying relationships
_____ Giving dynamic oral presentations
_____ Writing effective reports
_____ Listening responsively
_____ Giving effective feedback to others
_____ Solving complex group problems
_____ Reading nonverbal cues effectively

4. Finally, complete the following sentence by listing three specific goals that you would like to achieve once you have completed studying this text.

Upon finishing this text/course in communication, I want to be able to:

a. _____

b. _____

c. _____

Defining Communication

If you were asked to define "communication" during an important job interview, where would you begin? You might mention a speaker, a listener, sharing of information, transmission of symbols, or a variety of other descriptive terms. However, as you try to define this concept more completely, you may have problems in choosing the right words to express your ideas. You may also find it difficult to answer related questions that the interviewer might ask. The problem is that defining communication is akin to defining the concept of love. Intuitively, we feel we understand it, but it's difficult to put into words.

Interestingly enough, communication experts have never agreed on a single definition of communication. The reason is that it all depends on your perspective. For our purposes, we will define **communication** as a process in which interrelated elements work together to achieve a desired outcome or goal. Because we view communication as a process, we also perceive it to be dynamic, ever-changing, and unending. In other words, the conversation that you had with a friend yesterday affects you as a communicator today. Additionally, the hundreds of bits of information, ideas, and opinions that you process, evaluate, and store each day also change you to some extent. By tomorrow, you will have changed even more. Fortunately, this process is usually slow and subtle. Otherwise you might be in a constant state of confusion and frustration.

Another important key to understanding communication is to realize that communication events do not occur in isolation from one another. Each interaction that you have affects each one that follows, and not always in a simple, direct manner. For example, your girlfriend (or spouse) tells you without warning that she is seeing someone else. This "bombshell" may result in your lashing out at a friend or co-worker later that day when he reminds you of a project deadline that you must meet. The next day you are both less able to communicate effectively with one another because of your preoccupation with the previous day's communication experiences—and the process continues.

SELECTED PERSPECTIVES ON HUMAN COMMUNICATION

As you can see, communication is more than one person speaking and another person listening. This section will explain some of the complexities of communication by looking at the dimensions of verbal and nonverbal, oral and written, formal and informal, and intentional and unintentional communication. In addition, we will discuss two indirectly related dimensions—human-computer and animal communication. Finally, we will conclude the chapter with an examination of the basic elements of the communication process and with a look at six primary communication contexts.

Verbal and Nonverbal Communication

When we think of communication, we usually think of spoken messages. However, experts usually divide communication into two primary categories: verbal and nonverbal communication. **Verbal communication** involves the use of symbols that generally have universal meanings for all who are taking part in the process. As such, verbal communication may be spoken or written. These spoken or written verbal symbols are known as *language*. Additionally, verbal communication is highly structured and uses formal rules of grammar. (Chapter 2 covers language in detail.) **Nonverbal communication** involves the use of symbols other than the written or spoken word, such as gestures, eye behavior, tone of voice, use of space, and touch. Although nonverbal symbols have socially shared meanings, they have no formal structure or rules of grammar. (Chapter 4 is devoted solely to nonverbal communication.)

Nonverbal messages usually complement verbal messages. A service-station attendant usually points and uses other gestures while giving direc-

Man-machine communication has become a necessity of everyday life.

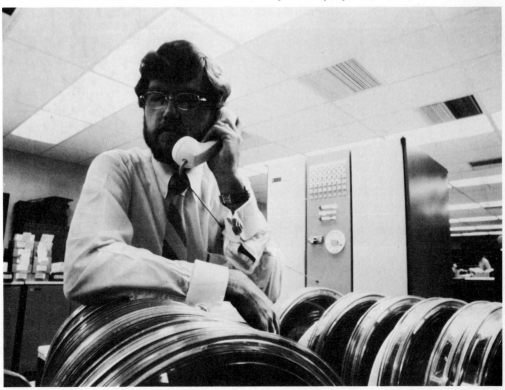

tions to a stranger from out of town. At other times, nonverbal symbols completely replace verbal messages. Teachers with cold, fixed stares can easily tell students to be quiet without uttering a word. It is important to note that when nonverbal messages contradict what you say verbally, others usually believe the nonverbal message. For example, when a husband tells his wife verbally that he is interested in hearing about what happened at a political rally as he continues to read the newspaper, he nonverbally communicates disinterest.

Oral and Written Communication

You probably already know many of the differences between oral and written communication. *Oral communication* refers to messages that are transmitted "out loud" from one person to another. Most messages are verbal, with complementary nonverbal messages. Each day we participate in oral communication either as speakers or as listeners when we answer the telephone, listen to a lecture, watch MTV, or turn on a compact disc player.

Written communication is taking place right now as you read this book. *Written communication* is primarily verbal, but nonverbal characteristics can affect written messages. We get a different feeling when we receive a personal, handwritten Christmas card than when we receive a mass-produced, printed one from an insurance company. Oral and written communications serve different purposes and are used both independently and in combination. Written reports or term papers use a formal style, while oral reports are usually more conversational with more informal language. Many television commercials use written reinforcement of an oral message when stressing the effectiveness of a new cold capsule, and a typed résumé presents an applicant more professionally than does a handwritten one.

Formal and Informal Communication

We have all been involved in formal and informal communication situations. In *formal communication*, such as public speaking or mass communication, we pay more attention to both verbal and nonverbal messages. Language use is more precise, with careful attention to grammar. People are more concerned with items such as dress, posture, or eye contact. Formal communication is also used with persons of higher perceived status. For example, during an appointment with a university dean, a student would probably avoid the use of slang, would sit up straight, dress neatly, and make eye contact.

In *informal communication*, such as interpersonal and small-group communication, people are more at ease and can be themselves. Observers would notice more hesitations and slang in verbal messages and less attention to nonverbal messages such as clothing, posture, and eye contact. When going to a party at a friend's house, you probably wouldn't hesitate to sit on the floor, go to the refrigerator for something to eat, or use the telephone. At a party at your boss's house, however, you probably would be hesitant to sit on the floor, go to the kitchen, or use the phone without asking permission.

Intentional and Unintentional Communication

Most communication has a purpose, but sometimes we take part in communication without realizing it. *Intentional communication* occurs when messages are sent with specific goals in mind. Comedians, such as Roseanne Barr, tell jokes to get laughs and entertain audiences. Radio spots are designed

Patty Hearst before her trial.

Patty Hearst in 1988.

to persuade people to vote for local candidates, buy products, or donate time and money.

Other communication takes place **unintentionally**, without the communicator's being aware of it. The greatest number of unintentional messages are nonverbal. Our nonverbal behaviors often speak louder than words. Students or employees who are continually late for class or work might be communicating that they are moonlighting, are irresponsible, or have unreliable alarm clocks.

Intentional communication is sometimes made to appear unintentional. Many lawyers tell their clients how to dress for the courtroom. For example, during her now classic robbery trial, wealthy socialite Patricia Hearst wore conservative, old clothing, which included a large, loosely fitted blouse, under the instruction of her attorney, F. Lee Bailey. The old clothing was used to de-emphasize the fact that she was wealthy, and the large blouse was used to give the impression of weight loss to arouse sympathy among the jurors.

Additional Communication Forms

Two additional forms of communication that are rapidly becoming of interest to communication scholars are human-computer and animal communication. Indeed, studies of humans and their relationship to computers are of growing concern, given the magnitude of recent advances in computer technology. Studies of animals are and have been important since the dawning of time.

HUMAN-COMPUTER COMMUNICATION.   The growth of human knowledge has escalated beyond belief in modern times. Information that was once conveyed verbally through stories and myths in ancient times is now transmitted through high-tech media such as image retrieval and laser-disc systems. Satellite communication, once a novelty, is now a well-established medium. Once a luxury, personal computers have become a necessity in the average American home. In short, computer technology has established its preeminence in this age of information. What remains to be seen is its impact on future generations.

Although a number of questions may be raised regarding the ultimate impact and effectiveness of various technologies, communication scholars are becoming especially interested in the effects of technology on human communication. For example, to what extent does computer-mediated communication depersonalize interactions and cause a loss of individualization? What effects do computerized conferences have on the group decision-making process? To what extent does computer mediation reduce /increase communication efficiency? Each of these questions ultimately will be addressed by communication scholars in coming years. We, too, will address them more completely in Chapter 13.

ANIMAL COMMUNICATION.   Although the study of animal communication has played a vital role in our understanding of human communication ever since the dawning of time, recent research in this area has revealed a number of striking similarities between animal and human communication. Specifically, researchers have discovered that animals share with humans a number of characteristics, including those associated with attraction and mating, territoriality, rivalry and play, familial ties, colony organization, division of labor, and a number of other traits that we once assumed were uniquely "human."

For example, like humans, chimpanzees use different nonverbal behaviors when greeting young chimps versus older ones: They greet younger chimps by protruding their lips and older chimps with a broad grin. Much as humans use different paralinguistic (vocal) cues when in the company of strangers versus "intimates," spider monkeys use specialized vocalizations for intimate within-group communication, including special sounds, gestures, and facial expressions. Another similarity between animals and humans lies in the dolphin's ability to avoid dangerous situations. So intelligent are dolphins, they can determine which boats to avoid by "remembering" bad past experiences and by discerning any similarities in approaching boats or ships. In turn, they can signal this information to other dolphins who are swimming nearby.

In short, like humans, animals use a wide variety of communication processes ranging from auditory, visual, and tactile systems to olfactory, thermal, and electrical systems. The primary difference between the two forms of communication seems to lie in humans' ability to use words or symbols—and to string them together into sentences that can build and present abstract ideas or that can tell a story about the past, present, or future. However, as researchers delve more deeply into questions regarding the communication systems of animals, new discoveries regarding their "language patterns" will emerge. Given the vast number of similarities that already have come to light between animal and human communication, it is certain that human communication scholars will be watching.

BASIC ELEMENTS OF THE COMMUNICATION PROCESS

Thus far in your reading you may have formed the impression that communication must be difficult, if not impossible, to study and understand. If it is ongoing, how do we stop it? If it has no beginning or end, how do we get hold of it? Although the task is not easy, it is not impossible. The communication process is a system that involves an interrelated, interdependent group of elements working together as a whole to achieve a desired outcome or goal. We can study communication in much the same way we study biological systems within our own bodies. We can determine the elements involved (circulatory and digestive systems, for example), analyze how those elements affect one another, and thus determine the nature of the process as a whole.

Applying this approach to the communication process, we find seven elements: (1) a source/encoder of communication, which sends (2) a message (3) through a channel(s) to (4) a receiver/decoder, which (5) responds via feedback with (6) possibilities of communication breakdowns in each stage

Figure 1–1
The Communication Process

of communication. However, none of these elements is meaningful outside of (7) a situation or context in which it may be interpreted. Figure 1–1 gives us a visual representation of the communication process.

The Source/Encoder

The *source*, or encoder, makes the decision to communicate. The source also determines what the purpose of the message will be to: inform, persuade, or entertain. You may ask how the message gets from the source to the receiver. First, the source must *encode*, or create, a message. That is, the information that the source wishes to convey must be put into a form that can be sent to the receiver. The source generates a message through his or her past experiences, perceptions, thoughts, and feelings. Every ounce of your being may tell you that you are in love, but until you code those feelings into a form that can be transmitted to the person you love, communication cannot take place.

Message

The second element of the communication process is the *message*, or that information which is being communicated. The source encodes an idea and then determines whether or not he or she wants to inform, persuade, or entertain. After deciding what message will be transmitted, the source uses symbols to get the message across to others. These *symbols* stand for other things. The eagle, the flag, and Uncle Sam are all symbols of the United States, for example. But the most important symbols are words, which can represent objects, ideas, and feelings. These words permit us to share our thoughts with other members of our species. Important as words are to us, they can be tricky. We must remember that words are symbols. They represent things, but are not the things themselves. That lanky, bearded old man we call Uncle Sam represents the United States, but he is *not* the United States— in fact, he doesn't even exist. The letters *a-p-p-l-e p-i-e* represent an all-American pastry, but they are *not* an apple pie.

   To increase the likelihood of successful communication, the source must try to encode in a way that the receiver understands, so that the receiver can properly decode (interpret) the message. For example, many American tourists in Paris have discovered that even though their command of French is minimal, it is sometimes easier to communicate in halting French than in English. Some Parisians, despite their fluent knowledge of English, refuse to decode an "inferior" tongue.

Channel

Channels are the means (that is, pathways or devices) by which messages are communicated. Channels may be described and analyzed in two different ways. The first involves the form in which messages are transmitted to receivers. Forms include both verbal and nonverbal channels of communication. We use our five senses to receive messages from others. We may hear a presidential address over a radio, watch an Olympic gymnast perform a routine on television, smell the aroma of Thanksgiving dinner when opening the door to our grandmother's house, taste the flavors in mint-chocolate chip ice cream, or hug a friend to congratulate her on her new job.

Channels may also be described according to the manner of presentation employed in communication. The source may speak face-to-face with the receiver, use a public address system to talk with one hundred listeners, or talk over radio or television to millions of receivers. Each of these examples would demand different manners of presentation. Depending on the situation, the source would concentrate on verbal and/or nonverbal channels of communication. If the speaker were on radio, physical appearance wouldn't matter, but if he or she were performing on a cable network program or before a live audience, personal appearance could easily influence the reception of the message. For example, when we go to watch a circus, we expect the clowns to have painted faces and appropriate costumes. If they were dressed in regular street clothes, their performances wouldn't be as effective. Whatever channels of communication are used, the source must learn to adapt the message to make use of the most appropriate channels available for the situation.

Receiver/Decoder

The person (or persons) who attends to the source's message is the *receiver*. The act of interpreting messages is called *decoding*. Receivers decode messages based on past experiences, perceptions, thoughts, and feelings. We receive messages through all our senses, but most often we decode messages by listening or seeing. We first have a physiological reception of stimuli (a noise causes sound waves to hit our eardrum or a movement catches our eye). We then pay attention to both the verbal and nonverbal stimuli and reduce all the stimuli bombarding us to one or two we can cope with more easily. Next, we try to understand the stimuli and interpret them into messages (we decide that the noise is a telephone bell or that the movement is a friend waving to us across campus). Finally, we store this information for later use so that next time we will be able to respond to the stimuli more quickly. It is important to remember that receivers make immediate decisions about what they will respond to in a given situation. During a lecture, an audience member may decide to take a nap. During an argument with your boyfriend or spouse, you may listen only to negative comments. During a crowded party you may watch the nonverbal behaviors of your date (yawning, standing off in a corner alone, and so on) to decide when it's time to leave. As sources of communication, we need to learn to analyze our prospective receivers to determine which communication messages will be most effective.

Of course, all of us are both encoders and decoders; that is, we are capable of both transmitting and receiving messages. When you receive a message, you must interpret it and then encode a response. The response may be silent, noisy, or somewhere in between, depending upon the situation and the existence of any barriers to communication.

Feedback

Another element in the communication process is **feedback**. Each party in an interaction continuously sends messages back to the other. This return process is called feedback. Feedback tells the source how the receiver has interpreted each message. For example, if at the airport you ask your departing friend about his itinerary, and he replies that he didn't pack one, you know your message has not been understood. This kind of feedback, which conveys lack of understanding, is known as **negative feedback**. **Positive feedback**, on the other hand, indicates that the receiver has understood the source's message. It does not necessarily mean that he or she agrees with the source, just that the message was interpreted accurately. Feedback can also be ambiguous, not clearly positive or negative. "I see" and "mm-hmm" can be examples of **ambiguous feedback**. The good communicator is always sensitive to feedback and constantly modifies his or her messages as a result of the feedback received. After a discreet pause, for example, you might ask your friend not about his "itinerary" but about the cities he plans to visit.

Feedback doesn't have to come from others. We can and do get feedback from our own messages. The fact that we can hear the words we speak and see the sentences we write sometimes lets us correct our own mistakes.

Barriers

The human communication system can be compared with a radio or telephone circuit. Just as in radio transmissions where distortion can occur at any point along the circuit (channel), there can be similar **barriers** in human communication. The source's information may be insufficient or unclear. (A love-struck hero may think he is ill rather than in love.) Or the message can be ineffectively or inaccurately encoded. (Our hero may know he's in love but can't find the proper words to convey his feelings until it's too late. That is, his signals may not be transmitted rapidly or accurately enough.) The wrong channel of communication may be used. (He may sing a love song or send flowers when she doesn't like love songs and is allergic to flowers.) The message may not be decoded the way it was encoded. (The

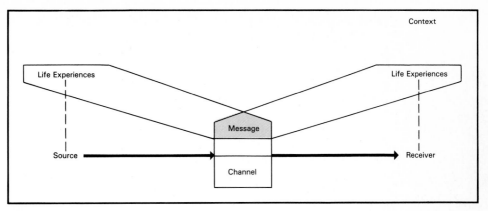

Figure 1–2
Interpersonal Communication

object of our hero's love loves him too—like a brother.) Finally, the receiver may not be equipped to handle the decoded message in such a way as to produce the response (feedback) expected by the source. (Our heroine skips town after receiving our hero's impassioned love letter.) Barriers to communication also occur if the sender and receiver are not on the same "wavelength." This is as true in human communication as it is in radio transmission. On the human level, being on the same wavelength involves shared experiences. That is, the source can encode only in terms of the experiences he or she has had. This is why two people from completely different cultures may find it difficult, if not impossible, to communicate. For example, imagine trying to convey the idea of a soap opera like *General Hospital* or *The Young and the Restless* to someone who has never even seen a television set. (In answer to your question, "Yes, such people do exist.") Figure 1–2 shows the necessity for overlapping fields of experience in communication.

Naturally, no two wavelengths can be exactly alike, because each human being's experiences are unique. Communication will be most effective, however, if the boxes that represent the fields of experience of the source and the receiver have a large area in common. If there have been no common experiences (that is, if the boxes don't meet), communication will be impossible.

Context or Situation

Intricately related to the concept of shared field of experience is the concept of **context**, or situation. This element of communication is, perhaps, the most important; it affects each of the other elements as well as the communication process as a whole. Look, for example, at the following communicative situation: While working in her office one afternoon, Debbie overhears her office mate Cindy saying to someone in the hall, "Not only do I not have time to see you now; in a hundred years I wouldn't find the time." Had Debbie not peered down the hall in amazement, only to see Cindy smiling and directing this comment to one of the latter's good friends, she probably would have completely misunderstood the message she overheard! With the context supplied, an accurate meaning could be assigned to Cindy's comment.

COMMUNICATION CONTEXTS

Communication is often thought of as an interaction between two people. However, we participate in several communication contexts each day. Communication transactions include (1) intrapersonal, (2) interpersonal, (3) small group, (4) public, (5) organizational, and (6) mass transactions. Figure 1–3 describes differences between the contexts of communication. Distinctions are generally made between communication contexts by the number of sensory channels available and immediacy of feedback.

      The number of communicators automatically affects the other dimensions of communication transactions. When watching David Letterman on television, we observe two contexts of levels of communication: interpersonal communication and mass communication. When Dave interviews one of his guests, he is involved in interpersonal communication. Since they are close to one another, all the sensory channels are available to them. They are face-to-face, free to shake hands and touch each others, able to smell cologne or body odors, and so on. They also get immediate feedback such as laughs, facial expressions, or verbal rebukes.

      With mass communication, all the situational categories are altered.

Figure 1–3
Distinguishing Characteristics of Human Communication Contexts

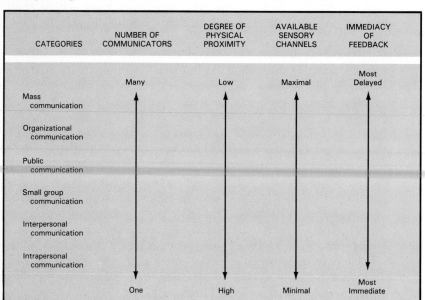

Source: Adapted from G. R. Miller, "The Current Status of Theory and Research in Interpersonal Communication," *Human Communication Research*, 4, no. 2 (Winter 1978), 316–23.

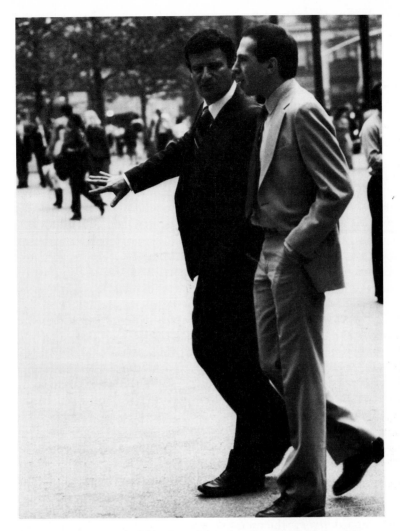

Communication can build both social and professional relationships.

Instead of being beside David Letterman, you may be in Auburn, Alabama, watching him on television. You become one of millions watching him each evening. Because you are so far from New York, where the show originates, there are only two sensory channels available: hearing and sight. Reception from these sensory channels is limited because cameras switch back and forth, commercials interrupt, there may be reception difficulties, or you may be watching black-and-white instead of color television. Finally, with mass communication, feedback is delayed. Nielsen ratings don't come out every month, and you cannot be sure that your personal letter will be read by anyone, much less by David Letterman.

    As we begin looking at communication, it is important to remember that it is a process. We begin with *intrapersonal communication* and gradually work up the continuum to mass communication. The most basic and important communication context is intrapersonal communication. This takes place when an individual sends and receives messages internally. Babies first communicate with themselves before they communicate with others by crying to say that they are hungry, wet, or in pain. Later in life we make conscious reminders to pick up the laundry, feed the dog, or water the plants. We also communicate with ourselves at an unconscious level. Usually we don't notice our heart rates, brain activity, or body tension, but they are essential to our survival and tell us about our internal processing (see Chapter 5).

Intrapersonal communication is the foundation on which interpersonal communication is based. Successful communication with others depends first upon effective communication with ourselves. **Interpersonal communication** is usually thought of as occurring between two people. When you call a friend on the phone, go for a job interview, or ask a professor about your last test grade, you are participating in interpersonal communication. The responsibility for successful interaction is shared between two people. The closeness of the communicators places greater attention on the nonverbal responses from others as we monitor feedback (see Chapter 6).

When you and a co-worker are talking and another person joins you, the three of you are involved in **small group communication**. Communication is more complicated with a group of three or more persons. Think about how confusing a meeting can be with everyone talking at once, or about the satisfaction you feel when the combination of individual talents results in an *A* on a group project. In successful small group communication, each participant has the potential to communicate and adds to the interaction, but this is not true with some communication contexts (see Chapter 7).

With **public communication**, one person addresses a group in a lecture or public speech, and the audience usually does not participate. Try to remember the last time you spoke before a group. It may have been during "show and tell" in the first grade, giving a toast at a friend's wedding rehearsal, or demonstrating the latest food processor to a group of homemakers. With public communication, a speaker is concerned about personal appearance, delivery, the message, and the audience and their response. Speakers learn to adjust their delivery styles to the type of audience they're addressing. A young architect showing some plans to a group of executives is more concerned about clothing, language, and reasoning than she would be if demonstrating Avon products to her immediate family. The public communicator controls the communication process almost completely (see Chapters 9 through 12).

Perhaps the area of communication that has gained the greatest amount of attention in recent years is **organizational communication**. Two books—*In Search of Excellence* and *Thriving on Chaos*—are examples of the many books that have addressed the current "management revolution." As a result of this newfound interest in maximizing communication effectiveness in the workplace, school systems, businesses, governmental agencies, and nonprofit groups are all interested in finding ways to achieve greater responsiveness to clients, improve leadership abilities, build effective self-management teams, create more efficient work environments, and optimize the flow of information. Organizations usually have a chain of command, with one or several top managers making decisions and controlling communication. More and more organizations are incorporating management training and development programs concerned with communication. Effective communication in organizations ensures efficiency for consumers. For example, the Prelude you order from a local Honda dealer will be made to your specifications, assembled properly, shipped on the appropriate date, and checked for safety and performance before you drive home (see Chapter 8).

The communication context with the most process control is **mass communication**. Types of mass communication include radio, television, newspapers, magazines, the recording industry, and so on. Mass communication affects every aspect of our daily lives. We wake up to music on the radio, read a newspaper over coffee, notice signs as we drive to school or work, study from textbooks, watch the news and favorite shows on television, and go for further entertainment to the local movie theater. Mass communication is everywhere, and it is difficult to turn it off even for a few minutes. The characteristics of mass communication include large audiences, message reproduction, rapid distribution and delivery, and low cost to the consumer (see Chapter 13).

After examining the six contexts of communication, you will see that communication involves more than just two people interacting with one another. Intrapersonal, interpersonal, small group, public, organizational, and mass communication each contain sources, messages, channels, receivers, feedback, and barriers. The interaction of these basic elements within their respective contexts leads to communication.

SUMMARY

Communication is a dynamic, ever-changing, unending process by which people transmit information and feelings to others. Communication plays a major role in all of our lives. By increasing your knowledge and understanding of the principles of communication, you will probably become a more effective communicator. Seven basic elements of the communication process are (1) source, (2) message, (3) channel, (4) receiver, (5) feedback, (6) barriers, and (7) context, or situation. The source of communication sends a message (made up of signs or symbols) through verbal and nonverbal channels to a receiver. As receivers decode messages, they respond through feedback, which causes them to be the next source of com-

munication. Effective communication can be hindered by barriers interacting with each element in the process.

The process of communication has many dimensions and occurs on many different levels. Four dimensions of human communication are verbal and nonverbal, oral and written, formal and informal, and intentional and unintentional communication. Human-computer and animal communication also must be considered.

The six contexts of communication include (1) intrapersonal, (2) interpersonal, (3) small group, (4) public, (5) organizational, and (6) mass communication. In an intrapersonal context, both the sending and the receiving of messages take place within one individual. Interpersonal communication, on the other hand, is characterized by a give-and-take between senders and receivers of messages.

Interaction among three or more communicators is known as small group communication. Small group communication involves a different set of communication roles and functions than those found in two-person communication, primarily because of the increased number of communicators present. Communication is almost entirely one way in the public communication situation. The public speaker holds a distinct advantage in that he or she controls the communication process almost completely. All communication contexts function in organizations. Differences between small group and organizational communication include a formal structure designed to achieve specific goals through managerial control, leadership, technology, and communication networks. The final context of communication, mass media, has developed communication to its fullest extent, exerting an immensely powerful effect on modern society. Today, more than ever, we are a media society because of audience interest, diversity in messages, rapid distribution, and low cost to the consumer.

The remainder of this book is designed to increase your knowledge and your understanding of communication. Chapter 2 begins by explaining the most basic components of human communication, language, and meaning.

EXERCISES

GROUP EXPERIENCES

Breakdowns

DESCRIPTION: The human communication system is a complex process in which breakdowns can occur at any point. In this chapter a simple seven-part model was presented, consisting of (1) source, (2) message, (3) channel, (4) receiver, (5) feedback, (6) barriers, and (7) situation, or context. The purpose of this activity is to identify the communication breakdowns that can occur at each stage in the communication process.

PROCEDURE: Think of an important communication you want to make to another person. For example, you may want to tell your parents that you plan to quit school for a semester. Whatever your communication, identify the (1) source, (2) message channel(s), (3) receiver, (4) types of feedback, and (5) barriers that could occur at each of these stages.

DISCUSSION: Were you able to identify a potential breakdown for each of the five parts of the model? By identifying various types of breakdowns, you should be able to analyze communication problems that you experience daily. The next time you encounter a communication problem, attempt to determine where the breakdown occurred. This should help you to avoid unnecessary breakdowns.

Walk a Mile in My Shoes

DESCRIPTION: Successful communication depends to a large extent on the source encoding a message in a way the receiver understands. In any communication transaction, both the source and the receiver have a field of experience that in some cases may be shared and in other cases completely separate. When the fields of experience for the source and the receiver are different, special attention must be given to the differences in the transmission of the message. An effective method is "to walk a mile in the other person's shoes." This activity is designed to demonstrate (1) the importance of shared fields of experience between the source and receiver and (2) a method for dealing with the different fields of experience of the two parties.

PROCEDURE: There are two stages in this activity. The first stage involves role playing in a situation in which the source and receiver do not share a field of experience. Although a sample situation is provided, you may wish to write your own. A three- to five-minute dialogue should take place between the following characters. Each character should be played as a person who not only does not share a field of experience with the other person, but who also has no understanding of the way in which the other person views the world.

Source	Receiver
A college freshman who wants his parents to sign a permission slip to allow him to live in off-campus housing instead of in a dormitory.	A parent who never went to college and who considers the purpose of college to be "education," not "socialization."

The second stage of this activity requires that the two role players switch roles. In other words, the college freshman should play the parent, in an attempt to see the world through the eyes of the parent, and the parent should now be playing the college freshman. In this reversed role playing, each person should attempt to understand the other's position based on his or her life experiences.

DISCUSSION: In the first stage of the role-playing situation, the characters had different fields of experience. Communication under these conditions is very difficult, if not impossible. In the role-reversal situation, each character tried to bridge the gap by seeing the world through the eyes of the other person. If you face a similar situation, try to step back and understand how the other person experiences the world.

Responding

DESCRIPTION: Feedback is an important element in the communication process. The three types of feedback include (1) negative feedback, conveying a lack of understanding; (2) positive feedback, indicating that the receiver has understood the source's message; and (3) ambiguous feedback, which is not clearly positive or negative. This activity will help you to identify the different types of feedback.

PROCEDURE: After reviewing the following example, write a negative, positive, and ambiguous feedback response to each of the three statements listed below.

Example

Statement: I would like to go to a private college. I have heard that you can get a better education there.

Positive Feedback: You might check into a private school and see how you feel about its educational program.

Negative Feedback: Private schools have poor athletic programs—why would you want to go there?

Ambiguous Feedback: I see.

Statement 1: I think people from the North weigh more than people from the South—probably because of the climatic differences.

Statement 2: If I had my choice, I'd never work for anyone but myself.

Statement 3: I hate taking basic course requirements. It seems to me that since I'm paying for my education, I ought to be able to decide what courses to take.

DISCUSSION: A good communicator is always sensitive to feedback and constantly modifies his or her messages in response to feedback received. Feedback can be conveyed through both verbal and nonverbal channels.

PERSONAL EXPERIENCES

1. Is it true that it is impossible **not** to communicate? Gather evidence based on logic or personal experience that proves or disproves this statement.

2. Select a person with whom you spend a great deal of time. Observe the type of feedback this person gives you. Is it mostly positive, negative, or ambiguous? Do you tend to like people who give you positive feedback? How do you respond to negative feedback?

3. Are you a good communicator? Take a day and find out. Determine your awareness of the various elements of communication by observing yourself. Do you attend and respond to both verbal and nonverbal messages?

DISCUSSION QUESTIONS

1. What is communication? Identify the basic elements of communication.

2. How does communication today affect communication tomorrow? Discuss the possible effects on the communication process or on you as a communicator.

3. How does a communication message get from the source to its destination?

4. Identify three different ways in which communication breakdowns occur.

5. How does feedback (negative, positive, and ambiguous) affect the communication process?

2
Language, Meaning, and Communication

KEY CONCEPTS AND TERMS

Language	Sense
Word	Referent
Labeling	Concrete
Interaction	Abstract
Transmission	Ambiguity
Innate	Vagueness
Imitative, learned behavior	Denotation
Language acquisition device	Connotation
Babbling stage	Style
Holophrastic stage	Communicator style
Analytic stage	Non-identity
Symbolic process	Non-allness
Semantics	Self-reflexiveness
Symbol	Semantic stereotyping

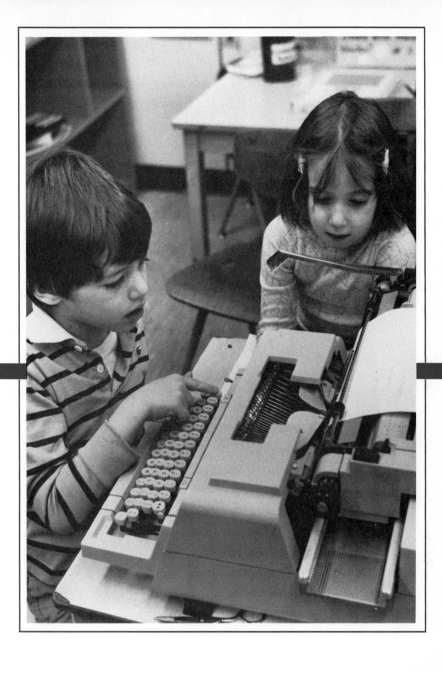

Both John and Sue joined the staff of a successful public relations firm in New York during the same year. They had just completed their PR degrees at a nearby university and were thrilled to be hired by one of the finest PR firms in the city. John's first assignment was to create a promotional campaign for a client who was putting a new game on the market. Initially, Sue was assigned to work with a sportswear company on a marketing concept for its newest line of clothing.

As time passed and work with their respective first clients became more and more difficult, John and Sue realized that they had been assigned two of the toughest accounts in town. Although John completed his assignment quickly and successfully, he was furious when he learned that the boss had deliberately assigned him a difficult account. In response, he not only complained to his colleagues but also to the boss's secretary. Sue, on the other hand, had a more difficult time satisfying her first client, and she took several additional months to actually complete the project. However, she just laughed when she heard through the grapevine that the boss had made the assignments purposely.

Over the next two years, John worked grudgingly with each assignment and problem that he encountered. Sue accepted each assignment cheerfully, and when problems arose she responded with her characteristic, "No problem—I can handle it." Although Sue always took longer to complete her projects than did John, and both were equally successful on assignments they completed, Sue was given the first promotion when the position was opened.

You may be asking at this point, "How could John's language alone have affected his job that way?" Or, better yet, "What does *this* have to do with a chapter on language?"

Whether you are working in a small accounting firm in Laramie, Wyoming, or a Fortune 500 company in New York City, you need to know the organization's "secret words" if you are headed to the top. So says Lois Wyse in her book *Company Manners: An Insider Tells How to Succeed in the Real World of Corporate Protocol and Power Politics.* What "secret words" is she talking about? They are ways in which each company likes to describe itself and think of its products, services, and employees. For example, a company's code word one year might be "innovation" and the next year "human resource development." Managers and executives on the rise know the importance of these words to the company and use them accordingly. In addition, these "secret words" include all words or phrases—like "no problem"—that reflect a positive attitude toward work and loyalty to the company.

As you can see, language *can* have an impact on others and on your future career. Thus, an understanding of what language is and how it operates in our daily lives can be useful to you. In this chapter we will focus on a number of topics that will help you to better understand how language works. We will begin with a discussion of the functions of language and how people actually develop personal language patterns. We will then address the concept of meaning and some of the features of language that affect our everyday lives, including abstraction and concreteness, ambiguity and vagueness, denotation and connotation, and language style. Finally, we will discuss the relationship between language and behavior. In this section we will address how language is often used to stereotype individuals or their behavior and look at several ways in which we can begin to make our everyday language more effective.

Before we launch head first into a discussion of these topics, let's begin with a working definition of language. ***Language*** is the communication of thoughts and emotions by means of a structured system of symbols. In our language these symbols are known as **words.** The word *innovation*, for example, is just an arbitrary combination of letters that, over time, has come to be accepted as a *symbol* for the introduction of some object or process that is new and exciting. Our ability to use these symbols defines our level of language skill.

FUNCTIONS OF LANGUAGE

Language fulfills three primary functions. We can use it to label, to interact with others, and to transmit information.

Identifying an object, act, or person by name so that she, he, or it can be referred to in communication is known as ***labeling.*** Once something is named, it takes on all of the characteristics and meanings that we associate with its label. For example, your meaning of the word "success" might include an $80,000-a-year salary and a new Porsche 911, while for someone else "success" may be defined as a $30,000-a-year job and time at night and on weekends to enjoy one's family. The same is true of our respective names. They are badges of our identity and symbols in their own right. That is one reason we become easily perturbed if someone misspells or (worse yet) makes fun of our names.

The next function of language, ***interaction,*** focuses on the sharing and communication of ideas and emotions. Language transmissions can produce sympathy and understanding or anger and confusion. For example, if a friend is in the middle of suggesting an idea for a Saturday retreat, and you believe that you have a "better" plan of action, you can use language more effectively by "holding your fire," letting her finish the idea, and beginning your response in a diplomatic, nonemotional way. For instance, you might say, "That's a great idea. Or we could . . . [your idea]. . . . Let's ask Don and April for their opinions." In this way, language can serve as the basis for a positive rather than a negative interaction.

Through language, information can also be passed on to other individuals. This function of language is referred to as ***transmission.*** Consider for a moment all of the information that you send and receive daily, from the first "good morning" that you hear until the last sentence you read before turning off the light at night. Books, lectures, electronic billboards, videodiscs, and satellites—there is no end to the many ways that language can transmit information.

Researchers have argued that transmission of information is perhaps the most important function of language in the history of human civilization. For example, language connects the past, present, and future. It also ensures the perpetuation of our culture and traditions. Older generations die, but they are able, through language, to leave behind their ideas, accomplishments, failures, and plans for the future. Thus, later generations do not have to repeat the trials and errors of their predecessors but can adapt and constantly improve upon the successes of the past. Just think how little of your present knowledge comes from your own experience and how much is based on long-accepted facts. It will certainly be apparent that language has enabled us to advance intellectually, psychologically, and culturally.

LANGUAGE DEVELOPMENT

Newborn babies have only a few ways to communicate—body movements, facial expressions, and sounds that are generalized to many needs. A cry, for example, can mean fear, hunger, pain, or any number of other things. As they grow, however, babies come to discover language and its importance in ensuring their personal well-being and development.

Babies discover that language is useful for expressing their own feelings and conveying the feelings of others. Their first "Ma-Ma" or Da-Da" evokes immediate smiles and caresses. Their later, more sophisticated expressions, such as "I love you" or "Go away," will continue the process of exchanging emotions through language. This aspect of language is quite important in creating psychological balance and adjustment.

During their early years, children also discover the meaning of "yes" and "no." No longer can they do everything they wish and still please others. Through spoken and, later, written symbols, they come to understand their culture and its expectations. Language thus serves as a means of socialization—teaching mores, norms, and accepted behavior.

In addition to creating psychological balance and teaching "acceptable" behaviors, early mother–infant interactions have been found to help the subsequent language and intellectual development of the child. For example, in 1982, researchers Roe, McClure, and Roe studied the vocal interchange of three-month-old infants with their mothers and with a stranger. Results of the study revealed that a high rate of vocal output by the infants in response to their mothers' vocalizations was associated with later performance on linguistic-cognitive and academic tests. It seems that these early conversations between parent and infant give the child an opportunity to develop vital cognitive processes.[1]

Theories of Language Development

From childhood to old age, we all use language as a means of broadening our knowledge of ourselves and the world about us. When humans first evolved, they were like newborn children, unable to use this valuable tool. Yet once language developed, the possibilities for humankind's future attainments and cultural growth increased.

Many linguists believe that evolution is responsible for our ability to produce and use language. They claim that our highly evolved brain

---

[1] K. V. Roe, A. McClure, and A. Roe, "Vocal Interaction at 3 months and cognitive skills at 12 years," *Developmental Psychology* 18 (1982), 15–16.

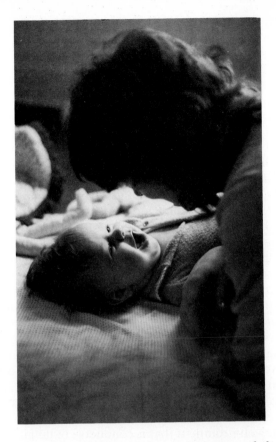

Early interactions between parent and child encourage language and intellectual development.

provides us with an innate language ability not found in lower organisms. Proponents of this **innateness theory,** most notably Eric Lenneberg, say that our potential for language is inborn, but that language itself develops gradually, as a function of the growth of the brain during childhood. Therefore, there are critical biological times for language development—once the growth of the brain is complete (during the early teen years), it is much harder to learn language.

Much evidence supports this theory. More and more schools are discovering that foreign languages are best taught in the lower grades. Young children can often learn several languages simply by being exposed to them, but adults have a much harder time of it.

Although some aspects of language are undeniably innate, language does not develop automatically, in a vacuum. Children who have been isolated from other human beings do not possess language. This demonstrates that interaction with other human beings is necessary for proper language development. Some linguists believe that this interaction is more basic to human language acquisition than any innate capacities. These theorists view language as **imitative, learned behavior.** In other words, children learn language from their parents by imitating them. Parents negatively reinforce inexact imitations and positively reinforce more precise imitations, thus gradually shaping their child's language skills.

There are elements of truth in both the innateness and the learning theories of language development. Currently accepted explanations tend to borrow from each viewpoint. Noam Chomsky, for example, says that we are all born with *language acquisition devices* (LAD, for short). This doesn't mean that grammar is somehow innately in our heads, but rather that these LADs help us sort out the language we hear and understand its grammatical rules. From listening to adults, American children learn, for example, that the usual sentence order is subject–verb–object. They will therefore begin to put words into this order. Children from another culture will learn the grammatical rules of their society. Thus, Chomsky's view suggests an interaction between innate (LAD) and learned aspects of language.

Children who, for one reason or another, have been isolated from speaking humans during the critical periods during which language usually develops find it very difficult, if not impossible, to acquire language abilities. Scientists explain that these children have passed crucial biological times in their neural development, critical periods during which language learning must occur. Once passed, these developmental stages can never be recaptured. Additionally, the quality of the language environment in which a child is reared has been found to affect his or her overall language development. Investigating whether quality of day-care environments and amount of interaction with caregivers affects language development, psychologist Kathleen McCartney found that children's scores on four intellectual and language development tests were significantly affected by the quality of their day-care environments. In addition, as the number of verbal interactions between the child and the caregiver increased, so did the children's language development scores.[2] Thus, it is important for parents and teachers to create a supportive, stimulating environment that is conducive to language learning.[3] Only in this way can the child successfully integrate innate and learned language "skills"—and become an articulate and competent member of society.

The Process of Language Development

Even when infants are surrounded by speaking adults, it takes about two years for them to actually learn to speak. In the first month or so, babies make many noises. Contrary to popular ideas, these sounds have no real meaning. This fact has been demonstrated in controlled studies of mothers who listened to their babies from behind screens. The mothers were unable to accurately link particular cries with specific situations, such as a wet diaper or an empty bottle. Investigators thus believe that the sounds newborns make are just reflexive attempts to exercise the vocal cords and related muscles. It is only at the age of two or three months that infants begin to make sounds that have specific meanings. During this **babbling stage,** as it

[2] K. McCartney, "Effect of Quality of Day Care Environment on Children's Language Development," *Developmental Psychology* 20, no. 2 (1984), 244–60.
[3] R. B. Simms, "But Teacher, You Went Right On," *Childhood Education* 62 (1986), 269–71.

is known, babies can make not only all the sounds of their own language but also those of all the languages in the world. For example, American infants may distinctly make the sound of a French *r* or German *ü*.

After a year, most babies begin to more closely observe their parents' speech, and their babbling begins to approximate their parents' sounds. As we mentioned, this imitation is usually reinforced by smiles and praise. From one year on, then, children learn more and more words. By age two they have built a speaking vocabulary of about three hundred words. Their comprehension vocabulary (words they understand but do not yet use) is even larger.

Until some time after the second year, children's speech is **holophrastic**; that is, they use one word to mean a number of things, or several words run together to signify one thought. For example, the word *hug* may mean "Daddy, I want a hug" or "I am hugging my teddy bear." *Mamagive* becomes a single word symbol that means "Mama give." It is not until the **analytic stage**, after the second year, that the child learns that *Mama give* consists of two separate units, and begins to experiment with this order: "Me give Mama hug," "Mama give me hug."

By the time children are six years old they seem to know all the grammatical rules that enable them to speak correctly. However, the learning process never ceases. Your vocabulary can continue to increase as long as you live; every new experience can increase it.

MEANING

Semantics

Our discussion of language thus far has focused on words. Once you have acquired language, you still must learn to use the words to communicate effectively. You gradually learn to combine your words in an infinite variety of ways to transmit an infinite number of messages. Still, transmission of messages is not enough. You also want them to be received and understood. Commonality of language between speaker and listener is, obviously, essential for this understanding. What is even more essential is commonality of meaning.

But what is meaning? To take an example, the word *jaram* does not exist in your vocabulary. It should have no significance for you whatsoever. It *means* nothing. Let's say, though, that you are now shown an object called a "jaram." Hereafter, the word *jaram* will bring to mind a picture of that object. Now the word has meaning for you. The use of words such as *jaram* as symbols representing objects and concepts is known as the **symbolic process.** The study of the relationship between these word symbols and their meanings is called **semantics.**

Semantics is quite a complicated area of study, since many symbols and dimensions of meaning exist. However, researchers generally agree that words have three dimensions of meaning. The **symbol** refers to objects in the real world, and the **sense** to subjective feelings we have about the symbol.

The quality of children's language environments significantly affects their language development.

The ***referent*** is the actual object as it exists in reality. Thus, your meaning of the word *football* is a function of the symbol (the word *football*), the sense (pleasant feelings brought on by the thought of last year's winning season), and the referent (an actual football). Of course, this analysis applies only to the linguistic level of meaning. We cannot forget that there are philosophical, psychological, and logical levels of meaning as well.

Language Features

At a minimum, meaning involves shared understanding or shared agreement regarding a symbol, its sense, and its referent. For example, we probably can all agree that an "office" is a place where business is transacted. However, the word "office" takes on a different dimension of meaning when it describes a large, beautifully decorated corner room with lots of windows—and when the word refers to a 6′ × 6′ windowless room located near an elevator. What features of language allow the same word to take on such a diverse set of meanings? Although the answer to this question is complex, semanticists have agreed on at least four factors that affect word meanings: (1) the extent to which words are abstract or concrete, (2) the amount of ambiguity and vagueness in a language, (3) the denotative and connotative dimensions of meaning, and (4) language style. Each of these topics will be addressed more completely in the following paragraphs.

ABSTRACTION AND CONCRETENESS.   Determining meanings is complicated when the words in question are not concrete. ***Concrete*** words symbolize objects or events that can be pointed to, touched, experienced, or felt. *Abstract* words, on the other hand, represent things we can't sense directly. How do we define abstract terms such as *freedom, honesty, religion,* or *politics*?

No matter how difficult it may be to define abstractions, they are very important to the communication process. With abstract words, we are able to extend the level of our thoughts and speech beyond the concrete, everyday world. We can talk about the complicated concepts of right and wrong, discuss things that we can't see, and consider the future as if it existed today.

AMBIGUITY AND VAGUENESS.   Two other language variables that affect understanding are ambiguity and vagueness. *Ambiguity* has been defined as the amount of doubtfulness or uncertainty in meanings. Generally, ambiguity arises for the simple reason that human language customarily assigns one symbol to several categories or things. To illustrate, consider the word *heavy*. One can have heavy luggage, a heavy yield of grain, a room heavy with moisture, a heavy odor, heavy gunfire, heavy food, heavy features, a heavy date, and a heavy book, both in weight and in profundity.

Vagueness can present even greater problems for language users than can ambiguity. A word or phrase is said to be *vague* if it lacks precision or clarity of expression. In other words, vagueness occurs when the language we use is unspecific or imprecise. For example, if you have been asked by your boss to pick up a job candidate whom you have never met, and you are told to look for the tall man at the train-station entrance, you may have difficulty locating the person because of imprecision in the description. The definition of "tall" for someone who stands 5'2" may be different for someone who is 6'2" in height.

Vagueness leads to trivial arguments, such as "I say it's green," which is countered by, "Well, I say it's blue." However, vagueness also may lead to more serious concerns, such as "Where does truth end and falsehood begin?" or "Where does business savvy end and corrupt practice begin?"

DENOTATION AND CONNOTATION.   Meaning is also affected by the denotation and connotation of particular words. *Denotation* is the objective reference of a word—that is, its factual, concrete meaning. Dictionary definitions present denotations. Some words are primarily denotative, but most words also possess less definable connotations. *Connotation* refers to meanings beyond the objective reference. The word *automobile*, for example, denotes a four-wheeled motor vehicle. Yet it may connote little or nothing to one person, anger to someone who has just been fired from an automobile factory, and pleasure to someone who has just bought a new sports car. Very specific words—*chair, desk, book,* and so forth—are usually without connotation for most people. Other words, such as *obsolete* and *respectable,* can fall either way, depending on context, while words such as *fantastic* and *horrible* are almost totally connotative in nature.

We acquire our connotations from social and personal experiences. The word *farm* means something different to a city dweller than to a country person. The more two people have in common—the more similar their backgrounds, past experiences, attitudes, and outlooks—the better chance they have of attaching the same meaning to a word or concept.

Consider the following situation. Greg is talking with his parents, and all is going well. They are communicating for a change. Then the conversation turns to the subject of drugs. Communication quickly comes to an end. Greg and his parents stop communicating because they have different connotations for the word *drug*. But the word is only a small part of a larger problem. Greg, his mother, and his father have different attitudes about many things, and this difference in attitudes influences the connotations they attach to words. The end result of these differing connotations is often only too similar to this example—breakdown of communication.

STYLE.   Another factor that influences meaning is *style,* or how we choose, organize, and use those features of the language that are open to individual selection.

The rules of our language dictate the arrangement of words in sentences (subject–verb–object) and frequently determine which forms of words must be used (present or past tense, singular or plural verb). These are not matters of style, but of grammar. Style, on the other hand, refers to an individual's characteristic tendencies to choose particular kinds of words (simple versus multisyllabic, factual versus descriptive), particular sentence constructions (short versus long, complete versus fragmentary), or even particular phrases ("you know," "I mean," "right on"). For example, assertive speakers have been found to use more words, phrases, and clauses than passive speakers. In addition, they use a significantly larger proportion of feeling verbs.[4]

Style is influenced by variables in the speaker as well as in the listener. Have you ever wondered why it seems difficult to talk with some people and easy to talk with others? Think for a minute about blind dates you've had, parties you've attended, or plane trips you've taken. Pleasant interactions are usually associated with people with whom you hit it off immediately. Even though you may have found commonalities, successful communication was probably based on more than just similar professions or common interests.

Personality differences do exist between communicators, and we tend to make positive and negative judgments based on specific communication styles. We often base first impressions more on how a person says something than on what is said: "She turned me off with her sarcastic comments." "The salesman sounded so sincere that I wanted to buy from him." "She really had a way of making people feel right at home." In fact, the first few minutes of interpersonal interaction often determine whether or not we will continue interaction. These minutes are also often the key to business achievement, social success, family harmony, and sexual satisfaction. Hem-

---

[4] A. H. Gervasio, H. B. Pepinsky, and A. I. Schwebel, "Stylistic Complexity and Verb Usage in Assertive and Passive Speech," *Journal of Counseling Psychology* 30, no. 4 (1983), 546–56.

ming and hawing, overusing profanity, and cutting off another person who is speaking all indicate the influence of personality on communicator style.

Although up to this point we have been discussing the concept of style in general, two specific groups of researchers have been specifically interested in *communicator style*. Robert Norton, for example, has defined *communicator style* as "the way one verbally and preverbally interacts to signal how literal meaning should be taken, interpreted, filtered, or understood."[5] As a result of his perceptions, he has discriminated ten variables, or components, that seemingly contribute to an individual's communicator style. These include the following:

1. Dominance, or tendency to take control in social interactions;
2. Contentiousness, or argumentativeness and aggressiveness;
3. Preciseness, or degree of concern with accuracy, documentation, and proof in informative interactions;
4. Attentiveness, or sensitivity to others;
5. Friendliness, or willingness to establish interpersonal relationships;
6. Openness, or willingness to reveal personal information or to express feelings and emotions openly;
7. Degree of anxiety or nervousness when interacting with others;
8. Animation, or amount of expressiveness and interest when conversing with others;
9. Dramatic behaviors, or degree to which he or she dramatizes events, creating closeness among interactants; and
10. The overall impression or image which a person presents when she or he interacts with others.[6]

To document the importance of these ten variables in style, D. A. Bednar examined the relationship between communicator style and managerial performance in both the corporate headquarters of a life insurance company and in a hospital setting. For supervisors in the life insurance company, "outstanding" and "above-average" managers were described as more open and precise. For hospital personnel, managers who rated high on attentiveness and low on argumentativeness were esteemed. Results of this study suggest that communicator style is an important dimension of communication in any organization. Despite the varying emphases placed on different style components across the two organizations, the overall image (or communicator style) of outstanding managers contributed to their high ratings by supervisors, subordinates, and peers.[7]

---

[5] B. M. Montgomery and R. W. Norton, "Sex Differences and Similarities in Communicator Style," *Communication Monographs* 48, no. 2 (1981), 121–32.
[6] Ibid.
[7] D. A. Bednar, "Relationships Between Communicator Style and Managerial Performance in Complex Organizations: A Field Study," *The Journal of Business Communication* 19, no. 4 (1982), 51–76.

Words in Wonderland

Lewis Carroll was an English mathematician and logician whose real name was Charles Lutwidge Dodgson. He is remembered, not for his contributions to mathematics or logic, but as the author of *Alice's Adventures in Wonderland* and *Through the Looking Glass*. These great works are sometimes called "nonsense" literature, but from the excerpts that follow we can see that even in wonderland Carroll was concerned with the logic of words and how they represent reality.

"Come, we shall have some fun now!" thought Alice. "I'm glad you've begun asking riddles—I believe I can guess that," she added aloud.

"Do you mean that you think you can find out the answer to it?" said the March Hare.

"Exactly so," said Alice.

"Then you should say what you mean," the March Hare went on.

"I do," Alice hastily replied: "at least—at least I mean what I say—that's the same thing, you know."

"Not the same thing a bit!" said the Hatter. "Why, you might just as well say that 'I see what I eat' is same thing as 'I eat what I see!' "

"You might just as well say," added the March Hare, "that 'I like what I get' is the same thing as 'I get what I like!' "

"You might just as well say," added the Dormouse, which seemed to be talking in its sleep, "that 'I breathe when I sleep' is the same thing as "I sleep when I breathe!' "

"It *is* the same thing with you," said the Hatter, and here the conversation dropped. . . .

Alice's Adventures in Wonderland

"I don't know what you mean by 'glory,' " Alice said.

Humpty Dumpty smiled contemptuously. "Of course you don't—till I tell you. I meant 'there's a nice knock-down argument for you!' "

"But 'glory' doesn't mean 'a nice knock-down argument,' " Alice objected.

"When *I* use a word," Humpty Dumpty said, in rather a scornful tone, "it means just what I choose it to mean—neither more nor less."

"The question is," said Alice, "whether you *can* make words mean so many different things."

"The quest is," said Humpty Dumpty, "which is to be master—that's all."

Through the Looking-Glass

As you can see, we need to be aware of our own communicator style so that we can communicate more effectively with others. Specifically, when we understand our style of communication, we can adapt to the styles of others. For example, we frequently "tailor" our language for a particular audience or to the purpose of our message. Additionally, we vary our language production, consciously or unconsciously, depending on our mood, and the constraints of the situation in which we find ourselves.[8] A nuclear physicist uses scientific jargon with colleagues, but not with people outside the profession. Physicians often have a habit of talking with their patients as if the latter were familiar with the latest medical terminology. As a result, patients sometimes feel alienated, especially when Latin terminology seems to change their simple complaint into what sounds like a fatal illness. A considerate physician uses terms that are easily understood by patients.

Korzybski's Laws

As we have seen in the previous discussions, language is a highly complex, yet powerful, phenomenon. However, we can all strive to become more aware of the subtle but powerful influence of words in our lives. Alfred Korzybski, a pioneer in the area of General Semantics—the study of the structure and function of speech and resultant behavior—observed that people often falsely identify with words. We sometimes respond to words as if the words themselves were the referent objects they symbolize. In fact, many individuals are tyrannized by words. For example, just hearing the word *spider* may cause someone with a fear of spiders to shiver. The spider itself does not have to be in sight; the symbol, not the referent, causes the response.

This observation led to Korzybski's law of ***non-identity,*** which says, simply, that a word is *not* the thing it represents. The word *cat* and the animal itself are not one and the same thing. (See Figure 2–1).

Korzybski's second law, that of **non-allness,** reminds us that a word cannot symbolize *all* of a thing. *Cat* may bring to mind your own pet and the expensive show animal you saw on TV last night. However, *cat* may symbolize something quite different for an African who has experienced cats of a larger and more ferocious variety than the string of "Fluffys" you have owned and loved. Neither you nor the African, though, might think of an Egyptian god or a Canadian lynx. Clearly, language never conveys *everything* about *anything.*

Korzybski's third law concerns ***self-reflexiveness.*** It explains that a word can refer not only to something in the real world but also to itself. The word *cat* not only refers to a kind of four-legged animal in the real world but also to the word formed in English by the letters *c-a-t,* or to the word formed in Italian by the letters *g-a-t-t-o.*

LANGUAGE AND BEHAVIOR

Our discussion of connotation and style revealed the effects of environmental and personal variables on an individual's language usage. It is also important

---

[8] J. P. Forgas, "Language, Goals and Situations," *Journal of Language and Social Psychology* 2 (1983), 267–93.

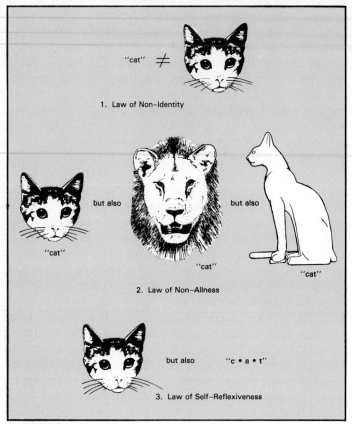

FIGURE 2–1
Korzybski's Three Laws

to recognize that our language affects the attitudes and subsequent behaviors of others.

We know, for example, that listeners can accurately identify or estimate, on the basis of speech alone, various characteristics of speakers, including their age, sex, race, socioeconomic status, personality, specific identity, facial and body features, and height and weight.[9] In addition, researchers have found that speech style contributes to a group's or culture's identity and cohesion. One illustration of this language principle was our discussion at the beginning of this chapter regarding organizational "buzz words" and their importance. Another example is the use of "secret" rites (and their corresponding language) that groups such as college fraternities and sororities employ.

Language patterns also have an effect on the degree to which people are perceived to be credible or powerful. For example, linguistic patterns typical of women have been found to be less powerful than those associated

---

[9] N. J. Lass, J. N. Thompson, and P. A. Kimmel, "Identification of Speakers' Occupations," *Perceptual and Motor Skills* 54 (1982), 93.

with men. According to recent research, women make greater use of indirect control strategies as is reflected in their use of a significantly greater number of questions (for example, "What's next?"). Additionally, women use justifiers ("The reason I say that is . . .") more frequently, apparently perceiving a greater need to provide a rationale for their opinions. Furthermore, they use more intensive adverbs ("I really think X") than do men, perhaps to increase the strength of what they are saying. Finally, women talk more about people than objects, as exemplified in their greater use of pronouns ("We, you, they . . .), and they employ a more indirect, qualified language style (for example, through the use of adverbs when beginning sentences, such as "Surprisingly, that test was a breeze").[10]

Conversely, men have been found to use a more direct, or overt, control strategy through the production of more interruptions ("Let's move on; we can come back to that point later"). They also have a tendency to use a greater number of directives ("Why don't you finish this report before we talk?") and maintain longer speaking turns through the use of more conjunctions and/or fillers when beginning a sentence ("and another thing we need to consider. . .").[11] According to C. M. Staley, such differences between men and women begin to arise as early as the age of four, with girls displaying more interpretive, emotional, and reflexive language styles than do boys.[12]

What impact do these language differences have on the attitudes and behavior of other people? One answer seems to lie in the differential language patterns that women and men use when speaking in same-sex as opposed to mixed-sex groups. According to research, when women converse with other women, they are rated higher on socio-intellectual status and aesthetic quality than men interacting with other men. In other words, when speaking to other women, females are perceived to be of high social status, rich, white collar, and literate as compared to men speaking with other men. Additionally, women who interact with other women are perceived to be more "beautiful, nice, pleasant, and sweet" than are men when interacting with other men.[13]

However, in mixed-sex groups (men interacting with women and vice versa), language patterns seem to change, and ratings of socio-intellectual status begin to increase for men and decrease for women. Additionally, when interacting with men, women are no longer rated more highly than are men on aesthetic quality. Instead, men are perceived to be more "beautiful, nice, pleasant, and sweet" than are women. To their credit, women are perceived to be more dynamic than men when speaking in mixed-sex groups.

[10] A. Mulac, J. M. Wiemann, S. J. Widenmann, and T. W. Gibson, "Male/Female Language Differences and Effects in Same-Sex and Mixed-Sex Dyads: The Gender-Linked Language Effect," *Communication Monographs* 55(4) (1988), 315–35.
[11] Ibid.
[12] C. M. Staley, "Sex-Related Differences in the Style of Children's Language," *Journal of Psycholinguistic Research* 11 (1982), 141–58.
[13] Mulac and others, "Male/Female Language Differences," 331–32.

In other words, women are perceived to be more strong, active, aggressive, and loud than men in mixed-sex communication situations.[14]

Linguistic Stereotyping

Although speech styles have a useful function, as we have seen, they may also serve their users in a negative way. Such a situation usually arises when nonusers of a major style or dialect come into contact with people who are unaware of their function and importance, or who tend to see things and people categorically. Perceptions regarding the Amish people of the Pennsylvania Dutch area illustrate this point. Although the people of this region may share both similar culture and beliefs, it is not necessarily true that everyone who speaks with a Pennsylvania Dutch accent will prefer old-fashioned clothes and horse-drawn wagons. Assuming such automatic relationships between particular linguistic styles and particular personal traits is known as **semantic,** or **linguistic, stereotyping.** For example, many people unfairly underestimate the intellectual ability of people who speak slow and halting English. Conversely, linguistic stereotyping may also produce a perception of intellectual superiority for a speaker with a crisp Oxford accent.

As you may have guessed by now, most semantic stereotypes are negative. They are particularly harmful for individuals who share easily recognizable (yet nonstandard) dialects such as Black English or Louisiana creole. Perhaps the greatest damage, however, comes when speakers of the standard or majority dialect of a culture believe that nonspeakers are somehow inferior. In fact, studies have shown that many employers in American businesses and industries today are guilty of such perceptions, which in turn has affected their hiring (and firing) policies.[15]

The question, then, becomes: What can we do, given this knowledge concerning linguistic stereotypes? For "native" speakers, the solution seems to reside in concern and awareness—awareness of the information we have presented and a concern for consistency in acting upon it, whether in interpersonal interactions or on the job.

For non-native speakers, the solution is more complex and will involve a weighing of alternatives and their consequences. To disregard the importance of competence in the standard dialect or style may result in diminished opportunities and rewards. At the same time, it is crucial that an individual be aware of the importance of his or her social identity, which is intimately tied to the language in which he or she takes an active part.

Perhaps one answer lies in the individual's ability to achieve some degree of linguistic competence in both communities. Although such an attempt would be both difficult and frustrating, it could provide a means by which the "bilingual" or "bidialectical" individual any more effectively communicate.

---

[14] Ibid.
[15] E. Anderson, "Language and Success," *College English* 43, no. 8 (December 1981), 807–12.

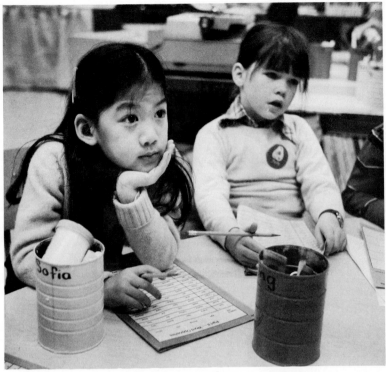

Our social identities are inextricably tied to the language we speak.

Making Language More Effective

When Clark Gable said "Frankly, my dear, I don't give a damn" in the film *Gone With the Wind* (1939), millions of people were either shocked or titillated. Times have changed. Four-letter words don't offend as they once did. New words come into the language almost daily, as they always have. As the norms and mores of a society change, so does its language. Both society and language reflect the "liberated" spirit of the twentieth century.

Unfortunately, liberated language often also means sloppy, imprecise language. Although people seem to be communicating *more* these days, they may be understood even *less*. As a student of communication (and now language!), you should be aware of the trend. You also can become a communication trendsetter by following these tips:

1. Try to speak clearly at all times (that is, use words whose meanings can be understood by those who are listening).
2. Relate to your listeners by being sensitive to their attitudes, beliefs, and experiences.
3. Avoid using slang and jargon (for example, computerese).
4. Minimize the use of regionalisms such as "y'all" or "you guys," especially in the professional world.

5. Converse without using habitual expressions, such as:

"you know what I mean?"

"uh-huh" (for yes)

"uh-uh" (for no)

"yeah"

"to be honest"

"truthfully"

6. Choose language that is appropriate to the purpose of the interaction and the communication setting—your language should be different when you are talking with a friend and when giving a presentation.

7. Avoid using vague and ambiguous language—learn to say what you mean and mean what you say.

8. Be careful not to overkill a subject by rambling on and on. Business people especially appreciate others who KISS: "*Keep it simple and short.*"

9. Avoid "I-trouble," or talking too much about you. A conversation of indefinite length about your accomplishments or problems will be perceived as rude and selfish.

10. Finally, be "other-centered"—and learn to be an effective listener. You cannot learn anything new when you are talking.

SUMMARY

Language is our most important tool of communication. It provides us with a means of labeling, or identifying by name, objects, acts, or persons. It is the basis of interaction, the sharing of ideas and emotions, and finally, the means by which we transmit information among ourselves and through the ages from one culture and generation to the next.

There are two major theories of language development: innateness theory and imitative theory. Innateness refers to the inborn ability to speak a language. The imitative theory holds that language is a learned behavior. While these are the two basic viewpoints, many other theories draw upon them. Language development occurs for the most part in early childhood.

Meaning is the essential part of any message. Understanding between individuals depends upon similarity of meaning.

Semantics is the study of the relationship between our words and their meanings. Abstraction is the ability to give symbolic meaning to those things that cannot be sensed—concepts, ideals, and so forth. Ambiguity and vagueness arise because one word or symbol can have several meanings, and meaning itself is relative.

Words are also denotative and connotative. They may have concrete and factual meanings, or they may represent something beyond the objective reference.

Meaning is also influenced by style. Each individual has his or her own characteristic way of communicating. Style is influenced by our personalities, our purposes, and our communication settings. In short, these variables and the laws of self-reflexiveness, non-identity, and non-allness (and their use) may drastically affect communication outcomes.

The variables of language also affect our attitudes and behavior. We sometimes assume relationships between linguistic styles and personal or cultural traits. This process is known as linguistic stereotyping and usually has a negative effect upon communication. Linguistic stereotyping plays a large part in racism and causes individuals to react to words and symbols as if they were reality itself. In order to overcome linguistic stereotypes, we must be aware of their existence and concerned with their effects. In addition, each of us should strive to make language more effective. Speaking as clearly as possible, using words that can be understood by others, relating to our listeners, and using language that is appropriate to ourselves and others are only a few of the ways in which we may begin to be more concerned and effective communicators.

EXERCISES

GROUP EXPERIENCES

Meanings Are in People

DESCRIPTION: The fact that a single word is used when referring to many different things (the example *heavy* was used earlier) points to the fact that people attach meaning to symbols: Symbols have no meaning in and of themselves. This activity will focus on the multiple meanings we attach to words.

PROCEDURE: Divide into groups of four to six. Each group should list as many different meanings as possible for the words given below. In listing the meanings, a phrase should be used to make clear the specific meaning of the word. Do as many as you can in five minutes. When the time is up, each group should read its list of meanings for each word. If a particular meaning is challenged, a standard dictionary or dictionary of slang should solve the argument.

Word List

cracked	book
spirit	black
lid	hot
down	fly
high	jam

DISCUSSION: What types of communication problems do multiple word meanings create? Do word meanings change with each generation? How can you use these and similar words in such a way as to make their meaning more explicit?

Do Your Symbols Convey Your Sense?

DESCRIPTION: Alfred Korzybski offers three basic laws, the first of which is the law of non-identity. This law says that the word is not the thing it represents. We often forget how inadequate language is in describing our emotional feelings, for example. This activity will provide you with the opportunity to explore the limitations of language.

PROCEDURE: Divide into groups of four to six. Each group should take the following common phrases and attempt to state them in more precise or explicit language. In other words, you will need to describe what "love" is, for example. After each group has completed the four phrases, they should be read aloud to the rest of the class:

Example	New Phrase
I really like him.	have a very positive feeling toward him.
I hate your guts.	
I love you.	
My head aches.	
My stomach is tied in knots.	

DISCUSSION: Do the new phrases sound funny? Are they more explicit than the common phrases? What does the law of non-identity mean to you?

Who's Talking?

DESCRIPTION: How does language affect our behavior? When compared to various languages, English has a distinctive feature. We use the word *I* as a general referent for all the "roles" we play. What "I" do in one situation may not be the same action "I" would take in another situation. Eskimos avoid the direct identification of the term *I* with "self" by using phrases such as "this woman believes" or "this man feels." Eastern philosophy suggests that using phrases such as "I am" or "you are" can be very misleading, for they infer that "you" are the thing, and, moreover, that "you" do not change your basic personality. This activity will provide you with an opportunity to see how often you make use of pronouns such as *I* or *you*.

PROCEDURE: Divide into dyads. You are to have a ten-minute conversation, during which time you cannot use the following words:

I YOU HE   SHE THEY WE

Instead, you should replace these words either with formal statements or with an alternative referent. For example

Normal: I think that . . . (*I* is unacceptable in this activity.)
Formal: It appears that institutions of education are not receiving the necessary financial support.

Alternate: This woman thinks that institutions of education are not receiving the necessary financial support.

In asking a question of your partner, you will also have to take special care with the wording, for example:

Normal: What do you think? (The use of the pronoun *you* is unacceptable in this activity.)

Formal: What are some alternative ways of viewing this situation?

Alternate: What does Dick think? (In this case you would use the name of your partner to replace the personal pronoun *you*.)

DISCUSSION: Did you experience much difficulty with this conversation? Did the "meaning" in the conversation change with the new referents used? Did you find the conversation more depersonalized when avoiding the use of pronouns? Is it difficult for you to avoid using the word *I*?

PERSONAL EXPERIENCES

1. Sit alone in a quiet room. Very slowly begin saying your name over and over. Do this for ten minutes and see if your name takes on a different meaning. Then consider whether or not you consider your "name" to be "you." Do you believe that a word in any language is not the thing but rather a symbol for it? Is your name simply a symbol for you?

2. Read the poem "The Jabberwocky" from *Through the Looking-Glass*. Then write your interpretation of this poem. Was Lewis Carroll making a comment on language in general? What do the words mean? Where did you find the meanings of the words (dictionary, context of the poem)?

DISCUSSION QUESTIONS

1. What are the two main schools of thought on language acquisition in children?

2. Discuss the stages of a child's acquisition of language during the first few months after birth, at one year, at eighteen months, at two years, and at six years.

3. What are the primary advantages and disadvantages of maintaining a nonstandard dialect or style of speaking? In what ways can "standard" users help to increase communication effectiveness between users and nonusers?

3
Listening and Feedback

KEY CONCEPTS AND TERMS

Hearing	Social listening
Listening	Serious listening
Attention	Appreciative listening
Postural adjustments	Conversational listening
Receptor adjustments	Courteous listening
Understanding	Critical listening
Remembering	Discriminative listening
Evaluating	Thinking-speaking time differential
Responding	Feedback
Active listening	Self-feedback
Passive listening	Listener feedback

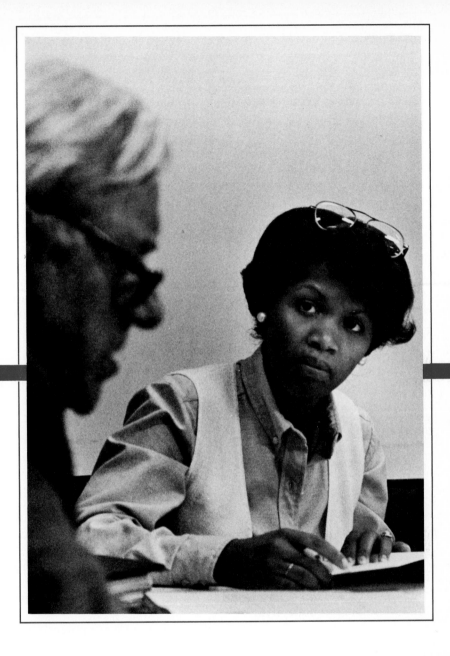

THE LISTENING PROCESS

A major computer consulting firm contracts with a Fortune 500 company to upgrade the latter's outdated computer facility. The consulting firm is asked to design and construct a new, more modern computer system and to develop a security program that will provide the company with a complete computer backup and recovery plan. To complete the mammoth task, the consulting firm subcontracts with an independent computer consultant whose fee is $7,500 a week, assigns three in-house consultants to the project at a cost of about $2,500 per person per week, and puts together a team of 20 in-house technicians at a cost of approximately $1,000 per worker per week. As the project is almost completed, one technician encounters a critical problem that threatens to delay the project and to subject the consulting firm to a heavy late penalty under its present contract.

To address the problem, the head of the project quickly contacts a member of the in-house consulting team and assigns the group to work with the independent consultant on a solution to the problem and to complete their work within seven days. At the end of the week, the project coordinator contacts a member of the consulting team, only to learn that they have "misunderstood the situation" and have designed a solution to a problem that does not exist. As a result, the project goes past the deadline, and the team of technicians and consultants must be hired for an additional week to complete the project. The cost of this listening error:

Independent consultant's fee for one week	$ 7,500
Salaries and fringe benefits of in-house con- sultants/week	$ 7,500
Salaries and fringe benefits of in-house techni- cians/week	$ 20,000
Late penalty under the company's contract	$133,000
Total loss to the company:	$168,000

Think for a moment about the last time you experienced the consequences of a listening mistake. Was it the time you showed up for a party that wasn't to be held until the following week? Or was it the day that the copy shop made eighty, instead of eight, copies of your résumé? If you haven't experienced either of these events, you probably have experienced similar mishaps due to errors in listening. In the world of business, even a $10 mistake by each of the 100 million workers in America would cost $1 billion to the industry, collectively.

As you can see, the costs of poor listening are potentially enormous. Listening errors such as those just described cost time, money, physical and psychological strain, human relationships, and sometimes even lawsuits. Given these costs (and the fact that we deal effectively with, at best, little more than one-fourth of what we hear!), it is essential that we find ways to increase our listening effectiveness and efficiency. In order to help you achieve this goal, Chapter 3 will focus on information concerning the overall listening process, on specific variables that affect our ability to listen effectively, and on ways in which we can learn to develop more effective listening skills. In addition—and related to the topic of listening—this chapter will also present information concerning the nature and functions of feedback, an important aspect of listening. We hope that once you have completed the chapter, you will be able to increase your listening skills a thousandfold. At the very least, you should be able to avoid those embarrassing little moments that result from ineffective listening.

The Hearing-Listening Distinction

Hearing, which is only one part of the listening process, refers to the physical act of receiving sounds. It is a passive process that occurs even when we're asleep. *Listening*, on the other hand, is work. It means not only hearing but also paying attention and understanding.

We all have probably had the annoying experience of telling what we thought was a fascinating story, only to discover that our "listener" may have heard our message but did not really listen to it. Several studies of college students showed that they could repeat only 50 percent of a message they had just heard. Effective listening is not a natural ability, but some people do it very well, even establishing reputations as good listeners. "You know, whenever I have a problem, I talk to Jesse. He really listens to what I have to say." There are also trained professionals, such as psychiatrists and social workers, whose jobs are to listen to the thoughts and feelings of their clients. Unfortunately, however, trained listeners and people such as Jesse are in the minority. The majority of us owe it to ourselves and others to improve our listening skills. To achieve that goal, we must seriously study and practice the art of listening.

Six Stages of the Listening Process

Our study focuses first on the listening process, which involves six stages: hearing, attending, understanding, remembering, evaluating, and responding (see Figure 3–1). The stages occur in sequence, but they are generally performed with little awareness and often in rapid succession.

HEARING.   As we mentioned earlier, the term ***hearing*** is often incorrectly used to mean listening. In fact, hearing is but one stage of the complex process of listening. Hearing refers to the response caused by sound waves stimulating the sensory receptors of the ear. This is a purely physical response. Therefore, the reception of sound waves, which we know as hearing, does not mean that there is any conscious perception of what is being heard. In other words, you must hear to listen, but you need not listen to hear. The perception necessary for listening depends on attention.

ATTENTION.   Our senses are constantly bombarded by countless stimuli from the world about us. Just as you may feel overwhelmed by the total environment at a circus or a carnival—flashing lights, loud voices, crowds milling about, smells of popcorn, cotton candy, and elephants—so, too, can your mind become overloaded by the barrage of everyday stimuli. However, your brain screens these stimuli and permits only a select few to come into focus. This selective perception is known as ***attention,*** an important requirement for effective listening.

Strong stimuli such as bright lights, sudden noises, or sharp bumps

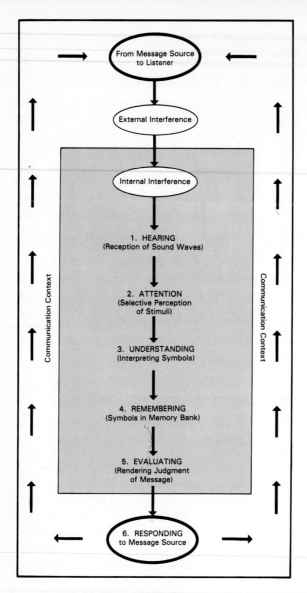

FIGURE 3–1
The Six Stages of the Learning Process

in the road are sure attention getters. Attention to more commonplace or less striking stimuli requires special effort. For example, you may unconsciously tilt your head to bring your ear closer to the source of a faint noise, or squint your eyes to make out a distant street sign. These ***postural adjustments*** are aided by physical changes in sensory receptor organs. Such ***receptor adjustments*** might include tensing of the ear's tympanic muscle for better response to weak sounds, or dilation of the pupils of the eyes to help you see better in a dark room.

UNDERSTANDING.   Hearing and perceiving a sound are still not enough to enable meaningful messages to be received. The next step is ***understanding***

Hearing is only one stage of the listening process.

the symbols we have seen and heard. To do this, we must analyze the meaning of the stimuli we have perceived. It is at this stage of the listening process, for example, that parents begin to tell the difference between a baby's playful babblings and attempts at meaningful speech. Italian and French, though beautiful and expressive languages, are only collections of pleasant sounds until we learn to understand the meaning of the word symbols.

When we talk about symbolic stimuli, we are talking not only about words but also about other sounds (applause, a fog horn, a siren) and sights (a blue uniform, a skull and crossbones, a flashing red light) that have symbolic meanings as well. The meanings attached to these symbols are a function of our past associations and of the context in which the symbols occur. Thus, we usually associate a siren with an emergency but feel no alarm when the same siren is sounded at midnight on New Year's Eve. For successful interpersonal communication, the listener must understand the intended meaning and the context assumed by the sender.

REMEMBERING.   The fourth stage of the listening process, *remembering,* is often omitted by communication analysts, who do not consider it essential to the process. Yet remembering is important to the listening process because it means that an individual has not only received and interpreted a message but has also added it to the mind's storage bank. Of course, anyone listening to the court testimony of eyewitnesses to an auto accident will immediately realize that what is remembered may be quite different from what was originally seen or heard. Just as our attention is selective, so too is our memory.

EVALUATING.   A fifth stage in which active listeners participate is the act of *evaluating.* It is at this point that the active listener weighs evidence, sorts fact from opinion, and determines the presence or absence of bias or prejudice in a message. During this stage the listener also renders judgment as a function of these criteria. The effective listener makes sure that he or she doesn't begin this activity too soon, however. Beginning this stage of the process before a message is completed requires that we no longer hear and attend to the incoming message. As a result, the listening process ceases— and so does our chance to participate as effective listeners.

RESPONDING.   The sixth and final stage of the listening process is that of *responding* to a speaker and his or her message. This stage of the process requires that the receiver complete the process through verbal and/or nonverbal feedback. Because the speaker has no other way to determine if a message has been received (all of your behaviors up to this point have been covert, or elicited intrapersonally), this stage becomes the only overt means by which the sender may determine the degree of success in transmitting the message. The feedback you return may range from silence (if you do not hear a message—or if you are angry), to smiling or frowning, to requesting clarification. By responding to a message in one of these ways, you will have made an active attempt to complete the listening process effectively.

TYPES OF LISTENING

Listening has been classified in a variety of ways by communication scholars. These classifications include the distinction between active and passive listening and, more specifically, distinctions among various types of social versus serious listening situations.

    Active listening may be distinguished from *passive listening* in a number of ways. First, in active listening, the listener has "a very definite responsibility." As Zerpa and Smeltzer point out, the listener does not passively absorb words or messages, with little personal involvement. Instead, he or she tries to grasp the facts and feelings in what the speaker has said. Passive listeners generally listen less discriminately and with decreased personal involvement.[1]

    Second, active listening is viewed as an approach to problems that arise from ordinary day-to-day events, rather than as the "wearisome" task of listening to someone's problems. Although active listening does involve placing yourself in the proverbial shoes of the speaker, it also involves an ability to step out of the person's shoes once the message exchange has been completed. In sum, active listening means listening to others with consideration.

    Third, active listening involves *wanting* to listen. If we are insincere

---

[1] J. J. Zerpa and L. R. Smeltzer, "Active Listening for Managers," *Credit and Financial Management* 86, no. 2 (1984), 21, 24.

and lacking in the general spirit of listening (a spirit which matches the worth of the speaker as a human being!), we may succeed in alienating the speaker and, perhaps, in making matters worse.[2]

Thus, active listening may be distinguished from passive listening by the extent to which the listener becomes involved in a given interaction. In his recent book, *Thriving on Chaos*, Tom Peters describes Roger Milliken as the definitive active listener. According to Peters, this 70-year-old chief executive officer of Milliken, Inc., "is like a kid when attending a session with dozens of team presentations from the 'front line' of his company." On one occasion when Peters was invited to attend the company's annual strategy meeting, Milliken turned to Peters during several presentations and "with stunned amazement" remarked: "Can you believe that? Look at what they did." According to Peters, "All news from the front is engaging to [Milliken] . . . especially if it comes from junior people who've caught fire and pushed Roger's vision further than anyone had a right to expect."[3]

Either active or passive listening may occur during social or serious listening situations, which are best distinguished by the structure of the communication setting in which they take place. If the setting is more informal and nonstructured than it is formal and structured, *social listening* will be more appropriate. Conversely, if the situation calls for a more formal and structured format, *serious listening* may potentially take place.

During informal, social listening the listener's responsibilities are limited to appreciation, conversation, and courtesy. Specifically, *appreciative listening* (the type of enjoyable, entertaining listening engaged in while attending a concert, playing a cassette, or attending a poetry reading) requires that the listener respond on a cognitive or affective level. During appreciative listening the listener remains a listener only. *Conversational listening,* however, implies a constant exchange in the roles of speaker and listener. *Courteous listening* also involves conversation, but of a more restricted type. For example, if you run into a friend of the family whom you haven't seen in years and never really cared for, you still feel obliged to listen as he fills you in on everything he has done for the last five years.

> A good listener is not only popular everywhere, but after a while he gets to know something.
>
> Wilson Mizner

The most important type of social listening in interpersonal relationships is listening to show affection, caring, and warmth. For example, your best friend has had an argument with her parents and needs to talk to someone. Sometimes you can provide support just by listening.

Some interpersonal listening occurs in formal contexts. One kind of

---

[2] Ibid., 21.
[3] T. Peters, *Thriving on Chaos: Handbook for a Management Revolution* (New York: Alfred A. Knopf, 1987), 437.

formal, serious listening is *critical listening,* which involves analysis and evaluation of what is heard. Critical listening requires certain skills, such as the ability to do the following: discern fact from fiction, separate fact from opinion, determine whether an argument is based on logic or emotion, maintain an objective attitude toward the source and the message, and clarify ambiguities. For example, as two candidates debate an issue, the critical listener will be concerned with what is said, rather than who said it, and with the logic and truth of the arguments.

Discriminative listening is another form of serious listening, the purpose of which is understanding and remembering. In order to understand what you hear, you must be able to tune in to the main ideas, follow the logic of the message, pinpoint important details, and recognize the purpose of the message. Discriminative listening is practiced by the student taking notes on a history lecture or by someone getting instructions from the florist about proper lighting for certain plants.

VARIABLES AFFECTING LISTENING

Although the six stages of listening are apparent in almost all listening situations, it would be wrong to think that these situations are all alike. The complex process of listening is affected by many variables, which operate differently in different communication interactions. Environmental setting is one such variable. For example, we are generally more excited—and listen more breathlessly—during a concert than when we listen to our favorite vocal artist at home on a record or CD. Another variable that affects how well we listen is the message source, or the person to whom we are listening. Indeed, we all have people to whom we listen and others whom we regularly "tune out." Of course, the message itself is also important. For instance, we react quite differently when we receive a call from the bank concerning an overdraft and from a friend with whom we haven't talked to for over a year. In addition, the personality and emotional state of the listener influences his or her responses (for example, we sometimes are eager to listen, and at other times we don't want to bother). Each of these variables can act either as barriers or as aids in the listening process and, thus, will be discussed more completely in the following paragraphs.

Environmental Setting

If you have ever tried to talk to a friend on a subway train or tried to enjoy a movie when a loud conversation was going on behind you, you know the extent to which noise can affect listening. Environmental noise is both distracting to your attention and detrimental to your ability to hear. Similar interference may be caused by crowding or poor acoustics, or by heat, cold, or precipitation.

A physical condition that affects listening behavior in groups and over which the listener may have little control is the seating arrangement of the people involved. A round table aids free-flowing communication and effective listening (see Chapter 4). Other seating arrangements may create barriers, however.

Your nearness to the other participants in the communication is also important. If you are seated at one end of a long table, it is almost impossible for you to listen to a conversation at the other end.

The Message Source

Research has shown that your impression of a person's status largely determines how well you listen to him or her. We all know that we listen closely to people we respect or admire, whereas we often pay little attention to those we feel are our inferiors. In addition, research suggests that females are at a disadvantage when they are a message source. Because they have a tendency to use deferential language (for example, they interrupt less often, ask a greater number of questions, and use polite commands and apologetic phrases), females are perceived to be more submissive, less assertive, and less willing to take a stand than are their male counterparts. In addition, they are viewed as less believable and, hence, are listened to less carefully.[4]

In addition, the speakers themselves determine how easy or difficult the listening situation will be for the listeners. As research suggests, it is much easier for an audience to listen to more fluent speakers (that is, those who use fewer vocal pauses such as "uh" and "um") than to speakers who are less fluent.[5]

The Message

Western Union advertises that mailgrams have more impact than ordinary letters. They are received much less frequently and thus benefit both from novelty and from association with messages of importance. These same factors of novelty and significance apply to all messages. Unusual signs catch your eye on the highway. Thundering brass bands make you stop to see what the parade is all about. In the same way, intense, emotion-filled messages also capture your attention. This explains the great effectiveness of a speaker such as Dr. Martin Luther King, Jr., in his "I Have a Dream" speech.

The Listener

No matter how excellent the acoustics, how prestigious the speaker, or how important the message, communication cannot occur unless a listener is present. The physical state of the listener can affect the listening situation. The deaf or hard-of-hearing listener can obviously be a barrier to communication. If the telephone has ever awakened you from a deep sleep, you know

---

[4] J. Liska, E. W. Mechling, and S. Stathas, "Differences in Subjects' Perceptions of Gender and Believability Between Users of Deferential and Nondeferential Language," *Communication Quarterly* 29 (1981), 40–48.
[5] L. K. Steil, L. L. Barker, and K. W. Watson, *Effective Listening: Key to Your Success* (New York: Random House, 1983), 66.

how sleepiness, too, can impair your ability to decipher a speaker's message. Less obvious, however, is the extent to which *psychological* attributes of the listener can also influence the communication process.

LISTENER ATTITUDES AND NEEDS.   Attitudes can become barriers to effective listening. If you see yourself as superior to others, with nothing to gain from listening to them, you have created a self-imposed barrier to communication. Often this causes adults to ignore what children say, just as a senior executive might ignore the suggestions of junior employees. On the other hand, if you feel a speaker is superior, you may be so willing to accept whatever is said that critical listening cannot take place at all.

Even in situations in which the status of the speaker has little effect, listeners are often guilty of prejudging. This point may be illustrated by the many times we find ourselves jumping to conclusions based on our own point of view, as opposed to what the speaker is actually saying. Sometimes we hear only what we expect to hear, no matter what is actually being said. While listening to a political debate, for example, we must be careful not to automatically hear our candidate's opponent make the stupid remarks we anticipate.

Then again, we often hear what we *want* to hear—motive is very important in the listening process. For example, an athlete who has suffered a leg injury consults a physician for advice. The physician says to avoid any great physical strain and to engage only in moderate exercise. The athlete goes out and plays an "easy" game of tennis—after all, the doctor said "moderate exercise," didn't she?

Another factor affecting listening is the shared experience, or recognition, factor. In a situation in which several conversations are going on at the same time, you will probably tune in to one of them if you hear something to which you can relate. If you are sitting in a crowded coffee shop and hear someone at the next table talking about a movie you have just seen, you will listen more closely than if you had not seen the movie. Suppose that you recognize your name being dropped in a conversation. Aren't you likely to listen very carefully to what is being said?

LISTENING HABITS.   Habits have a great deal to do with the way we listen. Throughout our lives we develop a series of listening habits, some of which may be undesirable. These habits create a barrier to communication. Early in our school careers, for example, we learn to fake attention in order to please teachers or parents. When these poor listening habits carry over to work situations, problems occur. Deadlines are missed, mistakes are made, and productivity is diminished. For this reason, many major companies now assess listening skills when considering employees for promotion. Faking attention is easily done by looking at a speaker, placing a hand under the chin, or using other gestures that suggest listening.

Another poor listening habit is listening only for facts, a habit that is often encouraged by teachers who test for content but not comprehension. While it is important to be able to separate important ideas and facts from

Your Listening-IQ

Instructions: Place an X or check mark in the blank that best describes the extent to which you exhibit these listening behaviors:

	often	sometimes	never
1. Prejudging topics and listening situations as unimportant, dry, or boring	_____	_____	_____
2. Criticizing a speaker's appearance or delivery	_____	_____	_____
3. Getting ego-involved with subjects and letting your emotions take control	_____	_____	_____
4. Listening only for facts (while overlooking intent, purpose, or structure of a message)	_____	_____	_____
5. Trying to outline everything when taking notes	_____	_____	_____
6. Faking attention to the speaker	_____	_____	_____
7. Tolerating or creating distractions during communication activities (e.g., turning on the television while talking at the dinner table or turning your desk to see what is happening in a hallway outside your office)	_____	_____	_____
8. Avoiding messages that are difficult to understand	_____	_____	_____
9. Reacting to specific words rather than the broader concept in a message (e.g., words like "abortion" that trigger word reactions)	_____	_____	_____
10. Letting your mind wander when you can somewhat follow what a speaker is saying	_____	_____	_____

less important ones, the listening process often suffers by a focus only on facts—some meanings and attitudes of the speaker may go unnoticed.

Another bad habit is avoding the difficult or uninteresting. The lazy listener just "changes channels" when something appears to be too dull or too difficult; or the listener assumes, if he or she doesn't understand an idea the first time it is presented, that it will be repeated later. We can miss a great deal of valuable information as a result of such laziness.

Although each of these poor listening habits may act as a barrier to effective listening, it is not unusual for several variables to affect any one

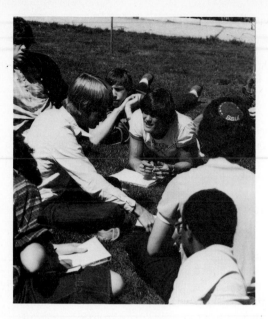

Habits affect the way that we listen.

listening situation. To determine the degree to which these factors affect your personal listening ability, take a moment to complete the above "questionnaire." By taking the time to assess the extent to which you currently exhibit poor listening habits, you can begin to overcome these problems and become a more effective listener.

DEVELOPING EFFECTIVE LISTENING SKILLS

If you completed the questionnaire on the previous page and discovered that you were "guilty" regarding any of these behaviors, you have completed the first step toward becoming a more effective listener—you have identified the poor listening habit(s) on which you can begin to work. Because so many of the factors that affect listening affect it in a negative way, it is important to work actively on developing effective listening skills.

As mentioned earlier, you listen best if you are motivated to listen, and it helps you to listen if you remind yourself of your motivation before the speaker begins: "If I am ever going to find this gas station, I'd better listen carefully to the directions." It also helps if you make a conscious effort to pay attention. You know when your mind is beginning to wander. If you let it go, you may miss the whole point of the communication; but if you make yourself pay attention at the beginning, it is more likely that you won't wander off in the middle. In addition, it is important to keep an open mind, free of prejudice. The speaker should be judged on what he or she says, not on what you wanted or expected to be said.

Listener Responsibilities

As an integral part of the communication process, the listener has specific responsibilities, the most important of which is not only to pay attention, as we've just mentioned, but also to show active signs of attentiveness. A speaker can usually judge the listener's level of attention by the facial expressions, gestures, and nods that express listening activity. A smile or nod can indicate support, while a frown or shake of the head suggests disapproval.

There are specific actions we can take to improve listening attentiveness. During the course of a communication, the active listener might choose to reflect the message back to the speaker by periodically interjecting comments such as, "What I hear you saying is that. . . ." Such comments enable you to play an active part in listening as well as to clear up any misunderstanding before it gets out of hand. By just passively listening, you may miss out on part of the communication or misinterpret the message being sent. The listener should also try to recognize the speaker's intent or purpose. You might be inclined to listen more sympathetically to a friend's seemingly endless description of the beach house she has rented for the summer if you suspect an invitation is forthcoming.

You normally have a certain amount of free time during the listening process because of the ***thinking-speaking time differential.*** Since you can think several times faster than someone can talk, you should have enough time to summarize and evaluate what is heard. While evaluating a speaker's message, you should try to figure out the speaker's view of the world and how that influences what he or she is saying. For example, if you know that the politician to whom you are listening believes that national defense is the government's first priority, you can evaluate how this view affects his or her stand on the particular issues being discussed—military spending, foreign aid, the draft, and so forth.

Above all, always attempt to use your powers of concentration to the greatest extent. The most effective way to overcome psychological or environmental barriers to listening is simply by good concentration.

To sum up, you can improve your listening behavior by being aware of what is happening in a communication situation. Chances are that you already know many ways to be a better listener, but the trick is to actually behave that way during a real listening situation. Some of the more desirable listening behaviors are listed in Table 3–1. These "effective listening habits" constitute ten tips for overcoming the ten worst listening habits listed in the questionnaire that you previously completed.

FEEDBACK

Communication is a circular process. As a message is transmitted from sender to receiver, a return message, known as ***feedback,*** is transmitted in the opposite direction. Feedback is a message that indicates the level of understanding or agreement between two or more communication in response to an original

TABLE 3–1 Tips for Effective Listening

1. When listening to "uninteresting" subject matter, look for benefits and opportunities by asking, "What's in it for me?"
2. Judge content—not the appearance or delivery of a speaker.
3. To avoid getting overstimulated by some part of a message, hold your fire: Avoid making a judgment until the message is complete.
4. Avoid listening only for facts by listening for central themes and ideas.
5. Be flexible when taking notes; take fewer notes and use different systems of notetaking depending on the speaker.
6. Overcome the temptation to fake attention by working hard to listen and assuming an active listening stance (e.g., lean forward, make eye contact with speaker).
7. Resist distractions by fighting or avoiding them; learn how to concentrate.
8. Seek out difficult material rather than avoid it; use "heavy" material as an exercise for the mind.
9. Keep an open mind when confronted with an emotional word with which you are uncomfortable. Work to interpret color words rather than to get hung up on them.
10. Capitalize on the fact that thought is faster than speech: Use them to summarize mentally, weigh evidence, and to listen "between the lines."

Source: Adapted from L. K. Steil, L. L. Barker, and K. W. Watson, *Effective Listening*: *Key to Your Success* (Reading, Mass.: Addison-Wesley, 1983), 72–73.

message. Feedback represents a listener's verbal or nonverbal commentary on the message being communicated.

Feedback is an ongoing process that usually begins as a reaction to various aspects of the initial message. For example, a definite response is being fed back to the speaker when we shake our heads affirmatively or look quizzically at the speaker. Feedback plays an essential role in helping us to determine whether or not our message has been understood, whether it is being received positively or negatively, and whether our audience is open or defensive, self-controlled or bored. Feedback can warn us that we must alter our communication to achieve the desired effect. If we are not aware of feedback or don't pay any attention to it, there is a strong possibility that our efforts at communicating will be completely ineffective.

To emphasize the importance of the feedback mechanism in communication, you need only imagine yourself growing up for the last 18 years or so, never having received any feedback. No one has praised you as you learned to walk or ride a bike. No one has warned you not to chase a ball into the street or to put your hand on a hot stove. No one has shared your tears or laughter. You probably would not function well at all. How would you appraise your self-concept? What values or morals would you possess? While such an existence is impossible, since a certain amount of feedback comes from you yourself as well as from others in the environment, this example does suggest the various functions and effects of feedback in the communication process.

Nothing that man possesses is more precious than his awareness.

Robert De Ropp

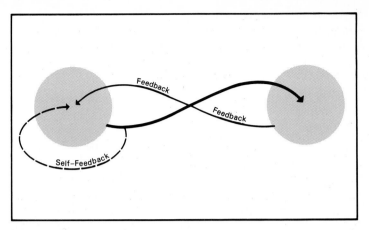

FIGURE 3–2
Self-Feedback and Listener Feedback

Types of Feedback

There are two types of feedback: self-feedback and listener feedback (see Figure 3–2).

Self-feedback applies to the words and actions that are fed back into your central nervous system as you perceive your own muscular movements and hear yourself speak. Feeling your tongue twist as you mispronounce a word or, in a library, suddenly realizing that you are speaking too loudly are examples of self-feedback. Another example would be hearing yourself use a word incorrectly, or reversing sounds—for example, asking, "Were you sappy or had?" instead of "happy or sad."

Research indicates that self-feedback plays an important role in the nature and form of our judgmental processes, especially when listener feedback is absent. For example, Hagafors and Brehmer have found that our judgments become more consistent when we are required to justify them to others and when no other form of listener feedback is present. In addition, under these conditions our judgments seem to become more analytical and less intuitive. It seems that self-feedback in the form of justification alters the nature and form of our overall judgmental process.[6]

The other major type of feedback, *listener feedback,* involves verbal and nonverbal responses. Verbal feedback may take the form of questions or comments. A listener may, for instance, ask a speaker to explain the last point or give praise for making the story so interesting. Nonverbal feedback may be transmitted by applause or laughter, to indicate approval, or by a blank stare, which might indicate disinterest or confusion. Even silence can act as feedback. If a teacher asks a question and no one answers, the silence may indicate lack of knowledge, misunderstanding, or perhaps dislike

---

[6] R. Hagafors and B. Brehmer, "Does Having to Justify One's Judgment Change the Nature of the Judgment Process?" *Organizational Behavior and Human Performance* 31 (1983), 223–32.

of the teacher. If a father asks his son if he has finished his homework and the son doesn't reply, that silence is meaningful.

Functions of Feedback

Feedback serves various functions in the communication process. The first of these functions is to evaluate what is right or wrong about a particular communication. If you give a speech to the class, your teacher will offer criticism and suggestions for improving your delivery. If someone is watching you hang a painting, he or she will give you feedback as you try various positions, to help you find the right place for it. As will be discussed in Chapter 4, nonverbal feedback, in the form of nods and hand movements, helps to regulate turn taking in conversation.

Secondly, feedback can serve to stimulate change. For example, a popular soft-drink company, after changing its century-old formula, received so much mixed feedback in the form of letters and phone calls that the company not only retained the new formula but brought back the original formula and placed both on grocery-store shelves.

A third function of feedback is to reinforce, to give reward or punishment. A father says, "I'm proud of you, son," or "Jim, can't you ever keep quiet!" When used in this way, rewarding feedback encourages certain behaviors, while punishing feedback is intended to discourage certain behaviors. Comedians rely on positive reinforcement from their audience in the form of laughter; their performance may improve if they sense that the audience feedback is positive.

Effects of Feedback

If you have ever made a phone call and found yourself talking to an answering machine, or prepared and sent a tape to a friend overseas, you may have felt somewhat uncomfortable, or even foolish. It is difficult to sound conversational when there is no one on the other end to respond. This example suggests that feedback is an essential part of the communication process. We can see this through the effects of feedback.

Probably the most important effect of feedback on the communication process is in improving the accuracy of understanding. For example, a teacher seeing only blank stares during a complicated lecture might make a conscious effort to repeat and clarify certain points until the audience shows signs of nodding in agreement. As this example indicates, feedback may increase the amount of time necessary for a communication interaction to be completed. Nonetheless, it ensures a more thoroughly and clearly transmitted message.

In terms of intrapersonal and interpersonal communication, the most significant effect of feedback, and one that is often long range, is its impact on self-concept. Surely you know people who have poor self-images and little feeling of self-worth. It is probable that such individuals have based this self-image on punishing feedback received from family and peers during crucial periods of identity development. On the other hand, an individual

Feedback serves to stimulate change.

who has had considerable rewarding feedback from family and friends is likely to develop a favorable self-concept.

Feedback also affects performance. As organizational psychologists Fay Walther and Susan Taylor have noted, feedback is essential to maintaining satisfaction and increased task performance. Because we often do not recognize our problems and deficiencies, we may feel justified in continuing a given level of performance. Through increased feedback (if it is timely and consistent), task performance may be improved. As a result, overall well-being and job satisfaction may be maximized.[7]

Feedback can work in two directions, however. For example, a beginning tennis player who has been praised for her skill at the sport (rewarding feedback) will probably perceive it to be an easier game than will a player who performs equally well but who has received harsh criticism (punishing feedback). Similarly, a student who fails a test (punishing feedback) may aim for just passing the next one instead of working for an *A*. Thus, we can see that feedback also affects performance expectations.

Another important effect of feedback on performance concerns task behavior, particularly in small groups. When people find themselves in small group situations in which they don't know the other members of the group,

[7] F. Walther and S. Taylor, "An Active Feedback Program Can Spark Performance," *Personnel Administrator* 28 (1983), 107, 109, 111, 147, 149.

they often suffer from feelings of rejection and hostility. Those negative feelings can keep the group from performing any type of cooperative work. Positive reinforcement from group members, as well as from outside observers, will help the group interact better and will ultimately improve performance. For example, a group of quarrelsome young children complimented on how well they are cleaning up their play area may continue the task with renewed enthusiasm.

Feedback can also affect your attitude toward your own messages or toward the messages of others. There is an extensive body of research on this aspect of feedback. Basically, the findings indicate that "we respond with positive motivation to feedback that is consistent and timely, and includes some positive information."[8] In addition, Taylor and Walther have also found that we do not generally experience adverse reactions to negative feedback as long as the information is perceived as accurate.[9]

We have all had experiences that, though less controlled than research studies, help to clarify the findings of these feedback studies. Perhaps you remember a time when you were in a theater, watching a comedy that you and the rest of the audience did not find amusing. No one was laughing. Yet when several members of the audience later began to laugh loudly, your reaction somehow became more favorable. Soon you were laughing, too. This is the reason for using laugh tracks in television situation comedies.

GIVING EFFECTIVE FEEDBACK

Feedback is often so spontaneous that you are unaware of giving or receiving it. Nevertheless, there are ways to consciously make your feedback more effective. One method is to focus on observations rather than inferences. For example, consider the following situation: A young woman passes a friend whom she had dated several times. She says hello, but her friend walks right on by. The next time she sees him, she asks, "Hey, are you mad at me? You ignored me the other day when I saw you downtown." She has assumed a negative motive for the man's action, although he may simply have been preoccupied. The woman's feedback to her friend would have been more productive if she had relayed the facts, and only the facts, as she understood them: "Hey, I saw you the other day and called to you, but you didn't answer." This would permit the man to make an honest response, rather than a defensive one.

Another method for increasing the effectiveness of your feedback is to use description rather than judgment. The captain of a basketball team would be more helpful in coaching her players if she said, "You're not running

---

[8] Ibid., 107.
[9] M. Taylor and F. Walther, "The Relationship of Feedback Dimensions to Work Attitudes and Behavior: Process and Practical Implications" (Paper presented at the Midwestern Academy of Management, April 1981).

for the ball and you're moving too slowly," as opposed to, "You're really getting lazy."

It is also important to give immediate feedback. We often delay our responses to problems and conflicts and wait for emotions to die down. It is better to deal with anger or hurt when it occurs, when you are in touch with your reactions. Feedback at the time is more specific and accurate than it can be, say, two months later. Yet sometimes extreme emotions make you overreact or respond in ways you later regret. Again, your feedback should be appropriate to the situation, and controlled to the extent possible.

Limiting feedback is another means of increasing its effectiveness, particularly in a one-to-one situation in which you are the listener. Constantly nodding or interjecting comments in such situations is interfering, at best, and may show superficiality and insincerity, at worst. Thus, it is necessary to guard against overresponding. A smile or nod of agreement to particularly significant statements does more to show that you understand than continuous "uh-huhs."

The act of using conscious feedback techniques may sometimes seem unnatural. It is important to remember, however, that effective feedback does improve the communication process. While feedback that is entirely calculated tends to be stilted, awareness of the feedback mechanism and the messages you are transmitting is an asset to communication.

SUMMARY

Despite the importance of listening in the communication process, studies have shown that many of us are poor listeners. We often take listening for granted and place little, if any, importance on developing good listening skills.

The listening process involves six distinct stages: hearing, the physical reception of stimuli; attention, the focused perception of verbal or nonverbal stimuli; understanding, the interpretation of stimuli into messages, which are then cognitively and affectively evaluated; remembering, the storage of these messages; evaluating, weighing evidence, sorting fact from opinion, and, on the basis of these, rendering judgment; and responding, completing the process through verbal and/or nonverbal feedback.

Listening may also be classified along an active-passive continuum, as a function of degree of involvement, as well as along a social-serious continuum, depending on the degree of formality and structure in the context. These classifications, in turn, may be categorized as courteous, appreciative, and conversational listening (on the social end of the continuum) and critical versus discriminative listening (on the serious end of the continuum).

Effective listening can be helped or hindered by factors related to the environmental setting, the source of the message, the type of message, or the personality variables of the listener. Because so many of these factors affect listening in a negative way, it is the listener's responsibility to try to improve his or her listening skills in both social and serious situations.

Perhaps the most important responsibility of the listener is to transmit effective feedback to the speaker. Simply stated, feedback is a reaction to various aspects of a particular message. It may be communicated through verbal comments or nonverbal gestures. While feedback is usually identified with reactions of the listener, there is also a certain amount of self-feedback, which takes place inside the communicator.

Both self-feedback and listener feedback function to regulate performance in communication processes, to stimulate change in listeners, and to reinforce selected behavior patterns. Feedback ensures greater accuracy in interpreting messages. On a psychological level, feedback affects our self-concept. If the information is consistent and timely, rewarding feedback tends to improve self-concept, task performance, and satisfaction. Negative feedback is effective if we perceive the information to be accurate. In addition, feedback in groups can help to improve performance of the assigned tasks. Finally, feedback can produce changes in a communicator's attitude toward his or her own messages or toward the messages transmitted by others.

While most feedback is communicated without your full awareness, it is possible to adopt conscious strategies to make your feedback more effective. These strategies focus on observations rather than inferences and on description rather than judgment. In addition, they stress immediate but controlled feedback. Remembering such strategies in everyday feedback situations ensures more effective communication and listening.

EXERCISES

GROUP EXPERIENCES

Do You Really Understand What I Am Saying?

DESCRIPTION: We use the word *understand* very loosely. Most of the time we mean that we are "hearing" something and translating it into the way we perceive the world—and then we call this phenomenon "understanding." The following experience is an opportunity to see how well you understand another person and how well he or she understands you.

PROCEDURE: Divide into groups of three. Persons A and B should discuss an issue they find controversial. Person C should observe the interaction and report on it after the exercise is completed. After each communication between Person A and Person B, the listening partner should attempt to paraphrase the speaker's position until the speaker accepts the paraphrase. An example of this interaction would be as follows:

Person A: I think that war is a waste in general. On the other hand, George Kennan claims that war can clear the path for a new form of government to emerge.

Person B: What I heard you say is that war isn't bad as long as it serves to clear the way for better forms of government.

Person A: I will not accept your paraphrase.

This process will continue until Person B provides an acceptable paraphrase for Person A. The person doing the paraphrasing should try to use different words than those of the speaker. The interaction should take from fifteen to twenty minutes. At the end of that time, Person C should offer an appraisal of what occurred.

DISCUSSION: When you have completed this activity, ask yourself these questions: How long did it take you to provide accurate paraphrases for your partner? How long did it take your partner to provide accurate paraphrases of your position? Was your verbal message clear? What are the implications of this activity? Does it suggest that most of the time we do not truly understand what another person is saying?

Did You See What I Saw?

DESCRIPTION: Our psychological makeup causes us to attend selectively to different stimuli, but we do not necessarily select the same stimuli as another person. We truly see the world through our own set of filters. The following activity demonstrates this idea.

PROCEDURE: Have one person arrange approximately 30 different items on a tray, such as a can opener, lipstick, a pen, a paperclip, and so on. Include (1) items that most people would not know the name of, such as a special tool; (2) items that are typically used by one sex as opposed to the other (pipe, lipstick); and (3) items that are taboo, such as underwear, a sanitary napkin, and so on.

Each individual may take 20 seconds to look at (not touch) the items on the tray. Immediately after you view the tray, try to list everything you saw. (Afterwards you may wish to check your list against a complete list of the items on the tray.)

DISCUSSION: The most obvious finding of this experiment is that people will remember different things. Were the first five items you remembered different from the first five items others remembered? Did you remember the male items? the female items? Did you attempt to describe the items for which you did not have a particular name? By comparison, did you remember more, less, or the same number of items as other people did? Do you selectively attend in listening as well as in seeing?

Silence Is Golden

DESCRIPTION: Most of us are poor listeners. We are usually thinking about what we want to say rather than about what the other person is saying. Try the following experiment, and check out your own listening behavior.

PROCEDURE: Divide into dyads. Person A should begin the conversation by describing a peak experience—a high point in his or her life. Person A should talk in short stretches, no more than 30 seconds at a time.

Person B must then wait 10 seconds before continuing the conversation. Person B should either respond to A or describe a peak experience of his or her own. The same guideline of length applies to Person B.

This process continues with each person waiting 10 seconds before speaking.

DISCUSSION: Does it feel awkward to wait before talking? At which point in listening do you begin to think about what you are going to say? Do you usually try to avoid these silent spaces? By the way, are you a good listener?

PERSONAL EXPERIENCES

1. Change the type of feedback you normally give people. For example, listen to a person in a one-to-one interaction without giving any verbal or nonverbal feedback. Make sure that you are not unconsciously nodding your head or shifting your position. Observe the person's reactions to the absence of feedback. After the conversation is over, ask how the person felt—if he or she noticed anything peculiar during the course of the interaction.

2. Take a ride with a friend in a car, on a bus, or on a bicycle. Ride for about 20 minutes and then discuss what each of you observed about your physical surroundings during the ride. Did you notice different things, people, places? Why did you observe different things? Do you tend to associate with people who select the same "stimuli" in the world as you do?

3. Observe yourself during a class of your choice—particularly one in which there is a lecture presentation. Watch the number of times your attention wanders—and for how long.

4. Sit in a public area, such as a library, a town square, or a park, and close your eyes for 10 minutes. Listen to the different sounds around you and try to determine what you are hearing. Would you normally be hearing these sounds if you had your eyes open? How aware are you of different sounds? Do you selectively listen during everyday activities?

DISCUSSION QUESTIONS

1. How do we distinguish *listening* from *hearing*?
2. What qualities does a good listener possess?
3. What effective methods of verbal and nonverbal feedback can you use as a good listener?
4. How does the type of feedback provided by a listener affect the communicator?

4
Nonverbal Communication

KEY CONCEPTS AND TERMS

Repeating
Substituting
Complementing
Regulating
Accenting
Deceiving
Leakage
Kinesics
Emblems
Illustrators
Regulators
Affect displays
Body manipulators

Proxemics
Intimate distance
Personal distance
Social distance
Public distance
Territoriality
Paralanguage
Quality
Pitch
Resonance
Tempo
Voice quality

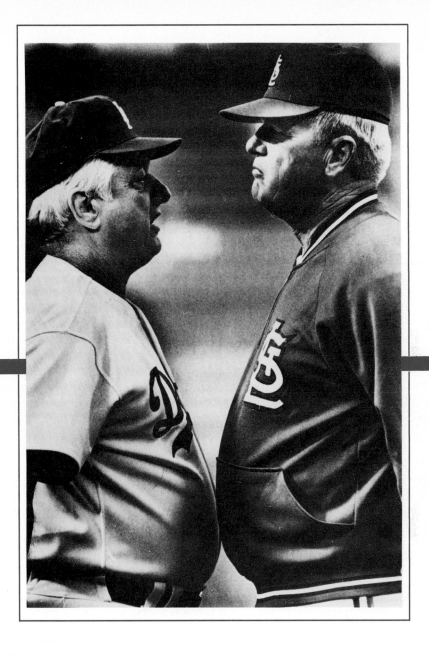

As more and more organizations enter the international marketplace, their executives and managers are rediscovering the importance of "minding their *P*'s and *Q*'s" and are turning to etiquette experts for refresher courses in corporate manners. Why has corporate etiquette become such a hot topic in boardrooms across the nation? According to Letitia Baldrige, America's first lady of etiquette, good manners are "cost-effective" because they

- increase the quality of life in the workplace,
- contribute to optimum employee morale,
- embellish the company image, and
- play a major role in generating profit.[1]

As a result of the importance of these variables to success in any organization, Baldrige and other experts have been jetting across America and consulting with corporate moguls on topics ranging from the etiquette of giving out business cards to seating arrangements at high-level dinners.

Interestingly enough, these two topics—and the hundreds of others that etiquette consultants are addressing in their seminars each day—have long been the purview of nonverbal communication experts as well. In short, the overriding message of both groups is: *How* we say something to others is often more important than *what* we say.

Although this chapter does not address the topic of corporate etiquette per se, it does address several related areas of interest—for example, the messages that we send to others through our facial expressions, eye behavior, body movements, gestures, clothing, and personal appearance. In addition, the chapter discusses the importance of touch, space, paralanguage, smell and taste, and environmental factors to communication. Because we acquire nonverbal behavior patterns early in life, we seldom have reason to think about them consciously. However, as Letitia Baldrige would agree, a great deal of information is communicated and can be learned from nonverbal expressions—both your own as well as those of people around you.

Before we continue, it is important to emphasize one point. No element of nonverbal behavior—be it a wink, a slouch, a tone of voice, or a gesture—can be interpreted in isolation. Verbal and nonverbal behavior are complementary; neither is really complete without the other. In addition, if we are to fully understand the nature of the nonverbal communication process, we must also consider the context, or the overall situation in which nonverbal behavior occurs, and its relationship to an individual's entire verbal and nonverbal behavior patterns.

FUNCTIONS OF NONVERBAL COMMUNICATION

Nonverbal communication plays a vital role in every communication event. From the clothes we wear during an important interview to the music we select to set the stage for a romantic evening, nonverbal cues send messages that are frequently more compelling and eloquent than any verbal statement. (*Note*: This statement assumes that each of you has worried—at least once— about "how you look" for an important date.) Although we are all aware to some degree of the impact of nonverbal communication, you may not be cognizant of the extent to which nonverbal messages function in our

---

[1] S. Gelles-Cole (ed.), *Letitia Baldrige's Complete Guide to Executive Manners* (New York: Rawson Associates, 1985), 3.

everyday lives. Specifically, nonverbal communication serves to repeat, substitute, complement, regulate, or accent our verbal messages. In addition, nonverbal cues often serve as a means for deception.

Repeating

> "Me?" said Danny, with wide, innocent eyes, pointing his index finger to his chest. "I'd never do something like that!"

When we communicate with one another, we use words and their nonverbal equivalents at the same time. For example, verbal statements of agreement or disagreement ("Right, right"; "No way"; "Are you kidding?") are often accompanied by a nod or shake of the head to indicate positive or negative feelings. We call these nonverbal gestures **repeating** messages because they convey the same meaning as the verbal message. Of course, either the words or the nods by themselves would be enough—but repeating messages are done almost without thinking. They are a very basic part of language behavior, occurring naturally, without conscious thought or intent.

Substituting

> They were not allowed to say a word, but we knew exactly how they felt by looking at their faces.

When hearing or speaking is impossible, nonverbal communication often replaces verbal messages. In such instances nonverbal messages are called **substitutes,** because they take the place of words. Thus, someone directing you into a tight parking space might substitute gestures for words when the car's noisy engine prohibits speaking. Another kind of substitution is made when someone with whom you've had an argument attacks you with "looks that could kill."

For nonverbal communication to act as a substitute, it must be recognized and, more importantly, interpreted in the same way by most of the people in a specific group, subculture, or culture. For example, people in the United States interpret the "thumbs down" sign to mean "no." Such well-known substitutes are so universal that they have been recorded in dictionaries of American gestures. Misunderstandings may occur, however, when we try to use our culture's nonverbal substitutes in another culture. Thus, Americans who say "I" by pointing to their chests would not be understood in Japan, where "I" is symbolized by pointing to one's nose.

Complementing

> "You don't believe it hurt, huh? Well, just let me shove you the way that idiot shoved me. You'll see!"

We also use nonverbal language to complement, complete, or accent explanations of how to do something or in descriptions of specific sizes or shapes.

To understand how important these **complementing** actions can be, just try the following without using nonverbal behavior: Teach a new dance step, explain how to tie a slip knot, or describe the shape of an hourglass.

Complementing behaviors are also used to emphasize emotional feelings or attitudes. The same complementing gesture can accompany quite different emotions, however:

> The five finalists in the essay contest stepped onto the stage. When the fourth runner-up was announced, the remaining contestants applauded loudly. When the winner was finally announced, the first runner-up applauded, but as she congratulated the new winner, tears streamed down her face.

In this example, the complementing gesture of applause was used in each instance—first to express a positive response (relief at still being "in the running") and then to accompany a negative response (disappointment).

Regulating

> Lily knew her father wanted to talk. She could feel his steady gaze upon her. As she turned and looked at him, he said, "Lily. . . ."

One of the most common purposes of nonverbal communication is **regulating.** Let's say that you and a friend are discussing a movie you saw the other night. Without regulating messages, you might sound something like this:

> "Hey, did you catch the movie at the Plaza the other night? O.K., I'm finished talking for the moment. You can speak."
> "Thank you. I wanted to answer your question. Yeah. Great. Especially that scene in the woods. . . ."
> "Can I talk?"
> "You want to talk again? Sure."
> "Thanks. I just wanted to say that I let out the biggest scream during that part!"

Fortunately, typical conversations don't require this kind of verbal permission to speak or respond. Instead, nonverbal cues automatically keep the conversation flowing between the turn-yielder (the person who has just spoken and is allowing the other to speak) and the turn-requester (the person who wishes to speak).

The nonverbal behaviors that mean "I want to talk" and "It's your turn to talk" are rules of interaction that we learn early in life. Nodding and looking at the area around the eyes of the other person are two examples of such nonverbal gestures. Speakers steadily increase the amount of time they spend looking at the listener as their speaking turn nears completion. There is also an increase in the amount of listener nodding as his or her turn to speak approaches. How fast the listener nods and whether or not the nods are accompanied by short verbal statements such as "sure" determine whether or not the listener is requesting time to respond. Slow, silent nods in response to the speaker's request for feedback usually increase the chances that the speaker will continue.

Accenting

> Sally slammed the book shut. "Oh, what's the use! There's no way I'll learn all this by tomorrow!"

Another function of nonverbal communication is **accenting,** the use of gestures, such as nods, blinks, squints, and shrugs, to help emphasize or punctuate spoken words:

> Adrienne's cocker spaniel just won first prize in the dog show. As she leads him out of the ring, friends and family congratulate both Adrienne and the dog with warm words, but also with pats on the back.

Accenting can also be achieved by changing the pitch or stress on a word or group of words. In fact, our entire meaning often depends on which words are accented:

> *I* want to dance with him.
> I want to dance with *him*.
> I want to *dance* with him.

Deceiving/Revealing

> "I'll see you and raise you five bucks," Kelly said with his usual poker face.

Sometimes we purposely deceive others or supply them with false information. You may not like a friend's new haircut, for example, but still say, "Your hair looks great!" to avoid hurting his feelings. At the same time that you are saying this and staring convincingly into your friend's eyes, you may be nervously pulling at your coat buttons. If your friend is sensitive to nonverbal behavior, he may pick up this contradictory message.

Deception cues (for example, an overly exaggerated smile or a too severe frown) suggest possible falsehood but do not tell what information is being withheld or falsified. **Leakage,** on the other hand, implies "spilling the beans" about the withheld information. For example, biting a fingernail can leak nervousness, or a clenched fist can leak the desire to fight.

Research on deception has demonstrated a relationship between the message-sending ability of a body part and the deception clues and leakage it reveals. Specifically, the face and the eyes are the best senders of messages. Their expressions are easily and quickly disseminated to the observer. Because so much attention is paid to our facial features, however, we all learn to alter these when we want to deceive someone. At the same time, little attention is paid to our hands, legs, and feet.

To demonstrate this statement, Cody and O'Hair asked male and female participants to either lie or tell the truth during a nonverbal communication experiment. Results of their study revealed that males who lied engaged in more facial touching and also exhibited increased leg and foot movements than male truth tellers. Conversely, female liars engaged in less leg and foot movements while lying, and used fewer hand gestures than female truth-tellers. It seems that the female liars attempted to control their behavior when lying and exhibited better control than did their male counterparts.[2]

> He that has eyes to see and ears to hear may convince himself that no mortal can keep a secret. If his lips are silent, he chatters with his fingertips; betrayal oozes out of him at every pore.
>
> Sigmund Freud

As you can see, unconscious movements of these appendages are often dead giveaways of our thoughts. In short, our faces and eyes are the most expressive but tell the most lies, while our hands and feet don't say as much but often tell the truth. Remember this the next time you really want to know what someone is thinking. Listen to the words, look at the facial expressions, but don't forget to look down at the hands and feet. Somewhere in the body's actions, the truth prevails.

TYPES OF NONVERBAL COMMUNICATION

Many people, because of popularized reading, consider body language to be the only form of nonverbal communication. However, nonverbal communication includes body language and much, much more. Each day we nonverbally signal our moods, attitudes, and values to others. Have you ever dressed up for a job interview, hugged a friend, been late for an appointment, wanted to sit in a certain seat in a class, or used your hands while talking? If so, you were communicating to others nonverbally. We are often unaware of our nonverbal behaviors. In our attempt to increase sensitivity to different types of our nonverbal behavior, we will examine facial expressions, eye behavior, kinesics and body movement, personal appearance and clothing, touching, proxemics, paralanguage, smell and taste, and environmental factors.

Facial Expressions

The face is perhaps the most obvious vehicle for nonverbal communication. It is a constant source of information to those around us. For example, a

---

[2] M. J. Cody and H. D. O'Hair, "Nonverbal Communication and Deception: Differences in Deception Cues Due to Gender and Communication Dominance," *Communication Monographs* 50 (1983), 175–92.

neuromuscular therapist uses nonverbal cues from a client's face to gauge the existence and subsequent release of "trigger points," or muscular tissue in which a great deal of tension has built up. Likewise, attorneys specializing in criminal law pay close attention to the face and eyes of future clients for clues to the latter's possible guilt or innocence.

How does the face send such nonverbal cues? When something makes you happy or sad (or produces any other emotion), your nerves immediately send a message to the face, which causes the muscles to contract or relax. The feedback you get from these muscle movements is one of the cues that tells you what emotional feeling you are having. This process is a form of internal self-feedback in intrapersonal communication, which will be discussed in the following chapter.

Think of all the things your face can say about you without your saying a word. Things such as wrinkles, baldness, and coloring comment not only on your age but also on the kind of life you lead—for example, we suspect that people with dark tans spend a considerable amount of time outdoors. The length and style of your hair and the amount of makeup you wear suggest your economic status, interest in fashion, and sometimes even your politics. All of these things, plus the facial expressions that reveal emotion, can speak for you before you ever open your mouth.

Charles Darwin first argued that many of our facial expressions evolved from lower animals, and scientists are still debating this issue. On one side of the debate, some research has yielded support for Darwin's theory about universal behaviors. For example, Paul Ekman and his colleagues have identified seven emotions that can be discerned universally from facial expressions: happiness, fear, sadness, anger, disgust, contempt, and surprise.[3] Identification of these emotions was based on a number of studies that demonstrated the recognition of emotions by adults across a number of cultures.

However, contradictory results have emerged in several cross-cultural studies, particularly those in which descriptions of situations have been supplied to individuals who are making judgments. For instance, using photographs that were identical to those used by Ekman in one of his studies, Niit and Valsiner conducted an experiment with Estonian and Kirghiz university students in the Soviet Union. Subjects were asked to describe the emotion that an individual in a photograph was attempting to convey—either with or without an accompanying description of the situation in which the emotional expression might occur. Results of their study revealed differences in students' recognition of the emotions when situational cues were supplied, while no differences from prior research emerged when situational descriptions were not provided.[4] Studies such as these support an alternative theory of facial expressions and their origins: It is the context of the event that supplies the meanings for facial expressions. Thus, one's culture is responsible for the ways in which its members encode and decode facial expressions.

---

[3] P. Ekman and W. V. Friesen, *Unmasking the Face* (Englewood Cliffs, N.J.: Prentice-Hall, 1975).
[4] T. Niit and J. Valsiner, "Recognition of Facial Expressions: An Experimental Investigation of Ekman's Model," *Tartu Riikliku Ulikooli Toimetised: Trudy po Psikhologii* 429 (1977), 85–107.

Although the debate concerning the origin of facial expression continues, some agreement exists regarding the universal ability of humans to encode and decode emotions via facial expressions. However, this "agreement" is qualified by the argument that cultures do differ in their uses of facial expressions and, hence, have a profound effect on how emotions are encoded and decoded. For example, research shows that Ekman's Facial Action Coding System offers a cross-culturally reliable set of units to describe expressions of basic emotions as well as their intensity.[5] However, Ekman, Roper, and Hager demonstrated that performances in imitating simple and complex facial expressions improve with age—especially when children have the benefits of practice, encouragement, and seeing themselves in a mirror.[6] This research supports the parental role in teaching facial expressions, as well as instructing children in their meanings. Thus, because of dissimilar learning patterns, members of two different cultures may react quite differently to the same stimulus. For example, one person might show disgust at the sight of an insect or snake, whereas another person might show elation because these animals are considered delightfully delicious edibles.

It also is important to note that cultural rules and societal pressures often inhibit spontaneous facial expressions. At early ages children learn which expressions are acceptable and which are unacceptable by hearing, "If you keep frowning, your face will grow like that" or "A shot is nothing to be afraid of; you've got to act like a big boy now." We also learn how to adapt our facial expressions to meet the expectations of others. How many times have you smiled politely when receiving an unwanted gift, held back tears after a bitter disappointment, or avoided laughing when watching someone trip over a curb? We all adjust many of our natural facial expressions to those considered to be more appropriate.

Eye Behavior

For centuries poets and painters have paid tribute to our expressive eyes. Modern-day researchers, too, have been intrigued by the eyes and the many nonverbal messages they convey. In general, eye behavior functions to provide information, regulate interaction, exercise social control, express intimacy, and facilitate goals.[7]

Certain eye behaviors are associated with definite moods, reactions, or attitudes. For example, consider the common negative connotation of "small, beady eyes." We also hold stereotypes about eye pupil size. Research indicates that people with large pupils are perceived to be happier and more attractive, whereas those with small pupils are viewed to be angry or unattractive.[8] However, as McAfee, Fox, and Hicks have argued, it is

---

[5] M. Wiggers, "Judgments of Facial Expressions of Emotion Predicted from Facial Behavior," *Journal of Nonverbal Behavior* 7 (Winter 1982), 101–15.

[6] P. Ekman, G. Roper, and J. Hager, "Deliberate Facial Movement," *Child Development* 51 (1980), 886–91.

[7] C. L. Kleinke, "Gaze and Eye Contact: A Research Review," *Psychological Bulletin* 100, no. 1 (1986), 78–100.

[8] E. H. Hess, "Attitude and Pupil Size," *Scientific American* 212, no. 4 (1965), 54.

important to realize that pupil variations occur in the context of other facial features.[9] Thus, the child with eyes with large pupils who seems to be nothing but innocence and sincerity can be "caught" in a lie if we attend to other nonverbal (that is, facial) cues.

Eye contact is another significant eye behavior variable. Speakers who never look up seem formal or nervous. Speakers who do look at their audience during a speech seem more relaxed and informal. We also tend to feel that their speeches are more genuine. Likewise, a listener who does not look at the speaker detracts from the speaker's image of authority and control. Perhaps this is why angry teachers or parents command, "Look at me when I'm talking to you." Little or no eye contact from a listener may not always anger you, but it does indicate lack of interest in what you are saying.

Our discussion of conversation regulators mentioned some examples of eye behavior. Visual interactions are indeed used to regulate conversation. The speaker usually catches the eye of the listener and thus the listener's attention. Before starting a long speech, however, the speaker will drop his or her eyes. Throughout the speech, periodic eye checks ensure that the listener is still there and attentive. Conversely, eye contact is avoided during pauses when the speaker is groping for the right words. When finished, the speaker turns his or her gaze to the listener, signaling that the listener can now have the floor.

Despite this general pattern, there are great individual differences in visual behavior during conversation. Depending on the speaker, gazes directed at the other person can range from about 10 percent to more than 70 percent of the conversation time. It has been suggested that these differences are related to the patterns of dominance and submissiveness we mentioned earlier. As Dovidio and Ellyson note in their study concerning power and visual dominance, attributions of power increase as the proportion of looking while speaking increases, and decrease as the proportion of looking while listening increases.[10] Thus, dominant, poised individuals look more at others during conversations than do submissive, uneasy individuals, particularly when speaking with other people.

Eye behavior also allows us to express our inner feelings to others—especially our interpersonal attitudes and the level of intimacy we are experiencing.[11] Think for a moment about the last time you gazed into the eyes of someone whom you love. If he or she responded in kind, you probably felt the "connection" associated with mutual gaze. If the person diverted his or her gaze to somewhere else in the room or to the floor, you probably

---

[9] L. J. McAfee, R. A. Fox, and R. A. Hicks, "Attributions of Male College Students to Variations in Facial Features in the Line Drawing of a Woman's Face," *Bulletin of the Psychonomic Society* 19, no. 3 (1982), 143–44.

[10] J. F. Dovidio and S. L. Ellyson, "Decoding Visual Dominance: Attributions of Power Based on Relative Percentages of Looking While Speaking and Looking While Listening," *Social Psychology Quarterly* 45, no. 2 (1982), 106–13.

[11] A. Abele, "Functions of Gaze in Social Interaction: Communication and Monitoring," *Journal of Nonverbal Behavior* 10, no. 2 (1986), 83–101.

felt that something was amiss. This communicative/monitoring function of eye behavior allows us not only to collect information but also to regulate the level of interpersonal intimacy that we are experiencing. In short, the eyes, indeed, may be viewed as "the window of the soul." Through them we can communicate additional—and often more "meaningful"—information not in the verbal exchange.

The fifth function of eye behavior, or the facilitation of goals, is another interesting aspect of eye contact. Specifically, it refers to our ability to communicate positive or negative reinforcement to others via mutual gaze and to encourage or discourage others from continuing with behavior that they are eliciting. One example of this function with which we are all familiar is our ability to stop someone from talking with a simple, straightforward glare. Another example lies in those instances when we can encourage someone with a warm glance and an accompanying smile.

Kinesics and Body Movement

The human body is so incredibly versatile that it can send thousands of nonverbal messages. In fact, it is hard to know just how to classify all of these nonverbal communications. Ray Birdwhistell, a pioneer in the field of nonverbal communication, coined the word **kinesics** to describe the study of body movement. Early researchers divided body expressions according to the part of the body involved—facial expression, trunk movements, hand gestures, and so forth.

Birdwhistell viewed body expressions as a language which, like French or Russian, could be studied, learned, and understood. Recent specialists such as Paul Ekman and Wallace Friesen have focused on the general functions of nonverbal communication discussed previously and have come up with five classes of specific body expressions: emblems, illustrators, regulators, affect displays, and body manipulators.[12]

EMBLEMS.   *Emblems* are commonly recognized signs (usually gestures) that communicate a message usually unrelated to an ongoing conversation. For example, if you and a co-worker suddenly realized that your animated conversation was disturbing an officemate, you might hold an index finger to your lips. This indication to talk more quietly serves to reduce the volume of your conversation without interrupting its flow. We learn such emblems early through imitation and continue to use them throughout our lives (see Figure 4–1).

> Beware of the man whose belly does not move when he laughs.
>
> Chinese proverb

---

[12] P. Ekman and W. V. Friesen, "The Repertoire of Non-Verbal Behavior: Categories, Origins, Usage, and Coding," *Semiotica* 1, no. 1 (1969), 49–98.

FIGURE 4–1
Can You Identify These Emblems?

ILLUSTRATORS.   These body expressions illustrate the verbal language they accompany. *Illustrators* may accent or add emphasis to a phrase, show the direction of thought, point to an object or place, depict spatial relationships, rhythms, or bodily actions, or demonstrate shape. You are using an illustrator when you point to someone across the room while shouting his or her name, or when you use your hands to estimate the length of the fish that got away.

REGULATORS.   As we explained in the previous section, *regulators* control verbal communication. Regulators such as gazes, nods, and raised eyebrows assist in the exchange of listening and speaking roles among participants in a communication setting. They provide smooth transitions in conversations.

AFFECT DISPLAYS.   Body changes that convey our internal emotional states are *affect displays.* These emotional displays can involve facial expressions,

Our bodies convey our emotional states.

such as angry stares or wide-eyed fear, or body movements, such as trembling hands or knocking knees. Affect displays are not always strictly tied to what we are saying at the time. For example, a ticket agent may be surprised by the deep sadness that lines the face of a man who has just asked for a ticket for the next plane to Pittsburgh, unaware that the passenger is going home to attend the funeral of a loved one. Because facial affect displays are easily simulated, they often function as deceptors—thus the expression "Smiling on the outside but crying on the inside."

BODY MANIPULATORS.   *Body manipulators* are movements that were originally associated with body functioning—for instance, scratching an itch or rubbing the eyes—but that have come to be used unconsciously and independently of bodily needs. We are all familiar with body manipulators such as rubbing the hands together or pulling an earlobe while talking. Other body manipulators involve the listener (patting someone's hand repeatedly while talking) or handy objects (using a pencil for doodling during a long phone conversation). Body movements such as these, however, are not body manipulators simply because there is contact among body parts.[13] Some may be classified as emblems or illustrators, such as placing the forefinger to the temple as an emblem for thought, or tapping the wrist as an illustrator of the question, "Do you have the correct time?"

BODY MOVEMENT AND POSTURE.   Body movements fall into one of several different categories and body expressions. How you walk, for instance, is often a strong indicator of how you feel. When you have a problem you may walk very slowly, with your head down and your hands clasped behind your back. You may even pause to kick a rock on the ground. On the other

---

[13] P. Ekman, "Three Classes of Nonverbal Behavior," in *Aspects of Nonverbal Communication*, ed. W. von Raffler-Engel (Lisse: Swets and Zeitlinger, B. V., 1980), 96.

We use our bodies to transmit messages about degrees of association and agreement.

hand, when you feel especially proud and happy, you may walk with your chin raised, your arms swinging freely, and your legs somewhat stiff—with a bounce in your step.

We all know how to "read" such obvious nonverbal cues, but conscious and sustained effort can help you to pick up even more subtle expressions of the nonverbal language. For example, you sometimes use your body parts to show that you are or are not associated with the people near you. Thus, crossing your legs in the same way the person next to you crosses hers may indicate identification with that person. Or, if you are standing and arguing with three other people, you may soon find yourself assuming the body posture of the person with whom you agree—both of you standing with your hands on your hips, for instance, while your two opponents may also assume like postures.

Other movements and gestures show openness and honesty. Holding the hands open while talking indicates sincerity; hands clenched into fists do the opposite. Similarly, if someone unbuttons or even takes off his or her coat in your presence, this conveys openness and friendliness toward you.

In contrast to these gestures of openness are those that indicate defensiveness. The crossed-arm-on-chest position is perhaps the best-known defensive gesture. Charles Darwin identified it as a universal trait in all societies, one that can strongly influence the behavior of observers. In fact, communication often comes to a complete halt when someone assumes this position, which says, in effect, "I have now withdrawn from this conversation." Of course, this is not true every time someone crosses his or her arms. However, if it happens during a conversation, you might examine what you have just said or done that would have prompted a withdrawal.

Even the way you sit communicates information. Someone speaking while his or her legs dangle over the arm of a chair might be saying, "I am not feeling cooperative. In fact, I am unconcerned or hostile to your feelings or needs." Similarly, people who sit backwards on chairs or put their feet up on a desk may be signaling their feelings of superiority, saying, "I am the dominant person here."

Such reflections of dominance seem to perpetuate sex role stereotypes. Men, for example, characteristically express dominance by taking up more space in a bed than a woman; crossing their legs at the thighs (which takes up a considerable amount of room); and looking into a woman's eyes while talking to her. Women, on the other hand, often use submissive gestures when they are with men: compressing their bodies into a small space in bed; crossing their legs at the ankles or sitting with uncrossed legs held tightly together (which takes up very little space); and looking down when talking to men. We shall explore such spatial relationships later in the chapter.

Personal Appearance

Each year Americans spend millions of dollars on cosmetics, weight control, and plastic surgery to increase their physical attractiveness. To become beautiful people, we starve ourselves to lose weight, spend countless hours in front of mirrors styling our hair and applying makeup, use special conditioners to halt thinning hair, and wear clothing to accent a bulge here and minimize a bulge there. We have been told that inner beauty is what counts in relationships, but research analyzing first impressions suggests that physical attractiveness affects interpersonal outcomes. Physical appearance influences job interviews, blind dates, consumer buying behavior, grades in school, and even courtroom decisions.

Although the face usually determines beauty, we are also judged by our body shapes, skin color, and hair. Every time television sets are turned on, advertisements are stereotyping people according to their physical attributes. Can you remember ever seeing an overweight, unkempt, scar-faced doctor recommend a leading aspirin? Advertisers usually hire neat, clean, attractive models to sell their products. Unattractive individuals are usually used only in advertisements that feature before-and-after sequences, such as when methods for increasing bust size or achieving younger-looking skin are being advertised. To look just right, we are encouraged to change our skin color and texture by applying makeup and medications, getting a golden tan, or using special skin softeners. Society also influences our views on hair. Men want to keep their hair because it is masculine to have hairy chests, beards, and mustaches. Women, however, are constantly finding ways to get rid of their hair. By electrolysis, depilation, and shaving, women eliminate unsightly hair under arms, on legs, over lips, and on eyebrows. Certainly, the way we look is important to ourselves and others. We manipulate our physical appearance so that we will be perceived as attractive rather than unattractive.

Clothing

It is often said that clothes make a person, but it may be more true to say that clothes *are* the person. Your clothes provide visual clues to your interests, age, personality, and attitudes. Even status information is gained from the clothes' age, condition, and fashion. Some of us are interested in clothing as a means of keeping up with the latest social changes. Others use clothing as a form of decoration and self-expression. T-shirt designs, for example, are a new communication channel between the wearer and the world.

> By a man's fingernails, by his coat-sleeve, by his boots, by his trouser-knees, by the callosities of his forefinger and thumb, by his expression, by his shirt cuffs—by each of these things a man's calling is plainly revealed. That all united should fail to enlighten the competent inquirer in any case is almost inconceivable.
>
> Sherlock Holmes

In the popular book *Letitia Baldrige's Complete Guide to Executive Manners*, Ms. Baldrige emphasizes the importance of clothing in the business community.[14] She suggests that clothing determines a person's job success. Thus, dress is an influential variable in the total system of nonverbal communication. It can fulfill functions ranging from protection, sexual attraction, and self-assertion to self-denial, concealment, group identification, and the display of status and role. To illustrate, have you ever thought of the impact that clothing color can have on evaluations of job applicants? Research indicates that both facial expressions and clothing color (light vs. dark) significantly affect evaluations of competence, power, character, and sociability in female job applicants. For example, in one study, Damhorst and Pinaire Reed asked male and female executives from 158 organizations in two major cities in Texas to judge photographs of six female job applicants wearing either dark or light colors and exhibiting either a smiling or serious facial expression. Results of the study indicated that, overall, smiling models were perceived to be more powerful and competent than nonsmiling models. Additionally, male subjects rated models who wore dark colors as more powerful and competent than those who wore light, pastel colors. When rating models on character and sociability, males again rated women in dark jackets more positively, but only when the models were placed in nonsmiling poses.[15]

Conversely, female raters did not base judgments of power and competence on color of clothing. Additionally, female executives rated those models who wore dark clothing and were not smiling more negatively on character and sociability factors. The researchers concluded that socialization factors may have been the root of the differences that emerged in the study. Since men have been socialized to perceive the dark business suit as a symbol of corporate achievement and power, they viewed female applicants in dark colors as more competent and powerful than those wearing pastel colors. Conversely, since women generally have not been socialized to pursue corpo-

---

[14] Sandi Gelles-Cole (ed.), *Letitia Baldrige's Complete Guide to Executive Manners* (New York: Rawson), 130–31.
[15] M. L. Damhorst and J. A. Pinaire Reed, "Clothing Color Value and Facial Expression: Effects on Evaluations of Female Job Applicants," *Social Behavior and Personality* 14, no. 1 (1986), 89–98.

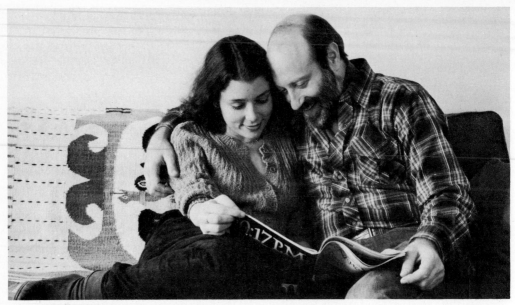

Intimate distance.

rate careers, they have not yet developed strong norms and expectations for women's business attire. Likewise, women have been allowed to experiment more freely with clothing colors and, consequently, do not perceive specific colors to be a symbol of business credibility.[16]

Touching

Do you often reach out to touch other people? Although ours is not a "contact" culture, touching is nonetheless the most basic form of nonverbal communication.

We all use touch at times. To emphasize a point or to interrupt another person, for instance, we may grab the speaker's elbow and interrupt with, "But you don't understand." Touching can be used as a calming gesture, too. We frequently try to comfort someone with a pat on the back and a "there, there." In other situations touching provides reassurance. Not only do we reach out to reassure ourselves of the presence of people we are fond of, but we sometimes do the same with objects—stroking the smooth leather of our gloves, for instance.

These behaviors suggest the importance of touching to human beings. In fact, physical contact with other humans is vital to healthy development. Lack of such contact in childhood may contribute to physical and psychological problems later in life. To understand this, consider how parents touch their children to communicate their feelings about the children's bodies. By stroking part of a child's body, parents are saying that that part is prized

---

[16] Ibid.

Touch is vital to healthy development.

and loved. If certain body parts are ignored or avoided, as is common with anal and genital areas, these areas may seem objectionable to the child and may eventually become a source of shame.

Proxemics

Just as we communicate with words, gestures, or facial expressions, so too can we transmit messages by placing ourselves in certain spatial relationships with other persons or objects. The study of these spatial factors—how we react to the space around us, how we use that space, and how our use of space communicates certain information—is known as *proxemics.* For example, the amount of space a person is allowed often communicates the status of that person. Let's say that a household has three sons but only two children's bedrooms. In recognition of the eldest son's status, chances are that he will have a room to himself while the other two children share a room.

SPATIAL ZONES.   Edward T. Hall, a pioneer in the study of proxemics, specified four spatial zones of interpersonal communication: intimate distance, personal distance, social distance, and public distance.

Intimate distance stretches from actual contact to 18 inches. A parent and child, two intimate friends, or other close pairs would have contact in this zone. Of course, even strangers can be thrown into this intimate zone—on a crowded elevator, for example. However, such forced closeness is usually countered by silence, averted glances, and other nonverbal messages that say, "O.K., this is fine for now, but it's only going to last for a minute, because I don't really know you."

Personal distance, from 1½ to 4 feet, is the zone we use for casual interactions. You would probably assume this distance when talking with a friend at a cocktail party. In contrast, *social distance,* from 4 to 12 feet, is used by people meeting for the first time or by people conducting business. *Public distance,* from 12 to over 25 feet, is most often used in formal address; for example, by a teacher lecturing students or by a politician speaking at a rally.

We also adapt our behavior when forced to interact in a different zone. For example, when even close friends are farther than 12 feet apart (public distance), they often speak in more formal phrases. On the other hand, casual acquaintances placed in an intimate distance usually whisper and use small, rather than expansive, gestures. Compare the gestures you use when sitting next to a friend to those used to shout a greeting to your neighbor across the street.

Consider also how people who are talking before they get on a crowded elevator usually stop abruptly when the doors close, then continue their conversation when they step out. It's interesting to note the reactions you get when you do keep a conversation going after entering an elevator. The other people in that confined space can't help hearing the conversation, but they will often turn away or lower their heads and pretend not to listen. It is even more interesting (despite the risk of some strange looks) to watch the response of others when you laugh out loud to yourself in this quiet atmosphere.

It is important to note that these spatial zones, though common for white, middle-class Americans, are by no means universal. Each culture has its own spatial needs. Thus, Arabs stand so close to each other while talking that they can easily touch and perceive body odors and heat—very different from our American "noncontact" culture. We may want to see and hear other people, but by no means do we wish to smell their body odor!

TERRITORIALITY.   Scientists have long observed the territorial habits of animals but are only recently beginning to understand that humans exhibit similar territorial needs and controls. In fact, all of us carry our own personal

Personal distance.

space around with us. This **territoriality**—the need to call space our space—is another facet of proxemics.

Territoriality implies a desire to possess or give up the space or objects around us. For example, different body parts permit us to claim temporary possession of an object. Thus, we often use our hands to reach out and grab an object (as in straightening someone's tie or holding another person's hand). Or, we employ our whole bodies as spatial indicators. Standing with hands on hips and elbows extended, for instance, claims all of the space around our bodies, saying, "Don't come any closer to me than my elbows, or else!" On the other hand, when we are kissing, we close our eyes, perhaps to break down spatial barriers. "It's okay," we imply. "Your kiss is not infringing on my territory." We also use objects to define our territory. Have you ever used books, paper, pencils, sweaters, and other objects to stake out your space at a library table? Such markers say, "This area is mine."

SEATING ARRANGEMENTS.   Did your father always sit at the head of the table in your house? The person who sits at the head of a table will usually be designated the "leader," whether or not that designation is appropriate. Have you ever avoided taking a chair at the head of a table for this very reason? The two ends of a table and the middle seats on the sides are "hot seats" in which people either do, or at least are expected to, talk more.

These examples illustrate the effects of seating arrangements on interpersonal interactions. Some spatial arrangements, such as a round table, encourage us to face each other and to communicate. Other arrangements—for example, a row of chairs in a theater or classroom—force us to face away from one another. These arrangements naturally produce less interaction.

Thus, different seating arrangements are desirable for different types of interactions. If two people are having a friendly conversation, they might

Seating arrangements affect our interpersonal interactions.

prefer seats at the corner of a rectangular table. When working together on a task, they might sit side by side. During competition (playing cards, for example) they would prefer to sit across from one another, thereby making it more difficult to see each other's hand and easier to establish strong eye contact.[17]

Similarly, spatial relationships in the classroom can influence student–teacher interactions. The three most popular ways to arrange classrooms are in rectangular, horseshoe, and modular arrangements (see Figures 4–2, 4–3, and 4–4). Most classrooms in America are rectangular, with desks arranged in straight rows. This arrangement is best for information dissemination or straight lectures. Horseshoe and modular arrangements are frequently used with smaller classes. Courses in disciplines such as home economics, architecture, horticulture, and speech communication would be likely to use these arrangements. Both the horseshoe and modular arrangements increase student participation. The grouping of the modular design allows for maximum interaction and is especially effective for teachers who need to work with groups and individual students.[18]

[17] T. R. V. Davis, "The Influence of the Physical Environment in Offices," *Academy of Management Review* 9, no. 2 (1984), 271–83.

[18] T. Hurt, M. D. Scott, and J. C. McCroskey, *Communication in the Classroom* (Reading, Mass.: Addison-Wesley, 1978), 95–99.

FIGURE 4–2

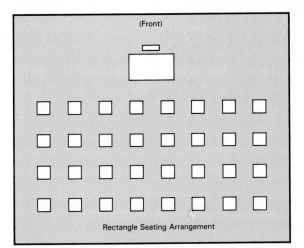

Rectangle Seating Arrangement

FIGURE 4–3

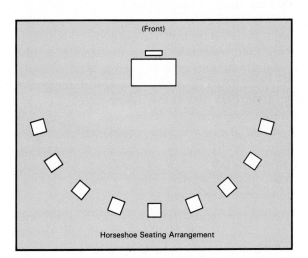

Horseshoe Seating Arrangement

FIGURE 4–4

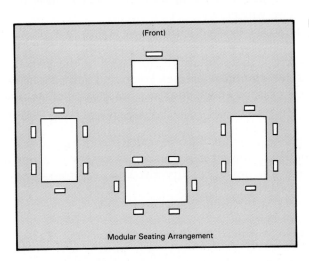

Modular Seating Arrangement

Most of us also have preferences about where we sit in classes. Have you ever been disappointed, on the first day of class, to find that you couldn't sit in the back row, in front of the teacher, or by the blackboard? A variety of factors, such as wanting to sit by the best-looking student, or wanting to be able to see the board, determine seating preferences. Investigations of interactions in classrooms reveal that while seating arrangement, or proximity to the teacher, generally is not strong enough to affect test performance, it is clearly related to student enjoyment, motivation, interest, and feelings of inclusion.[19]

Paralanguage

The next time you turn on the TV, close your eyes and listen to the actors' voices. What emotions are they portraying? Are the speakers male or female, British or American? How old are they? Try the same experiment while listening to a radio talk show. Is the caller nervous, tired, angry? *Paralanguage*—variations in the voice—is what makes it possible to answer these questions. Paralanguage is "a language alongside of language." It includes vocal characteristics such as pitch, range, resonance, tempo, and quality and various vocal sounds such as grunts, groans, and clearing of the throat.

Although paralanguage is closely tied to verbal expression, it is quite unlike the signs and symbols we know as language. Consider the various voice *pitches.* Some people use a wide range of pitches, talking now in a high voice, now in a low one, while others make few pitch changes, or even talk in a monotone. In addition, we all drop our voices at the end of a statement and raise our voices slightly at the end of a question. Ask, "Where are you going?" and notice how your voice rises on "going." These pitch changes are part of our paralanguage.

Other paralanguage cues relate to *resonance,* the variations from a thin and quiet voice to a loud and booming voice. For example, shyness or embarrassment can affect the voice: Have you ever begun an introduction to a large group of people only to find that nervousness has made your voice fade to a mere whisper?

Some people speak so fast that it is hard to pick up all their words; others speak very slowly. This paralanguage quality is called *tempo.* Good public speakers know that the ability to pause at the proper time and to draw out words for emphasis creates color and interest in what is being said. The nervous orator's short, choppy phrases and monotonous style are a real giveaway to the audience that the speaker is ill at ease and probably inexperienced.

Paralanguage cues are also revealed by the *quality* of a speaker's voice. Voice quality is most often associated with variations of harshness and breathiness in the voice. Quality also involves smoothness of delivery and other similar factors.

---

[19] R. J. Millard and D. V. Stimpson, "Enjoyment and Productivity as a Function of Classroom Seating Location," *Perceptual Motor Skills* 50 (April 1980), 439–44.

Environmental factors influence our behavior.

Although paralanguage, as we have described the concept so far, may seem to focus only on subtle nuances, paralinguistic expressions need not be subtle. For example, sounds such as sneezing, coughing, or crying all serve well-recognized purposes. Similarly, if you walk into a room in which two of your friends are deeply involved in a conversation, rather than standing there until one of them notices you, you might clear your throat. This simple noise communicates your presence, saying, "Hey, look at me. I'm here."

Paralanguage conveys information about age, sex, emotional states, personality variables, and other common attributes. Thus, it should not surprise you to learn that words in themselves account for only 7 percent of the communication of feelings. More important, researchers have found, are vocal cues, which account for 38 percent, and facial expressions, which account for 55 percent. To understand how true this finding is, consider a typical conversation. The speakers start out quite friendly but slowly build to a heated argument. As anger increases, voices become louder (intensity), the range of voices increases (pitch), and the speed of the exchange quickens (tempo). Even if you couldn't hear the speakers' angry words, paralanguage factors would immediately tell you that the two people were quarreling.

Smell and Taste

Every day we use our senses of smell and taste to receive information about the world around us. However, we also use the mediums of smell and taste to send out such information about ourselves. Think, for example, about the last time you were getting ready to go out with a very special person. After getting out of the bathtub, where you showered with deodorant soap and washed your hair with scented shampoo, you probably put on deodorant or antiperspirant and adorned yourself with after-shave lotion or perfume. You then proceeded to brush your teeth with a fresh-tasting toothpaste and, perhaps, gargled with a "germ-killing" mouthwash. Finally, you put on fresh-smelling clothes and odor-free shoes, the former having been washed in a freshly scented detergent and rinsed in a fabric softener, and the latter "fresh-ened" with "odor-eating" talcum power or foot pads.

It is interesting to note, however, that American perceptions of smells and tastes often differ from the perceptions of members of other cultures. For example, Americans have been conditioned to be ashamed of natural body odors. Have you ever kept your distance from someone for fear that the garlic on your breath would be offensive? Such a feeling of self-conscious-ness concerning a potential message such as this is only one example of how our culture differs from other cultures. Members of several cultures would feel quite insulted if you deprived them of your breath!

The sense of smell, however, is not the only "silent" sense that sends and receives messages. Our sense of taste allows us to receive messages of pleasure as well as warning and has the ability both to influence and to reflect our physical needs as well as preferences and attitudes. Do some odors and tastes make you happy, depressed, nostalgic? If you do not quite yet believe in the communicative power of these two senses, be aware of the processes involved the next time you sniff or taste an odor or flavor. You may open yourselves up to an awareness concerning two additional and viable channels of communication.

Environmental Factors

ARCHITECTURE AND OBJECTS.   Have you ever walked into a room and immediately felt at home, calm, and relaxed? Or avoided a building that made you feel nervous and insecure? Nonverbal messages from architectural structures and other objects around us can indeed influence our behavior. It is for this reason that dentists have comfortable chairs and pleasant decors in their waiting rooms—all to make us worry a little less. Nightclub, bar, and restaurant owners have also learned that interiors can greatly influence their customers. They realize that dim lighting, a quiet atmosphere, and soft music lead to greater intimacy, which encourages their patrons to stay longer.

These informal observations are supported by scientific studies. One classic experiment, for example, used three rooms: an "ugly" room, designed like a janitor's storeroom; a "beautiful" room, with carpeting, drapes, and other decorations; and an "average" room, decorated like a professor's office. While located in these different rooms, subjects were asked to rate a series of photographs of faces. Those in the beautiful room gave higher ratings to the faces than did those in the ugly room. While the beautiful room was found to stimulate feelings of pleasure, comfort, enjoyment, and the desire

TABLE 4–1   Association of Moods and Colors

MOOD	COLOR
Exciting, stimulating	Red
Secure, comfortable	Blue
Distressed, disturbed, upset	Orange
Tender, soothing	Blue
Protective, defending	Red, brown, blue, purple, black
Despondent, dejected, unhappy, melancholy	Black, brown
Calm, peaceful, serene	Blue, green
Dignified, stately	Purple
Cheerful, jovial, joyful	Yellow
Defiant, contrary, hostile	Red, orange, black
Powerful, strong, masterful	Black

From L. B. Wexner, "The Degree to Which Colors (Hues) Are Associated with Mood-Tones." *Journal of Applied Psychology* 38 (1954), 432–35. Copyright 1954 by the American Psychological Association. Reprinted by permission.

to continue the activity, the ugly room caused fatigue, headaches, discontent, sleepiness, irritability, and hostility.[20] Subsequent measures of recall and problem solving in these rooms showed better performance in the beautiful surroundings.

COLORS.   We all recognize clichés of color and emotion—"tickled pink," "feeling blue," "green with envy," and "seeing red," to name a few. It is well known that specific colors are associated with particular human moods. As one early study demonstrated (see Table 4–1), we tend to describe some moods in terms of a specific color, while other moods are associated with two or more colors. Additionally, research on achievement motivation has shown that highly motivated people prefer cool or somber colors and tend to be in a hurry, while people who are less motivated prefer warm or brighter colors, like red and yellow, and are generally less time conscious. To support these earlier findings, Charles and Carlota Salter investigated automobile color as a predictor of driving behavior. Specifically, they focused on color of car and propensity of the driver to speed at great velocities and to run red lights and stop signs. Results of their study revealed that drivers of cars with higher-achievement colors (such as blue and black) tended to speed at higher rates and to run red lights more often than drivers of cars with low-achievement colors (such as red or yellow). However, they did not tend to run stop signs more often.[21]

The difficulty with such research, of course, is in discerning whether people pick colors that are truly associated with specific moods or whether their choices actually reflect learned stereotypes. Do you respond to different

[20] A. H. Maslow and N. L. Mintz, "Effects of Esthetic Surroundings: I. Initial Effects of Three Esthetic Conditions upon Perceiving 'Energy' and 'Well-Being' in Faces," *Journal of Psychology* 41 (1956), 247–54.
[21] C. A. Salter and C. D. Salter, "Automobile Color as a Predictor of Driving Behavior," *Perceptual and Motor Skills* 55 (1982), 383–86.

"We want it done in tattletale gray."

colors in different ways? What colors are you wearing at this moment? Do they in any way reflect the mood you were in when you dressed? Answering these questions may give you some interesting insights into your reactions to particular colors. What about color combinations? Are there certain color combinations, say orange and red, that you would *never* wear? Why not? What nonverbal messages do you think you send by wearing such combinations?

TIME.   Americans are preoccupied with time. Just observe the many time-pieces around us—clocks in our homes, schools, and work places; church bells chiming every quarter hour; banks lighting up the time, second by second; radio stations announcing the time after every commercial; and almost everyone wearing a wristwatch (some of them even with alarms!). Time is also an important part of our verbal language—"kill time," "use time," "waste time," "it's high time," "time is of the essence," "now's the time. . . ."

Time is significant in nonverbal communication as well. Time is a valued commodity. Time is money—we are paid for the time we spend at work. Time is power—the more time someone gives you, the more important you are. Time is status—we are more punctual for an important business meeting than for a casual get-together. In short, we are compulsive clock-watchers—bound to our watches, time clocks, agendas, and timetables. Time keeps running on . . . running us.

Scientists have discovered that perceptions of time provide important nonverbal cues, cues that vary from culture to culture.[22] Western industrialized cultures, for example, think of time in linear-spatial terms related to past, present, and future. Thus, Americans think of moving "through" time, with the present as the intermediate point between past and future. In contrast, other cultures stress "felt time," the "now" of living for each day and not for the past or future. Greeks, for instance, see themselves as stationary. Time comes up behind them, overtakes them, and then becomes the past. Many American Indians have the same concept. Indeed, the Sioux have no words for "time," "late," or "waiting."

We also make certain assumptions about other people based on their time-consciousness. Those on time for appointments are considered most sociable and composed; those who are early are seen as least dynamic; and latecomers are usually viewed as least sociable, composed, and competent.[23] Bringing it closer to home, consider how someone else's time conceptions affect you. If you discover that your boss or professor is very time-conscious, keeps track of tardiness, absenteeism, and so forth, how might you modify your behavior? How would use of time affect such a boss or instructor?

MUSIC. Have you ever put on soft music to set the mood for a special date or wondered why some restaurants play classical music and others play disco? Maybe you haven't thought about the reasons behind the music selections, but whether you know it or not, music affects us and our interactions with others. Muzak Corporation, the largest producer of music for businesses, corporations, and industries, has provided evidence that music increases production and reduces errors, tension, and absenteeism. In addition, music has been reported to influence concept and skill learning, attention span, mental imagery, reading efficiency, and creative abilities.[24]

Music also plays a major role in our society. Americans spend more money on records than they do on textbooks for schools. The power of the music industry can be attributed to its diversity. With more than 8,000 radio stations, we have the freedom to tune into anything from jazz to punk rock. Tastes in music communicate information about others. Personality characteristics are often associated with the types of music people listen to. However, to assume that intellectuals listen to classical music, truck drivers enjoy country and western music, and long-haired liberals get into hard rock is to engage in dangerous generalizations. Just as there is diversity in the sounds of music, there is diversity in what people appreciate and like to listen to in music.

---

[22] R. E. Porter, "An Overview of Intercultural Communication," in *Intercultural Communication: A Reader*, 2d ed., ed. L. A. Samovar and R. E. Porter (Belmont, Calif.: Wadsworth, 1976), 318.
[23] L. A. Baxter and J. M. Ward, "An Exploratory Investigation of Diffused Point Arrival Time and Source Credibility" (paper presented at the Western Speech Communication Association Convention, November 1973).
[24] In L. Rosenfeld, "Setting the Stage for Learning," *Theory into Practice* 16 (June 1977), 167–73.

AWARENESS OF NONVERBAL COMMUNICATION

The previous sections have described some of the meanings attached to specific gestures, body language, expressions, and environmental stimuli. Again, we must assert that these nonverbal messages cannot be viewed in simple, black-and-white terms. Like words, nonverbal language has connotations as well as denotations. Just as each of us responds differently to a given word, term, or concept because of our different experiences, attitudes, and beliefs, so too do we respond differently to nonverbal messages.

Awareness of your own nonverbal behavior and that of others can increase your sensitivity in social interactions. Although we are usually attentive to nonverbal stimuli—we purposely wear clothes that evoke a particular response (positive or negative), we reach out and touch a friend who is unhappy to let him or her know that we are there—at other times we overlook or misread nonverbal cues that might enrich our understanding of interpersonal communications. Similarly, just as we may misinterpret the nonverbal behavior of others, they may do the same with us. Thus, you should consider questions such as, "I know what my beard means to me, but what does it mean to my parents?" "Does my being overweight influence her feelings about me?" "I wonder if they think I'm unfriendly because I don't go over and join them."

In the following section we will discuss the factors that affect our interpretation of nonverbal messages.

Context

Context influences our own nonverbal communications as well as our responses to other people's nonverbal messages. For example, when you are at home watching a movie on television, you probably prop your feet up on the coffee table or curl them under you on the sofa. You might noisily dig to the bottom of the potato chip bag, ignoring the crumbs that miss your mouth and fall to your chest. And, if the beer or soda you've been drinking should make you burp—so what? But what if you were watching the same movie in a crowded theater? Your behavior might differ considerably. Even if you wanted to slouch, the stiff theater seats might prevent it. If you insisted on potato chips rather than a less noisy snack, you would probably be more careful not to rattle the bag or scatter the crumbs. And, if the soda had the same effect on you it has at home, you would probably suppress the burp or let nature have its way—discreetly.

We learn appropriate context behaviors by negative reinforcement during childhood. How many times were you told as a child, "Don't put your feet on that table! You're not at home now!" Or, did you ever get stern looks because you talked too loudly in a movie theater or popped your gum in a library? After much scolding and some praise, we learn to vary our nonverbal behaviors according to whom we are with, where we are, and whether or not the situation is defined as formal or informal.

Just as context modifies your own nonverbal behavior, so too does it affect your response to nonverbal messages in your environment. For example, a simple gesture can have several different meanings, depending on the context in which it occurs. Let's say you are driving your car down the road and you spot someone hitchhiking. In a matter of seconds, you must decide whether to stop. What you do is based on contextual variables. First, your mood: Are you feeling helpful, or don't you want to be bothered? Are you in a hurry or on a leisurely drive? Are you afraid of all hitchhikers, never picking them up, or do you usually give them a lift? And what about the environment? Would it make a difference to you if it were daytime or night? On a crowded highway or on a country road? In the summer or during a snowstorm? What about the person himself . . . or herself? Would it matter to you if the hitchhiker were a man or a woman? Or perhaps a man *and* a woman—or a man with his pet German shepherd?

Would the hitchhiker's age and weight influence you? Or clothing, hairstyle, and other gestures? Finally, if and when you do pull over, would you take a few more seconds to change your mind after studying facial expressions, voice, and general demeanor?

Stereotypes

As you can see, the same gesture—"Hey, I need a ride. Please pick me up"—can be interpreted in many different ways, depending on the context and, of course, on your stereotypes.

Like it or not, most of us do have stereotypes about people and the way they act. These stereotypes play a large part in first impressions, for example. Whether or not the stereotypes bear any resemblance to reality, they do exist and must be considered when analyzing interpersonal behavior.

As our hitchhiking example demonstrated, we often make judgments about the personality and behavior of individuals just by observing their physical appearance or superficial actions. In fact, we sometimes make important decisions based on voice alone: "I didn't like the sound of his voice, so I. . . ." "As soon as she started to talk, I knew I could trust her." Researchers have verified this reliance on voice characteristics. In one experiment, students listened to two tape recordings of the same speaker. On one recording the speaker used a conversational delivery pattern—that is, a smaller range of inflections, a greater consistency of rate and pitch, less volume, and generally lower pitch than in the second recording, in which the speaker used a more dynamic delivery pattern. The students in this study did not realize that they were hearing the same speaker with two different vocal approaches. Instead, they rated the speaker who used the conversational delivery as honest and person-oriented, while the dynamic delivery elicited descriptions of tough-minded, task-oriented, self-assured, and assertive.[25]

Of course, we all have stereotypes about many aspects of behavior other than voice. Do you have certain beliefs about the way people should

[25] W. B. Pearce and F. Conklin, "Nonverbal Vocalic Communication and Perceptions of a Speaker," *Speech Monographs* 38 (1971), 235–41.

or shouldn't walk, smile, sit, stand, eat, laugh, sneeze, or cry? Ask yourself why the next time you jump to a conclusion based solely on some aspect of another person's behavior. Chances are your conclusion doesn't reflect the facts of the situation. Herein lies the danger of stereotypes: Too often they turn out to be assumptions completely unrelated to objective facts.

> I understand a fury in your words but not the words.
>
> William Shakespeare

However, the main point of this chapter is awareness: You cannot eliminate your stereotyped response to nonverbal messages, but you cannot disregard those stereotypes either. Thus, if you know, for example, that someone has a negative stereotype about blue jeans, you will either not wear them when you are with that person or will not be surprised or offended by the person's behavior when you do. In short, awareness improves understanding, and understanding improves communication—be it verbal or nonverbal.

SUMMARY

In addition to our spoken and written language, all of us communicate on the nonverbal level of body movements, gestures, facial expressions, tone of voice, and other related signs. Our interpretation of such nonverbal messages is a function of both their context and their relationship to the sum of the communicator's verbal and nonverbal behavior patterns.

The six basic functions of nonverbal communication are repeating, substituting, complementing, deceiving, regulating, and accenting. The body expressions that serve these functions are limitless. The language of facial expressions, eye adjustments, and related movements is responsible for a significant part of all human communication. In addition, specialists have organized body expressions into classes such as kinesics and body movement.

Some classes of body expressions include emblems, illustrators, regulators, affect displays, and body manipulators. These expressions, and the functions they serve, are the subject of the scientific discipline known as kinesics, or body language.

In addition to kinesic messages, we communicate through our personal appearance and our choice of clothing. Likewise, touch, the most basic form of nonverbal communication, is an important part of our communication system, and contributes to our overall sense of well-being.

In addition to these forms of nonverbal behavior, we communicate by our relationship to the space about us and our use of that space. Proxemics, the study of these spatial factors, specifies several distinct zones of interpersonal communication, which are affected by our territoriality.

The last three areas of nonverbal communication we discussed are paralanguage, our senses of taste and smell, and environmental factors that surround us.

It is important that we become aware of these factors and of the context in which nonverbal messages occur. In addition, we must recognize the perceptual stereotypes that always affect our interpretation of both verbal and nonverbal messages. This heightened awareness can help ensure understanding of others and improved communication on all levels.

EXERCISES

GROUP EXPERIENCES

How's Your Sign Language?

DESCRIPTION: As children, we used nonverbal communication as our direct statement of what we wanted, while verbal communication was the complement. As we grew older, this process became reversed, so that our nonverbal communication no longer served as a direct statement but as a complement to what we said verbally. Children depend a great deal on sign language (gestures that replace words, numbers, and punctuation). It has been found that children are easily able to transmit and interpret twelve frequently used gestures. Try this activity and see if your sign language is as good as a child's.

PROCEDURE: Divide into groups of four to six members. Each member should try to transmit a short phrase nonverbally. The following list of phrases is offered only as a beginning—these are the phrases mentioned above (that children are able to use quite easily).

Go away	Be quiet	Shape (round or square)
Come here	Give me attention	I don't know
Yes	How many	Goodbye
No	How big	Hi

The first person to accurately guess the message becomes the next transmitter. This process continues until all members have had the opportunity to transmit at least two messages.

DISCUSSION: How well do you transmit and interpret nonverbal messages? Consider this question in light of the activity you have just completed. If you have trouble transmitting messages nonverbally, this may suggest that you need to work on this to improve your communication. On the other hand, if you have trouble interpreting messages, you may be misinterpreting people. Problems with either transmission or interpretation of nonverbal messages may lead to communication breakdowns on an interpersonal or group level.

How Others Stereotype You

DESCRIPTION: Are you aware of how others stereotype you on the basis of your behavior and personal appearance? Not many people are. This activity will provide you with information about how others view you and should also help you to understand your own nonverbal behavior.

PROCEDURE: Divide into groups of four to six members. Each member should make a list of everyone in the group and put his or her name on the top of the list. Across the top of the paper, three categories should be written: books, dogs, and adjectives. Starting with yourself, select one choice from each category that most closely reflects you or the person for whom you are making the choice. When you are selecting, try to determine the specific behaviors that cause you to view a person in a particular stereotyped way.

Category A. Which book would you most likely find ___(insert name)___ reading?

a. How Managers Make Things
   Happen
b. How to Read the Stars
c. The Wild, Wild West
d. One Hundred Ways to Improve
   Your Golf Swing
e. The Prophet
f. How to Eat Better and Spend Less
g. How to Be Your Own Best Friend

Category B. What type of dog does ___(insert name)___ remind you of?

a. Poodle
b. German shepherd
c. Sheepdog
d. Cocker spaniel
e. Dachshund
f. St. Bernard
g. Chihuahua

Category C. Which group of adjectives most closely describes ___(insert name)___?

a. Open, optimistic, energetic
b. Meticulous, nervous, punctual
c. Soft-hearted, good-natured, loving
d. Competitive, dominant, authoritative
e. Closed, pessimistic, quiet
f. Fun-loving, ambitious, talkative
g. Introspective, spiritual, analytical

DISCUSSION: There are two ways to assess the results of this activity: Either start with a category and discuss each group member in the category, or start with a particular group member and discuss him or her in each of the three categories. Whichever method you choose, keep in mind that meanings are in people, not in the words. Therefore, it is very important that you try to provide information on *why* you made a particular selection. Focus on the personal appearance of the person and consider whether you stereotyped hairstyle or clothing in a particular way. If you find that the impressions others have of you are inconsistent with the way you view yourself, then you need to observe your own behavior and personal appearance to understand what you are nonverbally conveying to others. The expansion of nonverbal awareness begins with understanding how you project impressions to others.

It's Not What You Say, It's How You Say It!

DESCRIPTION: This activity can be conducted either in small groups of four to six members or as a demonstration activity in which the majority of the class serves as an audience while four or five individuals play roles in selected situations. Two partners will be needed for each role-playing scene. Two scenes are offered as examples of the type of drama that can be reenacted to illustrate the effects of pitch, rhythm, intonation, intensity, and other vocal qualities. The purpose of this activity is to clearly demonstrate that it's not *what* you say, but *how* you say it!

PROCEDURE: Two partners will be needed for each role-playing activity. Each team can either invent a scene they would like to portray or use one from the following list. In each scene only numbers are to be used—absolutely no words are permitted. For example, practice by reading the following numbers tenderly, angrily, and sadly: 42, 567, 3, 356, 8. Once you get a feel for this, try one of the following scenes. After a team plays a scene, the group should discuss the emotions and feelings that were being conveyed.

> *Scene 1.* Husband and wife. The wife comes home from work and the husband is irritable after spending the day watching the children and cooking. He displays his irritability the moment she walks through the door. The wife at first tries to be supportive, but then fights openly with her husband.
> *Scene 2.* A couple. In this scene the couple has been dating for a long time. Finally, after waiting for months, he pops the question. The scene is tender and romantic.

DISCUSSION: Are you aware of the subtle nonverbal cues that are transmitted through the voice? Consider how, even if the words are identical, a change in pitch, intensity, or even pause rate can dramatically alter the meaning of a message. After participating in this activity, you should be able to listen to your own vocal characteristics to see how you alter messages. Also consider the extent to which the vocal characteristics of others influence your interpretation of their messages. In other words, is it *what* they say or *how* they say it that counts?

Body Expressions

DESCRIPTION: The body and the face convey many emotional meanings in both speaking and listening. Most of us learn to convey emotions through our facial expressions but have more difficulty conveying emotions with other parts of our bodies. The following activity will provide you with an opportunity to determine how well you transmit and interpret the nonverbal display of emotions through the use of facial expressions and body movement.

PROCEDURE: Write each of the following body areas and emotions on separate cards.

Body Areas	Emotions
Whole face	Hate
Whole body	Love
Hands only	Anger
Face only	Surprise
Mouth only	Happiness
Eyes and eyebrows only	Distrust
Feet only	Disgust
Dyad (whole body with another person)	Contentment

Divide into groups of six to eight members (each group needs one set of cards). The first person should select one card from the body area category and one card from the emotion category. The person should then try to portray the selected emotion with *only* the body area designated on the card. The rest of the group has three guesses to determine both the correct body area and the emotion. If the group guesses correctly, the person receives one point. If the group does not guess correctly, the person loses one point. After the first person has finished, the cards should be returned to the appropriate deck. Go around the group until each participant has had three turns. (The number of turns may be modified depending on the number of participants in the group and the amount of time available for the activity.)

DISCUSSION: As a group, identify which emotions were most difficult to convey and which were easiest. Identify which body areas most accurately transmitted the emotional states and which least accurately. Which was more difficult—the transmission of nonverbal messages or the interpretation of them?

Conversation and Space

DESCRIPTION: Particular spatial arrangements may either aid or inhibit interactions. We are constantly readjusting our distance from other people and objects to match the nature of our conversations. The following activity provides you with the opportunity to experience the relationship between conversational topic and distance.

PROCEDURE: Divide into dyads. The members of the dyad should stand directly opposite one another at a distance of ten feet. Engage in a conversation on any topic you choose, but while you are talking, maintain the distance of ten feet between you and your partner for three minutes. After three minutes reduce the distance to five feet and continue to talk. You may change topics as many times as you wish. After another three minutes reduce the distance to two feet, then twelve inches, and finally six inches. Each distance should be maintained for a minimum of three minutes.

DISCUSSION: Discuss your reactions to the various conversational distances you maintained with your partner. Did the topic of the conversation or the intensity with which you discussed the topic vary with the different distances? Did certain topics seem inappropriate at particular distances? What types of topics do you consider to be appropriate at the following distances: ten feet, five feet, two feet, one foot, six inches?

PERSONAL EXPERIENCES

1. Strike up a conversation with a stranger while you are waiting in line, sitting in a bus, or walking on campus. After a couple of minutes, ask if he or she would be willing to participate in an experiment requiring no more than a few minutes. If the person is willing, ask him or her to relate the first impression of you. Stress the need for an honest appraisal of your personal appearance, nonverbal behaviors, and conversational qualities. Is the impression accurate? What was your reaction to the description of you? How aware are you of the nonverbal impression you create?

2. Select a person in one of your classes to observe. Watch your subject over a period of several days and see if you can classify his or her nonverbal behaviors as (a) regulators, (b) illustrators, (c) emblems, (d) affect displays, or (e) adaptors. What does this classification tell you about the person? For example, does the absence of the use of regulating nonverbal behavior suggest that the person may not provide adequate listening response for a speaker?

3. Watch television with a friend, but at separate locations. Have your friend watch the same program you do so that you can compare notes later. When you watch the program, however, turn off the sound completely. Watch the body movements and facial expressions very carefully and try to understand the story line. After the program tell your friend what happened—describe the emotions, the drama, and the interaction between characters in the program. Then listen to your friend's description. What were the major differences in your

descriptions? Did the absence of sound produce more information on the nonverbal level while reducing the content of the information, which is obtained through the verbal medium?

4. The next time you have a telephone conversation with someone you have never seen (telephone operator, salesperson), try to determine information about that person on the basis of vocal cues. For example, try to guess age, height, weight, race, sex, and the area of the country he or she is from. After you have made some tentative guesses, check your results by asking your telephone partner to verify the information. Try this several times and see how vocal cues help, hinder, or do not affect the identification of background and personality characteristics of an individual.

5. Observe yourself for a day to determine what relationship you have to time. Record the number of times you look at a clock, ask for the time, or refer to time in any manner. Next, go a step further and determine whether you live in present time, future time, past time, or linear time (no past, present, or future). How well can you relate to people who have a different time orientation than you?

6. Pick a task that takes approximately two hours to complete. Work on the task for one hour in an "ugly" room and one hour in a "beautiful" room. What effect did the difference in environment have on your productivity? Did you experience different physical feelings in each room? Are you sensitive to your environment?

DISCUSSION QUESTIONS

1. What is the difference between nonverbal communication and nonverbal behavior?
2. What are some of the ways (functions) in which we use nonverbal communication?
3. How is the formation of first impressions related to stereotyping?
4. Can you describe your nonverbal behaviors during speaking and listening?
5. What nonverbal behaviors do you use to defend your territory and personal space?
6. To what extent do nonverbal behaviors reflect our attitudes or emotions?
7. Do cultural norms regarding the use of space tell us anything about a given society?
8. How important do you consider paralinguistic cues to be in verbal communication?

5
Intrapersonal Communication

KEY CONCEPTS AND TERMS

Physical self
Emotional self
Intellectual self
Habit
Unity principle
Self-concept
Self-fulfilling prophecy
Reference group
Role
Ascribed role
Achieved role
Sex role
Social role
Hierarchy of human
  needs
Physiological needs
Safety needs
Need for love
Esteem needs
Self-actualization
Stimuli
Internal stimuli

External stimuli
Overt stimuli
Covert stimuli
Threshold of
  consciousness
Reception
Selective perception
Intensity
Cognitive processing
Memory
Sensory storage
Short-term memory
Long-term memory
Retrieval
Recognition
Recall
Sorting
Assimilation
Emotional processing
Physiological processing
Biofeedback
Transmission

External self-feedback
Internal self-feedback
Interference
Value
Attitude
Belief
Opinion
Prejudice
Trait
Locus of control
Manipulation
Dogmatism
Tolerance for ambiguity
Self-esteem
Maturity
Defense mechanism
Rationalization
Projection
Insulation
Reaction formation
Identification
Repression

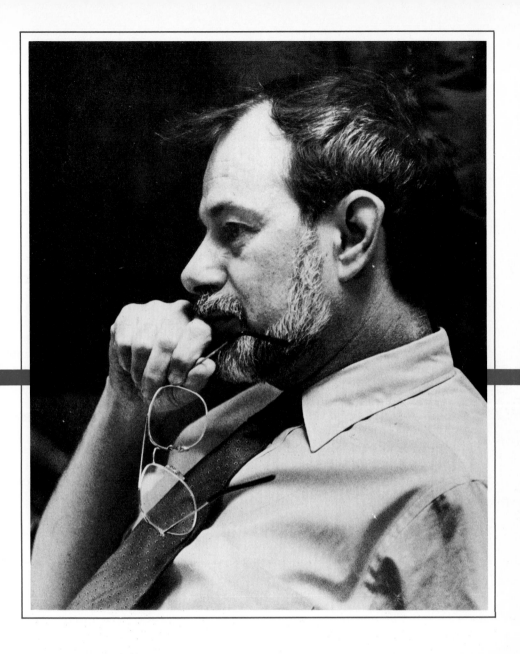

When Dr. James Black was hired as chief of pharmacology at the Welwyn Research Institute in Welwyn Garden City, England, little did the company know that Black—and a 14-year research effort on his part—would eventually bring to market the most successful drug in history. The drug that was developed at Welwyn for Smith, Kline and French Laboratories (SK&F) is called Tagamet, a wonder drug that heals ulcers quickly and painlessly. Tagamet became the first billion-dollar drug in pharmaceutical history and changed the course of SK&F from "the senior citizen of the drug business" into one of the world's foremost pharmaceutical research and development firms. However, the drug probably never would have emerged had it not been for Black's vision, scientific persistence, and defiance of the institutions for whom he worked. As a result of his argument that pharmaceutical researchers could move away from blending chemicals "like medieval herbalists" and could actually solve problems by designing combinations of atoms, Smith and a handful of SK&F "baton carriers" eventually introduced Tagamet to the world and ultimately moved pharmaceutical research into the twentieth century.[1]

How does this story relate to intrapersonal communication? Intrapersonal communication takes place whenever we evaluate and react to internal and external stimuli—and involves messages that are sent and received within ourselves. Thus, intrapersonal communication involves not only our intellect but also our physical and emotional sensations. To work 14 years on a single project required more of Dr. Black than his creativity, especially when he was fighting an uphill battle with the very institutions that supported him. To see his vision through to the end, Black had to deal with trillions of stimuli—from frustrations that must have mounted as he worked on the project to physical fatigue to outside input regarding his success or failure, to name just a few.

As you can see, intrapersonal communication is more far-reaching than just "talking to yourself." As you will read in the following pages, intrapersonal messages reflect your physical self, emotional self, intellectual self, and social self. They also reflect your habits, self-concept, self-related roles, and your attitudes, values, and beliefs. However, intrapersonal communication does not require 14 years to emerge during a person's lifetime. This form of communication takes place every moment that we live.

THE SELF

The study of intrapersonal communication begins with knowing yourself. As soon as you begin to examine *the* self, however, you discover that you are, in fact, *many* selves.

The Physical Self

The *physical self* is generally divided into three primary areas: internal functions, external movements, and body concept. Internal functions of the body include digestion, breathing, blood circulation, all the work of inner organs, the building of new cells, and the elimination of bodily wastes. Addi-

---

[1] P. Ranganath Nayak and J. M. Ketteringham, "Tagamet: Repairing Ulcers without Surgery," *Breakthroughs: How the Vision and Drive of Innovators in Sixteen Companies Created Commercial Breakthroughs that Swept the World* (New York: Rawson Associates, 1986), 102, 129.

tionally, the five senses (sight, smell, hearing, taste, and touch), sensations of weight and temperature, and all reflexes such as laughter and yawning belong to our body's internal functions.[2] We have all experienced messages from each of these areas of the body and responded to them accordingly. For example, if our stomach growls we head straight for the refrigerator; if we are a bit warm, we adjust the thermostat on the heater or air conditioner.

> The easiest person to deceive is one's own self.
>
> Edward Bulwer Lytton

The physical self also involves external movements, such as walking, talking, writing, eating, biking, and other movements of the body. External movements also include events such as unconsciously catching a falling object or talking to ourselves.[3] Again, in each instance, a message is sent from the brain to some other part of the body, and an external response of some form is elicited.

As infants, we do not recognize ourselves as being separate from the environment. Such physical recognition usually develops at around 18 months, as we acquire more accurate perceptions of our bodies. Such bodily concepts—better known as body image—are vital for normal mental and emotional development.

Body image is defined as a person's perception of his or her physical self. While this perception remains fairly constant in a normal individual, it is subject to change at times. If you feel hurt or depressed, you may actually feel smaller, more vulnerable. The reverse is true, too—a dieter may have a distorted body image each time he or she gains a pound or two. For the most part, however, a person with a fairly healthy personality will have a fairly healthy body image.

The Emotional Self

Another self is the *emotional self*. Emotions are conscious feelings that are accompanied by physiological changes, such as rapid heartbeat, tensed muscles, or raised blood sugar level. We are usually all too aware of the stimuli that prompt our emotional responses. Barely missing the car that darts out in front of you from a side street can tie your stomach in knots long after the stimulus is gone. At other times, before we realize it, our emotional selves take over. Crying for no reason at all, yelling at your best friend, or laughing out loud while others just smile are all examples of our emotions taking control.

---

[2] P. D. Ouspensky, *The Psychology of Man's Possible Evolution*, 2nd ed. (New York: Vintage Books, 1974), 26–28.
[3] Ibid.

The first step toward effective communication with others is successful communication with yourself.

The Intellectual Self

Your *intellectual self*, or the self associated with your mental processes, involves mental actions or behaviors such as concept and word formation, use of comparison and contrast, use of logic and reasoning, and the process by which we solve problems and make decisions. At this very moment your intellectual self is functioning as you read this text (that is, if your mind is not wandering to that upcoming weekend). In short, our intellectual self is our mental self—a self which we will learn more about in the following sections.

Habits

Each of us possesses *habits*, or repetitive behaviors, that become so automatic that we are hardly aware of them. You may have a habit of biting your nails or stroking your chin while you are thinking, even though you do not consciously choose to do so.

In contrast to these harmless habits, other unconscious behaviors have more serious consequences. Some individuals, for example, always fall in love with the wrong people. Psychologists say this happens not by accident but because there is some conflict within the individual that encourages this type of relationship. Such habitual behavior patterns usually continue as long as they fulfill certain needs within the individual.

Some of these behaviors directly affect our communication. Do you know people who constantly pepper their communication with misused words, or who have the knack of always saying the wrong thing at the wrong time? The characters of Rose and Sophia on television's *The Golden Girls* are perfect examples. Rose constantly interprets events through the eyes of innocence and Sophia through the eyes of a seventy-year old skeptic. Both end up making hilarious and often embarrassing remarks to Dorothy and Blanche.

The Unity Principle

At this point you may be asking, "If, in fact, I am a product of all of these selves, why am I not more aware of it?" The answer to this question lies first in our need to maintain a unified conceptual system,[4] as evidenced by our ability to process information that is inconsistent with our values, attitudes, and beliefs. Valerie, for example, loves to wake early in the morning, read the *Wall Street Journal*, and have several cups of coffee to start her day. As she rushes her way through a busy week in the office, she also likes to take time to sit, have several more cups of coffee, and talk with her supervisors about both problems and progress in their respective departments. Despite the large amounts of coffee Valerie consumes, what is the probability that a special program on the effects of caffeine on the human system would cause a behavioral change in Valerie's habits? Depending on several factors, there probably would be little or no change. She probably would not even believe the program could apply to her, and the information either would be lost in memory or would never be processed at all.

In addition to the impact that our need for perceptual unity has on our perceptions of the self, several other factors contribute to our illusions of a unified self. These include the use of words such as *I*, *me*, and *mine*, which also reflect unity; our sensations of having one body and one name associated with our bodies (both of which usually remain the same over time, once we reach adulthood); and our observations of the regularly recurring patterns of behavior that we associate with ourselves. Each of these contributes to the illusion of oneness.

Along with the innate function of our conceptual systems to maintain a unified and happy self, we can also consciously work toward a unified self by increasing our awareness of who we are—our many selves. One such method of increasing awareness is through the use of the Johari Window, a concept that focuses on increasing awareness of the private self and the public self.

---

[4] S. Epstein, "The Unity Principle versus the Reality and Pleasure Principles, or the Tale of the Scorpion and the Frog," in *Self-Concept: Advances in Theory and Research*, eds. M. D. Lynch, A. A. Norman-Hebeisen, and K. Gergen (Cambridge: Ballinger, 1981).

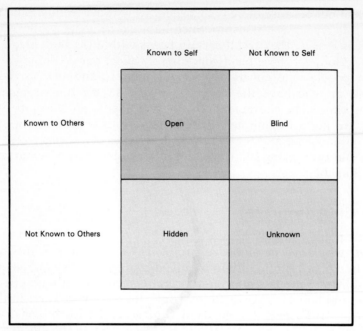

Figure 5–1
The Johari Window

Awareness and You

The distinction between our private and our public selves is well illustrated by the Johari Window, shown in Figure 5–1. Designed by Joseph Luft and Harrington Ingham,[5] the Johari Window compares aspects of open (public) versus closed (private) communication relationships.

The "open" section in the diagram represents self-knowledge that you are aware of and willing to share with others. The "hidden" section represents what you are aware of but not willing to share. The "blind" section represents information of which you yourself are unaware but which is known to others. The "unknown" section represents what is unknown both to you and to others.

Although each section of the Johari Window is conceptually the same size in Figure 5–1, in "real life" situations different proportions would be drawn for each relationship that we are in, depending on the amount of information that we share with that individual. In a close relationship, for example, our open area might be considerably larger than the hidden area. When communicating with a casual acquaintance, our hidden area would be the largest part of the window.

Let us see how this window applies to a particular communication situation:

[5] J. Luft, *Of Human Interaction* (Palo Alto, Calif.: National Press Books, 1969).

Linda and Tony are reunited after a two-month separation. Linda lets Tony know how much she missed him (open), but does not tell him that she has started to date someone new (hidden). Tony senses that Linda is upset, although she claims that she is fine (blind). The unknown in this situation is a whole range of feelings that are not clear to either of them. For example, both individuals are probably unsure about Linda's feelings toward Tony.

Again, you can use the concept of the Johari Window to increase your self-awareness. This, in turn, should improve your communication with others. As you strive to shrink the blind and unknown segments, you may begin to discover a self you only partially knew before, a self that may or may not resemble the concept you've always had about that person you call "me." The more information you can bring into the open from the hidden, blind, and unknown areas, the better your interpersonal communication will be.

SELF-CONCEPT

Before we begin a discussion of self-concept, take out a piece of paper. Quickly jot down the many roles that you play, using nouns that describe the most important aspects of who you are. The list might look something like this:

> Joanie: woman athlete, competitor, student, daughter, friend, animal lover
> Jerry: man, student, fiancé, gourmet cook, tennis player, lover, poet

What special descriptive words did you use? How varied were the roles that best describe you?

The first purpose we had in mind when asking you to develop this composite was to illustrate the highly complex and elaborate nature of our self-perceptions. Indeed, one need look no further than the number and variety of the terms to see that our composites reflect a host of ideas we have about ourselves.

Our second purpose was to demonstrate that this picture we have of ourselves—our *self-concept*—has a strong effect on both intrapersonal and interpersonal communication. For example, Crystal, who thinks of herself as a footloose and fancy-free swinger, would probably enjoy being asked on a cruise by a new man whom she recently met. However, Cindy, whose self-concept includes being a highly religious person, would probably be extremely offended by the same invitation. A good communicator is sensitive to the self-concepts of others and knows that their values and attitudes affect how they respond (that is, the effective communicator would be sensitive and respond quite differently to Cindy and Crystal when inviting the two women on such a cruise).

At this point you may be wondering how our self-concept came to exist. Self-concept is not inborn; rather, it is developed through interaction with people and the environment. Specifically, it develops as a function of three primary sets of variables: our past experiences, the reference groups with which we identify, and the roles that we play in our lives. The interaction between ourselves and these three variables has affected and will continue to affect our self-concept.

Past Experiences

Your past shapes the way you feel about yourself and the way you react to others. A small child may stop thinking of himself as Superman after falling down and finding that he is not indestructible. Sometimes past experiences shape your self-concept without your awareness. A child who is constantly criticized at home and made to feel worthless may develop a negative self-concept without realizing the reasons behind it.

Other early experiences can also color your self-concept. A child's school experiences are particularly important. The child who achieves success in the early grades will probably have a better self-concept than a child who has had constant academic failure. In turn, these positive or negative past experiences sometimes create a ***self-fulfilling prophecy***. Children who see themselves as inferior or dull may perform below their actual abilities. Similarly, children with highly positive self-concepts may prove to be over-achievers. Self-fulfilling prophecies can also reinforce self-concept. If a teacher is told that John is a discipline problem, the teacher expects John to misbehave. Sensing this expectation, John may very well cause the trouble that is expected of him. John's self-concept of being "bad" is thus reinforced.

Self-concept is particularly influenced by the socializing and dating experiences of adolescence. The boy who succeeds in getting a date with every girl he asks may come to view himself as a real ladies' man. On the other hand, frequent rejections might cause him to think of himself as a failure. Self-concept is often so shaky during adolescence that many boys

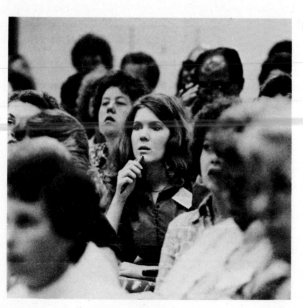

Unique among the masses—you!

ask someone out only when they are sure that the answer will be yes. Girls, too, are frequently unsure of themselves during adolescence, when changing bodies and social expectations can greatly influence self-concept.

Reference Groups

Groups that give you a sense of identity and help you establish your attitudes and values are known as *reference groups*. Reference groups contribute to your self-concept. Especially during adolescence, when a person's self-concept is so changeable, groups provide a certain amount of stability.

The adolescent group, like all groups, is characterized by a structure that defines the roles of group members in relation to other members and to those outside the group. The group also provides a set of values or group norms that are common to all the members and distinct from the values they share with outsiders. Thus, group membership enables a member to identify with an established whole. This identification is extremely important because individuals incorporate into their own self-concepts many of the ideas, attitudes and values of the people with whom they identify.

Roles

Whatever your self-concept, your behavior is strongly affected by the people with whom you interact. Typically, you assume different behavior patterns, or *roles*, in different social settings. In fact, the setting often dictates the roles other people are playing and to which you then respond.

ASCRIBED AND ACHIEVED ROLES. Some roles are *ascribed* to you and are thus out of your control. They are based primarily on sex, age, kinship and general place in society. For example, infants are expected to act in a certain way and grandparents in another. In recent years our understanding of ascribed sex roles has undergone striking transformations. Whereas our society once felt that being a female meant being gentle and passive, today many women reject these attributes as artificial and limiting and in no way necessary to being a woman.

Unlike ascribed roles, *achieved* roles are earned by individual accomplishment. We all possess different capabilities, and society recognizes these differences. A union steward, an athlete and a company president all occupy their positions at least to some extent because of their abilities and drive.

SEX ROLES. As we mentioned previously, *sex roles* are usually ascribed, defined, and encouraged by each culture. They are a product of the cues children pick up from their surroundings and from same-sex models in the community. In addition, sex-role identity is shaped by children's relations with parents and their relations with one another, the sexual taboos that exist in the culture and the social class to which the children belong. Obviously, these biologically and socially determined roles are extremely important to the development of self-concept.

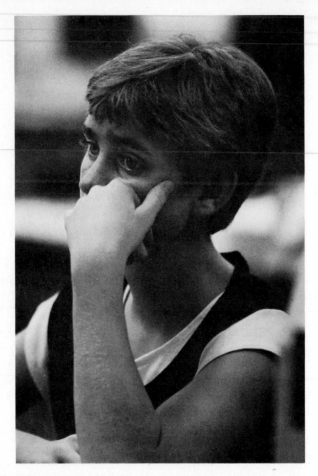

The ideas and attitudes of others strongly influence our overall self-concepts.

SOCIAL ROLES.   Each of us also assumes a number of *social* roles, defined by our environment. Sometimes an entire structure or organization is based on separate but complementary social roles. In the army, for instance, the roles of the enlisted personnel, the officers, the cooks, the military police, the medics, and so on are clearly defined and join together to form a working unit. Each role has its own duties, skills and established set of norms. If someone steps out of role, that person is subject to criticism and sometimes to punishment.

It is the combined interaction of your self-concept with these social, sexual, ascribed and achieved roles that determines your communication behavior in any given situation.

THE HIERARCHY OF HUMAN NEEDS

Before special holidays (Christmas, birthdays, and so on) many people make lists of all the things they want. If you were to make a list right now, it might include money, jewelry, clothes, a car, airline tickets, roller skates,

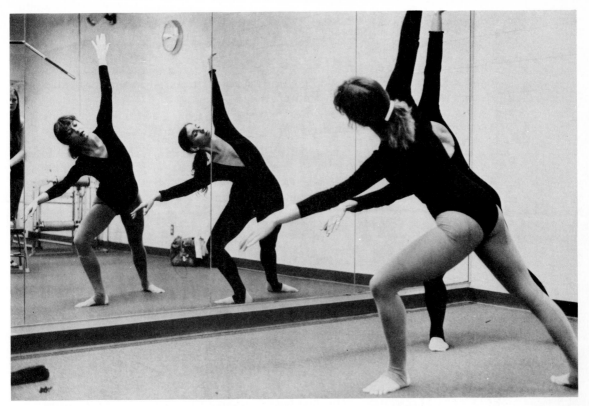

Self actualization: Being and doing all that we are capable of.

or frisbees. These are items some of us want, but what would you include if you had to make a list of your *needs?* Your list would probably look quite different. If you haven't thought recently about what you really need, take a few minutes to do so right now.

Some of our wants and needs are similar because we are driven by common internal motivations. Abraham Maslow, a well-known psychologist, examined hundreds of people and discovered five basic human drives. Each of us has physiological, safety, love, esteem and self-actualization needs. These needs, or drives, are known as the ***hierarchy of human needs***.[6]

PHYSIOLOGICAL.   Before we attend to other drives, we first have to satisfy desires for things such as food, water, shelter and sex. If you are hungry after not eating all day, it is difficult to think about studying or playing tennis before you've given yourself some nourishment. If you've pulled two all-nighters in a row, you're probably not interested in going out to have a beer with your friends until you've had some sleep.

---

[6] A. H. Maslow, *Motivation and Personality*, 2nd. ed. (New York: Harper & Row, 1970), 35–46.

SAFETY. After we've met all our physiological needs, our next concern is for safety. We like to feel secure, stable and in control. Many people work hard all their lives and save in every way so that they'll be free from fear and anxiety about money when they retire. All of us think of ways to protect ourselves from danger by doing things such as investing in life insurance, putting locks on doors, or installing smoke detectors.

LOVE. Many people would put love as their most important human need, but physiological and safety needs are usually met first or in combination with other needs. Some people feel insecure unless they are dating or married. In this case security and love may be taken care of simultaneously. Love involves another person and is not a one-way street. It is only through giving and receiving affection, care and concern that we gain approval and acceptance from others. To increase our sense of belonging, many of us get involved in various types of group activities, but generally we satisfy the love need through relationships with family, friends and lovers.

ESTEEM. After we feel loved and accepted, we look for esteem. Usually we must first acquire self-esteem or worth before others will attribute esteem to us. Esteem is a desire for dignity, achievement, competency and status. Some people get graduate degrees, others master difficult skills in sports, and still others do no more than be themselves to gain admiration and respect from their peers.

SELF-ACTUALIZATION. Our last basic human need is for *self-actualization*, or striving for all that we are capable of being. Self-actualization includes long-range goals for using our full potential and developing ourselves in all areas. Self-improvement is one form of self-actualization. Throughout our lives we meet small challenges such as winning a marathon (or just completing it), getting an *A* in physics, writing a novel, or sailing around the world. Our ultimate goal, however, is being and doing all that we are capable of—for personal satisfaction.

THE PROCESS OF INTRAPERSONAL COMMUNICATION

Intrapersonal communication is the foundation upon which interpersonal communication rests. Therefore, it is necessary to understand how you communicate with yourself before you approach the process of communicating with others. Figure 5–2 can help you visualize the intrapersonal communication process. The elements that set the process in motion are called *stimuli*.

Internal Stimuli

The brain is made aware of the state of the body by nerve impulses, *internal stimuli* that can prompt you to respond by communicating. Let's say you

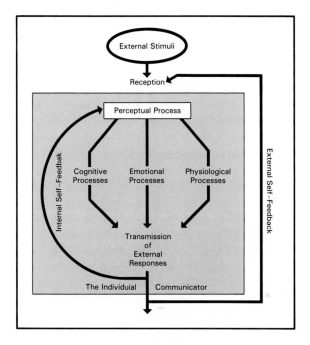

Figure 5–2
Intrapersonal Communication

have the flu. Your muscles ache, your fever is high, and you are depressed. Such a miserable state may prompt you to call a doctor to relieve your physical ills and a friend to relieve your depression. The internal stimuli in this situation have resulted in communication.

External Stimuli

External stimuli are, of course, those stimuli that originate in the environment outside of your body. There are two kinds of external stimuli. *Overt stimuli* are received on the conscious level. They are picked up by the sensory organs and then sent to the brain. More than one overt stimulus usually affects a person at any given moment. For example, the pizza being advertised on TV and the sounds and aromas coming from the kitchen can prompt an eager, "What's for dinner?"

Covert stimuli are external stimuli that are received on the subconscious level. Let's say you are getting dressed for work. One of your favorite songs comes on the radio, so you turn the volume up. The song ends and the news begins, just as you discover a gaping hole in your sock. You find another pair and finish dressing, but you're running late. Is it too cold for your lightweight jacket? You suddenly realize that the weather report has just ended but you have no idea what was said, despite the blaring volume.

The stimulus of the weather report was received and stored in your brain, but it was below the *threshold of consciousness*. Thus, you were not consciously aware of *what* was said, even though you recognized that you were hearing the weather report. Such covert stimuli have been shown to affect behavior and communication. Split-second presentations of the words, "Drink Smith's Beer" can indeed make a viewer feel thirsty.

> You do not need to leave your room. Remain sitting at your table and listen. Do not even listen, simply wait. Do not even wait, be quite still and solitary. The world will freely offer itself to you to be unmasked, it has no choice, it will roll in ecstasy at your feet.
>
> Franz Kafka

Reception

The process by which the body receives stimuli is called *reception*. In intrapersonal communication, both external and internal receptors send information to the central nervous system. External receptors for the five senses—sight, sound, smell, taste and touch—receive stimuli that are changed into nerve impulses and then sent to the brain. These external receptors are located on or near the body's surface and react to physical, chemical and mechanical stimuli to provide you with information about the environment. Internal receptors such as nerve endings, on the other hand, convey information about your interior state—the dryness of your mouth or the fullness of your stomach, for example.

Although your body receives every stimulus present in a particular communication setting, you could not possibly communicate in response to every one of them. The process that helps you to cope with this jumble of stimuli is called *selective perception*, the screening out of a huge number of stimuli present in your environment, which permits attention to just a few. What determines which stimuli we do perceive? The main factor is *intensity*: Loud sounds, bright colors, sharp smells, and so forth are often perceived when less intense stimuli are not.

Processing

Processing of internal and external communication occurs at three levels: cognitive, emotional and physiological. At each level of processing, some stimuli receive more conscious attention than others. This attention is a function of the particular stimulus and of the context in which it is presented. Some stimuli are perceived with full awareness (traffic lights, sirens, TV programs), while others may not be consciously noticed (background noise during a lecture, the hum of fluorescent lights in a room). Stimuli that are perceived consciously, or at least with some awareness, are the first to be processed. Stimuli that are perceived subconsciously are usually "stored" in your memory for later processing.

COGNITIVE PROCESSING.   *Cognitive processes* are associated with the intellectual self and include the storage, retrieval, sorting and assimilation of information. We don't know exactly how such processing occurs; our goal here is simply to describe these processes on both the conscious and subconscious cognitive levels.

MEMORY: The storage of information that we choose to remember is called *memory*. There are three forms of memory: (1) sensory storage, in which the information is held for only an instant; (2) short-term memory in which the information is stored for several seconds; and (3) long-term memory, in which the information is stored indefinitely. *Sensory storage* refers to our ability to hold some information for a fraction of a second after the stimulus disappears. For example, you are not aware of the gaps between frames when you watch a movie because each frame is held in sensory storage until the next appears. The major difference between sensory storage and *short-term memory* is that in the latter, data are analyzed, identified, and simplified so that they can be conveniently stored and handled. Short-term memory is a kind of "holding device" in which you keep information until you are ready to use it or discard it. If such information seems useful, you may transfer it to the permanent storage of *long-term memory* for future reference.

RETRIEVAL: Information is stored so that it can be used to help establish the meaning of later incoming stimuli. However, stored information is relatively useless unless it can be retrieved from memory. Such *retrieval* takes the form of either recognition or recall. *Recognition* involves awareness that certain information is familiar, having been experienced previously. *Recall* is more difficult, in that it requires reconstruction of the information that has been stored. For example, while we may recognize a certain word whose meaning we looked up last week, we may be unable to recall its definition.

SORTING: Your mind contains countless bits and pieces of information. In any particular processing situation, you must first select or *sort* the most relevant information from your entire storehouse of knowledge. Here again we know very little about the actual workings of our individual selection systems. We do know, however, that such selection processes occur. For example, when we read, we sort the letters until we are able to make words of them.

ASSIMILATION: Cognitive processing is not simply the sum of memory storage, retrieval and sorting functions. Rather, it involves *assimilation*, the process of incorporating some aspect of the environment into the whole set of mental functionings in order to make sense out of what goes on around us. To continue our reading example, your ability to read was first learned, then stored in long-term memory. Whenever you open a book, you retrieve this information, use it to sort the letters on the page into words and then assimilate the words into sentences and ideas that have meaning for you.

EMOTIONAL PROCESSING.   As mentioned at the beginning of this chapter, intrapersonal processing also involves *emotional processing*, or the nonlogical response of an organism to a stimulus. Later in this chapter we will take a closer look at the different variables that operate in emotional processing. However, it is important to mention here that variables, ranging from attitudes, beliefs, and opinions at the subconscious level to emotions at the conscious level, all interact to determine our response to any particular communication.

PHYSIOLOGICAL PROCESSING.   The third type of processing occurs at the physiological level and is associated with the physical self. Although ***physiological processing*** is of obvious importance in staying alive, its significance to intrapersonal communication is only beginning to be recognized. As we said earlier, some of the subconscious variables in this process are heart rate, brain activity, muscle tension, blood pressure and body temperature.

Brain wave activity has been given considerable attention lately as an aid in determining information processing. Have you ever wondered what parts of your brain process certain types of information? Research with an electroencephalograph (EEG) suggests that we alternate between our right and left brain hemispheres to process stimuli. Generally, if you are balancing your checking account, reading a textbook, or writing a term paper, you will be using your left hemisphere. The left hemisphere processes information logically and is concerned with speech and with mathematical and analytical tasks. The right hemisphere, in contrast, processes information abstractly and is involved with imagery and with spatial, musical and ***gestalt*** tasks. When you listen to your favorite album, imagine how you will look in a new outfit, or sketch a picture, you are using your right brain hemisphere.

Monitoring physiological variables makes it possible to control internal processes. First, we must be aware of what our states are. Awareness is much more developed in some people than in others. For most people, conscious physiological awareness is limited to sensations of pleasure, pain, tension and relaxation. Some people use ***biofeedback***, a form of external self-feedback, to help themselves become more aware of their physiological processing. Subjects are attached to instruments that provide information about physiological parameters such as pulse rate, muscle tension and skin temperature. In some manner, this information helps individuals to alter these levels. For example, biofeedback has been used to teach control of bodily functions such as heart rate, blood pressure and seizures. In addition, biofeedback has been shown to reduce tension levels in coronary-prone, or Type A, personalities. To illustrate the usefulness of biofeedback training in this area of study, Prior, Goodyear, and Holen gave biofeedback training to persons with either Type A or Type B personalities. (Type A personalities are usually highly competitive, achievement-oriented, time urgent and easily angered, while Type B personalities are more relaxed, feel less stressed and are less achievement-oriented, overall.) Following six weeks of training, their subjects were asked to perform a series of easy and difficult memory tasks. Results of the study revealed that, when compared to Type A and Type B personalities who were given no biofeedback training, biofeedback subjects maintained a greater degree of relaxation during their memory tasks. In

"It looks OK to me."

addition, they maintained significantly lower levels of tension both prior to and after their performance.[7]

Transmission

The process by which messages are sent from a source to a receiver is called *transmission*. In intrapersonal communication the source and the receiver are the same person. Thus, transmission takes place through nerve impulses in the brain rather than through sound waves in the air or words written on a page. The intrapersonal communication cycle is completed when the brain reacts to these nerve impulses by transmitting a message to smooth muscles, which regulate the movements of the body. As we described at the start of this chapter, putting a hand on a hot pan causes the individual's touch receptors to send a neural transmission to the brain, saying, "It's hot," which causes the brain to transmit a message to the muscles in the hand, ordering, "Move away from the pan immediately."

Feedback

We usually think of feedback as information from another person. In intrapersonal communication, however, there are two kinds of *self*-feedback—external and internal.

---

[7] D. W. Prior, R. K. Goodyear, and M. C. Holen, "EMG Biofeedback Training of Type A and Type B Behavior Pattern Subjects," *Journal of Counseling Psychology* 30, no. 3 (1983), 316–22.

External self-feedback is the part of your message that you hear yourself. This kind of feedback enables you to correct your own mistakes. For example, you would surely backtrack if you heard yourself say something like "external felf-seedback."

Internal self-feedback is usually picked up through bone conduction, nerve endings, or muscular movement. For example, you might perceive an awkward facial gesture without actually seeing it—simply by feeling the muscle tension in your face. Again, perceiving this information enables you to correct yourself.

Interference

Interference is another important variable in the communication process. *Interference* refers to any factor that negatively affects communication. It can occur at any point along the communication network and at any level of communication. For example, the blast of your neighbor's stereo or a splitting headache might make it impossible for you to read.

A special form of interference occurs intrapersonally when stimuli are processed at one level, although another level is better suited to dealing with them. For example, many people react emotionally to information that should be processed on a cognitive level. Have you ever started crying or gotten angry in response to a bad test score, when if you had remained calm, you might have been able to analyze and profit from the bad news? On the other hand, some individuals insist on processing information on the cognitive level when an emotional response would actually be more helpful. Often a good cry can relieve the pressure of a bad day better than a careful rehash of the day's events.[8]

THE EFFECTS OF INTRAPERSONAL VARIABLES ON COMMUNICATION

Even though a particular communication may focus on the here and now, your personality and past experience influence your interpretation of it. Thus, it is important to consider the intrapersonal factors that influence the communicators. For example, the experiences of someone who has recently lost a mate will no doubt affect that person's communication on the subject of death.

Personal Orientation

The way you react to the following situation will be determined by your personal orientation.

---

[8] L. L. Barker and R. Edwards, *Intrapersonal Communication* (Dubuque, Iowa: Gorsuch Scarisbrick, 1980), 7–8.

Warren and Jerry are interviewing for the job of advertising copywriter in a large advertising agency. Neither of them has had any experience, but both come to the interview prepared to show samples of the kind of work they are capable of producing. Jerry's samples represent many hours of hard work and a little talent, while Warren's show much talent but very little effort—he lifted them almost word for word from a textbook.

How do you feel about Jerry and Warren? Do you respect Jerry for his honesty and hard work, or do you appreciate Warren's craftiness in trying to get the kind of job he wants? Your reaction to this situation reflects the values, attitudes, beliefs, and opinions that make up your personal orientation.

VALUES.   Each of us maintains a set of *values*—moral or ethical judgments of things we consider important. Values can be a source of conflict within an individual as well as a barrier between people of opposing standards. Fearing a malpractice suit, for instance, a doctor who comes upon an accident victim may be reluctant to offer assistance. His or her values will determine what action is taken. Sometimes an individual will voice one set of values and be guided by another. For example, parents may scold their children for dishonesty but think nothing of cheating on their income tax.

ATTITUDES.   An *attitude* is a learned tendency to react positively or negatively to an object or situation. It implies a positive or negative evaluation of someone or something. Attitudes operate at three different levels: (1) cognitive, (2) affective, and (3) instrumental. The cognitive level involves a particular belief, the affective level involves a particular feeling, and the instrumental level involves overt behavior or action.

Let's examine a specific situation. Carlotta Ramirez, a member of the state board of higher education, is a strong opponent of free tuition. Her negative attitude can be broken down in this way:

1. Cognitive (belief) = People who value a college education should be willing to pay for it, even if it means going to work to get enough money for tuition.
2. Affective (feeling) = People who try to get something for nothing make me angry.
3. Instrumental (action) = I vote no on the proposal for free tuition at state universities.

BELIEFS, OPINIONS, AND PREJUDICES.   We have already used the term *belief*. A belief is anything accepted as true. Note that this definition does not imply either a positive or a negative judgment. For example, you may believe that there is life on other planets, yet this belief does not indicate a positive or negative attitude toward that idea. However, if you were to take your belief one step further to say that since you believe there is life on other planets, it would be in our best interests to increase space exploration programs, you would then be voicing an **opinion**. An opinion lies somewhere between an attitude and a belief. It implies a positive or negative reaction.

Not all our beliefs and opinions are well founded. Sometimes they are based on preconceived ideas and not on our own actual experiences. In this case they are, in fact, **prejudices**—preformed judgments about a particular person, group, or thing. None of us is free from prejudice, but certain prejudices are more harmful than others. Think for a moment about your own experiences with prejudice, when you were either guilty of prejudice or were its victim. Or consider this example of how foolish our prejudices can be:

> Although it was against her principles, Ruth had agreed to help a good friend out of a tight spot by accepting a blind date with the friend's uncle from Louisiana. Ruth, who had never been south of Philadelphia, just knew that an evening spent with this hick was going to be one of the most boring of her life.
>
> He arrived, and, sure enough, his accent was unlike anything Ruth had ever heard. By evening's end, however, she had changed her mind. Full of admiration for the most interesting and beautifully mannered man she had ever met, Ruth eagerly awaited their next date.
>
> He never called again. A few weeks later, Ruth learned from her friend that he had returned to New Orleans and, before leaving, had announced: "All Yankee women are alike—hard to please!"

Think about the groups toward which you may be prejudiced. Does this example suggest ways in which you may be oversimplifying to the point of prejudice?

Personality Traits

Another way the self affects our communication is through personality variables known as **traits**. Personality traits are those qualities that distinguish one personality from another. As the following examples indicate, some personality traits aid communication, but many are barriers to communication.

LOCUS OF CONTROL.   One important personality variable that affects the communication process is **locus of control**, or the degree to which we perceive reinforcement either as contingent upon our own efforts or actions (internal locus of control) or as a result of forces beyond our control and due to chance, fate, or some other external force (external locus of control).[9] There should be, for example, a difference in communication patterns between those who believe that they control events and those who believe that their desired outcomes will accrue as a function of the degree to which they fit in with the beliefs, desires, or attitudes of people who have power over them. The former person, with a more internal locus of control, would be

---

[9] H. I. Ayabe, A. R. Freese, K-J. Kim, M. Arakaki, and K. Y. Kameoka, "Feedback and Locus of Control," *The Journal of Genetic Psychology* 143 (1983), 141–42.

Self-esteem involves a readiness to accept the views of others.

more straightforward upon presenting new plans to an upper-level supervisor, while the latter person's communication (the person with an external locus of control) would be more indirect, vague and ambiguous.

MANIPULATION.   Related to the locus of control that a person exhibits is the degree to which he attempts to manipulate others. People vary with regard to the characteristic of *manipulation*, or the degree to which they attempt to achieve goals by dominating and controlling others. However, research has shown that people who have an external locus of control (that is, who believe that the world is ordered and controlled by others) often desire that control for themselves and tend to exhibit greater manipulative behaviors than do people who have an internal locus of control. Given that the latter believe that they control their own fates, they do not generally manifest excessive degrees of manipulation.

DOGMATISM.   One of the most difficult personality traits encountered in a communication situation is *dogmatism*. Dogmatic individuals have closed minds and are reluctant to accept new ideas and opinions. Yet they may accept without question the word of certain authorities and expect the same kind of blind acceptance from those they consider their inferiors. Dogmatic individuals often remain steadfast to ideas or opinions in spite of contradictory evidence.

TOLERANCE OF AMBIGUITY.   While some people can live with shades of gray, others insist on things being clearly defined and unambiguous. This varying **_tolerance of ambiguity_** frequently affects the communication process. Consider the following example:

> Phil and Max go to see the movie *Rain Man*. After the movie both agree that the film was extremely well done. However, Max is bothered by several inconsistencies that Phil didn's seem to notice. Max points out three areas in the film that he thought were ambiguous. When he asks Phil for clarification, Phil admits that he can't explain the confusing segments of the film.

Phil's tolerance of ambiguity is greater than Max's. Phil was able to ignore the ambiguities, while Max found them troublesome. Perhaps you have experienced a similar situation when reading a complex book or when trying to analyze a particular communication interaction.

SELF-ESTEEM.   Communication is also affected by the self-esteem of the sender and the receiver. **_Self-esteem_**, which is your enduring evaluation of yourself, often determines your confidence in what you are saying and your readiness to accept the view of others. Therefore, in the communication process, it is important to use your perception of another person's self-esteem as a means of evaluating certain messages. For example, individuals with high self-esteem may confidently state an opinion even without sufficient evidence. You might be quicker to question their veracity than that of speakers whose low self-esteem would prevent them from supporting unproven viewpoints.

MATURITY.   Of the many personality variables, the one that most strongly affects communication is level of **_maturity_**. It is difficult to pinpoint the stage at which a person matures psychologically, but we usually judge a person as mature when he or she is able to function independently in a social setting. One measure of such maturity is the individual's ability to satisfy psychological needs for things such as independence, approval, affection, and so forth. What this means in a communication setting is the absence of intrapersonal conflicts that might intrude on objective transmission and interpretation of messages.

Defense Mechanisms

We all suffer from varying degrees of anxiety. For most of us, anxiety stems from intrapersonal conflicts—conflicts between inner psychological needs and external realities. If severe enough, anxiety can distort your perception of yourself and your environment and thus act as a barrier to communication with others.

The self must find various ways to resolve the anxiety produced by such intrapersonal conflict. These methods, known as **_defense mechanisms_**, help us accept things that might otherwise cause emotional pain. Defense mechanisms, when used in moderation, aid our personal adjustment to the environment. If used to excess, however, they can become a crutch that distorts reality.

> We introduce ourselves
> To Planets and to Flowers
> But with ourselves
> Have etiquettes
> Embarrassments
> And awes.
>
> Emily Dickinson

RATIONALIZATION.   Defense mechanisms take many forms. Perhaps the best known is *rationalization*, an attempt to justify our failures or inadequacies. Most of us rationalize from time to time. For example, when Ellen was not hired for a job she wanted very badly, she rationalized her failure by claiming that the man who would have been her boss was threatened by her abilities. Tom rationalized his rejection by a law school by telling everyone that he really didn't want to go anyway.

PROJECTION.   Sometimes we ignore certain traits, motives, or behaviors in ourselves and attribute them to others. This defense mechanism is known as *projection*. Eleanor, who has a weight problem and is constantly dieting, goes to lunch with her friend Jan, a perfect size 8. When the women finish eating, Eleanor remarks, "I can tell you're still hungry." Actually, Jan is quite full. It is Eleanor who is still hungry.

INSULATION.   One way to resolve conflicts caused by contradictions is to isolate contradictory feelings and/or information. This defense mechanism is known as *insulation*. For example, a member of a radical group who protests police brutality by bombing a precinct headquarters has clearly insulated contradictory behaviors. This person is able to oppose violence on the one hand and participate in violence of a "different" sort on the other.

REACTION FORMATION.   Sometimes people deal with "undesirable" urges or behaviors with a defense mechanism known as *reaction formation*. This process involves denial of what you or society consider unacceptable feelings or behaviors, coupled with extreme advocacy of the opposite position. For example, someone who is easily aroused by pictures of nudes may deny this tendency by becoming an outspoken opponent of pornography.

IDENTIFICATION.   We have discussed the importance of identification in developing self-concept. The *identification process* can also be used as a defense mechanism against insecurity or inadequacy. Thus, adolescents, who often feel uncertain about themselves, may seek security by identifying themselves with stars of the entertainment or sports worlds. Such identification accounts for much of the popularity of personalities such as Elvis Presley, Madonna, Bill Cosby, and "Sting."

REPRESSION.   Some people deal with unpleasant or unacceptable feelings, desires, or experiences by repressing them. *Repression* is a defense mechanism that keeps certain thoughts and feelings beneath the conscious level. Thus, children brought up in overly strict homes, where outbursts are severely punished, often learn to repress anger.

SUMMARY

The most basic level of communication is intrapersonal, involving the sending and receiving of messages within one individual. This is the level on which you communicate with yourself.

Intrapersonal communication is a function of the physical self, the emotional self, the intellectual self, habits, and private versus public situations. In addition, the need for a unified conceptual system and the picture that you have of yourself—your self-concept—also strongly influence these self-communications. Your past experiences, reference groups, and accustomed roles combine in ever-changing relationships to form this self-concept. At the same time, internal and external stimuli affect the cognitive, emotional and physiological processing of intrapersonal communication.

An individual's intrapersonal communication must be considered in any analysis of interpersonal communication situations. For example, personality variables such as manipulation, locus of control, dogmatism, tolerance for ambiguity, self-esteem and maturity—and personal orientations, values, attitudes and beliefs—all intrude on objective transmission and interpretation of interpersonal messages. Communication is further hampered by the many defense mechanisms that people use to minimize anxiety.

EXERCISES

GROUP EXPERIENCES

Who Are You?

DESCRIPTION: Understanding the many selves that exist inside you is not an easy task. In this activity you will repeatedly be asked the question, "Who are you?" At first the answers may come easily, but after several minutes you may be surprised at the increased difficulty you experience in answering the question. The purpose of this activity is to provide you with an opportunity to explore your perceptions of yourself.

PROCEDURE: Divide into dyads. For the first five minutes, Person A should ask Person B the question, "Who are you?" Person B should answer this question with very short and concise phrases, such as "I am a student." As soon as Person B supplies an answer, Person A should once again repeat the question, "Who are you?" After five minutes the roles should be reversed, and Person B should ask the question.

DISCUSSION: How did your answers illustrate (1) your perceptions of yourself and (2) others' perceptions of you? Do you have "multiple" concepts of yourself? What do your answers say about the degree to which your self-concept is negative or positive? Ask your partner what he or she perceives you to be, based on your answers to the question. How does the way you see yourself affect your communication with others?

Cocktail Party

DESCRIPTION: Feedback from other people often plays an important role in the way we feel about ourselves—it may cause us to reevaluate our perceptions of ourselves. This activity provides you with an opportunity to experience the extent to which positive and negative feedback affects your responses to others and your perceptions of yourself.

PROCEDURE: Each participant should receive a self-adhesive label to be worn on the forehead for this activity. Each label will have a short phrase written on it, such as:

Criticize Me	I'm Boring
I'm a Clown	Give Me Your Sexiest Look
Frown at Me	Smile at Me

When you are ready to begin the activity, all participants should have labels placed on their foreheads. *No one is permitted to tell you what your label says.* Participants should move around and talk to people as if they were at a cocktail party. The "cocktail party" should last from 10 to 15 minutes, depending on the size of the group. As you talk with other people, you must respond to their labels (follow the directions on their labels), without actually telling them what their labels say. For example, if players are wearing labels saying, "I'm boring," you must act as if everything they say is dull. You can do this by yawning, walking away, closing your eyes, or using your voice to show disinterest.

DISCUSSION: Before you remove your label, try to guess what it says, based on the verbal and nonverbal feedback you have received. Next, classify your label—was it very negative, negative, neutral, positive, or very positive?

Begin the discussion by asking all those people who were wearing negative or very negative labels to share their experiences. Did they have an emotional response to the feedback they received? For example, did they become withdrawn, introverted, or depressed during the cocktail party? Then ask those people who had positive labels if they were talkative, extroverted, smiling and gregarious. How would consistent positive or negative feedback from significant others (parent, friend) affect your emotions and ultimately your perception of yourself?

PERSONAL EXPERIENCES

1. We all seem to be affected, to varying degrees, by the type of feedback we receive from others. Observe the amount of positive, neutral and negative feedback you receive during a two-hour period. How do the different types of feedback affect you? How would you react to a large amount of negative feedback?

2. Spend some time alone and consider people or groups with which you identify. Remember that identification is more than just imitation. When you identify with another person or a particular group, you see yourself as an extension of that person or group. What are the problems with identifying with another person or group? Why have you formed identifications with particular people or groups? What do your identifications reflect about your self-concept?

3. Keep a diary for a week. At the end of each day, record the feelings you experienced during the day. For example, you might write that you felt angry for most of the morning, but by the end of the day you felt very calm. At the end of the week, reread your log to determine if (a) you have experienced highly intense feelings that may properly be called emotions and (b) if those feelings were predominantly positive or negative. How does your inner world of feelings affect your communication with others?

DISCUSSION QUESTIONS

1. To what extent can you achieve effective communication with another person without understanding his or her self-concept, attitudes, and beliefs?

2. What effect does a positive or negative self-concept have on your communication with others?

3. What characteristics distinguish achieved roles from ascribed ones?

4. How would you draw the Johari Window for (a) an intimate relationship, (b) a casual relationship, and (c) an initial interaction with another person? Remember that you can change the proportions of any square.

5. How do you use the various defense mechanisms in your daily activities?

6
Interpersonal Communication

KEY CONCEPTS AND TERMS

Interpersonal communication
Dyad
Functional theory
Linking function
Mentation function
Regulatory function
Relational theory
Control
One-up message
One-down message
Complementary relationship
Symmetrical relationship
Trust
Trustworthiness
Intimacy
Coordinated management of
  meaning theory
Constitutive rule
Regulative rule

Self-disclosure
Feedback
Feedforward
Attraction
Initiating
Experimenting
Intensifying
Integrating
Bonding
Differentiating
Circumscribing
Stagnating
Terminating
Alternating monologue
S=R interaction
Interaction with feedback
Interaction with empathy
Conflict management

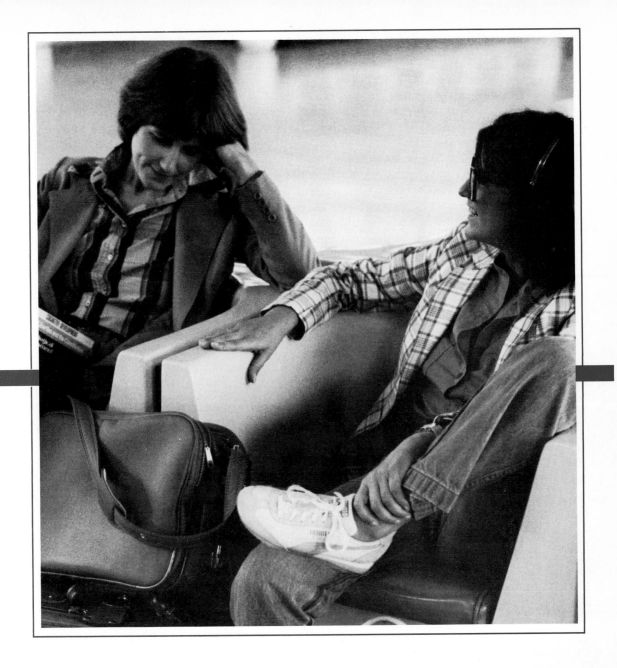

Margaret had just received a promotion to vice-president of research and development, a position for which she had worked for some 15 years. Not only had she been the woman behind one of the latest developments in aerospace technology but she had also brought to the company one of its largest accounts yet—worth $10 million the first year that the two companies would do business. To her excitement, she was instantly promoted to the "executive suite" and was given a raise of almost $40,000 per year. The only problem, however, was that it was 8:30 a.m. and she had just received the news that she had "edged out" her equally successful husband for the same position. Feeling delighted—yet ambivalent about the development—she didn't know quite what to do. Steve was not only her husband but also her lover—her best friend—and the president of the company had asked her to break the news to him.

Fortunately, the scenario you have just read is fictitious. However, it is based on a composite of events that friends and colleagues of mine have experienced. (You guessed it: The names were changed to protect the innocent.) Although most of us probably will never be placed in this position during our lifetimes, we all have had moments when we have felt alone and isolated. At these times, we feel the need to reach out to others and to share our feelings and ideas. This sharing of experiences—both positive and negative—is known as ***interpersonal communication.*** It is the extension of ourselves to other people and their extensions toward us.

In the previous chapter we examined *intra*personal communication and analyzed the messages that are sent and received within an individual. However, the term "communication" is most often identified with the transmission of information between or among individuals, or interpersonal communication.

AN INTERPERSONAL COMMUNICATION MODEL

Interpersonal communication can occur in any environment, be it formal (the lecture hall) or informal (the check-out line). Most interpersonal messages are informal, however, stemming from everyday, face-to-face encounters. Think of your own communication. From your first "Good morning" to your last "See you tomorrow," your interpersonal communication is usually spontaneous, unplanned, and loosely organized, probably even ungrammatical. With the exception of telephone conversations, most of this communication involves people close enough to see and touch each other. This makes sending and receiving messages much easier and eliminates the need for the kind of formal rules followed in debates, news conferences, or other public speaking situations.

DYADIC VERSUS SMALL GROUP COMMUNICATION

Much interpersonal communication involves a ***dyad,*** or two people in close contact. As a result, the potential for sending, receiving and evaluating messages is divided between the two halves of the dyad (see Figure 6–1). That is, both participants alternate from one role to the other—sometimes originating messages, at other times responding to them. Both roles provide a means for exchanging information, but neither is complete in itself; if one participant

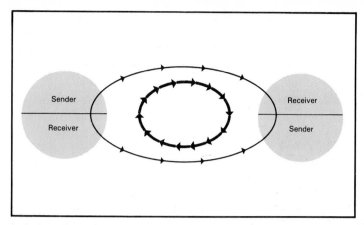

Figure 6–1 Dyadic Communication

only listened, and the other only spoke, communication would soon break down. Thus, communication in a dyad is very much a shared responsibility. This differentiates the dyad from the small group communication situations we will examine in the next chapter. In groups the balance of communication shifts. Because each participant has a different role and status in the group, the potential for receiving and transmitting messages is not evenly divided. Furthermore, group members serve not only as sources or destinations of messages, but they also function as channels to relay the messages of others.

What further differentiates interpersonal and group communication is purpose. Many groups are problem centered; that is, members are working together for a defined purpose, usually decision making or problem solving. In contrast, interpersonal communication in dyads focuses on the *sharing of meaning*. Although interpersonal dyads may also solve problems or make decisions, their messages convey a wider range of feelings and emotions. The information they exchange is not just the dry, factual material common, for example, in a sales meeting. Rather, it consists of meanings derived from personal experiences and observations. These interpersonal messages have a significant psychological impact: The process of translating thoughts into verbal and nonverbal messages increases the communicator's awareness of his or her feelings and self-concept. In turn, the listener's responses confirm or alter these feelings. With effective interpersonal communication, this process becomes reciprocal; both participants strengthen themselves and each other through the sharing of meanings and emotions.

To help you more clearly understand the process of interpersonal communication, this chapter will focus on various interpersonal communication theories, as well as on variables that affect interpersonal relationships. Additionally, we will examine the growth and decline of interpersonal relationships and discuss how we can more effectively manage interpersonal communication. By the time you have completed this chapter, we hope you will have taken the time to examine your own interpersonal behaviors. Such self-analysis is critical to the development and maintenance of healthy interpersonal relationships.

THEORIES OF INTERPERSONAL COMMUNICATION

Although the study of interpersonal communication may seem relatively straightforward when you first consider it, a perusal of the many different approaches to its study reveals the true complexity of the subject. For example, some communication theorists are interested in the functions of interpersonal communication, while others focus solely on dimensions of interpersonal relationships. Still other communication specialists are interested in how meanings are created and interpreted, while others address variables that affect interpersonal communication. In short, interpersonal communication may be viewed in a variety of ways—each of which can help us to better understand the overall communication process.

In order to introduce you to the study of interpersonal communication, the following sections will focus on three specific theories of interpersonal communication: functional theory, which addresses the functions of interpersonal communication; relational communication theory, which focuses on dimensions of interpersonal relationships; and the theory of the coordinated management of meaning. This final theory addresses meanings in interpersonal relationships and the rules through which we construct interpersonal communication.

Functions of Interpersonal Communication

According to the *functional theory of interpersonal communication*, we use interpersonal communication for a variety of reasons. For example, through interpersonal communication, we are better able to understand our world. Talking through a problem with a friend or business associate in order to better understand a situation is an illustration of this function. At other times, we communicate interpersonally in order to think and evaluate more effectively. For example, when Julie asks for input from her staff in order to help her make a more informed decision, she is illustrating another interpersonal function. We also communicate interpersonally in order to change behavior in some way, whether that behavior is our own or someone elses.

For communication specialists Frank Dance and Carl Larson, interpersonal communication saves precisely these three functions. More specifically, it (1) provides a *linking function* between a person and his or her environment; (2) allows us to conceptualize, remember and plan, each a part of the *mentation function*; and (3) serves to regulate our own and others' behavior, the *regulating function*.[1]

To illustrate the importance of these three functions, first imagine a world in which communication would not allow you to relate to the outside world, but instead would only let you communicate with yourself—intrapersonally. (Incidentally, you probably would be unable to communicate even

---

[1] F. E. X. Dance and C. E. Larson, *The Functions of Human Communication* (New York: Holt, Rinehart & Winston, 1976).

with yourself without interpersonal communication.) Then imagine a world in which you could not relate to other people. Not only would a world such as this be a very lonely place in which to live, but you also would probably be unable to survive for much longer than an hour. Through interpersonal communication, we are nurtured as infants—physically, emotionally and intellectually. In addition, we develop cultural, social and psychological ties with the world through interpersonal communication. In short, interpersonal interactions allow us to *function* more practically in life. The functional theory of interpersonal communication was developed for this reason.

Relational Communication Theory

Unlike the functional theory of interpersonal communication, which focuses solely on communication functions, **relational communication theory** addresses interpersonal communication by examining dimensions of interpersonal relationships.

According to communication theorists Edna Rogers-Millar and Frank Millar, three dimensions of interpersonal relationships are important: the control, trust, and intimacy dimensions of relationships. Created and sustained primarily through interpersonal messages, these three dimensions reflect and define the nature of the relationship.[2]

The first dimension, or the **control** dimension of interpersonal relationships, focuses on the distribution of power in a relationship, particularly the power to direct the nature of the interaction. This dimension is usually reflected in the number of messages we use to exert or relinquish relational control (for example, a message such as the following exerts control: "I'm really tired this evening, Jan. Let's stay home and watch a movie!"). In addition, "control" is reflected in our general tendency to accept or reject a source's statements of control. Look at the following conversation between Bob and Sandy:

Bob: (slamming door) Honey, I'm home. . . . Is anybody here?

Sandy: (coming through living room door) Hello, sweetheart. Yes, I'm home.

Bob: Good, I was hoping to find you here. We only have a couple of minutes before we have to go!

Sandy: Before we have to go where?

Bob: Let's talk while we're getting ready. The boss has invited us out to dinner at 7:00, and it's already 6:30. I can't believe he expected us to go on such short notice.

Sandy: That's O.K., honey. Dinner here can wait until tomorrow. I'll go and put it in the refrigerator before I change.

---

[2] F. E. Millar and L. E. Rogers, "A Relational Approach to Interpersonal Communication." In Gerald Miller (ed.), *Explorations in Interpersonal Communication* (Beverly Hills, Calif.: Sage, 1976), 87–103.

In the previous conversation, as you can see Bob used a set of messages that tended to exert control. Rather than asking Sandy how she felt about the change in the evening's plans, he took "control" of the situation and made the decision. (By the way, Rogers-Millar and Millar call such messages **one-up messages**.) Sandy, on the other hand, responded in a way that accepted Bob's control. As a result, she tended to use a greater number of messages that were **one-down** in nature. In other words, she used messages that relinquished control to Bob. The result of using such messages, particularly if they occur on a regular basis, is the creation of a **complementary relationship**, or a relationship in which one person is more dominant and the other less so. If Sandy had argued with Bob and had refused to accept Bob's control, the relationship would indeed be a very different one. Rogers-Millar and Millar would describe this type of relationship as **symmetrical** in nature. More specifically, the partners would mirror behavior more often.

The second dimension of interpersonal relationships is the **trust** dimension, which is, interestingly enough, defined quite uniquely when compared with other current definitions of trust. More specifically, trust is defined by Rogers-Millar and Millar as "the responsible acceptance of the control dimension." Although this definition may seem alien at first when we think about trusting others, trust indeed involves a belief that the other person will not exploit us. It is this aspect of trust on which Rogers-Millar and Millar base their definition of trust. For these researchers, *trusting* involves an admission of dependency on the part of the persons involved. In turn, **trustworthiness** is defined as the acceptance of an obligation not to exploit control. Both trusting and trustworthiness go hand in hand to create our feelings of trust.

The third dimension of interpersonal relationships, for Rogers-Millar and Millar, is the **intimacy** dimension, or the degree to which two can uniquely meet one another's needs. For example, if Hal meets all of Jennifer's needs and Jennifer doesn't feel the need for additional relationships, for Jennifer the relationship would be defined as an intimate one. However, if Hal is unable to meet all of Jennifer's interpersonal needs, the relationship for Jennifer would be described as lower in overall intimacy.

At this point, you may be asking yourself, "What does all of this have to do with interpersonal communication?" Although the answer may seem vague at first glance, Malcolm Parks has argued that the types of messages that we exchange in our interpersonal relationships can indeed predict both positive and negative interpersonal outcomes.[3] For example, Parks argues that the less often one-up messages are followed by one-up messages, the greater the satisfaction will be with the message exchange. However, the more often one-up messages are followed by one-down messages, the less often feelings of empathy will be exchanged. Additionally, mutual envy often results from complementary message exchanges. As you can see, relational communication theory has much to offer to communication students—it can make specific predictions about interpersonal outcomes.

---

[3] M. Parks, "Relational Communication: Theory and Research," *Human Communication Research* 3 (1977), 372–81.

The Coordinated Management of Meaning

Unlike the two theories of interpersonal communication we have already addressed, the ***coordinated management of meaning theory*** (CMM for short) is a meaning-centered theory of communication. In other words, its primary focus is on meanings in interpersonal communication, and on how we coordinate and manage meanings in everyday life.

Perhaps one of the most compelling arguments that CMM theorists make is that all communication is best viewed as coordination—primarily the coordination of rules for interacting with others.[4] For example, if you and I were to meet for the very first time, we both would bring to that initial meeting certain rules about interactions. To illustrate, my rules might include the following:

1. When meeting someone for the first time, I should smile and say, "hello."
2. When one meets another person, it is generally considered polite to shake his or her hand.
3. If I am interested in that person, I should maintain a fair amount of direct eye contact.

In turn, you also might bring these rules to our initial interaction. Once we move through the behaviors that are guided by these rules, however, what should we say to each other next? Should I inquire about your health? Your background? Whether you have read the latest edition of *Communication*? What meanings should I assign to your words and behavior—and should you assign to mine?

According to Pearce and Cronen, developers of CMM theory, two specific sets of rules should help to answer these questions-and will, we hope, allow us to coordinate the interaction. These rules have been labeled by Pearce and Cronen as *constitutive* and *regulative* rules. The first of these rules, ***constitutive rules***, define what a given act (or behavior) should "count as" and allow us to decide what each other's behaviors mean. In CMM notation, this type of rule would be written something like this:

$$
\begin{array}{|l}
\text{initial meeting} \\
\hline
\text{smile} \longrightarrow \text{sign of} \\
\qquad\qquad\ \text{friendliness}
\end{array}
$$

Or, "In the context of an initial meeting, a smile may be taken to count as a sign of friendliness." As you can see, the symbol ⌐————————⌐ simply designates the situation or context, while the arrow ————————→ is used to designate what the given behavior (in this instance, a smile) should "count as."

---

[4] W. B. Pearce and V. Cronen, *Communication, Action, and Meaning* (New York: Praeger, 1980).

Regulative rules, on the other hand, tell us how we should behave in a given situation. For example, the following regulative rule might apply during our initial interaction:

Or, "In the context of an initial interaction, if the other person smiles, then I should smile in return." At this point, the only unfamiliar symbol in this rule is the symbol ⊃, which says, "If you do *x*, then I should respond with *y*."

Although these examples are exceptionally simple, very complex acts may be described in a similar fashion. In addition, CMM theory allows us to see how these rules actually mesh—in other words, how we actually coordinate meanings. To illustrate this coordinated management of meaning, Figure 6–2 describes a potential sequence that might occur during our (same) initial meeting.

As you can see, if viewed in this way, communication may indeed be defined as coordination—the coordination of each of our individual rules and the meanings that we attribute to resulting behaviors. In short, for CMM theorists, effective communication is viewed as a function of two ingredients: (1) a mutually shared system of rules and (2) the coordinated management of meanings that results.

Figure 6–2

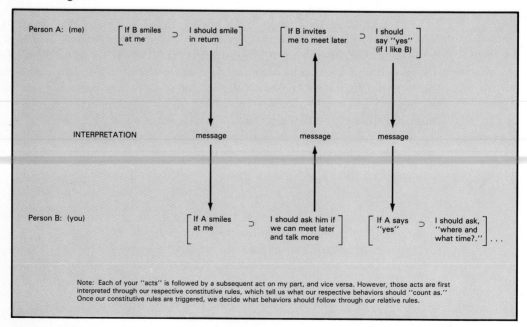

Note: Each of your "acts" is followed by a subsequent act on my part, and vice versa. However, those acts are first interpreted through our respective constitutive rules, which tell us what our respective behaviors should "count as." Once our constitutive rules are triggered, we decide what behaviors should follow through our relative rules.

Adapted from W. B. Pearce and V. Cronen, *Communication, Action, and Meaning* (New York: Praeger, 1980), p. 174.

VARIABLES AFFECTING INTERPERSONAL RELATIONSHIPS

In the previous section of this chapter, we identified three theories of interpersonal communication in order to show you how communication theorists currently conceptualize the interpersonal communication process. We hope that this discussion has helped to reveal the complexities associated with interpersonal communication. In order to help you to further understand interpersonal communication, this section will focus on variables that affect interpersonal relationships, including self-disclosure, trust, feedback, nonverbal behavior and interpersonal attraction. Our success or failure in addressing these variables in our own interpersonal communication determines how satisfying our interpersonal relationships will be.

> The uttered part of a man's life, let us always repeat, bears to the unuttered, unconscious part a small unknown proportion. He himself never knows it, much less do others.
>
> Thomas Carlyle

Self-Disclosure

Self-disclosure lies at the heart of the process of interpersonal communication. It is the vehicle by which others know what is going on inside you, what you are thinking and feeling and what you care about. In addition, self-disclosure is a primary source of satisfaction in long-term interpersonal relationships.[5]

Knowing these facts will not always make self-disclosure any easier, however. Our natural tendency is to hide feelings of incompetence, loneliness, guilt, anxiety over love and rejection, and conflicts over anger and resentment toward loved ones. According to VanLear and other researchers, these feelings are natural and are reflected in the very limited amount of private, personal disclosures that we make during early stages of a relationship. However, as the relationship progresses and greater trust is established, we usually begin to share information that is private and personal.[6] (There will be more later on relationship development.)

Even when feelings such as anxiety and guilt are not involved in a given relationship, self-disclosure may still be difficult because of well-learned habits that help us to avoid emotional pain. We all learn these evasive strategies as part of our socialization process. They are so rewarding that it becomes difficult to know when to put them away. Many people in our society are accustomed to hiding what they really want, think, or feel. For this reason,

---

[5] M. Argyle and A. Furnham, "Sources of Satisfaction and Conflict in Long-Term Relationships," *Journal of Marriage and the Family* 45 (August 1983), 481–93.

[6] C. A. VanLear, Jr., "The Formation of Social Relationships: A Longitudinal Study of Social Penetration," *Human Communication Research* 13, no. 3 (1987), 299–322.

Self-disclosure is vital to healthy interpersonal communication.

self-disclosure becomes a rare and valued gift. Confiding in others and receiving their confidences is, therefore, one of the most effective interpersonal communication tools.

Because of the importance of self-disclosure to the development of interpersonal relationships, communication researchers have explored the nature of self-disclosure and its relationship to other important interpersonal concepts. For example, psychologist Steven Broder explored the relationship between self-disclosure and liking with female roommates—focusing on these variables over a 13-week period.[7] Results of his study revealed that a relationship existed between self-disclosure and liking during the initial phases of acquaintanceship and friendship. Additionally, Waring and Chase found a positive relationship between self-disclosure and intimacy in married couples.[8] Although self-disclosure and intimacy were not viewed as synonymous, these researchers found self-disclosure to be a major determinant of intimacy for married couples.

As this research demonstrates, self-disclosure is a vital component of interpersonal communication. However, the work of these scholars should perhaps be qualified in at least two ways. First, as Caltabiano and Smithson have noted, self-disclosure should increase in scope and intimacy as a relationship develops, in order for self-disclosure to be seen as appropriate. Second, during the acquaintanceship stage, positive disclosure of information (in contrast to negative disclosure) is seen as more appropriate, with positive

[7] M. L. Caltabiano and M. Smithson, "Variables Affecting the Perception of Self-Disclosure Appropriateness," *Journal of Social Psychology* 120 (1983), 119–28.
[8] E. M. Waring and G. J. Chase, "Marital Intimacy and Self-Disclosure," *Journal of Clinical Psychology* 39, no. 2 (March 1983), 183–90.

disclosures viewed as more adjusted and emotionally stable than negative disclosures.[9] In short, during the initial stages of interpersonal relationships, it is best to avoid negative disclosure statements, particularly about oneself. Such disclosures reduce the chances that a relationship will be sought by the communication receiver.

Trust

As self-disclosure affects the nature of interpersonal relationships, so too does trust affect the quality of our interactions. For example, we all have experienced the satisfaction that results from learning that we can trust a new acquaintance. Likewise, we know the importance of being trustworthy in return, another important dimension of interpersonal trust. According to Rogers-Millar and Millar, both of these trust dimensions must be in operation before interpersonal trust can develop in a relationship. As we stated earlier, *trust* may be best defined as an interaction between trusting and trustworthy behaviors. More specifically, it involves (1) an *admission* of dependency by all parties involved, and (2) the *acceptance* of an obligation not to exploit control.

Although interpersonal trust indeed involves both of these dimensions, it is not a communication phenomenon (or state) that suddenly exists. Trust in another person develops over time. According to interpersonal communication experts Gamble and Gamble, interpersonal is accomplished in four major ways.

1. The individuals who are involved must be willing to disclose themselves to the person of interest—trust precipitates trusting behaviors in others.
2. One must be willing to let the other person know he or she is accepted and supported—reducing threats to another's ego increases trust.
3. A willingness must exist to develop a cooperative rather than a competitive orientation—working to win in a relationship can destroy it.
4. Finally, one should trust another individual when trusting behavior is appropriate—taking inappropriate risks can be as destructive as not taking a risk at all.[10]

In short, the "bottom line" regarding trust in relationships is threefold. First, trusting others generally encourages their trust in you. Second, you must be cooperative and supportive of the other person. Finally, trusting behavior may be appropriate or inappropriate, depending on the context

---

[9] M. L. Caltabiano and M. Smithson, "Variables Affecting the Perception of Self-Disclosure Appropriateness," *Journal of Social Psychology* 120 (1983), 119–28.

[10] Adapted from T. K. Gamble and M. Gamble, *Contacts: Communicating Interpersonally* (New York: Random House, 1982), 226–28.

or situation. Only you can decide when and how to trust another individual. We hope that this discussion will help as you make these critical decisions.

> The highest compact we can make with our fellow is—"Let there be truth between us two forevermore."
>
> Ralph Waldo Emerson

Feedback and Feedforward

So far, we have shown how different theories of interpersonal communication can contribute to our knowledge of the communication process. Additionally, we have argued that self-disclosure and trust are important variables that influence the effectiveness of interpersonal communication is the concept of feedback (and its related concept, feedforward).

Feedback, a term borrowed from computer technology, originally referred to a self-regulating mechanism that keeps machines running smoothly and efficiently. As we mentioned in Chapter 3, communication feedback keeps interpersonal relationships running smoothly. You provide this feedback by *paraphrasing* (thereby confirming or correcting your understanding of a message), by *asking questions* (thereby demonstrating your interest and your desire for more information), or by *responding with feeling statements* (thereby showing that you care about your partner). The following dialogue illustrates all three of these forms of feedback.

Andy: My trip to Paris last summer was the most interesting experience of my life.

Mark: You really enjoyed your stay in Paris. What did you like best?

Andy: Well, I lived in a dorm for foreign students and I got to meet people from all over the world.

Mark: I can appreciate your pleasure in meeting people from different backgrounds. Two years ago my family hosted an exchange student from Zambia and I really grew a lot from knowing him.

We often require feedback from others to shape our own behavior. This is especially true in social situations, in which we tend to monitor our own actions to conform to the behavior of the group. Social cues are the feedback for this self-monitoring behavior. At a party, for example, self-monitors would model their behavior on that of the other guests, talking quietly when others talk quietly, laughing at jokes that seem to amuse the other guests, drinking only as much or as little as others do. In contrast, nonconformists disregard this situational feedback. They are low self-monitors, following their own inclinations to start dancing while others are engaged in serious conversation, or limiting their own drinking while others do not.

Concern about social feedback also helps speakers to plan communication strategies. Suppose, for example, that you are nervous about asking a co-worker for a date. From casual conversations during coffee breaks, you know that she likes sports, and you hope she'll agree to meet you at next Saturday night's hockey game. On the other hand, you worry that she might consider Saturday night a "heavy" dating night, inappropriate for a first date. Your reasoning process in anticipating feedback is known as **feedforward.** Feedforward in this situation permits you to set up two possible plans: the evening hockey game and an afternoon gymnastics exhibit. If, when you call your friend, she expresses hesitancy about going to the Saturday game, you can then switch to your contingency plan.

Nonverbal Behavior

Nonverbal behavior plays a strong, necessary role in interpersonal relationships. So much can be "said" by a smile, hug, or handclasp that words are often not needed.

As we mentioned in Chapter 4, eye behavior is especially important in interpersonal situations. Studies have shown, for example, that eye contact between close couples is much greater than that between casually dating couples. Besides showing interest and caring, eye contact can also express hostility or the desire for dominance. Indeed, competing athletes use staring as an aggressive gesture and an indication of their confidence level. In contrast, the avoided glance often signifies submission.

Touching is another nonverbal factor important in interpersonal relationships. Touching usually communicates intimacy: couples walk down the street with their arms around each other; a father caresses his baby; a child hugs her dog. Touching can also communicate status and power. Ask yourself, for instance, who would be more likely to use a patronizing pat on the head or an aggressive poke in the chest: a professor or a student; the policeman or the accused; the physician or the patient; the boss or the employee. Status differences related to sex are also revealed in touching behavior. Who is usually the first to hold the other's hand or to demonstrate physical affection in a male–female relationship? Women have come a long way, but it is still rare for one to make the first move by putting an arm around her date in a dark movie theater.

Interpersonal Attraction

Self-disclosure, trust, appropriate feedback and nonverbal behavior all work together to increase your interpersonal effectiveness. Interestingly enough, this increased effectiveness somehow improves your interpersonal attraction, the "good vibrations," "magnetism," or "invisible force" that somehow draws people together.

What we mean by **attraction** is a positive attitude, movement toward, or liking between two people. What causes this attraction is rarely "love at first sight." Rather, the cause can be found in the complex mix of variables within ourselves and within the other individual. Research indicates that many of the factors that determine attraction relate to interpersonal communication. For example, Blass and Schwarz were interested in the relative

Physical proximity positively affects interpersonal attraction.

importance of four major determinants of attraction: attitude similarity, personality or need similarity, physical proximity or closeness to the other individual and frequency of exposure. To test the relative importance of each variable, the researchers asked students from both Austria and the United States to indicate the degree of importance of each of the factors in the formation of their friendships with same-sexed friends. Results of their study revealed that attitude similarity, personality (need) similarity, and frequency of interactions were more important than physical proximity to the other person. The only difference between the two cultures was that American students evaluated each of the dimensions higher than did the Austrian students.[11]

Although Blass and Schwarz found that physical closeness scored lower in importance than the other three variables in their study, friendships can arise as a function of propinquity or geographical closeness. For example, Leah started taking yoga lessons at the YMCA. In the class she met a couple of people who shared many of her other interests, such as Eastern religion, natural foods and meditation. The three students became close friends and continued to see each other after the lessons were over. Sharing a common territory, in this case the YMCA classroom, brought these students together. As Blass and Schwarz have noted, however, it was probably their similar attitudes and interests that sustained the relationships following their initial interactions.

---

[11] T. Blass and P. D. Schwarz, "The Relative Importance of Four Determinants of Attraction," *Journal of Social Psychology* 117 (1982), 145–46.

DEVELOPMENT OF DYADIC RELATIONSHIPS

We have thus far examined skills that are important in interpersonal relationships, but you may be wondering where these relationships begin. Recent popular literature suggests that individual personalities evolve through a developmental process. Just as personality types evolve through life experiences, acquired knowledge, and environmental factors, so too relationships evolved in similar ways through time. It may take years to cultivate a friendship made in grade school, or only a few seconds with "lovers at first sight."

Phases of Relationship Development

Think for a moment about the types of relationships you are a part of in your family, school, job and community. Each relationship has unique qualities that set it apart from others, even though the characteristics may be positive or negative. If we look back to the beginning of each of our relationships, we see that there are a variety of reasons for the involvement. Maybe at one time you needed special care (mother), information (teacher), service (postal carrier), or lover (girlfriend or boyfriend). According to Mark Knapp, relationships follow characteristic patterns of development (coming together) and disintegration (coming apart). His five phases of relationship development are: initiating, experimenting, intensifying, integrating, and bonding.[12]

INITIATING.   During the first stage of relationship development, we make conscious and unconscious judgments about others. Although we are cautious at this stage, we have usually sized up the other person within 15 seconds. David entered a singles' bar and scanned the room for prospective dancing partners. He stereotyped and classified available women according to personal preferences. After narrowing the field to two women, David determined his approach strategies. Finally, he began a conversation by asking, "Would you like a drink?" "Are you waiting for someone?" "You look like you need company," or "It was nice of you to save me this seat." Sometimes we initiate communication nonverbally. In the same situation the girl at the bar could easily signal for David to leave by looking away, turning her back to him, or moving to another stool.

EXPERIMENTING.   After making initial contact, we begin experimenting with the unknown. This stage is known as the "do you know" period of interaction. Most relationships do not develop beyond this superficial point. We all can remember situations in which we used small talk to establish a friendly atmosphere. For example, after being introduced to her blind date,

---

[12] M. L. Knapp, *Interpersonal Communication and Human Relationships* (Boston: Allyn & Bacon, 1984).

Renee attempts to find common interests by asking about Tom s major, family, favorite bars, job, and so on. Renee may not even be interested, but she asks questions to make the situation more comfortable. If initial interaction goes well, each person probes to determine whether pursuing the relationship is worthwhile.

INTENSIFYING.   As relationships develop into friendships, participation and awareness are intensified. Gradually, steps are taken to strengthen the bond by asking for and reciprocating favors. Through self-disclosure and trust, the two personalities begin to blend. Statements such as "I've never told anyone this . . ." or "There is something you need to know: I was arrested when I was eighteen . . ." become more common. The verbal relationship usually changes, with the couple using nicknames, pet names and slang. More time is spent sharing expectations, assumptions and experiences. Nonverbal behaviors begin to communicate just as effectively as verbal ones. As a relationship intensifies, you notice mutual winks, nods, touches, and so on.

INTEGRATING.   At this point in relationship development, we agree to meet the expectations of the other person. Two people begin to share many commonalities, such as interests, attitudes, friends and property. At this stage the people do not completely lose their identity; however, there is a need to please the other person by giving in to his or her way of life. Not only do the individuals treat each other differently, but the two are now seen as a unit. In a dating relationship, Jim and Candy would tend to dress for each other. Jim is interested in racquetball, so Candy joins a beginning racquetball class. Candy collects antiques, and to help, Jim subscribes to the magazine *Treasures in Your Attic*. When friends have parties, Jim and Candy are invited together rather than individually.

BONDING.   In the final stage of relationship development, serious commitments and sacrifices are made. In today's society "commitment" involves marriage or a verbal commitment to live together. Sacrifices usually include the provision of assistance to a person who is experiencing some personal problem, and the giving of gifts or favors that require a substantial expenditure of time, energy, and/or money.[13] The bonding of any relationship can become a powerful force in making the relationship better or worse. Marriage is the most accepted form of commitment and usually gains social and institutional support. However, the couple also usually has to agree to the rules and regulations of the contract. In many relationships, lasting commitment is seen as possible only in marriage. For this reason, many couples end up either splitting or getting married after years of dating. Trial bonding is also used at this stage. After living together secretly for two years, Bill and Amy decided to make their commitment legal by getting married.

---

[13] L. A. Baxter and C. Bullis, "Turning Points in Developing Romantic Relationships," *Human Communication Research* 12, no. 4 (1986), 469–93.

Phases of Relationship Disintegration

As children, we are led to believe that relationships last forever, but they don't. As Wheeless, Wheeless, and Baus have argued, "the end state of all 'earthly' interpersonal relationships must be, by necessity, termination." This ending state may be in the form of physical death or may involve the "passing away" or "sudden death" of the relationship on the social/psychological level.[14]

As we all have experienced at one time or another, even our closest friends may go their separate ways over trivial matters, and many job changes are the result of negative interpersonal relationships rather than job dissatisfaction. Just as with relationship development, relationship disintegration may take years—or it can take a few seconds. After their children were married, David and Betty found that they had nothing left in common after 36 years of marriage. Tom and Sam, identical twin brothers, never spoke to each other again after Tom saw Sam with his girlfriend, Lynne.

Thus far we have examined five patterns of relationship development. We will now look at patterns of disintegration. The five phases of relational disintegration are: differentiating, circumscribing, stagnating, avoiding, and terminating.

DIFFERENTIATING.   Integration in a relationship signifies a union, and differentiating signifies a separation, or split. Differences occur at every stage of relationship development, but with differentiating there is increased interpersonal distance. At this stage, differences become more and more apparent. The partners usually begin to want freedom and individuality. Both parties begin to play games that test the relationship and the other person's involvement. After Bob and Kathy had been dating for seven years, friends and relatives expected them to get married. During the last few years, however, the couple began experiencing different life-styles, and they began to want different things out of life. At one time each knew what the other person wanted, but now they weren't so sure.

CIRCUMSCRIBING.   When relationships begin to disintegrate, there is less total communication. Topics of conversation are controlled to reduce conflict and tension. On the surface everything appears to be all right, but underlying difficulties are evident. The presence of others increases interaction, and socially the relationship seems unaltered. Sally wondered, after having so much fun at her friend's party, why she and Chip sat in silence all the way home. At this stage of disintegration, there also tends to be less expression of commitment verbally and nonverbally. Affection is given only occasionally, and loving remarks are almost nonexistent.

STAGNATING.   During the stagnating stage, all efforts to communicate are abandoned. The interpersonal atmosphere is cold. Nonverbal messages are

[14] L. R. Wheeless, V. E. Wheeless, and R. Baus, "Sexual Communication, Communication Satisfaction, and Solidarity in the Developmental Stages of Intimate Relationships," *Western Journal of Speech Communication* 48 (Summer 1984), 217–30.

In interpersonal communication, participants strengthen themselves and each other through the sharing of meanings and emotions.

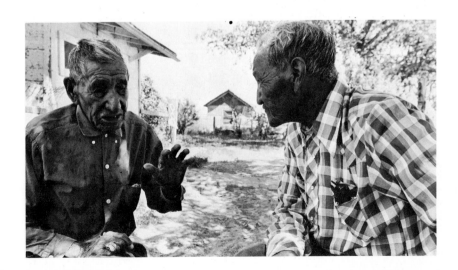

often the only feeling states expressed. As Jane got home from her dance recital, she was met with a cold stare from her husband. We wonder why individuals would continue a relationship that is so unrewarding. Many people stay in relationships because they want to punish the other person, they hope for reconciliation, or they want to avoid the pain of ending the relationship. Sandy was afraid she could not pay the rent on her own, so she continued to live with Angela, even though it was like having two room-mates because Angela was living with Ron.

AVOIDING.   At this stage, one or both parties act as though the other person doesn't exist. Each person tries to find ways to avoid interaction. Meetings are often arranged so that there is someone else around, or excuses are made for not being able to be with the other person alone. Toward the end of this stage, there is seeking for a permanent state of separation. Linda called John on the phone because they hadn't communicated in two weeks. She said, "John, we need to talk this thing through. Can we get together this weekend? How about Monday? Do you have a test on Tuesday? Okay, then you tell me the next time that you are free and I'll change my plans."

TERMINATING.   The termination of a relationship can be immediate or delayed. A friend may die of a heart attack, a marriage may dissolve because of an affair, or your company may transfer you to another city. Termination is dependent upon the type of relationship, perceived status of the relation-ship, effects of dissociation and timing. As with relationship development, the final stage of relationship disintegration can occur with heated words over a poker game, or slowly and unobtrusively by failing to make plans to get together. Methods of termination are usually dependent upon future goals and expectations.

The stages of relationship development and disintegration can occur in order, as we have just presented them, or they can start at any phase of development. In a crowded bar, a fight might end a relationship that was a minute old. If a person breaks into a movie theater ticket line, you quickly make a judgment and decide that this is a person to avoid.

MANAGING INTERPERSONAL RELATIONSHIPS

Our discussion thus far has emphasized the processes involved in interper-sonal communication. In this section, we turn our attention to the people involved and how we may best "manage" interpersonal relationships.

Types of Relationships

Just as individuals are emotionally healthy and productive, or sick and inef-fective, so too are interpersonal relationships. Manipulative involvements are a prime example. In such relationships, one or both members try to satisfy psychological needs by smothering the individuality or potential of the other. In manipulative relationships based on dependency, for example, one or both partners may be so "addicted" to the other that he or she drops all outside interests, activities and friends. Just as the single-minded pursuit of a drug addict destroys his or her life, so can the dependency relationship destroy self-identity, self-respect and all chances for growth and development. Many marriages suffer from these manipulative tendencies. Conversely, other marriages fail for the opposite reason: lack of involvement. When no effort is made to maintain a marriage, the relationship becomes boring and stale. Such marriages stifle personal growth and self-realization.

The ideal marriage, or any interpersonal relationship, is based on growth facilitation. The individuals involved are united but do not lose their identities. Through their shared communication, they achieve growth that they would not have reached on their own. In short, the whole exceeds the sum of its parts. The couple becomes not two separate individuals but a pair—more sensitive, loving, and stable than they had been before.

Levels of Social Interaction

Depending on the type of interpersonal relationship, different forms of communication or social interaction will take place.

ALTERNATING MONOLOGUE.   The least productive and least fulfilling kind of communication, often seen in manipulative relationships, is the *alternating monologue*. Each individual knows the other is speaking but does not listen openly to what is being said. Each person is so preoccupied with his or her own concerns that there is no sharing or understanding of ideas. The end of one statement merely signals the beginning of an unrelated reply:

Bob: You wouldn't believe what I had to do at work today.

Grace: Oh, yes. Tonight I have to go over to school and take that exam.

Bob: I almost quit, I was so angry at the boss.

Grace: I cannot believe how hard I've studied for this test.

Bob: Maybe I'll quit—get away from it all and have some fun.

Grace: Hey, now you're talking. Have some fun. That's what I'll do tonight after the exam.

STIMULUS-RESPONSE INTERACTION.   Stimulus-response communications are no better. In these interactions, the speaker proceeds in a set manner, independent of any responses the listener may make. The librarian who requests information to issue a card or the salesman who wants to know what size hiking boots you wear is participating in this type of interaction. They already know what questions to ask, and the responses do not change them.

INTERACTION WITH FEEDBACK.   Alternating monologues and stimulus-response interaction are alike in their neglect of feedback. Interactions *with* feedback are more common and more productive. For example, a political canvasser bases his comments on the responses he gets from the voter.

Canvasser: Excuse me, are you going to vote for Raymond Charles?

Voter: That socialist? No way would he have my vote!

Canvasser: Perhaps you received some wrong information about our candidate. Let me tell you a little about him.

Canvasser: Excuse me, are you going to vote for Raymond Charles?

Voter: I don't know. But I do know I don't want to be pestered.

Canvasser: Excuse me. I'll just leave this information with you, so you can read it at your leisure.

Even in these feedback situations, responses may be based as much on habit or learning as on interpersonal factors. Because the canvasser has had many similar experiences in the past, his answers may be automatic, requiring no feedforward or feedback.

INTERACTION WITH EMPATHY.   The most productive form of communication is interaction with empathy. Empathy means deep understanding of other people, identifying with their thoughts, feeling their pain, sharing their joy. Such empathy is typical of strong, healthy relationships. Indeed, empathetic communicators know each other so well that they can predict the responses to their messages. For example, Mario says to himself, "I know if I tell May that I'm not crazy about her new dress, she'll be hurt. So instead I'll say, 'May, that dress looks great on you, but I think the green one is even more becoming.' " This illustrates the special feedforward that empathy can produce.

Managing Interpersonal Conflict

People who care about each other will get angry, but their intimacy should ensure healthy, productive conflict and the use of words, not to hurt, but

Empathy means sharing others' joy and pain.

Successful conflict management aims at facts—not egos.

to find out what is bothering each person. Then, bottled-up tensions can be released.

There is a big difference between this type of arguing and the destructive variety. Whereas healthy conflict stresses the facts, destructive conflict aims for the ego, with statements such as "You're ridiculous," and "Me? You should see yourself." The goal of an argument should be conflict resolution, not character defamation. Better to say, "I hate what you said," than "I hate you because you said it."

Gamble and Gamble, two interpersonal communication experts, propose some other principles for managing interpersonal conflicts effectively and efficiently.

1. *Recognize that conflicts can be settled rationally.* A conflict has a better chance of being resolved if you do not pretend it doesn't exist, withdraw from discussing it, surrender to the other person, try to create distractions, find fault or lay blame, or attempt to force the other person to take your view.

2. *Define the conflict.* Ask yourself: Why are we in conflict? What is the nature of the conflict? Which of us feels more strongly about the issue? Then try to figure out a way that all can "win."

3. *Check your perceptions.* Perceptual distortions of the other person's behavior, position, or motivations can take place. At this time, attempt to determine whether you understand one another.

4. *Suggest possible solutions.* The goal at this stage is to put your heads together and come up with a variety of solutions. However, neither you nor the other person(s) should evaluate or condemn the suggested solutions at this time.

5. *Assess the alternative solutions and choose the best one.* Determine which solutions will let one party "win" at the other's expense, which solutions would allow both parties to lose, and which solutions let both parties win. Then choose the one which allows both people to win.

6. *Try out the solution and evaluate it.* Determine to what extent the selected solution is working or not working. Then make appropriate alternations in the plan.[15]

As you can see, interpersonal conflict can be managed successfully. However, doing so means taking the time and expending the necessary energy to talk through the conflict. We hope that the steps that Gamble and Gamble have listed will help you to be a more effective communicator. In addition, we hope that this chapter has provided you with the necessary "ammunition" to more effectively communicate in your interpersonal relationships.

SUMMARY

Interpersonal communication is the sharing of feelings and ideas with other people. Most interpersonal messages are informal exchanges in dyads—that is, between two people in close contact. The potential for sending, receiving, and evaluating messages is shared between the members of the dyad. The purpose of their communication usually focuses on the sharing of meaning, as well.

Three specific theories of interpersonal communication can help us to better understand the complexities of interpersonal communication. Dance and Larson's functional theory addresses the functions of interpersonal communication, while relational communication theory focuses on three specific dimensions of interpersonal relationships. These dimensions are control, trust, and intimacy. Finally, the coordinated management of meaning theory focuses on meanings in interpersonal communication, as well as on the concept of coordination.

Skills related to self-disclosure, trust, feedback and feedforward, nonverbal communication, and interpersonal attraction combine to determine how suc-

---

[15] From T. K. Gamble and M. Gamble, *Contacts: Communicating Interpersonally* (New York: Random House, 1982), 322–28.

cessfully meaning will be conveyed in such dyadic communications.

Another important topic in the study of interpersonal communication concerns the phases of relationship development. Of the ten stages, initiating, experimenting, intensifying, integrating, and bonding represent the growth in relationships. The five phases of relationship disintegration are differentiating, circumscribing, stagnating, avoiding, and terminating.

Managing interpersonal relationships involves a number of factors. For example, the people involved often bring personality and environmental factors into the interpersonal setting; they, too, influence the success or failure of the communicating process. For example, individuals with manipulative needs often destroy opportunities for communication that might aid personal growth and development of their friends and associates. Similarly, certain types of messages also limit effective social interaction. For instance, both alternating monologues, in which the speakers seem not to hear each other, and stimulus-response interactions, in which the speakers' set messages are unaffected by their listeners' replies, hinder effective communication. In contrast, interactions characterized by feedback and empathy build strong, healthy relationships.

Finally, managing relationships necessarily involves the management of conflict. Six principles that can help with this often-difficult aspect of relationship management are the following: (1) Recognize that conflicts can be settled rationally; (2) Define the conflict; (3) Check your perceptions; (4) Suggest possible solutions; (5) Assess alternative solutions and choose the best one; and (6) Try out the solution and evaluate it.

EXERCISES

GROUP EXPERIENCES

Positive–Negative

DESCRIPTION: One aspect of interpersonal attraction is the extent to which another person shares your attitudes and beliefs. Simply stated, we are more attracted to people who share our attitudes than to those who do not. Consider some of the relationships you have had with others. Those relationships that you remember as positive probably were ones in which your ideas were readily and willingly accepted or at least supported. When you have a falling out with another person you may both have reevaluated each other and may consider the attitudes of the other person to be strange. Because nobody wants to be considered strange, you leave the situation. The purpose of this activity is to magnify the emotional feelings a person has when their ideas are positively and negatively reinforced.

PROCEDURE: Divide into groups of four to six persons. Choose one person as the subject. Select a controversial topic of discussion or a topic that requires planning (such as planning a picnic). During your discussion, accept and support all ideas suggested by the subject. Listen carefully to everything he or she has to say. After five minutes select another subject. Then for the next five minutes, reject all comments presented by the second subject. Avoid listening to what is said by this subject. Let the subject know that you consider his or her beliefs to be strange, wrong, and worthless. The final part of this activity is a report from the subjects about the emotional states they experienced during the activity. The subjects should indicate how much they liked other group members, along with their reasons for liking or disliking them.

DISCUSSION: Most people surround themselves with people who agree with and reinforce their ideas. Let's face it—people who like us can't be all bad! The two subjects most likely had very different feelings about the group. It's hard to create in an exercise the actual emotional condition that you would feel in a real-life situation, because in the back of everyone's head is a little voice saying, "It's just an activity." But the next time you are in a group that evaluates you either positively or negatively, watch your emotional state. Do you tend to like people who like you?

Mr. and Ms. Wonderful

DESCRIPTION: Everyone has varying opinions as to what they regard as attractive. During different periods of time, being pleasantly plump was "in" and looking like Twiggy was definitely "out." In fact, history records periods of time when women were sent to "fattening schools" to prepare for marriage. Today everyone runs to the health farms to lose those extra 10 to 15 pounds. Even within a given period and culture, people simply have different ideas about beauty. This activity will provide you with the opportunity to identify what characteristics of attraction you want in your Mr. or Ms. Wonderful.

PROCEDURE: Now is your chance to become an author and to write a heartrending description of an attractive person at a cocktail party. The scene is set. You, the author, are watching this person from afar. Your attraction is immense, and you watch his or her every move. Write a paragraph describing those physical characteristics that are so magnetic to you. Be adventurous, and use the following lines as an example:

> I couldn't keep my eyes off his amber-colored hair as it fell feathered from his face. His deep brown eyes were penetrating, and I imagined that they were looking directly at me. I liked the way he moved—with assurance and yet lightness.

The above paragraph is just a beginning. Be creative and write about the physical characteristics you would find attractive in another person. Share your descriptions of Mr. or Ms. Wonderful with others in the class. Read them out loud with the same emotion you used in writing the paragraph.

DISCUSSION: You probably found some of the paragraphs funny— maybe even ridiculous; the question is, "Would you have been attracted to the same characteristics others wrote about?" Discuss the sayings, "Beauty is in the eye of the beholder," and "Love is blind." Are they true? Do you ever see couples that you think are physically mismatched? The final question: "What do you really want in a Mr. or Ms. Wonderful?"

PERSONAL EXPERIENCES

1. Make a list of three people that you like and three people that you dislike. Consider each person separately and determine how they respond to you. Are they enthusiastic about your ideas? Do they share similar attitudes and beliefs with you? After you have answered these questions, reflect on this one. Do you tend to like people who positively reinforce you, and dislike those who negatively reinforce you?

2 Using Knapp's ten phases of relational growth, chart the growth and decline of some relationship that you were a part of in the past. Then compare it with a chart of some relationship in which you are currently involved. How are the two relationships alike? How are they different? What factors affected the former relationship? How can you avoid those events in your current relationship? Does "knowing" the phases of growth and decline help in any way? If so, how?

3. Make a list of communication strategies that you can use to make your interpersonal communication more effective. Which suggestions do you find easy or difficult to practice? How can you be more aware of the communication strategies that you use each day? How can you learn to practice effective strategies more consistently? How can you learn to avoid detrimental communication strategies?

DISCUSSION QUESTIONS

1. What role do quarrels or arguments play in an interpersonal relationship?

2. How can theories of interpersonal communication help you in your day-to-day activities?

3. Explain how phases of development and disintegration evolve in interpersonal relationships.

4. What methods can be used to manage interpersonal conflict?

7
Small Group Communication

KEY CONCEPTS AND TERMS

Group	Maintenance role
Small group	Self-serving role
Primary group	Leadership
Discussion group	Leader
Private discussion group	Democratic leader
Open discussion	Authoritarian leader
Panel	Laissez-faire leader
Symposium	Cohesion
Forum	Intergroup conflict
Problem-solving group	Intragroup conflict
Fact-finding group	Conformity
Evaluation group	Circle network
Policy-making group	Wheel network
Quality circle	Y network
Bypassing	Chain network
Functional role	All-channel network
Task-oriented role	

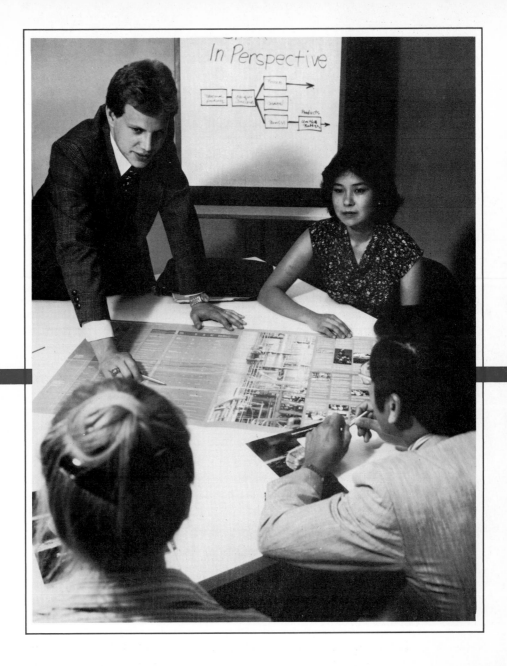

Jeanne, Bob, Trent, and Don were well into their third planning session when they heard the exasperating news. Trent, who had been appointed to brief the vice-president about the group's work, had not even mentioned to her that the group had been meeting. He also had neglected to tell Paul, their immediate supervisor, about the sessions, something each of them had agreed must be done before their initial meeting. After Trent had volunteered to talk to Paul about the group's plans, and the date for the initial meeting had been set, the group assumed that Trent had secured Paul's approval. Just as Trent blurted out the news, Paul knocked and entered the conference room. The group knew that the "look" on Paul's face could only spell *t-r-o-u-b-l-e*.

Problem-solving groups, such as the one described above, are common in American businesses and corporations. They may meet to discuss such issues as marketing strategies, team product/service development, or how to crack the international marketplace. However, as you have seen in the illustration above, each member of the group must pull his or her own weight if the group is to function effectively. Additionally, the group must be able to depend on each member regarding the roles that—either directly or tacitly—each member has agreed to play.

In the following pages you will learn a number of communication principles that will aid you during small group interactions. Following a brief overview, we will discuss some distinctions between small and large groups and the outcomes that will generally accrue from each. We also will address several types of small groups and the purposes and functions of each. Once we have made these distinctions, we will provide you with basic ammunition that will help you participate more effectively in group interactions. We also will provide you with the tools to become a more effective small-group leader and to optimize your contributions to the problem-solving process. From there, we will examine several factors that affect group outcomes and performance, such as personality, cohesion, and conflict. We will conclude by instructing you in the art of analyzing group interaction.

SMALL GROUP COMMUNICATION: AN OVERVIEW

Think for a moment about all the different groups to which you belong: whether they be social, political, family, academic, religious, vocational, or special interest groups. It is virtually impossible to exist independently of all groups. It has been estimated that the average person is a member of five or six groups at any one time and that the total number of small groups may be around 4 billion or 5 billion.

The existence of groups is a basic part of the democratic process. In a society such as ours, the group process plays a significant role in proposing and reviewing the laws that govern our land. The government does much of its work through various committees and subcommittees, which study and propose legislation. In addition, civic groups meet regularly to comment on the actions of government and ensure that the voice of the people will be heard. These groups protect the rights of the individual citizen.

The democratic aspect of the group goes beyond politics, however. The family that jointly decides where to go for winter vacation, the union members who meet to discuss contract demands, the student-faculty committee that determines college requirements and the consumer group that organizes a protest against dangerous toys are all participating in the democratic process on some level.

There are many different types of groups to which you can belong, and there are also many benefits to be gained from participation in groups, as well as from observation of group behavior. Participation in certain groups can lead to increased personal rewards, which include change and growth in personality, self-concept, and behavior. Well-known groups such as Weight Watchers, Alcoholics Anonymous, and Smoke Enders are self-help groups that enable people to overcome undesirable habits. As a result of interpersonal interactions, group members derive strength and support from others who are working toward the same goals. Different groups develop as different needs are expressed. Some groups, as in group therapy, can contribute to the emotional well-being of the participants. Others may serve social as well as psychological needs.

Participation in groups can also result in professional rewards. A person's ability is often measured by how effectively he or she functions in a small group. A student who participates in student government may be asked to head a campus committee; the parent who functions effectively in a parent-teacher group may be encouraged to run for the school board; or the president of a local chapter of a charity organization may move up to head a regional division.

On a very practical level, the study of the group process can help you function more effectively in the different groups to which you belong. For example, if you are aware of the various factors that can be barriers to decision making, you may be able to help your club, committee, or organization overcome them. As we said earlier, in this chapter we will discuss the group process and give explanations and guidelines to help you participate more fully and effectively in small group communication.

> I know of no safe depository of the ultimate powers of society but the people themselves.
>
> Thomas Jefferson

DEFINITIONS

The Group

Before discussing the group process, we must decide what we mean by the term *group*. A **group** is any number of people who have a common goal, interact with one another to accomplish their goal, recognize one another's existence, and see themselves as part of a group. To test our definition, let's consider an example—people in line outside a movie theater. Is this a group? Certainly these people have a common goal, for they are all waiting to see a particular film. But these people need not interact with one another to accomplish this goal, although each may be very aware of the presence of the others in line. Now, if someone were to try to sneak in at the front of the line and the people made a unified effort to keep the crasher out, we could say that during that period of time the random collection of people became a group. Looking at our definition, the unified effort to block the line crasher would call for group interaction and awareness of others.

The Small Group

Our main concern in this chapter is the small group. A ***small group*** is three or more people interacting face to face, with or without an assigned leader, in such a way that each person influences, and is influenced by, every other person in the group.

The small group may vary in size, but it is generally agreed that the best size in terms of total interaction and greatest efficiency is somewhere between five and seven members.

Certain generalizations can be made about small and large groups. For instance, small groups tend to be more informal and less structured, while larger groups may have to adopt formal rules to keep order. A small group can function effectively without a designated leader, but a large group may need such a person to maintain order and make sure the group peforms efficiently. Theoretically, an increase in size increases the group's resource pool, since more people means more information, ideas, and opinions. However, it has been found that the larger the group, the less chance there is for individual participation and the greater the tendency for several dominant or aggressive individuals to monopolize the discussion. This type of behavior causes the shy or less verbal person to withdraw from the interaction and feel a sense of frustration. After the group has functioned for some time, a number of cliques tend to develop, which often hinders the group effort. Therefore, as the group becomes larger, there is greater difficulty in accomplishing a particular task.

SOME SMALL GROUPS AND THEIR FUNCTIONS

The two major types of small groups are primary groups and discussion groups.

The Primary Group

The ***primary group,*** or ***psyche group,*** functions as a support system for its members. Neighbors who get together daily, friends with whom you go to the movies once or twice a month, and the coffee klatch at work are all groups that usually enjoy conversation as opposed to discussion. Conversation is much more loosely structured than discussion and covers a variety of topics without a particular objective in mind. It is neither unusual nor particularly harmful for one member of a primary group to occasionally dominate the conversation. In a discussion group, in which members have a common objective, however, it is essential that they maintain a balance between speaking and listening activity. Such "rules" are alien to the primary group, which is generally social and tends to be quite informal.

The Discussion Group

In addition to the formality of discussion groups as opposed to primary groups, there are certain other characteristics that make discussion groups unique. The *discussion group* is characterized by

1. *Face-to-face interaction.* A discussion cannot take place if group members do not respond, react and adapt to the communication of other participants. The interaction must be continuous and flow from within the group. If the people merely state preconceived ideas in isolation, apart from the interaction, fruitful discussion cannot take place.
2. *Leadership.* Generally, a discussion group is characterized by the presence of one or more leaders. Although many small-group experts insist that a designated leader must be present for a group to function effectively, our definition acknowledges the presence of leadership potential, or those instances in which one or more people assume leadership duties.
3. *Shared characteristics.* Discussion groups are distinguished from a "small aggregate" of people by the presence of a common characteristic. This common characteristic may range from similar religious beliefs to similar ethnic background, race, geographic location, social class, economic level, life-style, educational level, etc. A common characteristic may be assigned, assumed, or self-identified; however, as a rule, it does exist.
4. *Common purpose.* Ultimately, a common purpose or goal is the binding force of a discussion group, whether that goal is specific or broad in scope. Groups that are formed with no concrete goal in mind generally disband or disintegrate. Goal-directed behavior holds groups together. The more relevant the goal is, the more motivation that group members will have to maintain the group and their identification with it.[1]

Discussion groups can be either private or public. *Private,* or *closed, discussion groups* are those in which there is no audience to listen to or participate in the group discussion. An executive council or a cabinet meeting is an example of a private discussion. The *open* or *public discussion* takes place before an audience. The open discussion may take the form of a *panel,* in which a group of well-informed people exchanges ideas before an audience. A group of doctors, psychologists, and sociologists speaking about the effects of cocaine before a college audience would represent a panel discussion. Similar to the panel is the *symposium,* made up of experts who present their views one at a time. A group of physicians talking about progress in different types of organ transplants to an audience of colleagues is a sympo-

---

[1] L. L. Barker, K. J. Wahlers, K. W. Watson, and R. J. Kibler, *Groups in Process: An Introduction to Small Group Communication,* 3d ed. (Englewood Cliffs, N.J.: Prentice Hall, 1987), p. 43–44.

sium. If the audience mentioned in these two examples were to actively participate in the discussion, the group would then be called a *forum.*

THE PROBLEM-SOLVING GROUP.   One of the most important kinds of discussion groups, the *problem-solving group,* is usually private. The most basic of these groups is the *fact-finding group,* the purpose of which is to gather as much information as possible about a particular issue or problem. Such a task usually requires considerable research. The information collected by the group may then serve as the basis for future policy discussions. One example of a fact-finding group is a committee of university students who volunteered to study the circumstances that led to the closing of their library on weekends and evenings. The university cited lack of funds as the reason for reducing hours. The student group found out how much money was distributed throughout the school and where possible sources of relief money might be located. Government officials often appoint fact-finding committees to investigate particular incidents or problems. For example, after a number of schools report a sharp increase in vandalism, a commission might be established to investigate the situation.

A group whose task stems directly from the fact-finding group is the *evaluation group.* This type of group uses the information that has been made available through investigation to determine the scope of a particular problem and the priorities in finding a solution. It will then make recommendations to those who carry out policy. An example of an evaluation group would be a team of efficiency experts who are asked to make suggestions on how a factory's production might be increased while minimizing costs. After an evaluation group offers its recommendations, the *policy-making group* may make particular changes or take certain actions. Sound policy-making must be based on fact finding and evaluation.

We have described the various kinds of problem-solving groups as though they operate in a sequence but separately from one another. This is not always—in fact, not usually—the case. Any task group can perform any or all of these functions. Generally, the group involved in policy-making goes through the fact-finding and evaluation stages as well, to ensure a carefully considered decision.

One example of a task group that systematically performs any or all of these functions is the *quality circle.* A quality circle is defined as a group of persons, from three to ten in number, "who meet periodically to discuss and develop solutions for problems that relate to quality, productivity, or cost." As such, their primary emphasis is on democratic participation in the identification, analysis, and creation of solutions to problems. Quality circles are one of the most popular concepts to emerge from Japanese management practices during the 1980s. Currently, they exist in some form in over 2,500 American organizations.[2]

---

[2] J. R. Schermerhorn, Jr., J. G. Hunt, and R. N. Osborn, *Managing Organizational Behavior* (New York: John Wiley & Sons, 1985), 341.

PARTICIPATING IN SMALL GROUPS

Responsibilities

If a small group is going to function successfully, certain attitudes, actions, and behaviors are important. Your first responsibility as a group participant is to keep an open mind toward the issue or problem being discussed as well as toward the other members of the group. You should try to remain objective during the course of the discussion and evaluate information and ideas independently. This means being aware of personal biases to make sure that they do not interfere with a willingness to listen to the ideas of others.

Going one step further, it is important to show a certain sensitivity to the moods and emotional tone of individuals as well as of the group as a whole. Sometimes what people say and what they really believe are two different things—if you are sensitive to other members of the group, you may be able to pick up on this. A different tone of voice, changes in posture and body position, and other nonverbal cues help to either reinforce or contradict what is being said.

Individual members have an obligation to make sure that everyone participates in the group process. For example, a newcomer to the group may feel somewhat intimidated by the other members, particularly if they all know one another well and have worked together for a long time. As a sensitive group member, you should try to make the new person feel at ease and draw him or her into the discussion.

Participation in a group often requires preparation or homework of some sort. Sometimes the group may agree to think about a problem or do some research or reading on a particular subject before the next meeting. It is essential to follow through on such assignments. If not, time is wasted and those who have done their work feel frustrated and annoyed. For example, when the social committee of an organization was planning its Christmas party, each member of the committee was supposed to investigate the prices of different restaurants or catering halls where the party could be held. When only three of the seven members came prepared, the group's work was set back at least a week. As part of a group, you have an obligation to other people as well as to yourself.

Communicating

SPEAKING.   Because the group process depends on interaction among members, you must communicate your ideas and opinions as accurately and concisely as you can. Here are some ways to increase the effectiveness of your communication as a group member.

1. If you find yourself mumbling or rambling on, it may be because you yourself find what you are saying unimportant. If so, don't speak up until you have something you want to contribute.

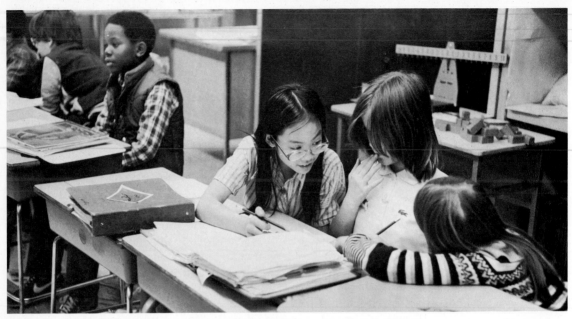

Effective small group communication involves speaking and listening.

2. Address your comments to the group as a whole—group involvement is very important in this process.

3. Organize your remarks whenever possible—although the discussion will be based largely on the interaction among different members of the group, and will therefore be spontaneous, certain comments can be prepared for the discussion and used when appropriate.

4. Relate your idea or opinion to what has been said, making the connection clear whenever necessary.

5. Try to state only one point at a time so that the group can digest what has been said. This will also help to keep the discussion on course and let the group respond to individual points.

6. To make sure everyone understands what you are saying, speak concisely and use language that the group members can relate to.

LISTENING AND FEEDBACK.   As a group member, you must be both a speaker and a listener. It is just as important to be able to listen effectively as it is to speak effectively. Jimmy Celano and Jeff Salzman, founders of CareerTrack, one of America's top business seminar companies, suggest the following guidelines for "listening" aggressively in dyads or groups.

1. *Consciously concentrate.* When you enter a situation in which you know you will have to listen, put yourself into a "tuned-in" mode. "Bear down, suppress other thoughts, and focus."

2. *Visibly respond to the speaker.* Act interested, maintain eye contact,

and demonstrate your interest verbally or nonverbally. The speaker will be far more likely to tell you what you need to know.

3. *Don't talk while you are listening.* This is like talking with your mouth full: highly rude. There's a difference between listening and waiting for your turn to talk.

4. *Create informal situations.* Formal communication settings can paralyze shy or less confident individuals. In informal settings, people will generally open up and reveal their true personalities.

5. *Avoid filtering out the negative.* When the news is good, we are "all ears"; when it's bad, we often tune out entirely. Effective listeners try to tune in during either situation.

6. *Sum up.* When you are listening for the purpose of understanding, paraphrase what's been said once the speaker comes to a natural pause. This will help to crystallize ideas, aid memory, and allow the speaker to clarify miscommunications.

7. *Interrogate—politely.* Asking questions will allow the speaker to know that you are serious about the information that he or she is sharing. It may also help a shy speaker to feel more important and, hence, more confident.

8. *Take notes, but not too many.* Listening and writing simultaneously may be difficult but is essential in the business world. To avoid missing what's being said, be selective: Write down key words, phrases, and statistics.

9. *Refuse to listen when a speaker is talking over your head or is incoherent.* Calculate the value of listening versus the consequences of not listening, and act accordingly.

10. *Avoid killing the messenger.* Whenever you hear bad news, avoid flying off the handle at the person who is delivering it. People will be less likely to cover up problems, and you will be able to keep abreast of the information needed to do your job. Welcome and reward the delivery of bad news—it's just as valuable as good news.

11. *Get to yes or no when you need a quick answer without the details.* If a quick response is impossible, use a "speeder-upper" such as, "Is it mostly yes or mostly no?" "Give me a headline." Or, "In twenty-five words or less, what is your opinion?"

12. *Listen to more than just the words.* Research indicates that 93 percent of a speaker's message is communicated nonverbally. When listening during a discussion or problem-solving session, consider the speaker's facial expressions, eye behavior, posture, and gestures for what's really being said.[3]

---

[3] Adapted from J. Celano and J. Salzman, "Listen Aggressively," in *CareerTracking: 26 Success Shortcuts to the Top* (New York: Simon & Schuster, 1988), 111–18.

Sometimes, even though people try to listen carefully, a certain amount of misunderstanding takes place. Sending feedback is one way to help reduce such misunderstanding, and, as Celano and Salzman suggest, questions can be a valuable form of feedback. Actually, the use of questions can improve communication throughout the group process. At the outset, it helps for members to ask questions relating to the goals and objectives of the group as a whole as well as to the purpose of any particular meeting. Once these goals are established, questions about procedures should be asked. Even when conclusions have been reached, carefully thought-out questions can often refine these decisions to a considerable degree.

BYPASSING.   A variety of questions can overcome barriers to communication in small groups. One such barrier is called *bypassing,* a situation in which people are actually talking past each other. In such a situation people argue or reach an impasse when, in fact, they are in agreement.

A major cause of bypassing is ambiguity, or vagueness, on the part of some group members. Questions relating to interpretation or calling for explanation can help bring out the intended meaning. On the other hand, sometimes a person will use stigma words, such as "indecent" or "foaming-at-the-mouth radical," that are emotionally loaded. The person who uses this type of vocabulary is trying to provoke the rest of the group and cause conflict. Without accusing or intimidating the member who uses such language, other members should be quick to ask for clarification.

ROLE STRUCTURE AND STATUS

Norms

Over a period of time, small groups develop a set of norms, rules, and expectations that are unique to that group, based on the interactions among its members. According to small groups researcher Daniel Feldman, these norms are developed and enforced for four major reasons.[4] First, such norms are established in order to facilitate the group's survival. More specifically, they help to protect the group from outside interference. Second, group norms are developed and enforced if they make more predictable the behaviors expected of group members. For example, when a group first convenes, some confusion may exist regarding which member(s) will keep the minutes. Consequently, a norm may be established that alternates the task among individual group members from meeting to meeting. Third, norms are likely to be developed if they help a group avoid embarrassing interpersonal problems. For instance, groups might enforce norms that prohibit the discussion of romantic topics during a meeting. Fourth, group norms are established if they "express the central values of the group and clarify what is distinctive about the group's identity." As a result, norms justify the group's activities and define and legitimize its power.

Sometimes members are unaware that group norms even exist until there is some specific change in the group. For example, members of a weekly scheduling meeting never realized that they followed a particular seating arrangement until at one session the group was short a chair and the usual pattern was disrupted. Similarly, members of a parent-teachers group were thrown off when a new member addressed them by their first names, which was not their usual practice.

These two examples concern norms that, while influential in terms of interaction among members, are outside the actual group discussion. Other norms actually govern the course of the discussion. For example, it was pointed out to members of an activities committee that during their weekly meetings Richard would always bring the discussion back on course if it seemed to stray, and Elsa would call for periodic summaries of what had been said. Although these behaviors were accepted norms, they were never realized by the group until they were pointed out.

Functional Roles

In the previous example, while neither Richard nor Elsa filled the official role of leader, each did, in fact, fill a leadership role. Role structure is one of the most important kinds of norm a group can develop. Sometimes a role is determined by a person's relative status or position. For example, a

---

[4] D. C. Feldman, "The Development and Enforcement of Group Norms," *Academy of Management Review* 9 (1984), 47–53.

student representative on the college personnel and planning board might defer to the head of a department because of his or her position relative to the student's own. Yet, while position is influential, role structure develops from within the group, and any and all members of a group can fill a variety of different functional roles. *Functional roles* are those that keep the discussion on course and aid the group in accomplishing its objectives.

The functional roles that develop within a group can be divided into two major categories—*task-oriented roles* and *maintenance roles.*

TASK-ORIENTED ROLES.   These roles are directly related to the group's goal, whether that goal is to gather information, make recommendations, solve a problem, or complete a project. In our example concerning the activities committee, Richard, who kept the discussion on track, and Elsa, who asked for summaries, were both filling task-oriented roles. These are only two of the several task-oriented behaviors of group members. A more complete list of such roles would include the following:

1. *Information or opinion giver*: In this role a group member provides content or well-considered opinions which will help the group move more smoothly toward the best decision. Richard, for example, knows of various fundraising activities which have worked well on other campuses. As an information giver, he would be aware of the salience of this information and would share any ideas that might contribute to his group's needs and set criteria.

2. *Information or opinion seeker*: The group member who takes on this role is usually the person who perceives that the group needs additional data. For example, John might ask, "Have we information that reflects the amount of money which might be raised through each alternative?"

3. *Expediter*: The individual in this role helps the group stick to its agenda and often leads the group back on course when it goes off on a tangent. As the activities committee begins to digress to an irrelevant topic, Elsa might state, "But weren't we in the process of deciding what criteria need to be applied?"

4. *Idea person*: The idea person is an imaginative group member who thinks originally, comes up with several alternatives, and quite often contributes an idea which serves as a basis for the final decision. In order to promote the carnival as the best decision, Jim and Carla might begin a debate on the pros and cons of the carnival as the best alternative.

5. *Analyzer*: This role is played by the individual who is highly skilled in problem solving, who moves the group rapidly to the core of the problem, and who, at times, examines the reasoning behind each contribution to the discussion. The analyzer is recognized by statements such as, "O.K., so far we've managed to narrow our choices

to a circus, a car wash, or an auction. But aren't we overlooking the potential of the raffle that Dave suggested?"[5]

MAINTENANCE ROLES.   Task-oriented behavior is essential in getting work done, but a group can only be productive if there is interaction among its members. *Maintenance roles* are concerned with the feelings of individual members and the emotional behavior of the group. Maintenance roles include the following:

1. *Active listener*: This role is played by the person who recognizes the contributions of others and who responds with specific verbal or nonverbal reinforcement. A nod of the head, a smile, or a verbal, "Great idea," represent the responses of an active and participating listener.

2. *Game leader*: The game leader is the individual who recognizes when the process is becoming tedious, when fatigue is setting in, or when the discussion is getting out of hand and who has a timely and uncanny ability to create an appropriate joke, digression, or comment to improve the spirits of the group. As tension begins to mount over the decision to be made, Andy might suggest, "Why don't we just quietly break into teams, with each team representing a solution, and let the winners of a pillow fight make the decision?"

3. *Harmonizer*: The harmonizer is the group member who is both perceptive and empathetic and who is able as a function of his or her contributions to reduce or reconcile differences and misunderstandings. When Steve and Karen seem almost ready to come to blows over the choice of a fundraising project, Julia might suggest that the two discover areas of agreement, rather than disagreement, and begin from there.

4. *Gatekeeper*: The role played by the gatekeeper is one of making sure that channels of communication are open and that everyone has a chance to enter the discussion. When Elaine notices that Alison is exceptionally quiet during a committee meeting, she might encourage Alison by asking her opinion.

5. *Compromiser*: During the course of a discussion in which two prominent positions emerge, it is often the compromiser who must act in order to make the decision. In cases such as this, when two decisions may work equally well, the compromiser may be spotted through statements such as: "How can we reconcile these differences so that we all can agree?" or "Rick, Andy, you both have good ideas, but if you look a little closer, you'll see some similarities between the two ideas."

---

[5] Adapted from R. F. Verderber, *Communicate*, 5th ed. (Belmont, Calif.: Wadsworth, 1987), pp. 228–231.

A leader, designated or not, is anyone who helps a group achieve its goals.

6. *Public relations—the front person*: The front person is the person who possesses skills at interacting with outside groups and individuals and who therefore is skilled in public speaking and interpersonal relations. Because the decision that any group makes will affect those around it, such a person is vital to solution implementation. Once our fundraising committee decides on the best way to raise funds, its public relations person's job only begins.[6]

SELF-SERVING ROLES.   Maintenance roles are extremely important in maximizing group efficiency, but sometimes members adopt *self-serving roles* that are counterproductive. These roles have a negative effect on the group's emotional climate as well as on its ability to reach its goals. Self-serving roles include:

1. *Aggressor*—the person who works for his or her own ends by criticizing or blaming others when things get rough.
2. *Blocker*—the person who blocks ideas from group acceptance by going off on tangents or rejecting suggestions on a personal basis.
3. *Competer*—the person who competes with others to gain attention.
4. *Special pleader*—the individual who has his or her own pet ideas and who, regardless of the group, works to integrate those into whatever is done.
5. *Joker*—the member of the group whose behavior includes clowning, mimicking, and generally disrupting the group. While the game leader plays a positive role in the maintenance of the group, the joker is only out for attention.
6. *Withdrawer*—the person who refuses to contribute or to be a part of the group.

[6] Ibid, pp. 231–234.

Small Group Communication   177

7. *Monopolizer*—the group member who feels the need to talk all the time.[7]

The different roles we have been discussing operate in almost all group situations. Awareness of task-oriented and maintenance roles can enable you to overcome self-serving behavior and accomplish the group goal in a positive manner.

THE DEVELOPMENT OF A SMALL GROUP

Although we have discussed the major roles that are a part of small group interactions, we do not want to suggest that effective small group communication takes place either easily or overnight. Every group has to spend both time and energy learning how to communicate and work together. As Giammatteo and Giammatteo have stated, "It takes time for members, each different, to learn how they can fit into the group and contribute best. Often things seem 'all mixed up,' and group members may quite naturally become disturbed and discouraged—even aggravated at each other."[8] To help people understand these natural "growing pains," these researchers have pinpointed the following descriptive stages in the development process of small group interaction:

1. *"Groping"*: When the group is first finding out how to plan and work together, they may not all agree. They don't know and understand each other well enough to really trust the others, and they still have to determine each others' skills, knowledge, situation and attitudes. They often feel uncomfortable and "lost."

2. *"Griping"*: The members become discouraged when they can't seem to work together, when there isn't much progress, and when their attempt are frustrated. They say the wrong things, play negative roles and block group action because they are uncomfortable. This is the place for more "self–other" understanding, for remembering that they are all different but that they all want to do a good job and to be liked by others. Maybe they can learn to understand why others are griping and learn to give themselves to work things out.

3. *"Grasping"*: Ideas and suggestions are beginning to fit. Members begin to agree and can start to see some direction to group activity. Everyone begins to feel more comfortable. Now they are getting somewhere.

4. *"Grouping"*: Members are getting to know each other and can understand and enjoy how each person works and fits into the scheme.

---

[7] Ibid, p. 234.
[8] M. Giammatteo and D. Giammatteo, *Forces on Leadership* (Reston, Va.: National Association of Secondary School Principals, 1981), 28.

Group tasks, building roles and maintenance roles come into play, and a surge of enthusiasm spreads through the group.

5. *"Group Action"*: Now the group is in full swing, with members playing constructive roles. Leadership is shared, and everyone is participating. While it was difficult at first, it was worth it to learn to work well together. They have shared in making plans and decisions, have learned together, and feel that this is a good group with which to work. They are busy making their group more democratic.[9]

Once a small group moves into the latter three stages, the members are ready to tackle other more important tasks. At times they will return to some of the early stages, but each time the process will be less disturbing and more effective.

LEADERS AND LEADERSHIP

In the example we have been discussing, we commented that both Richard and Elsa were filling leadership roles when they moved to keep the discussion on course and asked for periodic summaries. These task-oriented roles demonstrated leadership on their part, although neither of them was designated as the leader of the group. In the study of group dynamics, *leadership* is any kind of behavior that helps the group toward its goals, and a *leader* is any person who influences the group in this way. Therefore, according to these definitions, Richard and Elsa not only exhibited leadership, but by doing so became leaders of their group.

Sometimes one or more members of a group become leaders by assuming leadership roles, even if someone else has been assigned or elected to that role. Actually, it is possible for a group to demonstrate effective leadership even when there is no official leader. While it is most desirable for a group to have a designated leader to get things started, it is also good for a group to have shared leadership. For example, it is difficult for the person who assumes several task-oriented roles to assume maintenance roles as well. Sometimes one or two people will see to it that the social and emotional atmosphere of the group remains conducive to the completion of the goal, while another person will assume responsibility for task-oriented behavior.

Think for a moment about the groups to which you belong and the leadership roles you play. Are you more comfortable when assuming task roles, or are you more at ease when exhibiting maintenance behaviors? If you have not recently had the chance to "test" your leadership abilities (or if you have and wonder how well you may have done), take just a moment to complete the Leadership Assessment Questionnaire provided in Figure 7–1. This questionnaire will help you to determine your "leadership quotient."

---

[9] Ibid., 29.

FIGURE 7–1 Leadership Assessment Questionnaire

Leadership skills play a vital role in small group interaction and ultimately in your ability as an organizational or corporate manager. Primarily, leadership skills affect the way people perform and the results they achieve.

What kind of leader are you? The following questionnaire will help you to make an initial assessment.

1. Would you rather be
   a) the spokesperson for a group?
   b) the captain of a team?
   c) the commander of an army?
2. Would you consult with subordinates before making important decisions that will affect their work?
   a) Nearly always—I value their experience.
   b) Sometimes—it depends on how much time I have.
   c) Never—I believe a leader should lead.
3. Do you believe that people should be allowed to participate in setting objectives for a group or an organization?
   a) Always—I feel it's vital to get their commitment.
   b) Sometimes—usually for the less important goals.
   c) Never—they would simply try to persuade me to accept lower standards.
4. What do you consider to be the main benefit of delegation?
   a) Makes life easier for the leader.
   b) Helps to develop individual abilities.
   c) Allows the leader to concentrate on higher-level work.
5. How much authority would you delegate to subordinates? Would you prefer for them to
   a) check with you first before making important decisions?
   b) decide for themselves whether to consult you?
   c) act first and tell you later?
6. A subordinate turns in an outstanding performance on an important assignment. Would you
   a) congratulate him or her personally and right away?
   b) say nothing in case he/she might ask for more money?
   c) congratulate him or her if you happened to meet?
7. You have to announce a very important policy change to your group. Would you
   a) issue a memo or general circular, enclosing a copy of the new policy?
   b) brief one of your lieutenants and ask him or her to communicate with the rest of the group?
   c) call a meeting and explain the changes personally?
8. A subordinate's general performance begins to deteriorate sharply. Would you
   a) threaten him or her with tough action unless he/she improves quickly?
   b) discuss the problem to discover the cause?
   c) ask the personnel department to investigate?
9. A subordinate suggests a radical new idea—which you feel is unsound. Would you
   a) point out its weaknesses and encourage him or her to try again?
   b) tell him or her it's impractical, too costly, or not the right time?
   c) promise to think about it and then file it?

10. One of your people is depressed after missing a promotion. Would you
   a) tell him or her not to worry—everyone must expect an occasional setback?
   b) suggest what action he or she might take to become a stronger candidate for the next promotion vacancy?
   c) tell him or her the job wouldn't have suited him or her anyway.

Now that you have completed the questionnaire, let's determine your *current* standing in the leadership ranks. (Remember, many leadership qualities must be learned! If your score is low on the questionnaire this time, you simply have more work to do to increase your leadership skills.)

The Analysis

1. a – 0	3. a – 10	5. a – 0	7. a – 5	9. a – 10
b – 10	b – 5	b – 10	b – 0	b – 5
c – 5	c – 0	c – 5	c – 10	c – 0
2. a – 10	4. a – 0	6. a – 10	8. a – 0	10. a – 5
b – 5	b – 5	b – 0	b – 10	b – 10
c – 0	c – 10	c – 5	c – 5	c – 0

Leadership Ratings

80–100 You are an excellent leader who knows how to motivate people to give their best. Any group led by you will exhibit high levels of trust and commitment.

55–79 You have a positive attitude about managing people and major errors of judgment are rare. Occasionally, you could be more adventurous.

25–54 You are much too cautious and may tend to stifle your subordinate's development. Try to have more confidence in yourself—and in other people.

0–24 You shouldn't be in charge of people at all.

Adapted from T. Farnsworth, "Test your Leadership Skills." In J. E. Adair, "The Building Blocks of Good Leadership," *International Management* 38 (1983), 47, 50, 55, 77.

THEORETICAL APPROACHES

Operating under the assumption that leaders are born, not made, early investigators of leadership looked for traits that distinguish leaders from nonleaders. Many of these early studies revealed that leaders scored higher on measures of intelligence, scholarship, dependability, responsibility, social participation, and socioeconomic status. Dissatisfied with this personality-centered approach, later researchers turned their attention to the evaluation of the particular communication behaviors of both leaders and nonleaders. During the 1960s, for example, Geier reported the existence of five behavioral characteristics that prevented particular individuals from becoming leaders: being uninformed about the problem under discussion; not participating; being too rigid in opinions and approaches to the problem; being too authoritarian or "bossy"; and being verbally offensive—talking too much or talking in a pompous or overly formal manner.[10] Not surprisingly, still later investigators found that leaders are less opinionated and more agreeable than nonleaders.

A second, and significantly different, approach to the study of leadership focuses not on individual traits but on those behaviors that help the group reach its goals. This functional approach emphasizes the fact that anyone who learns these behaviors can contribute to the group's success. You don't have to be the designated leader of a group to discover that your group is straying from its agenda. Any member of the group who proposes a return to the agenda contributes positively to the group process. Similarly, any member who points out that there is a "hidden agenda" controlling group discussion (a disruptive ego battle or the promotion of special interests) contributes to the group process. Other major leadership behaviors include keeping the discussion centered on issues, insisting on the critical evaluation of evidence, and refusing to yield to social pressure. The experienced group member uses the issue-centered approach to rescue discussions that have fallen victim to personality clashes.

Styles of Leadership

There are three basic styles of leadership: democratic, authoritarian, and laissez-faire (see Figure 7–2). **Democratic** leaders guide, rather than direct, a group. Receptive to group members' suggestions, these leaders leave most of the actual decision making to the group itself. While this style of leadership is very popular, some less experienced groups feel lost when left on their own to this extent. The effectiveness of this type of leadership, like all others, depends on the power the leader has, the nature of the task at hand, and the interpersonal relationship's between the leader and group members. For example, one study has shown that democratically led groups do better than others on measures of creativity and consistency but fall behind in efficiency.

Authoritarian leaders are more directive than democratic leaders. They are strongly goal oriented and have firm opinions on how to achieve these goals. If their competency is respected by group members, the group works well and efficiently; if not, conflict is likely to arise within the group.

The third type, **laissez-faire** leaders, don't direct the group at all. As potential sources of information and feedback on group interaction, they function as observers and recorders, available for advice when the group wants it. This kind of leadership is especially appropriate for groups engaged in creative activity, where more direction would limit or stifle creativity.

Whatever the style of leadership chosen, positive evaluations of the group's performance depend on the degree to which each member contributes to the task and maintenance outcomes. In fact, as one study has shown,

[10] J. G. Geier, "A Trait Approach to the Study of Leadership in Small Groups," *Journal of Communication* 17, no. 4 (1967), 316–23.

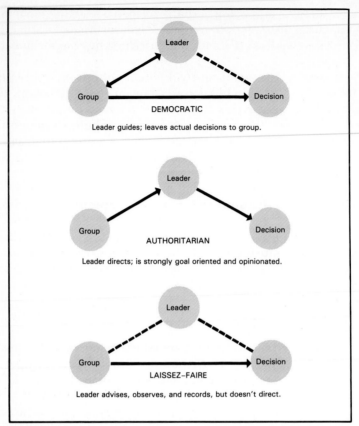

FIGURE 7–2
Three basic styles of leadership

group members are evaluated more positively by the leader, whatever his or her style, when the latter attributes the group's performance to the group members' efforts.[11] To the extent that leaders believe a performance is controlled by outside forces, such as the leader's direction, group members will be devalued by the leader.

EMERGENCE OF LEADERS.   In groups that have no assigned leaders, functioning leaders often emerge through a process of elimination, not through a process of selection. Interviews with group members reveal that during the first phase of the elimination process, members who are uninformed, quiet, or dogmatic are removed from consideration. In the second, longer phase of elimination, over-authoritarian or verbally offensive individuals are knocked out of the running. In most cases in which a consensus leader emerges (and this always happens in the most successful groups), a second person—a runner up, so to speak—becomes an auxiliary leader or lieutenant.

[11] D. Kipnis, S. Schmidt, K. Price, and C. Stitt, "Why Do I Like Thee: Is It Your Performance or My Orders?" *Journal of Applied Psychology* 66 (1981), 328.

SKILLS OF EFFECTIVE LEADERS.   As we have stated, earlier periods of research in the area of leadership emphasized the kind of person who would or would not make a good leader—the special traits or characteristics that were a part of effective leadership. More recently, leadership has been viewed in light of what effective leaders *do* rather than who they are. As a function of this more recent trend, several authors have attempted to summarize and categorize leadership skills. One such skill description is that of Giammatteo and Giammatteo (1981). They list and briefly describe five of these major skill areas:[12]

1. Skills of personal behavior. The effective leader:
     Is sensitive to feelings of the group.
     Identifies self with the needs of the group.
     Learns to listen attentively.
     Refrains from criticizing or ridiculing members' suggestions.
     Helps each member feel important and needed.
     Should not argue.

2. Skills of communication. The effective leader:
     Makes sure that everyone understands not only what is needed but why.
     Makes good communication with the group a routine part of the job.

3. Skills in equality. The effective leader recognizes that:
     Everyone is important.
     Leadership is to be shared and is not a monopoly.
     A leader grows when leadership functions are dispersed.

> The degree to which I can create relationships which facilitate the growth of others as separate persons is a measure of the growth I have achieved in myself.
>
> Carl Rogers

4. Skills of organization. The effective leader helps the group:
     Develop long-range and short-range objectives.
     Break big problems into small ones.
     Share opportunities and responsibilities.
     Plan, act, follow up and evaluate.

5. Skills of Self-Examination. The effective leader:
     Is aware of motivations and motives guiding actions.
     Is aware of members' levels of hostility and tolerance so that appropriate countermeasures are taken.

---

[12] Giammatteo and Giammatteo, 3–4.

Is aware of their fact-finding behavior.

Helps the group members to be aware of their own forces, attitudes and values.

Now that we have discussed leadership approaches, styles, and skills, we will turn to another important area of study in small group communication: the process of group problem solving.

PROBLEM SOLVING THROUGH GROUP DISCUSSION

We've all experienced the frustration that arises when a group of people can't seem to solve a problem that an individual would solve relatively easily—when, for example, four people spend all night trying to decide which movie to see. Researchers have discovered that the relative effectiveness of group—as opposed to individual—decision making depends on the nature of the problem at hand.

Groups do better than individuals in situations in which a pooling of data is necessary, in which more knowledge and a greater variety of approaches can contribute to more effective solutions. In policy decisions, group participation leads to wider acceptance and better understanding of the solution. The group decision-making process is, however, prone to the problems that arise from any process involving human interaction. For some group members, winning an argument may become more important than finding a solution. Other group members may try to dominate the discussion, while others may habitually give in, in order to win group acceptance. The four friends who can't decide which film to see may actually be arguing about social dominance—and not about movies at all.

A decision-making group is simply a group of people who work together to solve a problem by collecting information about the problem, reviewing that information and then making a decision based on their findings. While we may ordinarily think of decision making, as an unexciting or private process, decision-making groups and their decisions actually play a very central—and often very public—role in American life. During crucial strike negotiations, the media feature dramatic, up-to-the-minute accounts of union–management talks. If you are sensitive to the fact that decision making is a *process*, you can improve your own participation in group discussions and also contribute to the effectiveness of the entire group effort.

Kinds of Topics or Problems

Some topics or problems are better tackled by group discussion than are others. Those that are most appropriate to group discussion fall into three categories: problems of fact, problems of value, and problems of policy. It is important to be able to identify these three quite distinct types of topics; decision-making discussions often break down precisely because the participants don't understand the nature of the problems they're dealing with.

PROBLEMS OF FACT.   The first kind of problem or question that may be considered requires that the group investigate the truth or falsity of assertions about actual events or conditions. "Did last week's fatal DC-10 crash result from a defective cargo hatch?" "Do air pollutants from chemical-producing plants pose a health hazard to local residents?" "Is the nation going through a depression?" Panels of experts are sometimes assembled to decide crucial factual issues. Ideally, the beliefs, attitudes and values of group members don't affect the decision-making process here; instead, members act like detectives, defining their terms ("defective," "health hazard," "depression") and making logical deductions based on evidence. One group goal in discussions of problems of fact is to arrive at a correct and accurate description of the facts.

Interestingly, in this type of decision-making discussion, the fact that everyone agrees is no guarantee that the decision made will be the correct one; everyone may agree and still be wrong. Whether or not a good decision is made by a group considering a problem of fact is determined in large part by how well the members have analyzed and interpreted the information on which their decision is based. It is for this reason that it is so important for all group members to see the "facts" before them in more or less the same light. To avoid misunderstanding, it is necessary for members to ask questions relating to the interpretation of particular words or ideas.

For example, suppose a group was planning a party for a friend. The guest of honor's availability on certain dates would, of course, be one of the important facts to be considered. Also important would be clearing up the confusion created if one friend suggests that the group buy a "substantial" gift as opposed to each person giving something individually. Some friends might think in terms of high price, while others might think that the term referred to the gift itself, meaning something sturdy and practical. Someone has to clear up the confusion and ask for an agreed-upon definition of the word before the problem can be acted upon.

PROBLEMS OF VALUE.   Here facts are not the primary issue; instead of using hard evidence, group members base their discussion on attitudes, morals and values. "Is a citizen ever justified in refusing to fight in a war?" "Should abortion be legalized?" There are no correct or incorrect answers to these questions, but there are acceptable or unacceptable answers. It is the group's goal and responsibility to discover its own bases for acceptability and unacceptability.

Discussions concerning value will obviously differ greatly from discussions of fact; values are individually held, and they are not always formed (or defended) on the basis of logic. Also, more than one type of problem may, of course, be considered by any particular group. In the example just used to illustrate problems of fact, questions of value might easily surface and demand attention before consideration of the facts could occur. For instance, questions concerning an appropriate gift might reflect individual values. When one friend suggests that the group buy the guest of honor a fancy cigarette lighter, another friend might question whether the group should contribute to a bad habit. This question would reflect a difference in values.

On the other hand, often during discussions of value, definitions must be agreed on and facts must be determined: Are "undeclared wars" or "policing actions" to be considered in the same category as other wars? At what point is a fetus considered a human being? Problems often arise when groups fail to distinguish value from fact. It is also very important to remember that conclusions reached in discussions concerning values may be agreed to by the participants, but this in no way means that these conclusions have been proved.

PROBLEMS OF POLICY.   These problems are the most common type of topic for formal decision-making groups, and they are frequently used as topics for class exercises in decision making. Problems of policy are involved in determining courses of action: "How should we allocate our advertising budget this year?" "Should U.S.–Soviet trade agreements be affected by Soviet emigration policies?"

Discussions concerning policy inevitably involve discussions of fact and value. Before deciding on the allocation of their advertising budget, business executives have to identify their target audience, and they also have to know that audience's media habits: How much time do they spend watching TV, listening to the radio and reading magazines? In order to determine the basis for U.S.–Soviet trade arrangements, policymakers have to deal with a question of value: Does one government have the right to interfere in the internal affairs of another government? Because discussions of policy are liable to raise a great number of subsidiary questions, it is crucial that members of the group recognize when they are and are not addressing the same question. If one congressman, for example, is concerned with the adequacy of current U.S. grain supplies, another congressman is worried about disadvantageous wheat deals of the past, and a third congresswoman is concerned with civil rights in the Soviet Union, their committee's discussion on trade agreements may become disrupted or blocked entirely. If, however, the three concerned members are able to identify these issues separately and agree to discuss them one at a time, they can conduct an effective and productive discussion.

To bring things back to the level of our party-planning group, a question of policy might concern the nature of the party itself. For instance, should the party be a surprise or should it be announced? Should the group send out invitations or just telephone all the guests? These questions all suggest possible actions for the group to consider.

Research for Discussion

As the above has indicated, researching facts and evidence is sometimes a crucial part of the decision-making process. John K. Brilhart has divided this preparatory research stage into four distinct phases.[13]

---

[13] J. K. Brilhart, *Effective Group Discussion*, 5th ed. (Dubuque, Iowa: Wm. C. Brown, 1986), 81–92.

REVIEW YOUR OWN INFORMATION.   Whatever your topic for discussion, you will inevitably have some ideas and background information. Now is the time to jot down everything you know about the topic and its causes and effects. Move from a freewheeling kind of thinking to a more organized mode of thought in which you note main issues, subsidiary questions and supporting details. Make note of information that you don't know now but that would be useful for later discussion.

GATHER NEEDED INFORMATION.   This is the active phase of your research: Go out and observe the problem yourself. If your group is trying to come up with ways of reducing the theft of library books, go prowl around the library, watching for security leaks. A second source of information is interviews. Talk to experts; ask the head librarian for an analysis of the theft problem. More information about your topic can come from reading. Check magazines, professional journals and books for the latest data on your problem. Other informal sources of information are all around you. Ask friends for their ideas about your topic; check TV and radio shows that might give you some useful information; or go to a campus lecture that deals with your topic.

EVALUATE YOUR INFORMATION.   Now is the time for you to play the critic, distinguishing facts from opinions. As we noted earlier, statements of fact can be determined to be either true or false on the basis of evidence. Opinions can neither be proved nor disproved; they are not necessarily based on evidence, and they introduce the dangerous element of uncertainty into your discussion. While opinions may become useful in deciding questions of value or policy, it is essential that they be identified correctly. The head librarian's suggestion for installing antitheft devices may be a useful or expert opinion, but it is necessary to recognize it for what it is—an opinion, not a fact.

After you have separated fact from opinion, evaluate them both. To evaluate facts based on survey and statistical data, Brilhart suggests the following questions:

1. Are results based on a random or other scientific sample?
2. How are the questions asked? By whom?
3. Is the method explained by which the data used in computing the statistics were gathered?
4. Is the method of computing averages or trends described and appropriate?
5. Are the data interpreted and evaluated appropriately?[14]

Unless a member of your group is trained in research or statistical methods, ask a researcher or statistician to help you determine the answers to the last two questions.

---

[14] Ibid, 89–90.

To evaluate a source's opinions and their resulting implications, Brilhart advises asking the following questions:

1. Is the person (or other source) a recognized expert on the subject?
2. Does the source have a vested interest that might have influenced this opinion?
3. How well does the source support his or her opinion with documented evidence? Is the evidence well organized, with supporting statistics, tables, and clear reasoning?
4. How consistent is this opinion with others expressed by the source? If the statement is not consistent with other opinions and predictions from the same person, is there an acceptable explanation for the change?
5. What are the implications of the opinion?[15]

Finally, test your evidence for accuracy, recency, and completeness. Old or partial information is not useful and may be misleading.

REORGANIZE YOUR INFORMATION AND GATHER MORE, IF NECESSARY.
After you have weeded out useless or unreliable information, you can recognize the hard evidence and make a tentative outline of your analysis of the problem as well as suggested steps for its solution. It is important to remember at the close of this stage of the decision-making process that you are engaged in a cooperative effort. Don't regard your research material as weapons stockpiled for battle—view it instead as a collection of accurate and objective information that can be shared with the group to help provide the basis for informed problem solving.

THE PROBLEM-SOLVING PROCESS

Dewey's Reflective Thinking Process

When we are confronted with a problem, we often lose sight of the fact that decision making or problem solving is, in fact, a process. Studies have shown that people tend to respond to problems in an ordered series of steps. In his classic book *How We Think*, John Dewey identified five distinct phases in this pattern of goal-directed or reflective thinking:

1. Recognizing the difficulty.
2. Defining or specifying the difficulty.
3. Raising suggestions for possible solutions and rational exploration of the ideas.

---

[15] Ibid, pp. 90–91.

4. Selecting the best solution from among many proposals.

5. Carrying out the solution.[15]

A Standard Agenda for Decision Making

While Dewey's discussion of these five phases of reflective thought originated as a description of the pattern of rational thought, not as a set of rules for decision making, his influence has been so great that later scholars in the field of speech communication have adopted and expanded these steps to form the basis for a standard agenda for decision making.

STEP 1: DEFINING THE PROBLEM.   If a group has been given a very specific and clearly defined problem to solve, this step becomes unnecessary. In many—or most—cases, however, a group finds itself in the middle of a difficult situation, and working out a clear definition of the problem becomes an important part of the decision-making process.

Consider the following example: At a certain university, eating arrangements have become a problem for a large number of students; many students live off-campus, others have kitchens in their dorms, and still others, commuters, need only a few meals on campus a week. The university meal plan ticket is expensive, the cafeteria food is unappealing, and local grocery stores and restaurants are expensive and aren't open at convenient hours. A group of students concerned with this situation meets to share complaints. The students are aware of the situation, and some have vague ideas as to possible solutions, but they need to define their problem more clearly. At this stage they have two goals: They want to frame their definition of the problem so as to increase its "solvability," and they want to frame their definition in a way that will promote good discussion and effective interaction. Clearly, posing the question so that it can be answered by a simple "yes" or "no" doesn't help define the problem.

The most effective definitions are problem centered rather than solution centered. "How can we get local supermarkets to lower their prices?" is a solution-centered definition of our sample problem. Hidden in this question is the assumption that there is only one way to solve the problem; this kind of definition effectively short-circuits the entire decision-making process. An alternative definition of the problem—"How can we improve grocery buying and dining facilities?"—centers on the problem and does not limit the range of possible solutions from the beginning.

STEP 2: LIMITING THE TOPIC.   After the problem has been defined, limits to the discussion must be set up based on relevance to the group, the importance of specific issues involved in the larger problem and the amount of time available for discussion. Our hypothetical group, for example, is interested in the high price of groceries, but only in a certain sense. The group

---

[15] J. Dewey, *How We Think* (Boston: Heath, 1933), 106–15.

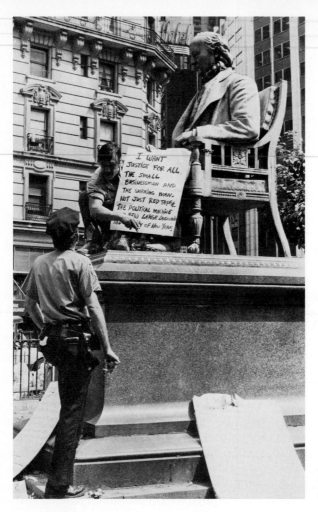

Which step of the problem-solving process could this be?

is not going to discuss a nationwide boycott of certain supermarket chains; it is interested in the problem of prices only in the immediate area. Similarly, the group has to limit its topic on the basis of the priority of specific issues: Should they focus on the problem of grocery buying, campus dining facilities, local restaurants—or all three? Obviously, the group's definition of the problem will also depend on the amount of time available—do they have only a few hours, or will they meet over a period of weeks or months, working slowly to find a solution?

STEP 3: ANALYZING THE DATA.   At this stage of the decision-making process, the group goes through its evidence, distinguishing relevant from irrelevant material, finding important details, searching for causes of the problem and working out the dynamics of the situation. Our sample group might at this point evaluate the quality of dining hall food in relation to its price, compare local supermarket prices with supermarket prices in other nearby towns, compile statistics on the number of students who do and do not have meal plan tickets, and collect figures on local restaurant prices.

STEP 4: ESTABLISHING CRITERIA FOR POSSIBLE SOLUTIONS.   The group must determine in advance what they expect from their proposed solutions. Our group might decide, for example, that its solution should meet three criteria: It should provide (1) nutritious and (2) tasty food to students (3) at prices they can afford. During this stage of the problem-solving process, group members must keep from judging which of the proposed criteria are acceptable until all suggestions have been heard. The group then selects those criteria that are acceptable to the majority.

STEP 5: SUGGESTING POSSIBLE SOLUTIONS.   During the "brainstorming" stage the quantity rather than the quality of proposed solutions is important. Again, the group must not try to come to a decision until all possible solutions have been heard. All possible approaches to the problem should be brought up and discussed: negotiating with the university to change dining hall policies, talking to local supermarket and restaurant owners about student discounts—these ideas and many more may prove worthwhile. Open-mindedness is the rule here. Even seemingly impossible proposals may yield solutions as they are worked over, improved, and modified by the group. An excited, "Hey, let's start our own grocery store!" may just provide the inspiration for the organization of a student cooperative supermarket.

STEP 6: CHECKING THE INDIVIDUAL SOLUTION AGAINST THE ESTAB-LISHED CRITERIA.   Does each solution satisfy the standards the group has already established? Do some of the proposed solutions satisfy the criteria better than others? At this point in the problem-solving process, the group will throw out those solutions that do not meet the established standards, and it will evaluate the remaining solutions in the light of the needs of the problem. In this stage the group must keep its discussion focused on issues, not personalities. Any proposed solution must be judged on its own merits— not on the popularity or loudness of its sponsor.

STEP 7: CARRYING OUT THE SOLUTION.   The group must decide how its solution may be carried out within the limitations of its authority, its power, its facilities and its budget. If our student group has decided to organize an alternative supermarket, should they hire an outside contractor to run the store, or should they run it themselves as a student cooperative? Do they have sufficient manpower, business expertise and financing to run it themselves? Which plan would result in the lowest food prices? The group must choose the most efficient and effective means of carrying out their solution.

STEP 8: EVALUATING THE EFFECT OF THE SOLUTION.   After the solution has been tried, various questions must be asked: Has it accomplished its purpose? Does the new student cooperative market provide better food at more reasonable prices? Has it satisfied the need—do enough students use it to justify its existence? Can improvements be made to increase the effectiveness of the solution? Should students work at the cooperative without wages in return for even lower food prices?

The standard agenda that we have described here is offered as a guide, not as a straitjacket. It is useful only insofar as all group members are aware of it and accept it as a useful and organized way to approach the problem-solving process. Despite the orderliness of the standard agenda, its use does not guarantee effortless solutions. Several other factors affect the operations and outcomes of problem-solving groups.

OTHER FACTORS AFFECTING GROUP PERFORMANCE

Personality

One of the most fascinating aspects of group behavior is the uniqueness of each and every group due to the nature of its membership. There are many variables that influence group interaction, but the primary (and ever-present) one is the different personality of each member of the group.

Each person contributes his or her own experiences, values, attitudes, and personality to the makeup of the group. For example, some people are basically shy and tend to sit back in a group situation, while more aggressive individuals may use the group as an audience for their assertiveness. While some people try to avoid conflict in a group, much the same as they would in a personal encounter, other people like to provoke conflict and enjoy the combative interaction that often follows. Perhaps you have participated in a group that you felt could have functioned more efficiently if one or two members had been less argumentative or if someone had been more dominant.

Undoubtedly, you have heard the expression "personality conflict" used to describe the irreconcilable clash of personalities. Such a difference in personality can sometimes cause a group to lose sight of its goal and remain unproductive. Yet differences in personality can have a positive effect on group interaction. For example, one person who is particularly task oriented may counterbalance the member who is primarily concerned with the effective behavior of the group. Similarly, a humorous individual can offset someone who is extremely serious or tense. The group is a complex entity because of the combination of different personalities. The next time you participate in a group or observe one in action, remember that the group is equal to and greater than the sum of the individual personalities of its members.

Cohesion

Groups develop personalities all their own. Some groups, for example, always seem to work smoothly and achieve their goals easily, while in other groups interaction is marked by conflict and progress is achieved slowly, if at all.

Highly publicized mountain climbs such as those up Mt. Everest provide an example of this second type of group. In the past, instances have arisen during which the climbers—who depend on each other for their survival—have not communicated effectively. Additionally, the overall groups have been divided into two subgroups with quite different goals: the climbers, whose goal was to reach the summit as quickly and safely as possible, and the film crews, whose goal was to capture exciting footage. As a result, teamwork between the two subgroups disintegrated—and ultimately jeopardized lives.

A communication expert would diagnose this problem as a lack of group cohesion or solidarity. **Cohesion** is the degree to which group members identify themselves as a team, as a whole, rather than as just a collection of individuals. Cohesion arises from and reinforces shared values, attitudes and standards of behavior. Cohesion is a crucial factor in a group's success, for highly cohesive groups are more likely to be productive, their members are more likely to feel personally satisfied by the group process, and their interpersonal communication is more effective.

Cohesive groups inspire feelings of loyalty because group members have an emotional investment in the life of the team; they share the same goals and are willing to make personal sacrifices for the good of the group. One compelling example of this aspect of group cohesiveness was the "bonding" reflected during the 1988 rescue of baby Jessica McClure from the well at her parents' Texas home. The awe-inspiring teamwork of rescue workers, family, and friends during the frightening ordeal succeeded not only in becoming an international media event but also in bringing the country together over the safety of the little girl. In short, group cohesiveness made the rescue of baby Jessica a reality.

Interaction in highly cohesive groups has several special characteristics. First, because individuals feel secure in these groups, they can tolerate some degree of productive conflict. Specifically, they feel free to offer both rewarding and punishing feedback to other group members.

Second, cohesive groups offer their members greater returns, or rewards, for their personal investment in the group. In the business world, these rewards may take the form of money; for example, a team assembling autos may be paid for the number of cars they produce each week, instead of being paid by the hour. In an academic situation, a professor may give the same grade to all students working on a group project, regardless of their individual contributions to the project. In both of these cases, cohesion increases as a result of a shared group goal. Members of the car assembly team will probably work harder to get more pay, and the students will most likely work harder to get a better grade.

Third, cohesive groups offer psychological rewards—feelings of belonging and the friendship and respect of other people. Cohesive groups also offer their members the reward of prestige, which comes either from the social status of the group or from some group accomplishment. In either case, group members share the reflected glory of the group. Finally, and perhaps most important, participation in a cohesive group allows each member to experience achievement rewards, the satisfaction that comes from

Cohesion is a major determinant of successful teamwork.

productive work, and the fulfillment that comes from contributing to a valuable and valued cause or goal.

Conflict

The ideal group is highly cohesive, but groups, like most other things in life, are rarely ideal, and conflict, rather than cohesion, often emerges from group interaction. Conflict between groups—***intergroup conflict***—often benefits the groups involved by increasing goal-oriented activity and causing group members to value their work more highly. An extreme case is war, in which conflict strengthens in-group bonds by providing an outlet for tension and focusing a group's goals. Conflict usually occurs when there are two or more competing or incompatible responses to a single event. Thus, conflict may occur both within the group itself, when individuals experience differing needs or values; or between groups, when the groups have competing interests over the accomplishment of a cooperative goal.[17]

In the past it was believed that all ***intragroup conflict*** (conflict within a group) had the opposite effect—that it had a negative influence, reduced cohesion, decreased productivity, and caused group members to discredit their own achievements. It is now believed that some degree of intragroup conflict is useful and productive. It is possible that when conflict is appropriately channeled, it can contribute to more effective results. Of course, the kind of conflict in mind here is not a pitched battle but an issue-centered form of open discussion and confrontation that uses group problem-solving methods to achieve better solutions.

[17] H. W. Cummings, L. Long, and M. Lewis, *Managing Communication in Organizations: An Introduction*, 2d ed. (Dubuque, Iowa: Gorsuch-Scarisbrick, 1987).

At times, intragroup conflict cannot be avoided. To cope, the group must be willing to work through its problems. The first step in this process is determining whether a conflict exists. To aid in the completion of this step, small-group researchers Schultz and Anderson suggest that group members should be willing to address four specific questions. First, do the parties involved believe or know that a conflict exists? A conflict is not a conflict unless all parties are aware of it. Second, are there incompatible goals? Conflict is almost always the result of one party's particular goals. For example, one group member may believe that the scope of a project is far too broad, while the leader of the group may feel that the project is manageable. Third, are scarce rewards involved? Conflict often results when rewards are perceived as limited or scarce (these include both tangible and intangible rewards, such as money or respect). Finally, what degree of interdependence and independence exists among the parties in conflict? Conflict seldom occurs if one of the parties is capable of functioning independently of all other group members. If the members could function independently, they probably would not be members of the group.[18]

Once the real source of conflict has been identified, the process of managing the conflict can begin. First, the group should determine the issues of the conflict at hand. An examination of every conceivable issue from all sides should be considered. (In our earlier example of group conflict, the scope of a particular group project was the issue. At this stage, the group would listen to the speakers representing both sides.) Once the issues are identified, the group can translate the issues into goals and can rank them according to practicality and desirability. For example, Jeannie might suggest that the project be completed in two stages rather than one, given that the scope of the project is broad. Finally, the group should determine the direction and strategy that would best achieve the goal(s). At this point, the problem solving process can be resumed.[19]

Conformity

Another important variable that influences groups is pressure to conform within the group. In and of itself, **conformity** is not a negative force. Sometimes, however, when consensus inhibits dissent, the pressure to conform, or "groupthink," can cause serious errors in decision making.[20] As previously discussed, many of the norms to which a group conforms are productive for the group, enabling it to function more effectively. Actually, conformity, when it occurs naturally, without force, is quite desirable, since consensus is one of the objectives of the group process.

While pressure to conform is sometimes so subtle that a group member may be totally unaware of it, at other times the pressure can be quite

---

[18] B. Schultz and J. Anderson, "Training in the Management of Conflict: A Communication Theory Perspective," *Small Group Behavior* 15 (1984), 333–48.

[19] Ibid., 339–42.

[20] I. L. Janis, *Victims of Groupthink: A Psychological Study of Foreign Policy Decisions and Fiascos*, 2d ed. (Boston: Houghton Mifflin, 1982).

open. Group members may be pressured to conform, even when it means going against their better judgment or even their conscience. This sort of overt pressure can result in dissonance, which can erupt in open conflict or take the form of defiance.

For example, an individual may verbally yield to group pressure but then exhibit contradictory behavior. Examine the following situation: Gil's bike club was going to sponsor a charity drive for an undetermined organization. Gil was anxious to support the local animal shelter, but the group made its final decision to support the nearby children's hospital. Gil reluctantly agreed, and the group believed that it had won him over to its side. Yet when it came to active participation in the collection drive, Gil was nowhere to be found. In this case Gil gave the group what it wanted to hear when it wanted to hear it, but he refused to conform in his actions.

The consequence that may result when group members are pressured to conform will vary depending upon the situation, the force of the pressure, and the people involved. Consider another example: After three weeks of testimony, a jury was asked to determine the guilt or innocence of the accused. From the very outset, most of the jurors were convinced that the defendant was guilty. After three days and endless hours of discussion, all but one of the jurors voted to convict the accused. The holdout was subjected to group pressure, both overt and subtle. Everyone was tired and anxious to go home. On the next day the twelfth juror gave in to the group pressure, and the accused was found guilty. This is obviously an instance in which group pressure—whether for good or ill (depending upon the actual guilt or innocence of the accused)—greatly affected a group's decision.

Some group members are more susceptible to group pressure than are others. The following personality characteristics identify those who are most vulnerable to group pressure:

1. *Level of self-confidence.* The better one's self-concept, the more resistant one will be to group pressure.
2. *Regard for authority.* A closed-minded person, defined as one who relies on the accuracy and correctness of authority, will be more apt to conform to group pressure.
3. *Intelligence.* The greater one's intelligence, the less likely one is to conform.
4. *Need for social approval.* As you might expect, the greater one's need for approval, the more apt one is to conform.

Other variables that influence conformity concern the situation in which the group finds itself. Situational variables include:

1. *The size of the group.* Conformity usually increases as the size of the group increases, but only until there are four members; thereafter, conformity decreases as the group increases.
2. *Group structure.* Group structures that permit a great deal of interac-

tion between members produce more conformity than those that limit interaction.

3. *Difficulty of the task.* Conformity usually increases as the task becomes more difficult.

4. *Degree of crisis or emergency.* The old adage that there is safety in numbers may account for the increase in conformity during a crisis situation. For example, a group of shipwrecked survivors floating on a raft in the middle of the ocean would probably exhibit a high degree of conformity since deviation from the norm could mean disaster.

Whatever the mechanisms affecting a particular group—personality, cohesion, conformity—it is the responsibility of each and every group member to try to make the most of the positive potential of these forces. By becoming a member of a group, you and the others have elected to pursue certain objectives as a team. When what needs to be accomplished is kept firmly in view, individual differences can often be recognized as the stumbling blocks they are and can be temporarily shelved while the solution is sought in an open-minded way.

Communication Networks

Another variable that influences the process of small group communication is the network of communication channels used in the group. The five most common communication networks are the circle, the wheel, the chain, the Y, and the all-channel networks. Distinguished by the concepts of *distance* among members and *centrality* of information flow, communication networks vary as a function of the transmission and reception of information from member to member. Figure 7–3 illustrates the most common communication networks in a five-member group.

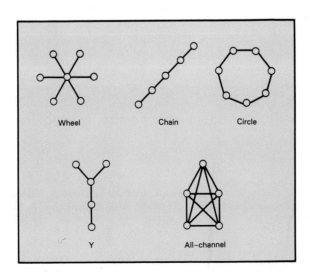

FIGURE 7–3
Common communication network structures

In the **circle communication network,** members pass information from side to side. No one person has greater access to group members than any other person. Unlike the wheel, which has a leader at the center, each group member in the circle is viewed as the leader at different times. Equal access to information means higher group morale and satisfaction. The circle network is especially effective when solving complex problems.

Perhaps the most unique characteristic of the **wheel network** is its highly centralized flow of communication. The person at the center of the network controls the communication flow. Because all information is primarily sent and received from a central source, the wheel is especially suited for solving simple problems. Speed and efficiency are the hallmarks of the wheel. However, this network tends to produce less group satisfaction and poorer morale than the circle network.

Much as the wheel is viewed as a highly centralized communication structure, so are the *Y* and the *chain* characterized as more centralized. In both the Y and the chain, the person in the center is viewed as the leader, due to the flow of information that he or she sends and receives. Perhaps the most interesting aspect of the Y is its ability to identify coalitions. Thus, the Y structure is more characteristic of groups that have developed over time. As with the wheel, these communication networks are more adaptable to solving simple problems. Again, speed and accuracy are the name of the game.

The final communication network that is illustrated is the **all-channel structure**—generally considered to describe a leaderless group discussion. An example of an all-channel communication network might be the first meeting of a group of concerned citizens who wish to raise money for the needy in their community. No leader may emerge during the initial meeting of such a group. Over time, however, another communication network will emerge (for example, a circle or a wheel). In short, the all-channel network may be considered to be "no network" at all. It is most often used to describe an initial group discussion.

Although this discussion of communication networks may seem a bit alien at first, you need only look to the small groups of which you are a member to discern their existence. The important thing to remember, however, is that satisfactory groups take time to develop. At first, group members may "jockey" for varying positions in the network, thus changing its form. Once the group is established, however, the particular pattern of communication should become of little consequence. The group's time can then be used to complete a project or to solve the problem at hand.[21]

---

[21] For a more complete discussion of communication networks, see B. A. Fisher, *Small Group Decision Making: Communication and the Group Process*, 2d ed. (New York: McGraw-Hill, 1980); and J. Luft, *Group Processes: Introduction to Group Dynamics*, 3d ed. (Palo Alto, Calif.: Mayfield Pub. Co., 1984). Portions of this discussion were adapted from these sources.

ANALYZING SMALL GROUP INTERACTION

The explanations and guidelines presented in this chapter will, we hope, help you participate more fully and effectively in small groups. One way to apply these principles is to observe group interaction. We should now be able to recognize characteristics of effective and ineffective small groups by examining group goals, member participation, types of listening and feedback, group roles and styles of leadership.

Groups are often evaluated based on the outcomes and products the members produce. Group membership can be beneficial to some and detrimental to others. Alcoholics Anonymous is beneficial to a person who attends and never drinks again. The Humane Society may be seen as unsuccessful when animals have to be put to sleep because they are not adopted.

Groups are also evaluated based on what actually takes place during a group interaction or meeting. During the 1970s, Bales and Lashbrook developed quantitative (number and amount of member participation) and qualitative (evaluation of a member response in terms of benefit to the group) methods to analyze group interaction. Their guidelines are still used today to evaluate group effectiveness.[22]

For example, Figure 7–4 shows a five-member group with ten possible channels of communication (or an all-channel network). Using Lashbrook's method of group analysis, the lines among the group members represent group members' ability to respond (verbally and nonverbally) back and forth. Donald can initiate a conversation with Kathy just as easily as he can with Larry, Janice, or Wayne. By examining the number of times a person speaks, you can evaluate factors such as leadership style, member participation, roles, and so on. The small slashes on the lines in Figure 7–5 indicate the number of times each person spoke to another member during a specified period.

If this were a family trying to decide where to go for a vacation, who do you think would have the most say? Probably the parents. In Figure 7–5, you'll notice that more communication is directed to Donald than to anyone else. We could assume that he is the father and that Janice is the mother. What would you guess about Kathy, Larry, and Wayne? Maybe Larry is the oldest child, because he interacts more than Kathy and Wayne, or maybe he is more assertive than they are. We might guess that Wayne is a small child or baby since no communication is directed to or from him.

---

[22] Guidelines for group evaluation can be obtained from the following sources: E. M. Bodaken, W. B. Lashbrook, and M. Champagne, "Proana 5: A Computerized Technique for the Analysis of Small Group Interaction," *Western Speech* 25 (1971), 112–15; R. F. Bales, *Personality and Interpersonal Behavior* (New York: Holt, Rinehart & Winston, 1970); R. F. Bales and S. P. Cohen, *Symlog: A System for the Multiple Level Observation of Groups* (New York: The Free Press, 1979).

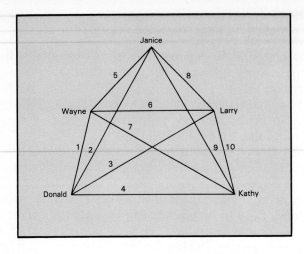

FIGURE 7–4
Channels of communication
in a five-member group

If this were a business meeting, we might assume that Donald was the designated leader or chairman of the board. We could also guess that his leadership style is authoritarian. We would probably be concerned that Wayne did not participate, but he may have another function (for example, recorder, trainee). Much can be assumed from these simple diagrams. However, it is often important to determine the quality as well as the amount of interaction.

Decisions about the quality of communication are based on a number of factors. It is important to know whether the group's purpose serves a social or task function. For example, if the group meets socially to celebrate a member's birthday, then no one would expect organized, purposeful conversation. On the other hand, if a group meets with a specific goal, then the functions of group members are important. A group of surgeons deciding which patient will receive an eye donation would need to get to the point

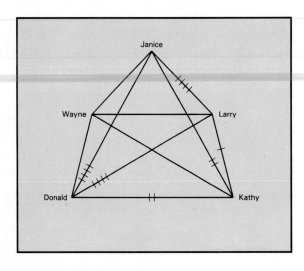

FIGURE 7–5
Number of times group
member spoke

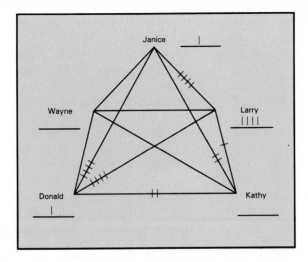

FIGURE 7–6
Diagram to determine
productive group members

immediately without sharing the tales of their latest golf game or fishing expedition.

When observing a group that is task oriented, we need to be aware of member functions. Does a member tell a joke just to get attention or to release tension? We also need to observe types of listening behavior and feedback. Do members listen to what is being said, or do they go off on a new tangent each time they speak? When a group is involved in brainstorming, are members accepting of others, or do they (verbally and nonverbally) chastise others for "far out" suggestions? Diagrams can be used to determine which members are most productive or meet group goals.

Figure 7–6 includes a space for interactions that are not beneficial to the group. For example, if Larry started talking about a song that he wrote when the group was assigning duties for a dance marathon to fight muscular dystrophy, he would not be adding to the group purpose and would be involved in nonpatterned interaction. A slash would be drawn beside his name and not on the line between members because he didn't add useful information or respond to a comment from another member.

SUMMARY

It is almost impossible to exist independently of all groups. Understanding the group process can help you get more out of your participation in groups. As a participant in a group, you have certain responsibilities. These include keeping an open mind to all ideas, showing sensitivity to other members, communicating ideas, opinions, and information as accurately and honestly as possible, using appropri-

ate questions when necessary, and doing all the homework or preparation required.

It is also helpful to be able to analyze the role structures, norms and outcomes that function in your group. Attention to the norms that develop will enable you to determine which of these are beneficial to the group and which are counterproductive. To further increase productivity, you and the other group members should assume various task-oriented roles, including information or opinion giving, information or opinion seeking, expediting, contributing ideas, and analyzing. These kinds of actions keep the discussion on course and aid the group in accomplishing its objectives.

You should also be concerned with the emotional behavior of the group. Concern for the social and emotional climate of the group is shown when members assume maintenance roles, which include active listening, game leading, harmonizing, gatekeeping, compromising, and "fronting" for the group. Indifference to the group and its goals often results in self-serving roles, which can obstruct the group's progress. Although each member in the group has his or her individual role to play, effective group interaction does not take place automatically. The group must go through several stages of development, including groping, griping, grasping, grouping, and group action.

Although some people seem to be good leaders by nature, specific leadership skills can be learned. Good leaders tend to have skills in the areas of personal behavior, communicating, equality, organization, and self-examination.

The three basic styles of leadership are democratic, authoritarian, and laissez-faire.

When approaching a problem, it is usually best to follow an orderly sequence to arrive at the best possible solution. Problems of fact, value and policy can all be discussed by groups, but it is extremely important for the group to understand the agenda, which is based on John Dewey's pattern of reflective thinking. These steps are defining the problem, limiting the topic, analyzing the problem, establishing criteria or standards, suggesting possible solutions, checking individual solutions against all the criteria, carrying out the solution, and evaluating the effect of the solution on the problem.

Cohesion can be the key to effective group discussion and action. Groups that are not cohesive often fail to solve problems effectively. Loyalty and allegiance are fostered in cohesive groups. Conflict can destroy cohesion in a group, but at times it may also contribute to more effective results. It is the responsibility of all group members, not just the leader, to deal with conflict in an objective and reasonable manner. Conformity, when it is not forced, is very desirable, since consensus is one of the objectives of the group process.

Finally, the type of communication network in place in a given small group can affect overall performance. Highly centralized networks are more accurate when solving relatively simple problems. More complex problems are best addressed by less centralized communication networks.

EXERCISES

GROUP EXPERIENCES

Group Roles and Behavior

DESCRIPTION: Task-oriented and maintenance roles in groups are related to the roles people play in life. This activity is designed to explore the relationship between behaviors and roles. If you receive a "behavior" that seems contradictory to a role, try it anyway. They may work together better than you think!

PROCEDURE: Divide into groups of six. Write each of the following behaviors and roles on separate index cards:

Task Behaviors	Maintenance Behaviors
Expediter	Harmonizer
Analyzer	Gatekeeper
Opinion seeker	Public Relations—the front person

Roles

Mr. Garcia: Runs a small grocery store.
Mrs. Garcia: Wife of Mr. Garcia and mother of seven children.
Father Hollen: Priest, and dedicated missionary of his faith.
Dr. Redding: Scientist, winner of several international awards.
Ms. Valentine: Sales manager of Honeywell, Inc.
Elaine Warner: M.D., general practitioner.

Each group member should select at random a role and a behavior. Take five minutes and look up your behavior in the chapter to make sure you understand what it involves. Do not show anyone the cards you selected.

All six members should meet as a group, playing their assigned parts. The problem you face as a group is to decide which two people can leave the island where you are stranded. Only two people may leave, and there is no guarantee that they will be able to send help or that they will reach their destination. For the people who stay on the island, there is plenty of fresh water, but food is scarce. Decide in 15 minutes.

DISCUSSION: Read aloud your role and describe the behavior you were asked to portray. Did you have trouble combining the role and behavior? Did you recognize the roles and behaviors that others were playing? Can you draw any conclusions regarding the relationship between roles and behaviors in groups?

The Power Trip

DESCRIPTION: The distinction between leaders and leadership has been discussed in this chapter. Leadership behavior (any behavior that helps a group clarify and achieve group goals) can be observed on both the verbal and nonverbal levels. This activity explores the relationship between power and influence and, subsequently, power and leadership. During the activity you should pay particular attention to the nonverbal behaviors that communicate influence, power and dominance.

PROCEDURE: Divide into groups of six to eight members. Each group member should be given an equal amount of money. Although many variations are possible at this point, one method is to distribute ten pennies, one nickel, one dime and one quarter to each participant.

Stage 1. For the first five minutes of the exercise, group members should be instructed that they may give some, all, or none of their money away to other members. However, during this time period they may not physically take money from another member. (A distinction is made between "taking" money and "receiving" money.) This means that they may not take money from any player, but they can accept money that is given to them.

Stage 2. The second stage of this exercise is the "taking" period. During the next five minutes, group members are instructed that they may "take" money from any group member, but they may no longer give money away. (This part of the exercise may become very lively, because group members may forcibly try to take money from a resistant member. This is an anticipated part of the exercise.)

Stage 3. At the end of the second five minutes, group members are told to stop and count the money they have. The group member who has accumulated the largest amount of money then becomes the group leader. All the members of the group must give the group leader their money so that the leader then has all the money for the group.

Stage 4. The leaders from each small group now come together to form their own "power" group. Their group members can stand around them and give them advice during the rest of the activity, but their group leader may not respond verbally to the comments.

Stage 5. Stages 1 and 2 (five minutes of giving, five minutes of taking) are repeated for the group leaders.

Stage 6. Each group leader should count the final amount of money collected. Each leader can decide whether to keep the money or to distribute it in some manner to the fellow group members. The decision of each group leader should be verbalized and carried out.

DISCUSSION: Now here is an interesting question: Is the person with the most power likely to be the leader? How are we persuaded to entrust other people with leadership authority? Is the use of money realistic and meaningful as a source of power? Is "power" a characteristic of a leader?

To Lead or Not to Lead

DESCRIPTION: The three types of leadership styles—democratic, authoritarian, and laissez-faire—are explored in this activity. The democratic leader guides rather than directs the group; the authoritarian leader is more directive than the democratic counterpart; the laissez-faire leader does not direct the group at all. In the following activity you will have an opportunity to experience the effects of all three types of leadership.

PROCEDURE: Divide into groups of six to eight members. The group should identify one person to play the democratic leader, one person to play the laissez-faire leader, and one person to play the authoritarian leader. The leadership should rotate every five minutes so that all three leaders have an opportunity to direct (or not direct) the group. Each group should select a task, such as planning a hike, a dance, a clean-up project for the city, or a recycling project.

DISCUSSION: After 15 minutes, each group should evaluate (1) its task orientation and (2) its social dimension (cohesion) during each type of leadership. Which type of leadership provided a balance between the task orientation and the social dimension? Did any particular type of leadership promote either the task orientation or the social dimension? Which type of leadership do you prefer? Why? Under which conditions would each of the three types of leadership be effective?

Questions As Feedback

DESCRIPTION: Questions can be a valuable source of feedback when they are used appropriately. Questions involve a matter of choice in terms of timing and the nature of the question itself. Sometimes a lack of questions can leave many issues unresolved in the minds of group members. This activity should help to make you aware of the appropriate use of questions of fact, value and policy.

PROCEDURE: Divide into groups of five to seven members. There are two parts to this activity. The first part is to be done individually. Complete the "situations" given below by providing an example of a question of fact, value and policy. After each group member has completed the situations, you should engage in a discussion to compare responses. The following situation and responses are offered as a sample.

> *Sample Situation.* A group member's parent has recently passed away. Sandy suggests that a large arrangement of flowers be sent to the funeral home. Richard suggests that the money would be better used if it were sent to the American Cancer Society. Carol, somewhat concerned about the decision, suggests that the decision be postponed until all members are present.

Question of fact: What is meant by "large" in reference to an arrangement of flowers?

Question of value: Why the American Cancer Society? Why not another organization that has a broader appeal?

Question of policy: Should all members be asked to contribute a given amount of money, even if they do not support the final decision?

> *Situation 1.* Michael was named as chairman of his department's picnic committee. Fulfilling his role as an authoritarian leader, Michael decided that the picnic should be held at a nice park that had good athletic facilities. In addition, he stated that it would cost $50, leaving $20 in the fund for the next six months. He pointed out to the committee members that the decision was entirely in the hands of the committee and was not subject to a vote by the student body. What questions of fact, value and policy should be asked to clarify the issues?

Situation 2. Richard is sitting around with a group of old college friends, trying to plan a five-year reunion. The group is having difficulty locating the addresses of approximately 20 of the 200 classmates. Don suggests that they place an advertisement in the newspaper to attract these people. Carol and Sandy respond that it would be a waste of money and that the reunion should be planned with the 180 people for whom addresses are available. What questions of fact, value and policy should be asked to clarify the issues?

DISCUSSION: Compare your responses with those of the other members of your group. Do you feel that in some cases a specific type of question is more appropriate? For example, is a question of fact more appropriate than a question of policy in a given situation? What are the repercussions for the group when questions are not asked? Do questions of fact, value and policy help the group communication process in terms of clarifying its goal?

How Do You See the World?

DESCRIPTION: Decision-making discussions often break down because the participants do not understand the nature of the questions being raised. A breakdown may also occur simply because each member is viewing the problem from a different perspective. A specific example is when one member argues an issue from the basis of factual information, another from a value position, and another from the basis of policy. Although these three perspectives can be integrated in the discussion process, they may often hinder effective discussion when members refuse to acknowledge the existence of another perspective for viewing the problem or issue. This activity will demonstrate how a breakdown of communication can occur and will suggest alternative methods for avoiding and resolving breakdowns of a similar nature.

PROCEDURE: Divide into groups of five. Each participant should be given one of the roles described below. The audience should be informed as to the context of the situation but, if possible, should not be informed of the individual roles. The context of the situation is as follows: The student government has decided to take some type of action relating to off-campus housing. A subcommittee has been given the mandate (1) to determine if unfair and discriminatory practices by landlords against students exist and (2) to suggest a plan of action to bring problems to the attention of the community. The following roles should be assigned to the participants:

Person A: You are a laissez-faire leader for the discussion group. You see your role as primarily one of observing and repeating what is happening and recording notes for the group.

Person B: You are concerned with facts and facts only. Before you commit yourself to resolving this problem, you will need to know if there is a problem. Examples of questions you might ask include, "What are the landlord–tenant regulations?" and "What is meant by 'unfair' or 'discriminatory' practices?" Do not argue issues unless they involve sound facts that you can relate to. Always bring the discussion back to the facts that are either known in this case or need to be determined.

Person C: You are concerned with attitudes, morals and values. "Are students justified in not paying rent when they feel that they have been treated unfairly?" "Does society have a right to treat students differently from other people who rent apartments?" Consider all issues from the humanistic point of view by raising questions of justice and injustice. Do not allow yourself to be pulled off these grounds during the discussion.

Person D: You are concerned with policy issues. "How much time and energy should be devoted to this problem relative to other pressing issues in student government?" "What authority do we have as a subcommittee to recommend or carry out particular solutions?" "Are there events in landlord–student discrimination that have already set a precedent?" In order to both ask and answer the type of questions you raise, you will need information based on facts and values. Probe the other discussion members to determine which issues are important to them. Find out how you can use their information to answer your questions.

Person E: For the first five minutes of this discussion, you should ask questions for clarification, to determine whether you understand the other points of view. After that point, urge committee members to discuss separately each kind of issue that arises. Try to direct the decision-making process so that all issues are fairly but distinctly considered.

DISCUSSION: Did Persons B, C, and D continue to discuss separate issues of fact, value and policy? If they did, you probably had an opportunity to see how the decision-making process breaks down. If each participant is discussing the same problem, but from a different perspective, it is unlikely that an acceptable resolution of the problem will be reached. Was Person E effective in convincing committee members to resolve issues of fact, value and policy separately? If so, did this help the decision-making process? How can a discussion leader avoid the problems that result from trying to argue, simultaneously, issues of fact, value and policy?

Group Discussion Contest

DESCRIPTION: This activity will provide you with an opportunity to either observe or participate in a group that uses a standard agenda for solving problems in a logical and objective manner. In this activity the group will be given a time limit to move through all the stages of discussion. In natural group discussion settings, it is unlikely that you would see a group move through all stages during one meeting, since most groups progress through the stages over longer periods of time. This activity can be considered a "speeded-up" version of a group engaged in a problem-solving task.

PROCEDURE: Divide into groups of five to seven members. Half of the groups should be observers, the other half participants. The following instructions are written for (1) the problem-solving groups and (2) the observation groups.

INSTRUCTIONS FOR PROBLEM-SOLVING GROUPS.   You have 40 minutes in which to discuss a problem from Step 1 through Step 8. The eight stages include

Step 1: Defining the problem
Step 2: Limiting the topic
Step 3: Analyzing the problem
Step 4: Establishing criteria or standards for possible solutions
Step 5: Suggesting possible solutions
Step 6: Checking the individual solutions against all established criteria
Step 7: Carrying out the solution
Step 8: Evaluating the effect of the solution upon the problem

Prior to the discussion, each member should have a thorough understanding of these steps. In addition, a problem area, such as downtown parking, low-income housing, quality of education, or medical services, should be selected by your group. Your 40 minutes officially begin *after* you have selected the problem area. Your primary task is to systematically evaluate the problem, using the steps just listed, in order.

INSTRUCTIONS FOR OBSERVATION GROUPS.   The purpose of your group is to observe how effectively and efficiently the problem-solving group goes through the eight stages of problem resolution. In addition, you should observe leader emergence, group cohesion, and conflict resolution among group members. Focus your observation on the following questions, in addition to other questions that you feel are important:

1. Did the group discussion cover all eight stages of problem solving?
2. Was any stage either dismissed or given too much time? Why?
3. During which stage in the problem-solving task did you observe (a) leader emergence, (b) group conflict, and (c) group consensus?
4. What criteria would you use in determining whether the group was effective in its problem-solving task?

DISCUSSION: At the conclusion of the 40 minutes, each problem-solving group and its observation group should meet together for a 15-minute debriefing period. The observation group should have approximately five minutes to report its findings. The problem-solving group should then have an equal amount of time to respond to the observations. Finally, both groups should reach a consensus regarding (1) the effectiveness of the group discussion, (2) the identifiable leaders in the group, and (3) the efficiency with which the group proceeded through the eight stages of problem solving.

PERSONAL EXPERIENCES

1. Attend a group meeting for the first time. Keep your participation to a minimum as you observe the task-oriented and maintenance behaviors used by other group members. Pay particular attention to whether members maintain the same role or change roles. Do any patterns emerge? For example, is one group member consistently a blocker when dealing with another member?

2. Pick a task-oriented or maintenance role that you can play in a group that you have been part of before. Carefully study the behavior you select so that you can consistently display your chosen role. Following the meeting, ask other group members to respond to your behavior in the group. Then explain your experiment to the other group members so that they can understand what you did and why.

3. Select a group to observe for 30 minutes. While you are observing, apply the criteria you think are important for an effective group discussion. Then answer the question, "To what extent was the group effective during its discussion or problem-solving task?" After you have answered this question, reevaluate your criteria and make any revisions you feel would be appropriate.

4. Select a day during which you can observe your personal decision making. As you watch yourself making decisions, ask yourself the following questions: Which problems could be better resolved by a group than by an individual? What types of decisions do I usually seek advice on? When do I feel the need to share my decision making with another person?

5. Watch a television program that involves a lot of decision making (for instance, a detective program). To what extent were the decisions affected by (a) an authoritarian leader, (b) group pressure, or (c) a democratic or laissez-faire leader?

Group Discussion

1. How do you distinguish conversation from discussion in your everyday life?
2. How does bypassing affect the group process?
3. What distinguishes someone who exhibits leadership behavior from a leader?
4. In your opinion, to what extent is group pressure to conform in decision making instrumental, as contrasted to group pressure to carefully evaluate the evidence and options? Consider various types of decision-making groups, such as a jury, a senate subcommittee, and social groups.
5. Why is it important to understand the distinction between questions of fact, value and policy in reference to group discussions?
6. Under what conditions would the three types of leadership (democratic, laissez-faire, and authoritarian) be most effective? Consider various types of groups, such as a shipwrecked crew, a dance committee, and a jury.
7. Think for a moment of the groups of which you're a member, and see if you can identify the communication networks that characterize them. Are those networks the most appropriate ones, given the nature of the task at hand? If not, which network might be most effective?
8. Why is it important to analyze small group interaction? Consider differences between quantitative and qualitative analysis.

8 Organizational Communication

KEY CONCEPTS AND TERMS

Organization
Division of labor
Power center
Substitution
Interdependence
Coordination
Mutual benefit organization
Business organization
Service organization
Commercial organization
Coercive organization
Utilitarian organization
Normative organization
Formal communication structure
Informal communication structure
Channel
Immediacy
Series transmission
Leveling
Sharpening

Assimilation
Network
Downward communication
Upward communication
Lateral communication
Informal network
Manipulator
Exploiter
Hustler
Professional
Networking
Interview
Employment interview
Appraisal interview
Exit interview
Directive interview
Non-directive interview
Business conference
Formal presentation

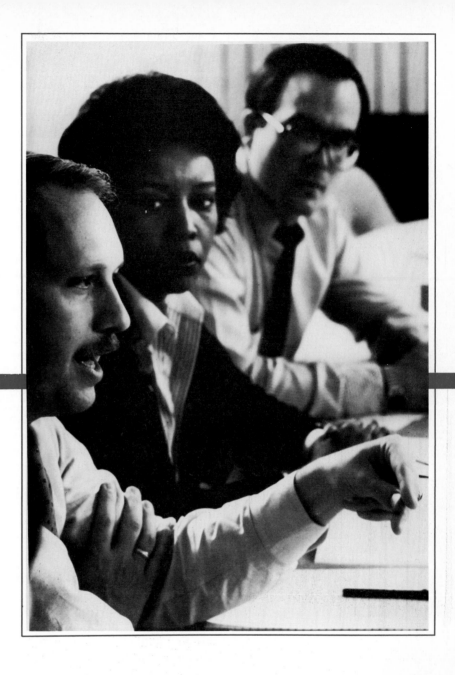

As Jane scurried down the corridor, past the door to the auditorium, she overheard the chief executive officer (CEO). His voice was unmistakable—booming and intense—and now legendary at Madison Securities. Unable to resist the temptation, she opened the door, ever so slightly, and saw the CEO giving his annual report to the company's stockholders. Like clockwork, he was making his usual glowing remarks about the company's employees. Jane smiled and whispered the words "most valuable resource" in unison with him as he got to that part of the speech. He often used those words to describe his staff—and always seemed to mean them.

That is why Jane and others were surprised when the CEO called a meeting of his staff one month later on a Monday morning. His meetings always were held on Friday afternoon after his usual round of golf. As Jane listened intensely to the CEO's unusually quiet voice, she knew that something was amiss. Then it hit—those bitter words that no one expected. The company was cutting the staff by 20 percent. As Jane looked around the room at the faces of her colleagues, she could gauge nothing less than shock. Why had last month's message to the stockholders told such a different story?

Executives and managers all across the nation are often guilty of sending mixed messages. Mixed messages are those in which separate messages go to different audiences, one audience hears two different messages, or one's words contradict one's actions.[1] Although the use of mixed messages is not limited to serious situations such as that described above, they breed mistrust and reduce motivation in all communication contexts.

In short, effective communication is the key to success in any organization or workplace. In fact, research indicates that people with more highly developed communication abilities tend to be found at higher levels in the organizational hierarchy and tend to be promoted more often than people with less developed communication abilities.[2] Any job you take, whether as an attorney, construction worker, manager, salesperson, minister, psychiatrist, teacher, or patrol officer, requires the ability to communicate. This chapter is designed to help you understand communication in organizations and to provide you with guidelines for securing and maintaining a professional position most suitable to your needs.

WHAT IS AN ORGANIZATION?

In Chapter 7 you learned that a group consists of three or more persons with a common goal and the potential for interaction between members. You also found that you are a member of five or more groups simultaneously. Now you may be wondering if these groups are also organizations. Not necessarily. **Organizations** are defined as collected groups of individuals constructed and reconstructed to strive for specific goals that could not be met by individuals acting alone. Although there are similarities in our definitions, an examination of five characteristics of organizations should help explain the differences between casual and organized groups.[3]

---

[1] V. McClelland, "Mixed Signals Breed Mistrust," *Personnel Journal* 66, no. 3 (1987), 26.

[2] B. D. Sypher and T. E. Zorn, Jr., "Communication-Related Abilities and Upward Mobility: A Longitudinal Investigation," *Human Communication Research* 12, no. 3 (1986), 420–31.

[3] J. E. Baird, *The Dynamics of Organizational Communication* (New York: Harper & Row, 1977), 15.

CHARACTERISTICS OF ORGANIZATIONS

Organizations are characterized first by **_divisions of labor_** and responsibility that help to facilitate specific goals. One goal of Delta Airlines, for example,

Interdependence is essential to effective organizational communication.

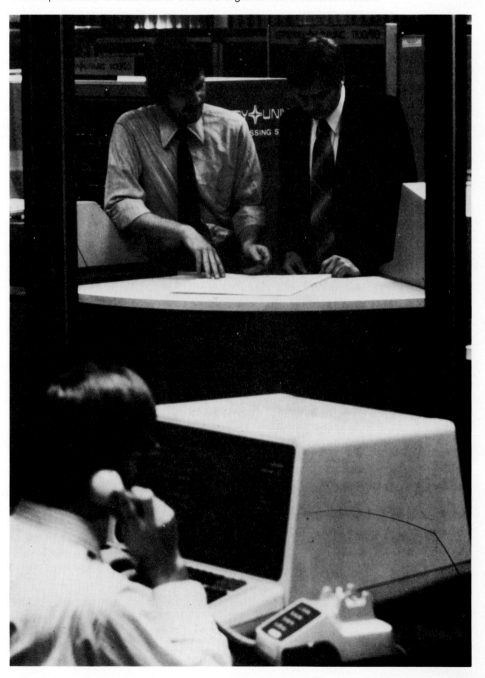

is to provide transportation. By flying, a casual observer can easily identify major departmental divisions, such as reservations, ticketing, baggage, and personnel. The divisions or departments are created to help the organization perform more efficiently. As the size of the organization increases, so does the number of necessary departments.

A second characteristic of organizations is the presence of one or more *power centers.* Top individuals review and direct organizational control and leadership. If the baggage department manager at Delta gets complaints from several passengers about lost luggage, then it is the manager's responsibility to locate the source of the difficulties and make the necessary improvements.

Third, organizations are characterized by ***substitution*** of personnel. People who retire, are fired, accept promotions, move to other companies, or take leaves of absence must be replaced so that the organization will continue to function properly. If a passenger is injured because a flight attendant fails to give instructions about the proper use of safety equipment, the attendant may be fired or placed on probation. As a result of this decision, someone else would now be needed to fill this position.

Interdependence among organizational components is a fourth characteristic of organizations. Departments don't act in isolation, and the performance of one department affects the performance of all other departments. You may have a tight schedule in making a connecting flight from Atlanta to Boston, and as you receive your boarding pass, the ticket agent may inform you that the flight will be an hour late. That would make it impossible for you to make your connecting flight to Boston. Although you appreciate the fact that the mechanic found a faulty wing structure before takeoff, this discovery affected you and the decisions of many others in the Delta organization.

Fifth, organizations are characterized by ***coordination*** among their components. Coordination is made possible in an organization by different channels of communication, such as word of mouth, phone calls, and letters. To make sure that a flight takes off at the appropriate time, passengers must be ticketed, ground crews have to service and load the aircraft, pilots and navigators must be informed of their destination, mechanical functions of the plane must be in operation, and the control tower must radio that all is clear.

Another important characteristic of organizations is organizational structure. ***Organizational structure*** is created when individuals systematically interact with one another.[4] When the marketing department at Apple Computer meets to discuss the effectiveness of its latest Macintosh campaign, the members of the group rely on organizational roles, norms, and rules established through communication. An unorganized group of people getting together for dinner will assume different roles and responsibilities, based on the goals of the host, the mood of the group, and interpersonal interactions.

---

[4] R. D. McPhee, "Formal Structure and Organizational Communication," in *Organizational Communication: Traditional Themes and New Directions,* eds. R. D. McPhee and P. K. Tompkins (Beverly Hills, Calif.: Sage Publications, 1985), 149–78.

The structure of an organization is reflected in its current annual report, employee manual, organizational chart, and policies/procedures. These descriptions tell employees about the organization, including its values, norms, and formal rules. (*Note*: Informal rules of conduct are generally un-written—more later). Additionally, these documents allow the organization to address its communication patterns directly.[5]

From this discussion you have probably identified differences between social groups and organized groups, even though social groups often possess one or more characteristics of organizations. In your family, for instance, a childhood responsibility might have been helping with the dinner dishes, mowing the lawn, or washing the family car. Your parents or older brothers and sisters probably shared one or more power centers. Your family may have used substitution of personnel by adopting a child or marrying someone, and some family members may have been "fired" through divorce. The differences between groups and organizations lie in the purposes for which organizations are constructed and in repetition of interaction. Now that you have a clearer understanding of organizational characteristics, we will examine the types and functions of organizations.

TYPES OF ORGANIZATIONS

You may already have an idea about what type of organization you would like to work for or with after graduation, but before making a final decision, you should examine organizational goals and power structures. By examining organizational goals, you will be able to determine who benefits most from membership. For instance, in a ***mutual benefit organization*** the members get the most out of participation. Mutual benefit associations include political parties, professional organizations, labor unions, private country clubs, and religious/fraternal organizations.

In a ***business organization*** the owners receive the greatest benefits or profits. Examples of business concerns are banks, hotels, retail stores, insurance companies, restaurants and public utilities. Clients usually receive the most benefits from ***service organizations.*** Civil rights groups, hospitals, schools, social work agencies, reformatories, and mental health centers are classified as service associations. Finally, there are ***commercial,*** or ***common-wealth, organizations,*** which are designed to serve public interests. Commercial associations include law enforcement agencies, post offices, public transportation systems, city recreational departments, the armed services, and educational radio and television stations.

Another way to classify organizations is by examining their means of control. This approach was formulated during the 1960s by Etzioni and still has pertinence today. In his now classic book, *A Comparative Analysis*

---

[5] R. D. McPhee, "Organizational Communication: A Structurational Exemplar," in *Re-thinking Communication: Vol. 2, Paradigm Exemplars*, eds. B. Dervin, L. Grossberg, B. O'Keefe, and E. Wartella (Beverly Hills, Calif.: Sage Publications, 1989). For a summary of literature concerning this characteristic, see S. W. Littlejohn, *Theories of Human Communication*, 3rd. ed. (Belmont, Calif.: Wadsworth, 1989), 243–46.

of Complex Organizations, Etzioni classified organizations as either coercive, utilitarian, or normative.[6] A ***coercive organization*** uses force over its members as a major means of control. Prisons, custodial mental health centers, and governmental dictatorships are examples of this type of organization. The Nazi concentration camps' primary method of control was coercion. A ***utilitarian organization*** controls its members through wages earned, advancement potential, tenure, and reward. Examples of utilitarian organizations are industries, business unions, and farmers' cooperatives. Some organizations also have internal, organized groups (labor unions), which attempt to provide greater rewards and benefits. In states that have right-to-work laws, labor unions provide benefits for all employees, not just those who are members of the union. This is one reason why labor groups are against right-to-work legislation. Finally, a ***normative organization*** controls the actions of its members through compliance with social norms. Members usually think about what ideas should be implemented to benefit society as a whole. Religious, political and voluntary organizations fall into this category. Many religious groups, for example, try to ban X-rated and other controversial movies from theaters because they feel that the effects will be detrimental to society.

It is difficult to classify an organization as having only one goal and power structure. Most organizations have combinations of goals and power centers. For example, the American Red Cross has mutual benefit, service, and commercial goals while having both utilitarian and normative power structures. During university blood drives, donors help others and themselves with plasma donations. The Red Cross determines where the blood is sent, at what cost, and when it will be used. Whatever its goal and power structure, it is important for you to understand what type of organization you join and to be aware of communication channels and networks in the organization.

COMMUNICATION DIMENSIONS IN ORGANIZATIONS

Think for a minute about the different organizations and businesses you've come in contact with in the last week. Now try to remember all the different channels of communication you used to get your message across to others. You may have called the power company to have electricity turned on, written a letter to a personnel director to ask about a summer job, told a salesperson nonverbally that you are just looking and don't want any help, or ordered a hamburger and french fries over the intercom at a fast-food restaurant drive-thru.

You can probably think of a variety of other situations, but now focus your attention on the internal workings of an organization. How do companies communicate with their employees and customers? Organizations have structured ways of operating efficiently. At a supermarket, for example,

---

[6] A. Etzioni, *A Comparative Analysis of Complex Organizations* (New York: Free Press, 1967), 31–67.

a sign over the door reads "Customer Satisfaction Guaranteed." A customer gets home with a carton of milk and finds that it is sour. The customer returns the opened carton to a cashier, who refunds the money and tells a supervisor, who, in turn, tells the dairy manager, who tells the assistant store manager, who notifies the general store manager about the spoiled product. All organizations have divisions of power to make sure that everything functions smoothly. To help you better understand communication in organizations, the next section will examine the functions of communication in organizations, formal and informal communication structures, channels of communication, and communication networks.

Functions of Communication in Organizations

Communication in organizations takes various forms. According to Koehler, Anatol, and Applbaum, communication serves either an (1) informative, (2) regulatory, (3) persuasive, or (4) integrative purpose.[7]

THE INFORMATIVE FUNCTION   Both employers and employees in an organization need an enormous amount of information in order to function efficiently. Essentially, they need information about (1) the job itself, including information focusing on the organization's goals, procedures, and rules; (2) organizational success, such as benefits, profits and work standards; and (3) the socioemotional state of the organization as a whole.

THE REGULATORY FUNCTION   Communication also acts as a means of control and regulation for the organization. This type of communication usually takes the form of orders, perceived expectations, and company restrictions. Also, this type of communication proceeds from the top of the organization in a downward flow. Its content is usually task related.

THE PERSUASIVE FUNCTION   Closely related to the regulatory function of communication is the persuasive function. This is usually reflected in interpersonal compliance-gaining interactions and is ordinarily in the form of face-to-face requests and personal interactions.

THE INTEGRATIVE FUNCTION   Communication in an organization also acts in an integrative capacity, operating to give the organization unity and cohesion, and identity and uniformity. Included are the coordination and scheduling of activities, the establishment of provisions for channeling information and authority, and the recruitment and training of employees.

Formal and Informal Communication

Messages that are sent through organizations may be classified as formal or informal. As we mentioned earlier, an organization's *formal communica-*

[7] J. W. Koehler, K. W. E. Anatol, and R. L. Applbaum, *Organizational Communication: Behavioral Perspectives*, 2d ed. (New York: Holt, Rinehart & Winston, 1981), 8–10.

tion structure functions through rules, regulations, and procedures, and is characterized by more "formalized" channels of communication (see Figure 8–1).

At most universities, for example, students must petition for grade changes. Students first go to their instructor, the instructor then goes to the department chair, the department chair sends a memorandum to the dean of academic affairs, the dean sends notification to the records department, and the records typist finally notifies students about appropriate grade changes. Failure to properly follow the steps results in confusion, no grade change, and, ultimately, no action through the normal channels. Other organizations work similarly, with office workers reporting to supervisors, supervisors reporting to managers and so on.

On the other hand, the *informal communication structure* of an organization is created wherever and whenever people meet and interact.

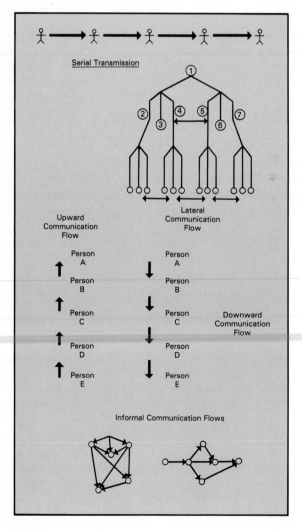

FIGURE 8–1
Networks showing the various flows of communication

An informal communication structure.

It emerges on its own from interpersonal relationships within the organization.[8] Social groups such as the water cooler crowd, the coffee lounge gang, or the lunch-hour jogging crew do not appear on any organizational chart; however, they serve at least eight vital organizational functions:

1. They provide employees with a sense of belonging, security, and recognition.
2. They provide a way for employees to discuss their concerns in an open, friendly manner, thereby reducing stress and pressure.
3. They maintain a sense of personal integrity, self-respect, and free choice.
4. They facilitate formal communication.
5. They provide an informal network of interpersonal and group communication.
6. They provide an opportunity for social interactions.
7. They can be a source of practical information for managerial decision making.
8. They can produce future organizational leaders from within the ranks.[9]

In short, formal and informal communication structures work like the blades of a pair of scissors. Without both, an organization could not function effectively. The following section will explain how channels are used specifically

---

[8] P. E. Han, "The Informal Organization You've Got to Live With," *Supervisory Management* 28 (1983), 25–28.
[9] Adapted from P. E. Han, "The Informal Organization You've Got To Live With," *Supervisory Management* 28 (1983), 27–28.

to disseminate information in both formal and informal communication structures.

Communication Channels in Organizations

Organizations are linked through a series of communication **channels.** The Bell Telephone System would have consumers believe that the telephone is the most effective channel of communication, when, in actuality, that organization uses face-to-face interaction, letters, memoranda, and computerized messages to get information to others. Communication channels are often taken for granted, and we usually use the channel that is most economical and convenient. Currently, in order to save time, many people use the telephone to check facts like product prices, locations of businesses, and whether or not an establishment stays open on weekends; in the past, many people hopped into their cars and actually drove to the business in question.

According to organizational consultant Roger D'Aprix, however, "the oldest (and best) way to communicate" within a given organization may be face-to-face, even if corporate presidents and supervisors have to leave executive suites and dining rooms to make contact with employees. As he argues, executives in large, modern organizations have isolated themselves in order to preserve their time and busy schedules. In so doing, however, they have forgotten that leadership does not exist in a vacuum. Leaders must "see and feel what their followers are experiencing; otherwise they become literally out of touch."[10] To illustrate, would you be more likely to vote for a candidate who placed a flier on the windshield of your car or one who knocked on your door asking for your vote? Would you be more responsive to a form letter requesting your presence at a court hearing or to a uniformed policeman with a subpoena?

Thoughtful consumers and organizations are becoming more aware of how channels affect the reception of messages. The channels we use to transmit messages send cues to receivers about how sources view the receiver and the message.

How the message is sent affects its degree of **immediacy,** or the degree of liking or disliking for a person or task. For example, rather than having to face a boss, an employee might write a letter of resignation. The employee uses a less immediate channel of communication to avoid a personal confrontation. Channels of communication can be ranked in degree from the most to the least immediate.[11]

1. Face-to-face
2. Picture phone
3. Telephone

---

[10] R. D'Aprix, "The Oldest (and Best) Way to Communicate With Employees," *Harvard Business Review* 60 (1982), 32.
[11] A. Mehrabian, *Silent Messages,* 2nd ed. (Belmont, Calif.: Wadsworth, 1981).

4. Interactive computer

5. Telegram

6. Letter

7. Direct intermediary

8. Leaked rumor through an intermediary

As mentioned in Chapter 1, the most immediate channel of communication is face-to-face interaction. With face-to-face communication, participants are concerned with verbal as well as nonverbal behaviors, and receive direct feedback, which allows decisions to be made more quickly than with other channels. A customer who returns a camera in person is notified immediately that the camera will be repaired or replaced or that the money will be refunded. The use of picture phones also allows for verbal and nonverbal exchanges, but differences lie in the mechanical nature of the communication and in the power each person has to disrupt the communication process. The president of the textile company may use a picture phone to tell the personnel department that a hundred people must be laid off. Instead of listening to and watching the negative reactions, the president may then quickly sign off.

The next most immediate media include telephones and interactive computers. With the telephone, listeners attend to verbal and vocal cues, but there are no visual messages. Conversely, using interactive computers, communicators send and receive visual/verbal messages, but do not have the benefit of vocal cues. With telegrams and letters, we are even one more step removed. Nonverbal messages and direct feedback are eliminated with these two message forms. Because telegrams arrive more quickly than letters, however, they are considered more immediate. The immediacy of a letter is determined by whether or not it is handwritten, typed by the source, or typed by an intermediary. Job applicants feel more encouraged when a recruiter sends a hand-signed letter of acknowledgment rather than a signature-stamped form letter.

An ***intermediary*** is a messenger between the source and the receiver. When a direct intermediary is asked to deliver a message, immediacy is decreased because most of the original message is altered by the messenger. The least immediate communication channel is a leaked rumor through an intermediary. The message can be intentional or unintentional. An executive accountant, for example, may tell local freight lines in passing that the Internal Revenue Service will inspect the books of shipping companies in the near future, in hope that the companies will be prepared. Other information is leaked inadvertently, as when employees overhear news about promotions, new policies and personnel shortages and tell other employees before official notification is given.

Most communication in organizations occurs in a series. **Series transmissions** take place through a number of individuals who first act as receivers and then as transmitters of messages to others in the organization. Difficulties arise when intermediaries transmit messages inaccurately. How many times have you had to explain what you actually said when your message was taken out of context by someone else? For example, telling a friend that you don't want to go to a party could be misinterpreted to mean that you don't like the people giving the party. In fact, you might be tired, have an exam, or have other plans. Similar serial transmission problems often occur in organizations.

Research has shown that messages are distorted in one of three ways: leveling, sharpening, or assimilation. **Leveling** minimizes or omits information that may be important. For example, employees may say that they take only 15-minute breaks, when they actually take 20- to 30-minute breaks. **Sharpening** magnifies some details of the message. A secretary who overhears that there could be layoffs if production doesn't pick up might tell other secretaries that they are going to be laid off. The third and most important method of distoring messages is **assimilation.** When people assimilate, they transform messages to fit personal attitudes and expectations. Managers often ask assistant managers to give suggestions to new employees about selling techniques. The new employees could take the message as reinforcement or condemnation depending on their perceptions of the manager's and the assistant manager's motives. A desire for consistency in our attitudes and beliefs makes awareness of assimilation particularly important. Consistency of attitudes will be discussed more completely in Chapter 10.

NETWORKS

Channel selection and organizational network usage affect communication effectiveness. **Networks** are the interconnected channels or lines of communication used in organizations to pass information from one person to another. The flow of communication operates in downward, upward, lateral and informal networks (Figure 8–1).

Downward networks direct information messages to subordinates. Messages include job instructions, individual evaluation (feedback), organizational procedures, training, and company-directed propaganda. Downward communication is solicited by employees who want feedback about their job performance, similar to the ways students seek results from tests, papers, and projects. Problems occur when information doesn't filter down to appropriate organizational levels. In addition, messages are often distorted and disrupted before they reach lower levels of the organization. For example, information may become distorted when the word "leaks out" that a company is planning layoffs, or when the chairman of the board is abruptly asked to resign by the board of directors.

Because downward communication is also seen as potentially threatening to employees, "open" communication between supervisors and subordinates becomes essential to organizational effectiveness.[12] For example, when a supervisor calls and asks you to come to her office, you usually feel

[12] For a more complete discussion of this topic and the variables that dictate decisions regarding "open communication," see E. M. Eisenberg and M. G. Witten, "Reconsidering Openness in Organizational Communication," *Academy of Management Review* 12, no. 3 (1987), 418–26.

anxious because you are unsure of what issues are involved (job evaluation, promotion, and so on). Top management officials should also be selective in choosing the types of messages sent to subordinates. A personnel director who calls departmental meetings every Monday morning for the same pep talk will eventually be tuned out. Employees get bored with redundant information and tend to listen more carefully when meetings are scheduled only when necessary.

Upward communication is another network used in organizations. Managers need to encourage subordinates to send upward communication freely because it is an important indication of how effective downward communication has been. Since managers and superiors control the rewards of their employees through promotion, salary increase, or tenure, upward communication is offered cautiously by subordinates. Just as students refrain from criticism about courses and instructors until their grades have been posted, employees hesitate to criticize because they are afraid that what they say may influence their upward mobility. Through upward communication, however, subordinates can keep their supervisors informed of trends, incidents, changes and feelings. Additionally, by sending communication upward, they can inform supervisors of actual and potential problem areas— as well as opportunities for cost savings and increased output.[13] The most useful way to improve upward communication, however, is by developing trust in the organization. With interpersonal trust at all hierarchical levels, employees feel free to comment both positively and negatively without fear of reprisal, and this freedom builds cohesiveness.

Lateral, or *horizontal, communication* takes place between peers at the same hierarchical levels. Intralevel communication coordinates departments and increases emotional and social bonding between peers. Lateral communication often acts as a substitute for upward and downward communication in organizations. Although lateral communication is essential, it becomes dangerous if it replaces other communication networks. For example, employees may complain among themselves about an assembly-line inspector who doesn't check safety equipment, when more would be accomplished by skipping this level and using upward communication. The more communication there is between superiors and subordinates, the more likely it is that jobs will be completed on time. Without proper supervision, many employees lack the discipline and motivation to continue performing at high levels. It is interesting to note that subordinates talk more to those above them than to those below them. One reason for this is that people are trying to make a favorable impression on those at higher levels to ensure promotions and raises in the organization.

As was stated earlier in this chapter, other unstructured, *informal networks* exist in organizations, of which the "grapevine" is the most popular. The grapevine was once thought to be characterized by disorganized, poorly defined lines of communication, when evidence actually reveals that grapevines operate quickly and more accurately than formal lines of communica-

---

[13] T. Halatin, "Upward Communication," *Supervisory Management* 27 (1982), 7.

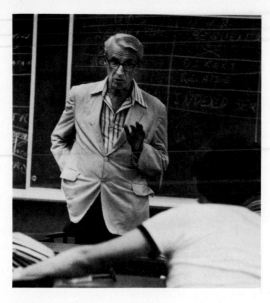

A classroom situation can use both upward and downward communication channels.

tion. In fact, some studies have shown the grapevine to be 80 to 95 percent accurate, with the inaccuracy usually taking the form of incomplete, rather than wrong, information.[14] During periods of excitement and insecurity, the grapevine becomes exceptionally active. For example, the installation of word processors in a secretarial pool may be perceived as a threat to overall job security. At times such as these, the grapevine will buzz with activity, and should be fed by managers with accurate information to keep the situation from getting out of hand.[15] Should the situation become explosive, the results could be poor employee relations, decreased production, and employee layoffs.

> The boundaries of all human organizations are defined and limited by the reach and efficiency of their communication networks.
>
> Otto Lerbinger

PROFESSIONALISM AND THE ORGANIZATION

The first part of this chapter examined organizational communication and the networks that exist in the organizational setting. We now turn to a consideration of professionalism in organizations. This section will examine how people relate in organizations (in other words, employee styles), as well as "office politics," and the concept of networking. In addition, we will address the importance of personal appearance. Upon completion of

[14] V. D. Arnold, "Harvesting Your Employee Grapevine," *Management World* 12 (1983), 25, 28, 37.
[15] Ibid., 27.

this section, we hope you will have a clearer understanding of professionalism in the organizational setting.

Professionalism

What is a professional? A professional may be the punter for the Dallas Cowboys, the president of the Exxon Corporation, an FBI agent, a CBS newscaster, an editor in a publishing company, a criminal lawyer, or a physical therapist. All professionals, no matter what their line of work, have one common characteristic: commitment to their jobs. Although new employees see themselves as professionals, it is often difficult to maintain a professional attitude. Climbing the ladder of success requires an understanding of how employees' styles, office politics, and networking affect communication and professionalism in organizations.

EMPLOYEE STYLES. Successful managers realize the importance of interpersonal trust and high morale in effective communication systems. Managers at all organizational levels must try to increase subordinates' feelings of individuality and self-esteem. Chapter 2 discussed differences in communicators' styles of language, and this chapter will look at differences in how various people relate to others in the organization. Employees are viewed as manipulators, exploiters, hustlers, managers, or professionals.[16]

Manipulators are individuals who seek to control people and events. Some clever methods they employ to get what they want include using scapegoats (intermediaries accomplish tasks so that if they fail, they—not you—take the rap), passing the buck (saying that someone else should do the work), or using self-effacement (pleading ignorance, sickness, or ineptness so that someone else will do the task). Barbara has worked for a prestigious magazine for three years. She tried an advertising campaign that failed, but now she wants to persuade a new employee to try it again so that she can receive the glory if it is successful. If the new employee fails, this time she won't look bad.

The goal of the *exploiters* is personal gain or profit. They usually live in the future and see opportunity as their big chance. Exploiters communicate in terms of lies that might be true. Exploiters sometimes come across as pioneers (seeing opportunities everywhere), record setters (first is best, more permanent, and more successful), or simplifiers (giving exactly what someone wants to gain).

Another communicator style is that of the *hustler*. Hustlers are usually gifted compromisers who win over others through cleverness, wit, and charm. You could imagine a hustler trying something like psyching ("I'm mentioning it to you first, because you're the type we can trust") or documenting evidence

---

[16] T. Frank and D. Ray, *Basic Business and Professional Speech Communication* (Englewood Cliffs, N.J.: Prentice-Hall, 1979), 111–14.

("Look what happened last year; if we don't invest now, we'll lose even more").

Unlike exploiters, manipulators and hustlers, the ***professional's*** main goal is to help others "find themselves" and reach their fullest potential. The professional is adept at social exchange and communication. Professionals characteristically trust others because they trust themselves. Also, they give and accept objective appraisals, decentralize authority and responsibility, take risks on people's abilities, believe in constructive work, find pleasure in others' successes, see others as potential leaders, and recognize others' need to be stimulated.[17] Most of us have one or more of these employee communicator styles, and each has its appropriate uses; but for overall communication efficiency, we should strive to act as professionals.

OFFICE POLITICS.   We've all heard statements like: "She got the job because her father is a golfing buddy of the president," "He didn't deserve a promotion, but the top brass were snowed," or "There's no need to work hard, it's all political anyway." Like it or not, office politics do exist, and many bright, highly capable people fail at jobs because of their inability to cope with the situation. Professionals succeed by adapting to office politics and by establishing a power base that will allow themselves and others to function effectively. Such a power base may be developed by emphasizing and/or expanding your level of expertise—and by creating liaisons with individuals who have access to pertinent information. Additionally, professionals can develop positive feelings and perceptions of relevant others, such as staff members and superiors. A third means of establishing a power base involves maximizing credibility with significant others. This not-so-difficult feat may be accomplished by joining outside professional groups from which one may receive recognition and support.[18]

However, once a power base is established, the professional must develop a set of strategies for implementing ideas and change—often the heart of success in any organization. Virginia Schein, a noted consultant in the area of organizational development, suggests use of the following ten "power" strategies for overcoming office politics and implementing change:

1. *Present a nonthreatening image to others.* Learn the repertoire of acceptable arguments and highlight those aspects of your proposal that are most pertinent to your organization.
2. *Diffuse opposition by bringing out conflict.* Inviting criticism and open discussion can enhance the process of organizational change. Doing so also allows you to keep up with your opposition and monitor resistance.

---

[17] A. Maslow, *Eupsychian Management: A Journal* (Homewood, Ill.: Richard D. Irwin and Dorsey Press, 1965), 17–33.
[18] Adapted from V. E. Schein, "Organizational Realities: The Politics of Change," *Training and Development Journal* 39 (February 1985), 37–41.

3. *Align with a powerful other, if possible.* Gaining management approval is another way of acquiring power and getting ideas off the ground.

4. *Develop liaisons* that maximize information flow and interactions with significant others.

5. *Trade-off* short-term goals for long-term changes. By solving a small problem for someone else, you will enhance your stature and set the stage for your ideas. In this way, "credit" can be cashed in later on projects in which you are interested.

6. *Strike while the iron is hot.* Follow up successful implementation of an idea with a request for approval to expedite a somewhat less popular program in which you believe.

7. *Conduct the necessary background research* in order to implement an idea successfully. Information is power. Additionally, it enhances credibility and esteem.

8. *Use a "neutral cover."* Associate your idea with an already approved and noncontroversial companywide program (that is related). Then, build on the similarities that exist between that program and your more controversial idea.

9. *Inch along.* Begin with small changes and then "inch along" to more expansive aims. Avoid taking an "all-or-nothing" stance.

10. *Know when to withdraw.* If you find yourself competing with someone who you know is incapable of succeeding, an unusual strategy is to withdraw openly and abruptly from the competition. If your hypothesis is correct about the competition, "higher-ups" may later come to you to implement change. (*Note*: This option may not be possible in many situations; however, it can be effective, given the appropriate circumstances.)[19]

Networking

A third vital dimension of professionalism is reflected in the concept of **networking,** or the process of developing and using contacts for information, advice and support.[20] Male members of organizations have used informal networks for years to promote themselves professionally. These networks have taken the form of social clubs (like country clubs), civic organizations (Kiwanis clubs, for example), and athletic groups.[21] Recently, however, women have taken networking one step further. As researchers DeWine and Casbolt have noted, women have deliberately formalized the activity by establishing "freestanding networks"—networks that link women with other women—in an attempt to expand organizational contacts. The major objectives of such networking activities are fourfold: (1) to provide women with

---

[19] Ibid., 37–41.
[20] Adapted from M. S. Welch, *Networking: The Great New Way for Women to Get Ahead* (New York: Harcourt Brace Jovanovich, 1980), 15.
[21] S. DeWine and D. Casbolt, "Networking: External Communication Systems for Female Organizational Members," *The Journal of Business Communication* 20 (1983), 57–58.

opportunities to make organizational contacts, (2) to provide successful role models for women, (3) to generate solutions to problems, and (4) to effectively disseminate information.[22]

Whether you are male or female, just getting started or well underway in a professional career, networking with other professionals, both within and outside of your organization, is important. Networking has become an important key to promotion and professional growth in organizations. As such, it is a vital concept to the professional.

PERSONAL APPEARANCE.   Personal appearance has already been discussed in Chapter 4, but its importance cannot be overestimated. First impressions made by professionals serve a public relations function for organizations because appearance sends signals to others about attitudes, feelings and personality. For many years IBM salespeople were required to wear dark suits or dresses, which stereotyped them as conservatives. Most companies no longer have stringent dress requirements for their employees, but clothing remains an important aspect of an organizations's image. Thus, appropriate appearance is necessary for upward mobility within an organization. Observing people in higher management positions will indicate what attire is considered appropriate. When deciding what to wear to your first job interview, it would be a good idea to find out how others dress who work in the position for which you are applying. Regardless of your size or sex, clothing should be coordinated in terms of color, line, texture, and style.

COMMUNICATION SITUATIONS

As a professional, you must be aware of the various communication situations in organizations. From what you have read thus far, you may think that succeeding in an organization involves little more than getting along with others and understanding office politics. While interpersonal relationships are important, the most important form of communication for upward mobility is the formal, structured communication in an organization. The three most common structured communication situations are the interview, the business conference, and the formal presentation.[23]

The Interview

If you have answered survey questions for a public opinion firm, tried to get information from a local politician about foreign policy, answered questions when applying for a job, or talked about job preferences with a career planning counselor, you have participated in an interview. *Interviews* are the most common form of planned communication and are often defined

---

[22] Ibid.

[23] R. A. Vogel and W. D. Brooks, *Business Communication* (Menlo Park, Calif.: Cummings, 1977), 4–5.

Gaining pertinent information is one major goal of employment interviews.

as "a process of dyadic communication with a predetermined and serious purpose designed to interchange behavior and involving the asking and answering of questions."[24] Although interviews take place for a variety of purposes and in a variety of situations, we are most concerned with interviews in organizations.

TYPES OF INTERVIEWS.   There are several different types of interviews, each requiring its own skills and offering its own benefits. During an ***employment interview,*** the employer tries to gain as much pertinent information about the applicant as possible. This kind of interview is usually broad in scope, dealing with all areas of the interviewee's background and personality. The interviewer wants to find out about the applicant's work history, work habits, ability to relate to others, health and other areas not covered extensively in the résumé or application form. Interviewees, however, do not become merely answer-producing machines. They have their own interests in mind and ask about things such as the working situation, benefits, salary and opportunities. Thus, information is given and sought by both participants.[25]

In most companies employees are given ***appraisal interviews*** on a regular basis. In such an interview the worker's past performance and future potential are discussed. The discussion may cover a variety of topics, such as salary, job improvement, outside schooling, or physical health. The objective is clear—to let employees know how they are doing, where they need

---

[24] C. J. Stewart and W. B. Cash, *Interviewing: Principles and Practices*, 3rd ed. (Dubuque, Iowa: Wm. C. Brown, 1983), 5.
[25] For a more complete discussion concerning preparation for job interviews, see Appendix A.

to improve job performance and where they are headed. If conducted properly, appraisal interviews also let employees know that their employer cares about their work and their well-being.

When employees plan to leave their jobs, they are often given an *exit interview,* which is designed to find out how they feel about the company, the working environment and other job conditions. The company can use this information to assess itself and make changes where necessary.

APPROACHES TO INTERVIEWING.   Be it an employment, appraisal, or exit interview, the participants can adopt one of two possible communication strategies: directive or nondirective. As interviewer in a *directive interview,* you must have not only a general plan of what you wish to accomplish but also a step-by-step outline to follow. Although this type of interview has the advantage of being thorough, it may be so abrupt and impersonal that the interviewee is uncomfortable. As the following dialogue illustrates, when you are a directive interviewer, you use frank, matter-of-fact questions, which gives you complete control over the discussion:

Interviewer: (Manager of men's store with opening for salesperson) By looking at your résumé, I can see you already have experience in the retail business. What exactly did your job entail at the department store?

Interviewee: At first I was at the register, but later I waited on the customers and wrote out sales slips.

Interviewer: What did you enjoy most about the job?

Interviewee: I like people and especially helping them out. So, I really enjoyed giving them some help with their purchases and answering any questions they had.

Interviewer: Is there any particular reason for your leaving the job?

Interviewee: Since the store was so large, it was sort of impersonal. I want to work in a smaller place where I can deal more with the customers. The department store is often self-service.

Interviewer: Do you have any plans beyond salesperson?

Interviewee: Yes, I hope to advance to store manager some day.

In a *nondirective interview,* although you have a plan and purpose in mind, you give interviewees a great deal of leeway in their responses. This kind of interview is not entirely unstructured, however. If an interviewee strays from the subject, he or she is redirected back to the topic. The conversation may run freely, but the major points are developed by the interviewer. The disadvantage of this approach is that you may not obtain all the needed information. The advantage, though, is that an informal atmosphere relaxes the interviewee, encouraging him or her to speak freely. Here is an example of a nondirective exit interview:

Interviewer: John, I'm sorry to see you leave, but I hear you have a good job offer.

Interviewee: Yes, B&G Steel Company is looking for a foreman.

Interviewer: So, tell me all about it.

A business conference.

Interviewee: Well, I'll be managing about fifty people and getting a lot more money. This will help the problems with the family.

Interviewer: Problems?

Interviewee: Yeah, you know how it is with two teenage kids . . . braces, sports, and school supplies. I liked this job and I really don't want to leave, but I didn't see any chance of promotion. And I couldn't wait any longer. Oh, and the new place is located pretty close to home, so I don't have such a long drive. The car is getting pretty run down, and just last week I thought it was a goner—couldn't start it up for hours!

Interviewer: You said you liked your job here. Why?

Interviewee: Well, the fellows in the shop are friendly, and the shop foreman is a good guy.

This sample shows both the strengths and weaknesses of the nondirective interview. Although the interviewee certainly feels relaxed, the interviewer has learned a lot about his personal problems but relatively little about working conditions at the shop. The ability to communicate effectively can obviously pay off in an interview situation. Other aspects of interviewing will be covered in greater detail later in this chapter when we discuss steps in securing your first professional position.

The Business Conference

After you join the work force of an organization, the business conference will be your most frequent formal communication interaction. The **business conference,** or small group discussion, usually involves five to ten people who interact about organizational concerns. Meetings are usually designed to disseminate information or to develop solutions to current organizational problems. A union spokesperson may explain to a small group of unionized

Video teleconferencing is widely used as a method of formal communication for nationwide and multinational corporations.

automotive-employee leaders the latest features of their negotiated contract, while management personnel get together to discuss methods of dealing with union demands. The business conference is essential to every organization, and the principles presented in Chapter 7 concerning small group communication should provide information to help you participate more effectively both as a group member and as a group leader.

The Formal Presentation

The most structured form of organizational communication is the *formal presentation.* The responsibility is placed on one person to create interest and to motivate the audience to listen. The speaker transmits a message orally with the aid of visual and audiovisual materials. A young architect showing a proposal for a new community sports arena to more established architects in the firm will carefully plan a verbal presentation explaining benefits, square footage, energy conservation features, space usage, costs, and so on, including visual aids to ensure clarity and receptivity of the message.

As an employee, you may be asked to explain new organizational policies, teach other employees about the proper use of technical equipment through demonstration, attempt to persuade employees to accept new ideas, and try to motivate employees to greater productivity. Individuals in organizations are unique, and you must understand them before preparing a message to meet their needs. Chapter 9 explains methods of audience analysis that should make your job easier. For a formal presentation you will also be concerned about your delivery, types of communication purposes, organization of messages, and how to secure the information to be included in your presentation. Careful consideration of the principles in Chapters 10, 11 and 12 should improve your formal presentation ability.

Visual aids can be an informal part of a formal presentation.

SUMMARY

Organizations are groups of individuals constructed and reconstructed to strive for specific goals that could not be met by individuals alone. Organizations differ from groups in their division of labor, presence of one or more power centers, substitution of personnel, interdependence, and coordination among organizational components. Organizations are also characterized by repetitive interaction.

Although organizations have characteristics in common, their goals differ. The Exxon Corporation is a business organization with the goal of making money, while a service organization such as the Humane Society helps animals, without concern for profit. Methods of control also differ among organizations. Coercive organizations (such as prisons or reformitories) use force to keep order, whereas utilitarian organizations control their employees

through wages and benefits. Finally, normative organizations control the actions of their members through expectations of compliance.

Related to the types of organizations and to the form of communication they stress are the functions of communication. Communication serves four major purposes in any organization: information exchange, regulation, persuasion, and integration.

These four communication functions are brought about through formal and informal communication structures. The formal structures function through organizational rules and regulations, while the informal structures function through interpersonal relationships among employees. The importance of a message within the organizational structure determines the immediacy of the channel used, with important messages being delivered through oral channels, either alone or in combination with written channels.

Networks are the channels or lines used to transmit messages from one person to another. Communication networks operate in downward, upward, lateral, or informal networks. Because of the serial nature of communication in organizations, information is often distorted by leveling, sharpening, or assimilation.

After you have familiarized yourself with an organization's communication patterns and structures, it is important for you to understand professionalism and its role in the organization. Professionalism increases job satisfaction and productivity. Understanding the effects of employees' styles, office politics, networking, and personal appearance should improve communication in organizations.

Employees communicate with others as manipulators, exploiters, hustlers, or professionals. Knowledge of office politics should help remind you to select group affiliations carefully. Professionals succeed by establishing a power base and developing a set of strategies for implementing ideas and change.

Networking is also a valuable tool for professionals growth in organizations. Networking involves the development and use of contacts for information, advice and moral support. Likewise, maintaining a "professional" personal appearance contributes to others' perceptions of you as a professional.

Office politics is usually part of the informal communication structures, but for upward mobility, the formal, structured situations are most important. The most common formal communication situations are interviews, business conferences, and formal presentations. Knowing what to expect and which guidelines to follow should help you perform effectively.

EXERCISES

GROUP EXPERIENCES

Organizational Networks

DESCRIPTION: Organizations use a variety of networks to communicate with employees. Supervisors use downward communications to give instructions. Subordinates send upward communications to complain about working conditions. Peers communicate laterally to establish interpersonal bonds, and at times everyone communicates at once in haphazard informal networks. Networks are essential for interdepartmental coordination, but networks are often used inappropriately. This exercise is designed to provide experience in dealing with communication networks within organizations.

PROCEDURE: Divide into groups of five to seven persons. Within the groups come up with a topic that could be used in the four communication networks. For example, each network is used in training programs in which new employees are instructed on the proper use of copying equipment, regulations, and so on. After the groups decide on topics, get group members to line up in rows (like a train). Exchange topics between the groups. With downward communication, the first person in the row should pass detailed instructions through channels until they reach their proper destination: person seven. (No feedback should be given, and all communication must move downward.) Next, divide the row into groups of two to three persons and discuss the message laterally; but again, remember that no interactions should take place with others in the chain. After a few minutes, form the rows again and send upward communication about the initial interaction. Finally, let members discuss the topic with whomever they wish.

DISCUSSION: Which communication network was the most satisfactory? You probably found that each situation contained unique problems. What problems were encountered with the networks? When would the use of one network be most effective? How could organizations improve their internal communication? What organizational network would you like to work in when you graduate?

Getting a point across first requires getting the group's attention.

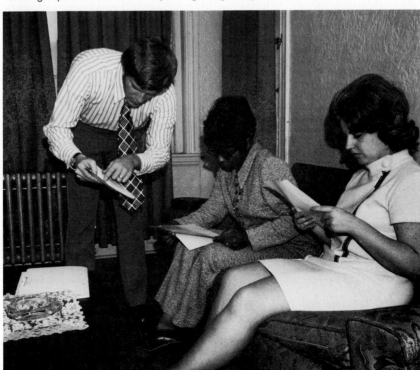

Conference Compatibility

DESCRIPTION: One of the most important formal communication situations within an organization is the conference. Interaction patterns during conferences are affected by the purpose of the meeting, the methods of control during the meeting, the group membership. This exercise shows how people participating in conferences affect conference outcomes.

PROCEDURE: Divide the class into male and female groups of five to seven people. Select a controversial topic that encourages active discussion (such as sexual freedom, the Equal Rights Amendment, or homosexuality). Each group should discuss the topic for five to ten minutes. Finally, change groups so that there is only one member of the opposite sex per group; again discuss the selected topic. After the second group discussion, have each member choose the group in which he or she felt most comfortable.

DISCUSSION: Share individual group selections with the rest of the class. What differences were there between the first and second group interactions? Why were there differences? How was the atmosphere affected by different-sex participants? How did your responses change with different group members? What does this exercise tell you about organizational conference effectiveness?

PERSONAL EXPERIENCES

1. Find a local organization to observe for one day. Try to analyze the formal and informal communication structures. Determine the purposes and power structure of the organization. How would you fit into this organization? What kinds of office politics would you have to avoid? After you've decided whether or not you would feel comfortable in this organization, make a list of personal criteria that organizations must meet to satisfy your needs.

2. Set up an interview with someone in middle management in an organization. During the interview, ask that individual to discuss the concept of professionalism from his or her point of view. What is a professional? What behaviors does he or she elicit? What examples does this person give of nonprofessional behavior? Then, examine your behavior in light of the talk you've had. How do you see your own behavior? How could you improve?

DISCUSSION QUESTIONS

1. How can organizations improve their formal and informal communication structures?
2. What communication channels exist in organizations, and what role does immediacy play in their effectiveness?
3. How are messages distorted within an organization's structure? Formally? Informally?
4. Why is it important to understand office politics?

9

Ethics, Intentions, and the Speaker-Audience Relationship

KEY CONCEPTS AND TERMS

Public speaking	Value
Public communication	Instrumental values
Ends-justifies-means approach	Terminal values
Social utility approach	Casual audience
Credibility-centered approach	Passive audience
Speech to inform	Selected audience
Persuasion	Concerted audience
Speech to entertain	Organized audience
Audience analysis	Polarization
Demography	Social facilitation
Belief	Circular response

J amie had worked on her presentation for weeks. Her head virtually reeled as she put down her pen and wearily glanced out the window that overlooked the bay. As she watched the distant sailboats bobbing lazily on the water, she imagined herself dressed in her new red suit—making a splash with her boss and the other advertising executives who would be present. How could she lose? Her ideas were fresh; the facts and figures impressive. "At last," she said out loud, as she reached for her favorite chocolates, "everything has fallen into place."

The next day Jamie rose, showered quickly, and threw on her clothes. As she turned, she caught a glimpse of herself in the full-length mirror. "Ummm . . . ," she purred, "now go out there and knock their socks off." With a danish in one hand and her briefcase in the other, she dashed out the door and headed down the steps toward the car. Between bites, she practiced her opening lines . . . then the statistics that would provide the foundation for her entire presentation.

Upon arriving at the office, Jamie quickly disposed of her purse and headed down the long, austere corridor that led to the conference room. The expensive, Titian artwork that lined the walls reminded her of the illustration she would use about halfway through her "act." As she entered the room, everyone turned to greet her. Jamie smiled and made a point to address each person who was present by name.

At last, after the joking and laughter subsided, Jamie began her well-researched presentation. Knowing that teasing and off-color jokes characterized the beginning of all such presentations, she launched into a slightly "blue" story designed to make the transition. As she finished with the punch line and a devilish grin, she felt her smile melting and a silence descend on the room. Attempting to recover from the icy stares, she moved awkwardly but swiftly to the first major argument of the presentation.

As Jamie moved from point to point—attempting to captivate the others at every turn, the only feedback she received was a coolness that virtually permeated the air. Feeling slightly nauseous as she made her closing remarks, Jamie realized the fatal error she had made. Her research had been brilliant—her ideas beyond compare. But she had lost her audience at the outset by trying to be "just one of the boys."

As you can see from the above illustration, public speaking involves more than simply preparing a message. This form of communication also involves an ability to analyze your audience as well as to adjust a given message to its overall purpose. To aid you in learning how to succeed at these two tasks, this chapter focuses on a variety of topics ranging from the general purposes of a message to audience analysis. Additionally, you will discover some of the ethical responsibilities that you have as a speaker and the moral dilemmas that you may encounter along the way. Upon concluding this chapter, it is hoped that you will be well on your way toward success in public-speaking settings. At the very least, we hope that you can avoid situations such as the one Jamie got herself into.

PUBLIC COMMUNICATION: AN OVERVIEW

Communication theory is relatively new, but the study of public speaking dates back to ancient Greece, when Aristotle and his contemporaries defined and practiced the principles of rhetoric. While these principles still provide the foundation of public speaking theory, modern styles of public speaking and public speaking situations are much less formal than they were in Aristotle's time. Even in our own relatively relaxed culture, however, public speaking situations can intimidate people who are usually very talkative and outgoing. Although public speaking includes many of the same communication skills as other speaking situations, some who are comfortable in small group communication feel anxious and experience stage fright in a public setting.

Perhaps these difficulties arise because **public speaking** differs from other forms of communication in two ways. First, a public-speaking situation includes two distinct and separate roles: speaker and audience. Second, in this speaker-audience relationship, the speaker carries more responsibility for the communication interaction than does the audience. In other communication situations, speakers and listeners exchange roles and share this responsibility.

A public-speaking situation need not be overly formal and imposing; it doesn't necessarily require a stage to separate the speaker from the audience. All of us participate in public speaking when we contribute to a class discussion, when we make a suggestion at a staff meeting, or when we tell a story at a party.

Public communication, like other forms of communication, serves several purposes. When a karate instructor gives a demonstration on self-defense, she uses public communication to instruct. When Ralph Nader speaks on the need for better consumer protection laws, he uses public communication to advocate his point of view. The mayor who delivers an annual Fourth of July speech to the townspeople uses the "soapbox" to stir feelings of patriotism. Public communication can also be used to praise and to blame, to accuse and to defend. When a local political candidate speaks to a community group, he may use public communication to blame the current office-holder for everything that's wrong with the community, while the minister who delivers a eulogy at a memorial service uses the same form of communication to praise the deceased. The prosecuting attorney who addresses a jury uses public communication to accuse the defendant of a crime. To accomplish the opposite end, Oliver North used his testimony during the Iran-contra hearings as a means of defending his honesty and actions.

Since public speaking is such a useful tool for accomplishing a wide range of purposes, it is important to clear up some popular myths about speech making. The first is that the ability to make speeches is natural and cannot be learned. While some people do have a talent for it, effective public speaking can be learned through training and practice. Students who take speech courses generally improve their speech-making ability and increase their self-confidence.

Effective public speaking depends on content and delivery. Contrary to popular opinion, good intentions are not enough when it comes to making a speech—they do not guarantee an effective presentation. Although someone may have something valuable to communicate, the message will be lost if the delivery is poor. Another misconception, however, is that it is not what you say that is important, but how you say it. The most eloquent delivery cannot save a meaningless message. Both content and delivery are important in achieving effective communication.

Finally, effective public speaking requires that the speaker be respon-

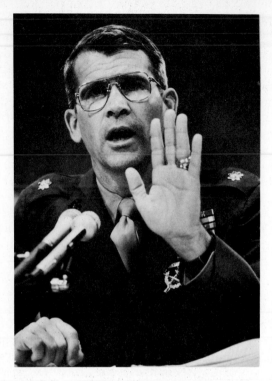

Oliver North successfully used public communication to advocate his point of view.

sible for the message he or she presents. Although people who "speak their minds" are often praised for their stamina and courage, the effective speaker knows that, by virtue of gaining the opportunity to speak, she or he also acquires the chance to influence others. Reckless, irresponsible, or unethical speakers can cause great harm both to the members of the audience and to subsequent decisions they might make.

We turn now to one of the most important statements concerning public speaking: An effective speaker is one who begins with a sense of responsibility. Once we have considered the nature and implications of this statement, we may return to a discussion of the overall purposes of public speaking—to inform, to persuade and to entertain.

ETHICAL RESPONSIBILITY AND THE PUBLIC SPEAKER

It would be naive to believe that all speakers possess the morality and good intentions included in Aristotle's concept of ethos. One need only study the persuasive tactics of someone like Hitler to be reminded that public communication can be used for evil as well as good. While ethical problems in communication are most often thought of only in a persuasive context, they apply to informative speaking as well. The student of communication must consider the ethics involved in all public communication.

Think for a moment about the nature of American politics today. Party candidates clash both between and within their ranks, and independent candidates clash with proponents of both. Although such "openness" is not inherently negative, speakers of one group often hurl insults at members of the opposing groups, and the recipients of these insults often respond in a similar manner. Because of the amount of time spent in such activities, the issues themselves are overlooked in many instances, and disenchanted voters who are genuinely concerned can do nothing but attempt, with little knowledge or trust, to choose the best candidate for a job.

American politics, however, is not the only arena in which ethics are problematic. In everyday life, ethics, morals and responsibilities are called into question, leaving many to believe that ethical principles should be left to the individual. However, at least four different approaches regarding the bases of ethical behavior exist in this country today. These include the *ends-justify-means* approach, the *social utility* and the *situation ethics* approaches, and the *credibility-centered* approach to ethics and responsibility.[1] Before discussing each of these positions, however, we need a definition of *ethics*. For us, *ethics* will be defined as questions concerning the concepts of right versus wrong and good versus evil; in addition, ethics focus on the nature of moral obligation.

Likewise, before we continue our discussion of ethical approaches, we must understand the nature of rhetorical (persuasive) principles themselves, or the means by which arguments are developed, understood, and critiqued. Principles of persuasion (or rhetorical principles)—like all principles addressing human behavior—are *amoral* in and of themselves. More specifically, they can be used for purposes that are evil or good. When applied to our discussion of the bases of ethical responsibilities, the same principle of amorality again applies. Each of these approaches can be used for right or for wrong. Armed with this understanding, we turn to the four approaches to ethics. As you will see, each approach has its merits and its potential pitfalls.

Ends-Justify-Means Approach

When speakers believe the **ends justify the means** in attaining their goals, they adopt the position that any available means of persuasion may be used as long as the end result is honorable, just, or desirable. As a result of such a belief, however, speakers who take this position may distort the truth, conceal motives, twist reasoning, or make emotional appeals in order to prevent their listeners from making their own rational decisions.[2] The major flaw in this approach to ethics is that the speaker often believes that she or he has either the right or the ability to make such decisions. The wholesale slaughter of innocent women and children during wartime is one instance

---

[1] Bert E. Bradley, *Fundamentals of Speech Communication: The Credibility of Ideas*, 5th ed. (Dubuque, Iowa: Wm. C. Brown, 1988), 48–53.
[2] Ibid., 48–49.

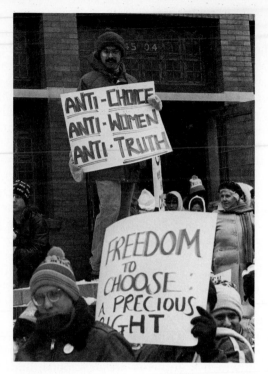

Ethical concerns play a major role in our everyday lives.

in which the ends do not justify the heinous means. In short, if we condone the use of such an approach to ethics, we must also be able to ensure that the end is in fact a good and justifiable end. Thus, it is imperative that the speaker who takes this approach be certain that the aims are justifiable and that the choice of rhetorical strategies is not based solely on the desire to achieve the aims or goals.

Social Utility Approach

When taking a *social utility approach* to ethics, the speaker determines which programs to advocate, based on his or her perceptions of the needs of a particular group. More specifically, he or she addresses two major questions in developing a program or message: (1) What program (or message) would most benefit the target group? and (2) What are the possible effects on other groups involved? If, for example, the president of a college decides that campus beautification is the most important priority, what is the best possible option to achieve that goal? This question would be the first that she would consider. Second, she would need to determine how that decision could affect the needs of other campus groups—for example, groups that advocate the need for faculty raises and stipend increases for graduate teaching assistants.

Situation Ethics Approach

The approach taken by a proponent of **situation ethics** is that consideration must be given to the nature of each individual situation before determining the "best" or "most loving" things to do. As a function of such goals, four factors are usually taken into account: (1) the desired end, (2) the means that are to be used to achieve that end, (3) the motive behind the act, and (4) the consequences of the action.[3]

Although on first sight such an approach seems reasonable and rationale, it can often lead to diverse decisions about particularly complex problems. If lives are at stake, for example, should one share confidential information in order to save them? For some people the answer would be clear-cut; for others, it might not be so clear. In addition, the use of this approach requires both sophistication and objectivity on the part of its user or proponent—a sophistication and objectivity that the speaker may not possess.

Credibility-Centered Approach

The final approach on which we will focus is the **credibility-centered approach.** In using this approach, the speaker comes to the public communication setting with the objective of demonstrating, through particular methods, his or her competence and trustworthiness. As a result, the speaker

1. Constructs a rational basis for argument based on a thorough review of all available information;
2. Presents evidence accurately;
3. Uses sound reasoning;
4. Retains objectivity with regard to groups or organizations with which she or he is affiliated;
5. Gives credit to all sources of information;
6. Stands firm on convictions;
7. Acknowledges when information is incomplete;
8. Avoids oversimplification;
9. Avoids the arousal of emotions on irrelevant bases.[4]

Perhaps this approach to public speaking contains the most effective overall treatment of ethics. However, it is up to the individual speaker to determine his or her own approach to achieving specific goals and objectives—*after* addressing the ethical considerations.

As a nation, we have come to expect politicians to make public prom-

---

[3] Ibid., 50.
[4] Ibid., 52–53.

ises that are all too often forgotten. We are all familiar with the Watergate era, during which high-ranking officials were found to have violated the public trust. We have also witnessed countless advertisements making misleading or exaggerated claims for products and services. We have seen newspapers, television, and radio select which news to report according to their editorial bias. Each of these examples represents an affront to our integrity and our sense of fairness and decency. Yet most of these affronts occur within the limits of the law. It is difficult to propose legislation that would protect our integrity but not infringe upon our basic rights. For example, how can a law govern campaign promises without infringing upon freedom of speech? How can a law determine on what page a particular news story should be printed? Aside from being impossible in a practical sense, the very idea suggests a violation of freedom of the press.

As students of communication, we must remember that ethics are separate from law and are based on our moral, and not our legal, system. It is up to every speaker to examine his or her own ethics and those of the speech before it is presented.

PURPOSES OF COMMUNICATING IN THE PUBLIC SETTING

General Purposes

In order to be successful in a public-speaking setting, you must have a clear purpose in mind: As speaker, you must know whether you intend to inform, persuade, or entertain the listeners. Although these three goals will be more fully discussed in the following chapter, we now take a brief look at each.

INFORMATION EXCHANGE.   The exchange of information is basic to public communication. All of us have participated in this type of communication situation. The *speech to inform* can take place in a variety of locations: on a football field, in a classroom, or in a convention hall. Similarly, the speech to inform can use a number of formats: instructions, reports, lectures and demonstration talks are but a few examples. The coach explaining the strategy and tactics of a particular play informs the team through instructions. The surgeon informs colleagues about a new kidney transplant technique by delivering a report on the subject. Airline attendants inform passengers how to prepare for a sudden emergency by demonstrating lifesaving equipment. All of these examples represent public speaking situations in which the speaker's main purpose is to inform.

Since the informative speaker's goal is to successfully transmit information, he or she must present the information in a way that holds the attention of the audience. Perhaps you can remember teachers who could put you to sleep even though they were talking about a topic that interested you. Or perhaps you have had the opposite experience, in which a professor brought to life a subject you had previously considered fatally boring.

The success of an informative speech depends on how well the material is understood. Even if the audience is motivated to listen and the speaker is dynamic, the final evaluation of success must be based on what was learned by the audience. A brilliant speech on newly discovered subatomic particles can be a failure if the audience cannot understand it.

Therefore, you must organize your speech to aid audience learning and aim for clarity and accuracy in your presentation.

PERSUASION.   The purpose of persuasion is to influence an audience's behavior or way of thinking. The art of persuasion has been a subject of interest throughout history; it is a powerful tool that can be used for both good and evil. In defining persuasion as a means of bringing about behavior change, Aristotle said that a speaker could accomplish his or her end by using logos (logic and reasoning), pathos (an appeal to the emotions), and ethos (proof of the speaker's morality and credibility). We will define **persuasion** as a deliberate attempt by one person to modify the attitudes, beliefs, or behavior of another person or group of people by transmitting a message.

ENTERTAINMENT.   We can define the **speech to entertain** as one that is intended to bring the audience pleasure. Such a speech is usually humorous, or at least characterized by some degree of humor. A humorous speech may be gently amusing or boisterously funny. The effect depends upon the speaker's personality, delivery and brand of humor. A speaker can use exaggeration, sarcasm, witticisms, or burlesque humor when presenting a speech to entertain.

Listeners expend much less effort during a speech to entertain than during an informative or persuasive speech. The very nature of the entertainment speech creates speaker-audience rapport. Usually, such a speech is considerably more informal than other forms of public speaking.

THE SPEAKER AND THE AUDIENCE: AUDIENCE ANALYSIS

Once you have determined your general purpose, it's time to take a look at the audience to whom you are planning to speak. Janet Elsea, president of a successful Washington, D.C., communication consulting firm, divides audiences into four major types: those that "love you," those that "think they are impartial," those that "could care less," and those that "love you not." Because communication focuses on the mutual exchange of meanings, it is important to develop strategies and adjust content appropriately to each.[5]

Audiences that "love you" are those that are friendly and predisposed to you, your topic, or your viewpoint. With these groups, Elsea advises that you use an "open and warm" delivery, including increased eye contact, smiles, gestures, and body movement. She also recommends that you vary

[5] J. G. Elsea, "Strategies for Effective Presentations," *Personnel Journal* 64, 9 (1985), 31–32.

your overall speech rate and loudness—and use examples, illustrations, humor, anecdotes, and personal testimony as supporting material.[6]

Most of us like to believe that we are calm, rational, and objective when, in fact, research indicates the opposite—that is, we generally approach controversial topics with our minds made up. Because audiences *think* they are objective, however, their perceptions should be honored. Thus, when attempting to speak to an audience on a controversial topic, use a delivery style that is dispassionate, even, and controlled. Additionally, focus on facts and figures, expert testimony, comparisons and contrasts as primary forms of evidence. Avoid humor, personal stories, and flashy visual aids, and organize your materials in the most precise and least controversial fashion possible. Finally, allow time for a question-and-answer session.[7]

The third type of audience to which we, at times, must speak is that which could basically "care less." (If you think for a moment, you probably can identify at least one instance when you—yes you—were a member of such an audience.) As a speaker in such a situation as this, your ally is a dynamic speaking style. According to Elsea, dynamic speakers are those who vary their speech rate, loudness levels, movement, gestures, facial expressions, and eye behavior. Additionally, they limit themselves to brief and interesting remarks. Supporting materials that will attract such audiences include the use of humor, cartoons, and anecdotes; interesting visual aids; metaphors; quotations, and startling statistics. Conversely, you will lose an apathetic audience if you stand behind the lectern without moving, pass out reading materials, or use boring overheads. Finally "fewer than three major points" should be the rule.[8]

Audiences that "love you not" represent the fourth type of audience that Elsea identifies. Such audiences look for chances to ridicule you and to spin the situation out of control. To handle this type of audience, remain calm, and speak slowly and evenly. Force yourself to use gestures purposefully and to avoid random movements. Select supporting materials that are data-based and derived from expert testimony. Avoid anecdotes and jokes, for they may anger or irritate your audience. If possible, avoid question-and-answer sessions, but, if they are a must, insist on a moderator, written questions, and a definite time frame. Elsea also suggests that you make a final statement after you have taken the last question.[9]

As you can see, communication in the public setting is much like that in other settings: It too involves both a listener and a speaker. A speaker's ideas, speaking style, and nonverbal behavior are only a part of successful delivery—the listener is equally important. How do you determine what type of audience to whom you will be speaking? The answer lies in the concept of **audience analysis,** or the act of acquainting yourself with your listeners before giving a speech.

---

[6] Ibid., pp. 31–32.
[7] Ibid., pp. 31–32.
[8] Ibid.
[9] Ibid.

> For of the three elements in speech making—speaker, subject, and person addressed—it is the last one, the hearer, that determines the speech's end and object.
>
> Aristotle

Of course, it is impossible to know everything about the members of your audience, but you can aim for a realistic assessment of the overall situation. First, try to learn about those aspects of the audience that will have the greatest effect on its listening behavior. Then, if time and circumstances permit, acquaint yourself with other factors. Let's say that you are going to give a speech on current unemployment problems. It would be more important to learn about the socioeconomic occupational backgrounds of your audience than about its religious affiliations.

Keep in mind that your own attitudes and stereotypes can influence the way you relate to your listeners. You should overcome your biases so that they will not limit your ability to judge how others think and feel.

Remember, too, that people change with time, and so will your audiences. An analysis made several weeks before you speak may not alter drastically by the time you are heard, but some minor changes will naturally occur. Even if you have done a careful job of audience analysis before you walk to the podium, your listeners may change their attitudes *while* you are talking. Prior analysis is only the beginning of understanding and relating to your listeners. While speaking, you must continue your examination, looking for audience reaction to the ideas you are presenting. What clues are your listeners giving you? What are their facial expressions? Are their eyes on you? Are they squirming in their seats, laughing, whispering, applauding? A successful speaker knows how to pick up on such cues, accept them, and then adapt the speech accordingly.

Demographic Analysis

What are the ages of the members of the audience? What is their average salary? Is one sex more represented than the other? What kinds of jobs do the people hold? What is their level of education or religious background? These are some of the questions asked when analyzing the demographic characteristics of an audience. **Demography** is the statistical study of populations. In the demographic approach to audience analysis, specific factual information is recorded upon which probable audience reaction is based.

AGE.   Consider the ages of your audience members when planning your speech. People of different ages like different clothes, listen to different music and have many different attitudes and beliefs. It is hardly surprising, then, that young, middle-aged, and older people react differently as audience members.

Winston Price, a writer of popular songs for all age groups, was often called on to talk about his career and about music in general. His speeches usually resulted in a strong, positive reaction from the audience. One of the reasons for his success was his ability to alter the approach and content of his speech depending on the average age of his audience. When speaking to teenagers, he dealt primarily with "top ten" hits and popular rock groups, but these were quickly put aside when he spoke to senior citizens, to whom he talked about entertainers such as Frank Sinatra, Lawrence Welk, and Guy Lombardo. If Price spoke to an audience composed of all ages, he approached the subject in more general terms, giving examples that appealed to all members instead of a select few.

EDUCATIONAL LEVEL.   Before giving a speech, try to estimate your audience's educational level. This will help you to know what vocabulary, sentence structure, and abstract ideas will be appropriate. Also, it will let you know how many examples and definitions you will have to give in order to be understood. If you speak below your listeners' educational level, they more than likely will not only be bored but will also be angry when they discover they are being patronized. Likewise, if the audience is not as educated as you are, keep the vocabulary and structure of your speech at the audience's level. Too many speakers throw in technical, difficult terms to show how much they know. Your purpose as a speaker is to communicate, not to boost your ego.

Remember, there is not necessarily a correlation between the amount of education your audience members have and their degree of understanding and knowledge of a specific subject. Besides knowing your audience's educational level, you should, if possible, determine the amount of information it already has on the subject you will discuss. Before giving your speech, try to find out whether or not your listeners have done any reading on the

What are some of the demographical characteristics of this audience?

subject, observed it, or perhaps even participated in it. You might want to talk about hang gliding because you went once or twice, but there could be members of the audience who are real pros and could speak more knowledgeably about the sport. Through analysis of your audience's knowledge, you will be able to take advantage of what your listeners already know and give them the additional information they need.

SOCIOECONOMIC STATUS.   Many of your listeners' values and attitudes are based on their economic background, so this aspect should also be taken into consideration when planning your speech. If, for example, you are asked to discuss the school budget for the coming year, a subject that influences tax level, you should be aware of the economic status of your listeners, and the weight of their current tax burden.

Audience members are also influenced by their social background and experiences and by the attitudes and values they have developed. No one can totally escape his or her past. Social background, in fact, is often considered to have the strongest effect on listeners, being more important than religion, age, or sex.

OCCUPATION.   People's occupations often give clues to their educational level as well as to their information on and interest in certain subjects. Although both car mechanics and accountants may be interested in future modes of transportation, the former group would probably be more interested in a new engine part.

Knowing the interests and hobbies of your audience can help you to target them more appropriately.

Different occupational groups may be concerned about different aspects of a topic. For example, postal clerks might want to know how a postal law will affect their present salaries, while publishers may be interested in how the law will influence their mailing costs. Similarly, newspaper editors may be interested in learning the facts about a new superhighway, urban planners about the ways it will change the city's environment, and construction workers about the possibility of new job openings.

SEX.   In the past men and women were often thought to be interested in entirely different things. With the advent of the women's movement and the entrance of women into every field of endeavor, this "obvious" generalization about men and women is no longer appropriate. Some women are not only interested in automobiles but they also race them. Some men are not only appreciative of needlework, but they produce it, too. Therefore, it is harder to differentiate audience interests on the basis of sex than it was in the past.

Nonetheless, the sensitive speaker may still be able to discern meaningful, if sometimes subtle, differences between audiences composed of men or women. For example, as a result of early socialization, males have been taught to listen more for facts, while females have been reinforced for effectively decoding relational cues. As a result, men may often attend more closely to men—and women to their female counterparts.[10] The implications of this difference in listening goals, and overall socialization, is that a speaker may need to take these variables into account. However, you must keep in mind that generalizations are just that—and that there are countless exceptions.

GROUP MEMBERSHIP.   If you are asked to speak to a specific group or organization, such as the Young Republicans or the American Medical Association, you are one step ahead of the analysis game. The groups people belong to give you many clues to their other demographic characteristics. Most clubs or associations have certain guidelines they wish all members to follow—religious groups follow certain moral codes, political associations advocate certain partisan positions, and so on.

Referring to your audience's association in your speech can sometimes create a closer speaker-listener bond. Let's say you are trying to persuade a group of women faculty members at the local community college to support with financial assistance and volunteer service a newly established women's health center. You might draw a parallel between their fierce battle against the college administration for more equitable salaries for male and female faculty members and your own group's attempt to provide good, low-cost health services despite the opposition of the community's medical hierarchy, composed mostly of men. If you are able to identify the group memberships

---

[10] M. Booth-Butterfield, "She Hears . . . He Hears: What They Hear and Why," *Personnel Journal* 63 (1984), 36–42.

Awareness concerning political affiliations is critical to speaking effectively in public.

of audience members, you may gain insight into their attitudes and determine in advance what their reactions will be to your speech.

Psychological Variables

BELIEFS AND VALUES.   According to psychologist Milton Rokeach, *beliefs* are probability statements about the existence of things, or statements about the relationships between an object and another quality or thing. For example, we may "believe in God" or believe that God is omnipotent—the former being a belief in something and the latter being a belief in a quality-object relationship. *Values,* on the other hand, are specific types of beliefs that are central to our lives and act as life guides. According to Rokeach, values may take one of two forms: those that are guidelines for living and on which we base our daily behavior (*instrumental values*), and the ultimate aim or aims toward which we work (*terminal values*). An example of terminal values might be the desire to have a comfortable life. Being ambitious or cheerful is an example of an instrumental value.[11]

Many of our beliefs and values are acquired early in childhood and, although somewhat altered by new experiences, remain the basis of many of our thoughts and actions. As a speaker, you must therefore pay close attention to these elements when analyzing your audiences. As we mentioned

---

[11] Discussion adapted from S. W. Littlejohn, *Theories of Human Communication*, 3rd ed. (Belmont, Calif.: Wadsworth, 1989), 90–91.

earlier, you can appeal to an audience's values in order to persuade them to accept your point of view; but in order to achieve this end, you must be sensitive both to your own value structure and to that of the members of your audience. You must seek out the common ground that will give clues to their value structure. Let's suppose that you are going to talk to the Veterans of Foreign Wars about capital punishment, but you do not know their basic convictions. Before delivering your speech, you could read recent newspaper and magazine articles about the VFW's reaction to present-day political issues. From these you would be able to infer some of their basic beliefs and adapt the approach of your speech accordingly. Remember, however, that group associations do not always present the whole picture. The views of Democrats and Republicans, for example, often overlap on specific issues; not all Democrats feel one way and all Republicans another.

Audience Attitudes

TOWARD THE SPEAKER.   No matter how well you know your subject and how capable you are of speaking about it, you will not be effective if the audience dislikes you or strongly disagrees with your ideas. An audience's attitudes about the speaker often determine his or her success or failure in communicating the desired message.

What criteria influence an audience's decisions about a speaker? Studies show that audiences base their attitudes on a variety of things. Some are meaningful, such as the person's experience, and others petty, such as the speaker's physical appearance. For example, researchers have found that attractive communicators, compared to unattractive communicators, are more consistently liked, are perceived in more favorable terms, and have a greater positive impact.[12] In most cases, however, a speaker's success depends on the listeners' confidence or faith in him or her and what they feel is the speaker's worth or competence. As was pointed out earlier, this is usually referred to as speaker *credibility*, or ethos.

As difficult as it may be to "see ourselves as others see us," it is extremely important for you as a speaker to try to estimate what the audience will think of you. Whether this information is uncovered through informal conversation or through direct questioning of prospective audience members, you should seek out both the positive and the negative expectations of the audience. With this information you can make a deliberate effort to structure the message in such a way as to reinforce the positive expectations and diminish the negative ones.

TOWARD THE SUBJECT.   As stated earlier, if your audience's attitude toward the subject of your speech is favorable, your task is easier. All you have to do is give the subject a fresh approach and reinforce your ideas. But what

---

[12] J. W. Benoy, "The Credibility of Physically Attractive Communicators: A Review," *Journal of Advertising* 11 (1982), 15–24.

An audience's attitudes about a speaker often determine his success or failure.

do you do if your audience is neutral? People who have no opinions on a particular topic will probably listen to both sides of the issue and keep their minds open to all information and attempts at persuasion. At the same time, though, they may be critical toward everything they hear. Neutrality toward a subject does not mean indifference to it. Neutral listeners are concerned about the subject but have not yet made any final decisions about it. As politicians have discovered, these open-minded audience members may be very important to the outcome of a persuasive speech: They can still be moved to either side of an issue. This movement is possible, however, only if the speaker presents sound evidence to support his or her ideas, relates to the audience by sharing experiences, and answers all questions from the floor.

If you feel that your audience is indifferent to your topic, make your speech as interesting as possible. You can do this by finding an appealing, exciting way to cover the topic, by using attention-getting devices, and by playing upon other interests the members of your audience may have that are related to your subject area. The yacht club members might not be concerned with world politics, but they could be interested in the political implications of maritime law. Mathematics might be exciting to elementary school students when related to their everyday adventures or to magic tricks.

If you know that your audience is negatively disposed toward your subject, remember Elsea's advice to be calm and controlled. Additionally, for audiences that are extremely hostile, public-speaking expert Toby Katz urges proceeding with caution and using the five following steps:

1. Identify the exact cause of your listeners' hostility, to the extent doing so is possible.

2. Select a point of agreement with your listeners in order to attract their attention.

3. State their arguments fairly and sincerely.

4. Demonstrate the merits of your position.

5. Build arguments that lead toward your conclusions.[13]

Take for example, Career Day at George Washington High, a ghetto school. Rose, a dance instructor, had been asked to talk about the career of a professional dancer to an assembly of high school juniors. Long before she approached the podium, she knew she was going to face an uninterested, if not antagonistic, audience. But Rose was prepared.

> You know, many football players, such as Hershel Walker, learn ballet in order to limber up and play better. Those who have tried ballet have found that it has made them more agile and has enabled them to run faster and kick farther. But football players aren't the only athletes who learn ballet; it is practiced by many gymnasts, track stars, and swimmers, as well.

By approaching her speech in this way, Rose was able to accomplish several purposes: She lessened the opposition to her topic, gave the students someone with whom to identify, and dispelled some of the negative stereotypes connected with her subject area.

Other ways to combat audience indifference or opposition include adjusting your message, such as by omitting key discrepant statements, making the message less specific, taking a less extreme position, or using weaker language; and spending more time on issues and problems rather than on solutions. The most important thing to remember when confronting a negative audience, again, is to remain as calm as possible. If you hope to persuade your listeners, be careful not to show anger or impatience with their differing viewpoints. It is quite possible for you and your audience to disagree without losing respect for one another's opinions. If you present yourself and your speech in a fair and reasonable way, you may not only be able to get people to listen to your different ideas, but you may gain some converts as well.

TOWARD YOUR PURPOSE. Every speech you make should have a definite purpose. Without the focus a well-defined purpose provides, your speech may be nothing but a collection of statements with no overall meaning. You will recall that the purpose of any speech is to inform, persuade, or entertain.

Speeches can, of course, have aspects of all three purposes, but there should be only one specific, unifying goal. If you give a speech in support of the liberalization of marijuana laws, you may inform your audience of the history of the drug's use, and perhaps relate some interesting anecdotes,

---

[13] T. Katz, "Hostile Audience. Proceed With Caution!" *Training and Development Journal* (February 1984), 82.

but these are only means to help you accomplish your primary goal of persuasion.

The purpose of your speech will often directly depend on the audience's attitude toward the topic. Let's say that your listeners are already in favor of decriminalizing marijuana. Your purpose then is not to persuade but rather to reinforce their beliefs and inform them of the appropriate actions they can take in support of their beliefs. If your listeners are rigidly opposed to your topic, however, it might be best to not try to persuade them but simply to inform them of the facts and hope that as a result, your audience will have obtained a more well-rounded impression of the topic. If your audience is neutral or only partially opposed, persuasion would probably be the best approach, while the interest and attention of a totally indifferent audience can often be focused on a particular issue by an entertaining delivery.

A good speaker will try to base the purpose of his or her speech on the desires and expectations of the audience. Listeners are more apt to pay attention to a speech they are prepared for and consider appropriate to their beliefs and the situation. The chances of a speech's success are greater if both the speaker and the listeners have the same purpose in mind.

Nothing angers an audience more than believing that a speaker's purpose is one thing and finding out that it is something entirely different.

> The presentation of a well-known black poet was eagerly awaited by an audience composed mostly of admirers of his works and would-be writers. Their disappointment was tinged with anger when instead of discussing his poetry, he delivered a powerful attack on white middle-class attitudes toward black Americans.

> Charles Marsden, a fashion designer, was asked by a woman's club to speak on the history of clothing. The members felt resentful when the lecture turned out to be a sales pitch for Marsden's latest line of women's fashions.

The irritation of the audience members in both cases did the speakers much harm. Had the poet and the designer given the expected information in a pleasing manner, they would have related well to their listeners and greatly furthered their personal causes.

If, prior to your speech, you can discover your audience's purpose and demands, you will know how to adapt your speech to increase the likelihood of a successful outcome.

METHODS OF INVESTIGATING YOUR AUDIENCE

When preparing a speech for one of your college classes, you already know the age, sex, relative economic status, and race of the class members. You can also make accurate guesses about their opinions on issues such as reinstitution of the draft, job opportunities and higher education. Difficulties occur when you are asked to speak to groups of people that you know relatively little about (in terms of their demographic characteristics, values, beliefs, and attitudes).

Invitation Committee

The most obvious place to begin seeking information is from the people who invited you to speak. Immediately, questions will come to mind, such as: How many people will attend? Are there any specific time limitations or expectations? What does the audience know about the subject? Will they be required to attend? What are their ages? At first, being startled by the invitation, you may not ask all the necessary questions. If this is the case, don't hesitate to ask for additional information about your prospective audience.

Mass Media Sources

Other valuable audience information comes from reading community newspapers and magazines, listening to local radio stations and watching local television programs. It may even be a good idea to subscribe to various publications for a few weeks before you speak, to get an idea of important issues in the geographical area. Through the mass media you'll find the concerns that are uppermost in the listeners' minds, such as police or teachers' strikes, sports playoffs, or human interest issues such as the activities of the local humane society. Even if your topic is not one of general community interest, being informed about local concerns can aid you in preparing examples and illustrations relevant to your audience.

Public Opinion Polls and Surveys

Over the years we have seen the importance of polls in predicting election results. Politicians are extremely concerned about how their platforms are accepted and how popular they are in particular areas. The information received from polls and surveys helps the candidates determine the best method of presenting their arguments and themselves. Beginning speakers can also gain insight from similar information without going to the expense of conducting actual surveys. References such as the *Gallup Opinion Index*, *Public Opinion Polls*, and *Public Opinion Quarterly* provide useful data on a variety of topics for different geographical regions of the country.

Personal Interviews

If you live nearby, much can be learned about your prospective audience by talking with local people. Interviews with local leaders and citizens can give you a clearer picture about who is being affected on issues such as waste water facilities, local parks and recreation departments, and health facilities. Even if you don't live nearby, after arriving in a particular area, you can talk to people with whom you come in contact (for example, taxi drivers or hotel managers) to find out the latest issues of concern and even language styles that might be appropriate for your particular speech.

OTHER AUDIENCE CONSIDERATIONS

Audience Types

In 1935, H. L. Hollingworth developed a classification system that described audiences on the basis of their organization and orientation toward the situation in which the speech is given.[14] This now classic approach to audiences is still highly pertinent today. As you will see, speaking before each of these audience types entails unique problems and responsibilities.

CASUAL AUDIENCES.   Frequently, in large cities, people walking down the street will stop and listen to a soapbox orator preaching religion or some other cause, or watch an entertainer such as a magician or musician. Hollingworth calls such pedestrian audiences *casual.* These so-called audiences show very little, if any, homogeneity and, in fact, are barely audiences at all. They are just small groups of people who have gathered for a short time at the same place.

Soapbox orators or street entertainers who address casual audiences must first get the attention of the pedestrians passing by. This means that they have to spend a lot of time on their speech preparation and delivery. Each street orator attempts to develop his or her own unique speaking style—a specific way to hook the attention of the pedestrians. But, more important, these speakers have to *keep* the casual audience there. This means getting the listeners involved. The orator will perhaps fire questions into the crowd, and the entertainer may ask listeners to participate, emotionally or physically.

PASSIVE AUDIENCES.   The second type of audience is *passive,* or *partially oriented,* and is usually composed of captive listeners. The people who make up this kind of audience have no choice but to listen to the speaker. A church congregation listening to a sermon or club members listening to the after-luncheon speaker are examples of passive audiences.

Speakers who confront passive audiences must gain the attention of the listeners and arouse their interest in the subject matter. In order to accomplish this, they can appeal to one or more of the interests that almost all audiences have in common. All people share basic primary interests or needs. Financial security, for instance, is one of the most basic needs of all persons. Almost everyone wants to hear about ways of earning or saving money. If you are trying to get the attention of your audience members, use some examples that are close to home and, especially, close to their wallets.

---

[14] H. L. Hollingworth, *The Psychology of the Audience* (New York: American Book, 1935), 19–32.

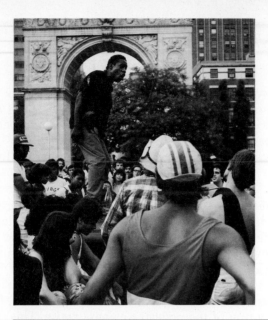

A casual audience.

A comedian can only last till he either takes himself serious or his audience takes him serious.

Will Rogers

There are other common interests that, although not vital to personal welfare, appeal to audiences. Sports and hobbies are examples of such *secondary interests*. Suppose you are making a speech about an area of land you think should be converted into a state park. You might draw upon the secondary interests of your audience to advance your argument. If you have ascertained beforehand that audience members are outdoors enthusiasts, you could talk about the hiking trails, camping sites, and observation points that could be made available by such a state park. Or, if they are animal lovers, you might list the types of animals that would be protected in the park. Which secondary interests you draw on will depend on your specific audience and the results of your analysis.

Momentary interests are things that concern us for only a short time and are then replaced by other issues. A new television show or news event may be on everyone's lips for a couple of days. A speaker's reference to such a topic can be used to arouse the attention of the audience. An awareness of the momentary interests of an audience can be a great asset to the speaker.

SELECTED AUDIENCES.   Audiences who have collected for a specific purpose are referred to as **selected** audiences. These listeners normally attend a speech because they have some previous interest in the subject. Examples of such selected audiences are environmentalists who come to hear a lecture on the ozone layer, students of the occult attending a talk on witchcraft, and members of the Farmers of America learning about a new irrigation technique.

While "interest catchers" are helpful with passive audiences, what are your responsibilities toward selected audiences that have met for a specific purpose? First, you need not try to attract attention; you already have it. Instead, you should strive to make a strong impression on your listeners so that they remember what you have said after your speech is over. A group of parents who wish to impress upon their fellow PTA members the seriousness of conditions existing in the school might invite an engineer first to inspect the buildings and then to come to the next meeting to discuss the leaking roof, unsafe staircases, and broken windows.

CONCERTED AUDIENCES.   At the General Motors Cadillac engine plant in Livonia, Michigan, "business teams" made up of eight to fifteen persons meet at least once a week as a group to discuss scheduling, training, problem solving, and other related activities.[15] These teams make up a *concerted* audience, one that has an active purpose and mutual interests, but no set separation of labor or strict organization of authority. Furthermore, the concerted audience has a high degree of orientation toward the speaker and his or her purpose. An Alcoholics Anonymous meeting is another example of this kind of audience.

Concerted audiences are already impressed and are ready to be led to action. The speaker must therefore enforce the audience's convictions—persuading members and directing their action. Audiences may have very strong attitudes, but having such attitudes and acting on them are two different things. For example, many women who attend National Organization of Women (NOW) meetings have definite pro-liberation views. This does not always mean that they are taking action, however. A vibrant speaker may be needed to motivate these women to take legal action in cases of discrimination, for example.

ORGANIZED AUDIENCES.   Finally, there is the *organized* audience, in which listeners are totally directed toward the speaker and all labor and authority lines are strictly designated. A Minnesota Vikings coach lecturing his football team on the upcoming game against the Green Bay Packers is speaking to an organized audience.

Organized audiences are ready for action, but they often have no direction. The speaker's responsibility in this case is to give the listeners specific instructions on the action plans. The Minnesota Vikings coach will discuss specific football moves before the big game with the Packers. The labor leader will advise the union members about where and when they should picket.

Effects of the Environment

Is your speech being given in a large room or in a small one? Are the chairs comfortable? How are they arranged? What kind of lighting is there, and

---

[15] T. Peters, *Thriving on Chaos* (New York: Harper & Row, 1987), 358.

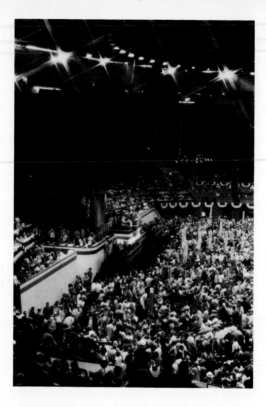

The size of an audience affects its behavior and reactions.

how good are the acoustics? All of these questions deal with the physical setting of your speech, which will greatly influence your audience's behavior.

Take the room itself, for instance. People will act differently if they are sitting in a large auditorium, a small classroom, or a house. Compare an audience listening to a formal lecture in a classroom to one that listens to the same speech in a coffee shop or outside under a tree.

The noises or other distractions around you must also be taken into consideration. Is the room quiet, or must you compete with the sounds of traffic outside and distractions such as air conditioning inside? You should learn how to adapt to such situations. You can project your voice over the noises, pause to let an intrusion pass, or incorporate the competing stimuli into the speech.

While in office, President Ronald Reagan often used noise from his helicopter to his advantage when dealing with members of the press. Rather than shout over the noise or approach the press corps close enough to hear them, he would simply cup his hand over his ear, shrug, and mouth the words, "I can't hear you." In this way, Reagan made use of the competing stimuli and avoided answering questions that he may have been unprepared to address at the time.

The atmosphere in a large auditorium with hundreds of unrelated people is, of course, very formal. Listeners usually sit in straight chairs, and all face the speaker. Compare this to a small, informal gathering in someone's home, where the listeners and the speaker have a much more intimate relationship. The listeners are more prone to ask questions and offer comments on the speaker's ideas. The speaker, in turn, is more at ease, uses more informal speech patterns, and relates better to the audience.[16] He or she can show more concern for the listeners and can come across with more sincerity.

The size of the audience is a physical condition that affects both your audience's behavior and your reactions to it. You will probably be more formal with large audiences than with small ones. You will also have to use more pronounced gestures and a louder voice when addressing a large audience so that members in the back rows get the full impact of the message. In a smaller group, your facial expressions and small body movements will communicate much more effectively.

Many social psychologists, rhetoricians, and educators believe that audience density and anxiety are related. For example, McKinney, Gatchel, and Paulus found that highly anxious speakers were relatively more anxious and depressed after speaking before a larger audience, and speakers with low anxiety levels were relatively less anxious and depressed. However, both groups of speakers showed similar physiological increases in arousal during their preparations for speaking and during the actual speaking event.[17]

The Speaker-Audience Interaction

What distinguishes an audience from a random collection of people? Three things happen when groups of people progress from a mere gathering to audience status.

POLARIZATION.   The first thing that happens is ***polarization,*** which provides the structure for an unorganized group of people. It is at this point that audience members recognize their role as listeners and accept someone else as a speaker. Two distinct roles, then, come into existence. While the polarized audience is separate from the speaker, it is also connected to him or her by the communication that occurs. Various aspects of the public speaking situation contribute to polarization, such as seating arrangements in which the chairs face the speaker, or the stage or platform from which the speaker delivers the speech.

Polarization is both normal and necessary in public-speaking situations. However, polarization can become too extreme when either speaker or audience becomes alienated from the other. Shortly after his inauguration, President Bush accepted invitations to attend meetings at two elite, "males only" professional clubs in Washington, D.C. By doing so he drew fire from

---

[16] R. L. Street, Jr., R. M. Brady, and R. Lee, "Evaluative Responses to Communicators: The Effects of Speech Rate, Sex, and Interaction Context," *The Western Journal of Speech Communication* 48 (Winter 1984), 18.
[17] M. E. McKinney, R. J. Gatchel, and P. B. Paulus, "The Effects of Audience Size on High and Low Speech-Anxious Subjects During an Actual Speaking Task," *Basic & Applied Social Psychology* 4 (March 1983), 73–87.

Mutual feedback heightens the participation of communicators.

the American press and damaged his credibility with feminists all across the country. Additionally, he created the potential for polarization in future meetings with this latter, highly influential audience.

SOCIAL FACILITATION.   The influence that one audience member has on another is called *social facilitation.* If you are watching a TV comedy alone, you may not laugh out loud, even if you think the program very funny. With friends, however, you may be prompted to laugh long and loud. Social facilitation may not occur immediately. It often takes a formal audience, the kind in an auditorium or theater, some time to warm up. Few people want to be the first to applaud, cheer, clap hands to the music, or stand for an ovation. Audience members look to one another for reinforcement.

Imagine that you are watching the performance of a Russian dance troupe. At the beginning of the performance, the members of the audience may be very quiet. A few people tap their feet or drum their fingers in time to the music, but most are relatively unresponsive. But as the rhythm of the music and the exuberant movements on stage affect more and more of the members of the audience, a drastic change can occur. Before you know it, you, like everyone else, may find yourself stamping your feet, clapping your hands and cheering. Even listeners who are usually very quiet and reserved can be influenced by the excitement of an audience.

CIRCULAR RESPONSE.   When the kind of communication that happens between listeners occurs between the audience and the speaker, the phenomenon is called *circular response.* The speaker says something and the audience responds with nods, applause, or frowns. From these responses the speaker knows how best to slant what he or she says next to hold the attention of the listeners. If the response is favorable, the speaker may exert more effort, which in turn leads to more audience responses, and so on. This mutual feedback heightens the participation of both speaker and listeners and strengthens the bonds between them.

Audience Analysis Checklist

Audience analysis is an art, not a science. Just think of all the variations and combinations that can occur in an audience's demographic and attitudinal characteristics. It is plain to see how difficult, if not impossible, it is to set down specific step-by-step rules to cover all the variables of any particular audience. However, Table 9–1 provides a checklist of some of the basics of audience analysis that can help you construct an effective speech.

1. Before choosing my speech purpose and topic, do I know the demographic characteristics of my audience, including age, education, occupation, personality and so forth?
2. Have I a fairly clear notion of how much and what kind of knowledge my audience has about my topic? Will the range of knowledge among audience members be broad or narrow?
3. Have I discovered those basic religious, political, social, and moral beliefs, values, and attitudes that could affect this audience's understanding of my speech topic? Are there likely to be beliefs, values, or attitudes that may interfere with the audience accepting my point of view, arguments, evidence, or examples? Have I taken these into account in planning my speech material?
4. Have I made an objective attempt to learn my audience's attitudes toward my intended purpose, my speech topic, and myself?
5. Do I know what type of audience I will be facing? If I know, have I chosen the level and emphasis of speech materials appropriate for a casual, passive, selected, concerted, or organized audience?
6. Did I consider environmental factors that could affect the comprehension and/or acceptance of my ideas? Can I describe and analyze the physical setting and note its good and bad points? Are there any potential competing stimuli for which I can plan adjustments?
7. What is the occasion for which I am to speak? Is this a regular monthly meeting of Athletes in Action or an annual honors banquet? Is it the Fourth of July, or Valentine's Day?

The answers to these questions will provide you with the information you need to increase the chances of a successful presentation.

TABLE 9–1 Audience Analysis

SUBJECT AND PURPOSE

Subject:	Your general subject area.
Purpose:	To entertain, persuade, or inform.
Specific purpose:	What you want your audience to learn; what action or response you want.
Expected purpose:	What your audience thinks the purpose is.

GENERAL CHARACTERISTICS

Personality:	Open/closed minded, active/passive, tired/alert, calm/angry, other, mixed.
Knowledge of subject:	None–little, moderate, professional.
Knowledge of speaker:	None–little, same background, family member, friend.

DEMOGRAPHICS

Age:	Up to 12, 13–21, 22–40, 65, over, mixed.
Education:	Elementary, high school, college, graduate school, mixed.
Environment:	Rural, town, small/large city, urban, industrialized, suburbs, other, mixed.
Economic:	Poor, lower middle, upper middle, wealthy, mixed.
Occupation:	Unemployed, student, homemaker, mixed, trade, professional, other, mixed.
Sex:	Male, female, mixed.
Group membership:	Sports clubs, lodges, occupational clubs, interest clubs, other, mixed.
Classification:	Casual, passive, selected, concerted, organized.

ATTITUDES, BELIEFS, VALUES

Political:	Republican/Democrat, liberal/conservative, independent, other, mixed.
Religious:	Catholic, Protestant, Jewish, other, mixed.
Attitude toward speaker:	Favorable, opposed, neutral, indifferent.
Attitude toward subject:	Favorable, opposed, neutral, indifferent.
Attitude toward purpose:	Favorable, opposed, neutral, indifferent.

ENVIRONMENTAL FACTORS

Physical setting:	Formal/informal, large/small room, indoors/outdoors, other.
Competing stimuli:	Quiet, moderate, noisy.
Size:	Small, moderate-sized, large.
Density:	Scattered, moderate, compact.
Proximity:	Audience close to speaker/far from speaker, seated in front row/back row/sides.

Adapted from G. Wiseman and L. Barker. *A Workbook for Speech/Interpersonal Communication* (San Francisco: Chandler, 1967).

SUMMARY

Public speaking differs from other forms of communication in two essential ways: (1) Public-speaking situations require two distinct roles, that of speaker and audience, and (2) in the speaker-audience relationship, the speaker carries more responsibility for the communication interaction than does the audience.

Perhaps the most important consideration to be made before speech preparation is ethical responsibility. There appear to be four approaches to ethics: (1) ends-justifies-means approach, (2) social utility approach, (3) situation ethics approach, and (4) credibility-centered approach. After dealing with ethical considerations, the speaker should select both general and specific purposes. The selection should be based on the speaker's own knowledge and interests as well as on a thorough audience analysis.

One system of audience analysis is the demographic approach. This involves the gathering of particular and factual information to predict audience reaction. A speech may be planned according to factors such as the age, educational level and socioeconomic status of the audience. Other useful considerations are the occupations, gender, or group affiliations of audience members. It is important to avoid stereotyping the audience, however. Demography is best used in a factual, impartial and nonprejudiced manner.

Other variables that the effective communicator should consider are the beliefs, values, and attitudes of the audience. Familiarity with the political or religious character of the audience may provide many clues about listeners' basic beliefs and common values or convictions.

Effective communication is not likely to take place if listeners are alienated by the speaker, the subject, or the speaker's purpose. A good speaker must present the speech in a way that will emphasize the positive attitudes of the audience while minimizing its negative reactions. A message that is geared to the desires and expectations of the audience will be received more readily than one that is not.

Speaking situations vary according to audience type. There are casual, passive, selected, concerted, and organized audiences, and the responsibility of the speaker is different in each case.

The person who speaks to the casual or passive audience must first attract and then hold the attention of the listeners. The select audience is a group that has met for a specific purpose, and the goal of the speaker should be to strongly impress the intended message upon them. The concerted audience is already impressed but has not yet been directed to action. In this case the speaker may try to reinforce established attitudes and motivate the listeners to take action. The final kind of audience is the organized audience. In this situation the listeners have already been persuaded of the necessity for action and are willing to carry out the specific directions of the speaker.

An intelligent public speaker must be aware of the effects of environment upon communication. Audiences react differently in large, small, formal, and informal speaking situations. Audience density is a factor in successful persuasion. Therefore, conflicting noises and distractions should be taken into account and prepared for, in order to make the smoothest possible presentation.

Those who wish to understand how a group of individuals becomes an audience and how audience reaction works should study the speaker-audience relationship. Polarization, the division of roles, establishes the speaker as separate from the listeners and establishes the connection between the two. Social facilitation involves the internal reaction of an audience. Audience members reinforce the reactions of one another. Circular response involves the speaker in the sharing of excitement.

Audience analysis is an art, and like all arts must be practiced and developed by each speaker. Students of audience analysis who keep in mind the characteristics and values of the listeners, the type of audience they are addressing, and the environment in which they are making the speech are on the way to becoming effective communicators.

EXERCISES

GROUP EXPERIENCES

Ghostwriting

DESCRIPTION: Many audience variables need to be considered when preparing a speech or presentation for a group. Analyzing the audience is a key element in public presentations. This activity will give you the opportunity to "advise" a speaker on the elements that should be considered for a given audience and topic.

PROCEDURE: Divide into groups of four to six members. Write each of the following topics and targets on a separate piece of paper.

Topics

1. The use of marijuana should be decriminalized.
2. Women should serve their husbands.
3. All families should be limited to two children.
4. Wearing seat belts should be required for all passengers in cars and buses.
5. Wearing helmets should be required for all motorcyclists.

Audiences

1. Veterans groups, 50 males, ages 25–50.
2. College students, 30 males and females, ages 18–30.
3. Feminist group, 40 females, ages 18–60.
4. Hell's Angels, 30 males, ages 20–35.
5. Daughters of the American Revolution, 25 females, ages 30–80.

Each group should select one topic and one target audience and should prepare a list of recommendations for things the speaker should consider. In preparing this list, the following factors should be considered:

Demographic characteristics	Group membership
Educational level	Psychological characteristics
Socioeconomic status	Audience beliefs and values
Personality	Audience attitude toward the
Sex	subject and purpose of the speech

Although you have not been given all of the information just listed, you will have to make inferences about these variables.

Examples of recommendations include:

1. Avoid the use of idiomatic expressions. This is a professional audience who will expect the use of professional language.
2. You will need to loosen the group up so that they will feel comfortable with one another, since they do not know one another.

Each group should identify its topic and target audience. Then the list of recommendations should be read. Finally, the other groups should evaluate each list.

DISCUSSION: Did the group make logical inferences about the given audience? Did the recommendations reflect the appropriate concerns for the given audience? Were any important recommendations omitted? Do you think that the consideration of audience variables is important in writing an effective speech?

Audience Types

DESCRIPTION: Hollingworth developed a classification system that described audiences on the basis of their organization and orientation toward the speech situation. His audience types include casual, passive, selected, concerted, and organized audiences. This activity will give you a chance to use the Hollingworth classification system.

PROCEDURE: Each person should make up an example of two audience types. The examples should be collected and read aloud to the class. As each example is read, you should classify it as casual, passive, selected, concerted, or organized. After everyone has classified each example, the correct answers should be determined by class discussion. Check your score to see how many correct classifications you made.

DISCUSSION: Beyond the classification of audiences, of what value is the Hollingworth system? How could you use it in preparing a speech for a particular group?

Warm Up

DESCRIPTION: One of the most difficult tasks for a speaker to perform is to try to "warm up" a formal audience. Few people want to be the first to yell, clap hands to music, or even stand for an ovation. This activity will give you an opportunity to develop various warm-up techniques for different audiences.

PROCEDURE: This activity can be done either by groups or by individuals. The procedure is the same for both formats. Two descriptions of specific audiences are provided below. You are to write down all possible alternatives for warming up the given group. Your suggestions should be specific. Some examples include the following:

1. Tell a joke related specifically to the audience.
2. Bring several members of the audience in front of the group to participate in a demonstration.
3. Socialize with the group before your speech in an effort to relax them.

Setting 1. You have been asked to speak on malpractice insurance before a group of physicians. You are an attorney and have been active in lawsuits against physicians. Some members of the group resent the fact that you have been asked to speak to them. These members see you as the enemy.

Setting 2. You work for the Total Woman franchise. Your message to all women is that they should consider their husbands to be first and foremost in their lives. You have been asked to address a group of husbands who are experiencing some marital difficulties.

DISCUSSION: Have you given careful consideration to the techniques you have selected? Do any of your techniques involve nonverbal behavior, such as smiling or standing close to your audience? What are some indications that an audience is warming up to you as a speaker?

PERSONAL EXPERIENCES

1. Observe a speaker in action, but spend most of your time watching for audience response. What cues did you observe that indicated attentiveness, boredom, interest, or anger? Could you tell when (or if) the speaker won or lost the audience?
2. Have you ever considered how much information you have about people based on age alone? Consider each of the following time periods during which people were born: What do you know about people who were born during 1931–1940; 1941–1950; 1951–1960; 1961–1970? Who were their idols? What was the political climate they experienced?
3. Can you remember a speech that was well received by the audience? To what extent did the speaker's adapting to the audience make the speech a success?

DISCUSSION QUESTIONS

1. How does group membership provide you with clues for presenting an effective speech?
2. What audience factors do you consider important in preparing a speech?

3. What environmental effects should be considered in preparing a speech for a selected audience?
4. How can you assess audience attitudes toward (a) the speaker, (b) the subject, and (c) the purpose of the speech?
5. How might an awareness of the concept of social facilitation affect your preparation of a speech for a formal audience?

10
Communication Goals
Information Exchange, Persuasion, Entertainment

KEY CONCEPTS AND TERMS

Intrinsic motivation

Extrinsic motivation

Repetition

Visual aid

Platform

Speech to convince

Speech to stimulate

Speech to move audience to action

Logos

Deductive reasoning

Inductive reasoning

Pathos

Reward appeal

Fear-arousing appeal

Qualification/expertness

Safety/trustworthiness

Compliance/dynamism

Normative/identification

Social judgment theory

Latitude of acceptance

Latitude of rejection

Latitude of noncommitment

Ego-involvement

Balance theory

Cognitive dissonance

Belief

Attitude

Value

One-sided presentation

Two-sided presentation

Forewarning

Primacy effect

Recency effect

Speech to welcome

Award presentation

Acceptance speech

After-dinner speech

Farewell speech

Eulogy

Impromptu speech

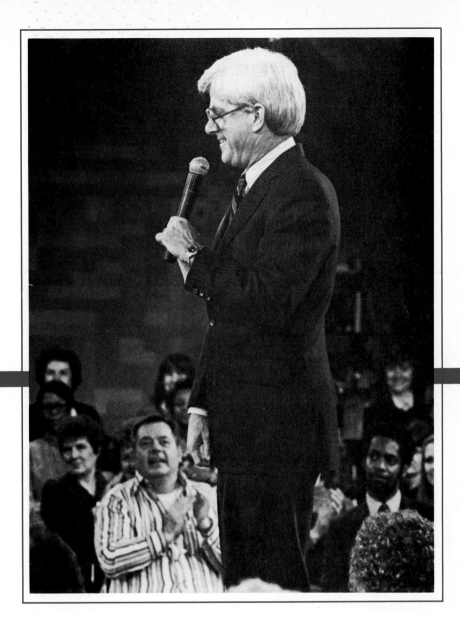

When the Xerox Corporation first explored the distribution of its copy equipment nationwide, it began with the knowledge that the company was short of salespeople with professional sales skills. To meet the company's growing needs, Xerox created a training program that is still recognized as a leader today. Developed by a team of psychologists and the most experienced and successful members of its sales force, the training program was built on the premise that sales calls would be more effective if they included an "initial benefit statement." This statement would act not only to introduce the company's equipment by delineating its positive attributes, but it would also catch the customers' attention and give them a reason to buy.[1]

Since its development, this technique has played a major role in sales training programs across the nation. Because of their persuasability, benefit statements are employed successfully in a variety of business presentations. From their subtle use in television commercials, which suggest that we will be more happy, successful, or sexy if we use a particular product, to their more direct use by salespeople, activists, and politicians, this technique gives a targeted audience a strong incentive to listen and pay attention.

In this chapter we will focus a number of techniques for presenting a persuasive message. However, our discussion will not be limited solely to *persuasion* as a goal, but will also focus on two other purposes of public speaking: *information exchange* and *entertainment*. As you saw in the previous chapter, you must not only know who your audience is but you must also have a specific purpose in mind in order to be a successful speaker. Armed with this knowledge and a clear understanding of the three primary purposes of public speaking, you can begin to construct messages that win the enthusiasm and support of any audience.

INFORMATION EXCHANGE

Ways to Increase Learning

In order to facilitate audience learning, a major goal of informative speaking, you must organize your speech for clarity and accuracy. However, there are several additional ways in which a speaker can increase audience learning while presenting a speech to inform. Careful attention to these areas not only improves the chances that an audience will remember what is said but also can contribute to the ease with which the speaker is able to deliver the message.

MOTIVATION.   The most significant factor in increasing learning is motivation. Before you can learn you must listen; and before you listen you must be motivated to do so. The motivation may come from within (intrinsic motivation) or from an outside source (extrinsic motivation). For example, when Maria attended a seminar on crime prevention, she went because she wanted to learn how to protect herself. On the other hand, her roommate Stephanie went because her sociology professor promised to give extra credit to students who wrote reports on the seminar. Maria's motivation to listen and learn was intrinsic; Stephanie's motivation was extrinsic. Although learning theorists disagree as to which form of motivation creates a greater increase in learning, we do know that an individual needs some type of motivation to listen to and then to learn the information being conveyed by a speaker.

---

[1] J. MacLachlan, "Making a Message Memorable and Persuasive," *Journal of Advertising Research* 23, no. 6 (1983–84), 51–59.

If a speaker gives an audience a reason or reasons for learning the information, ideas, or skills presented, the audience gives more effort to the learning process. For example, when a representative comes to speak from the American Cancer Society and encourages the women in the audience to have a Pap smear and breast examination and then teaches them how to conduct self-examinations, she would probably tell them that doing so will increase the chances of early detection of cancer.

ORGANIZATION.   It is also the speaker's responsibility to organize his or her ideas so that the information presented to the audience is logical and easy to follow. There has been considerable research on how the organization of a speaker's message can affect listener comprehension, speaker credibility, and listener frustration. In general, the findings of these studies support the claim that the organization of a message influences the audience in its interpretation and evaluation of a message. In studies designed to test the effects of message structure and style on listener evaluations, results indicate that messages which are more organized, logical, predictable, and factual are perceived as more comprehensible and persuasive than messages without these particular attributes.[2] You would probably reach a similar conclusion based on personal experience. Undoubtedly, you find it much easier to understand a speaker who presents ideas clearly and logically than one who is disorganized. Most of us have trouble grasping the main idea of speakers who jump ahead of themselves or who backtrack to fill in information they left out.

EFFECTIVE DEVELOPMENT OF IDEAS.   Speakers who are presenting new information must develop their ideas effectively to sustain listener attention and motivation and thereby increase learning. There are specific techniques speakers can use to do this. One technique is to mix new and familiar ideas. Although the purpose of the speech may be to present new and useful information, it is important to connect this information with something that the audience already knows. It is always easier for listeners to understand something they have experienced or can relate to. A person discussing the detrimental effects of television violence on small children would include examples of shows the audience has seen to make the information more meaningful.

Another technique a speaker can use to sustain listener attention combines the elements of conflict and suspense. If a speaker can emphasize opposition or competition through an appropriate image, the audience is more likely to note and remember that particular point. For example, an ecologist might refer to the "race" among the industrial nations to exhaust the earth's resources.

A strong image can serve as a focal point for a speech and give the listeners a major concept upon which they can hang other important bits

[2] V. Hazleton, W. R. Cupach, and J. Liska, "Message Style: An Investigation of the Perceived Characteristics of Persuasive Messages," *Journal of Social Behavior and Personality* 1, no. 4 (1986), 565–74.

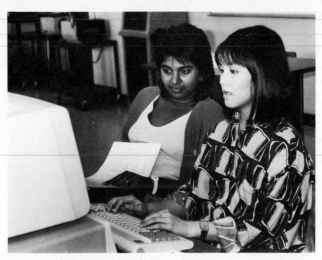

Computerized information exchange.

of information. One key phrase can later trigger a listener's recall of important, related information. A historian describing the circumstances that led to the American Civil War could use the image of a fork in the road, one path leading to an urban industrialized North, the other to a rural, agrarian South.

In recent years educators have talked about the need for relevance. You have no doubt sat through many speeches wondering what the information being conveyed had to do with you and your life. A speaker who can take ideas and associate them with the audience's present concerns will increase listener attention and interest. For example, an anthropologist could add interest to a discussion of primitive tribal rites by comparing them to some of the customs and rituals of various modern cultures and societies.

Another way in which a speaker can develop ideas effectively and increase learning is through the use of concrete, specific images that convey a sense of realism and vividness. A student delivering a speech on the World Trade Center in New York emphasized the enormity of the structure by pointing out that the building had close to 40,000 doorknobs. Although this bit of trivia is not in itself important, it made a more vivid and lasting impression than would have been made if the speaker had just informed the audience of the building's dimensions.

REPETITION.   In every information speech, regardless of subject, some information is more important than the rest, and it is the speaker's responsibility to convey this to the audience. An effective speaker will increase audience learning by emphasizing the most important information through *repetition.* A speaker can mention a point, underline its importance, mention it again in the middle of the speech, and repeat it at the conclusion. A recording engineer giving a talk to a class of would-be studio technicians might want to emphasize the need for organization during a recording session. He may mention it in the introduction simply as a "crucial factor." In the body of

Effective visual aids help make ideas more clear, vivid and concrete.

the speech, the engineer might quote the current hourly cost of studio time, pointing to the need for an organized use of every single minute. Finally, in the conclusion, organization might once again be stressed as a necessary element of good production.

VISUAL AIDS.   In addition to using verbal pictures created through imagery, the speaker may improve a presentation by using a variety of diagrams, graphs and photographs.

There are several advantages to using visual aids during a speech to inform.

1. By showing the audience an object or a representation of it, the speaker can make her ideas more clear and vivid.
2. Visual aids can help make abstract ideas more concrete.
3. The interest level of the audience can be increased by using visual aids.
4. By using visual images, the speaker can aid the audience in retaining information for longer periods of time.[3]

Visual aids, then, can be of great value when a speaker is presenting information; however, they must be used effectively. The following guidelines can help you use visual aids to your advantage:

Don't:

1. Talk to the visual aid instead of the audience.
2. Put materials in the hands of listeners until you've finished speaking.
3. Display visual aids until you reach the point in the speech that relates to them.
4. Overdo the use of visual aids during the speech.

---

[3] S. E. Lucas, *The Art of Public Speaking* (New York: Random House, 1983), 240–41.

Do:

1. Explain the significance of each visual aid and relate it to your speech.
2. Give the audience sufficient time to view and understand the visual aid.
3. Think of all possible hazards before using visual aids.
4. Come prepared with all necessary materials (tape, thumb tacks, projectors, etc.).
5. Prepare visual aids in advance.
6. Use the hand closest to the visual aid as a pointer to avoid turning your back on some audience members.
7. Make sure that the visual aids are clearly visible to all audience members.
8. Be creative to increase interest and variety in the use of visual aids.

A park official may decide to use color slides of various national forests in his presentation. As he talks of the size of the forests, he may show aerial shots to emphasize the number of square miles covered with trees. While describing the wildlife protected in the national parks, he may show slides of various animals and birds. When he wants to make clear the necessity of preventing forest fires, he may follow a series of beautiful images with one of the blackened and smoking ruin of a forest. By means of contrast, and by leaving this last image on the screen for a number of minutes, he will surely give his audience a clear idea of the damage and waste caused by a careless camper.

Audience Participation

While most of our discussion of the informative speech has focused on the presentation of information by the speaker, we should mention those situations in which the audience participates in the exchange of information. One popular format in which this occurs is the *platform.*

A platform format might be used at a public hearing on drainage problems, when citizens report on property damage from recent flooding, and officials relate their efforts to deal with the situation. Similarly, there may be an exchange situation on campus, when the college financial advisor gives an informative speech on how to earn money part time, after which a number of students relate the various ways they have found to earn money for tuition.

The classroom also offers an opportunity for the presentation and exchange of information. Examples would be a home economics class in which students share their special recipes; a crafts class in which students do demonstrations of macramé, needlepoint, and pottery; and a philosophy class in which students explain their orientations to life. In each case, while the primary speaker may be the instructor, the audience also participates in the exchange of information.

PERSUASION

The degree to which an audience is actually persuaded will, of course, vary. A speaker who intends to persuade may (1) convince, (2) stimulate, or (3) move the audience to action. A person who attempts to *convince* intends to get the audience to think, believe, or feel a certain way. A person engaged in a debate, a minister preaching on the evils of materialism, and a business executive who thinks the company should merge with another firm may all use persuasion to convince their audience of a particular belief.

Another type of persuasion comes in the form of *stimulation*. Generally, a person who wants to stimulate an audience will attempt to reaffirm or strengthen preexisting beliefs or feelings. For example, the union leader who addresses members as they march on a picket line is trying to reinforce their belief in the importance of the strike while strengthening their feelings of solidarity.

The third level of persuasion is the speech that uses persuasion to *move members of an audience to action*. For example, when coffee prices skyrocketed, different consumer groups addressed communities to gain support for an immediate boycott.

Although we make a distinction between the different degrees of persuasion, keep in mind that these purposes overlap. Obviously, before you can successfully move an audience to act, you must convince them. Because it is easier to get an audience to believe in something than to get them to act on it, the speaker who wants to activate an audience must use different techniques than the speaker who merely wants to convince.

Informative Versus Persuasive Communication

Perhaps the best way to understand persuasive communication is first, to contrast it with informative communication. Persuasive communication differs from informative communication in three ways:

1. *Climate or environment.* When a speaker delivers an informative message, the relationship between the speaker and the audience is usually neutral. However, when a speaker delivers a persuasive message, there is an emotional atmosphere that may be hostile or inspiring, depending upon the situation.

2. *Response sought.* In general, a persuasive speech will aim for a higher degree of audience involvement or action.

3. *Goals to be achieved.* The goal of an informative speech is to present an audience with new and useful information which they will understand and learn. The goal of a persuasive speech can be either to change an attitude or belief, or to bring a person to act. The goal of an informative speech on what to look for in buying a fur coat is much less controversial than a persuasive speech in which the speaker's goal is to gain support for a boycott of furs of endangered species.

There are several approaches to persuasion that can help you more clearly understand the persuasive process. These include the Aristotelian approach as well as the more contemporary approaches of social judgment theory, cognitive consistency theories, and Milton Rokeach's theory regarding attitudes and beliefs. Given the relevance of these approaches to our understanding of persuasion, we will begin by discussing each of them.

APPROACHES TO PERSUASION

The Aristotelian Approach

According to Aristotle, a speaker who wishes to create a persuasive message can choose among three persuasive modes, or appeals, in order to make his or her message effective. Aristotle labeled these appeals *logos*, *pathos*, and *ethos*.

> Rhetoric may be defined as the faculty of observing in any given case the available means of persuasion.
>
> Aristotle

LOGOS: REASONING.   *Logos* refers to a rational approach to persuasion. Based on logic and argumentation, logos is intended to appeal to an individual's sense of reason. For example, a physician trying to convince her colleagues of the value of an experimental surgical technique would do so most successfully if she uses a rational approach. Citing research studies and including statistics of successes and failures might persuade the listeners to adopt the technique. A member of a consulting firm trying to persuade a business person to adopt an efficiency plan must present hard facts and solid figures to show how the proposed plan will either increase productivity or eliminate waste.

Aside from facts and figures, logos includes the use of two basic types of reasoning: deductive and inductive. **Deductive reasoning** moves from the general to the specific. The best known form of deductive reasoning is the syllogism. The following is a classic example.

All men are mortal.
Socrates is a man.
Therefore Socrates is mortal.

A syllogism illustrates the deductive process very clearly; the final conclusion follows logically from the first generalization.

Inductive reasoning moves from the specific to the general. If your favorite disc jockey plays two enjoyable selections from a newly released record album, you may induce that the entire album is good and decide to buy it. Sherlock Holmes was known for his ability to draw accurate conclusions about a crime on the basis of specific information or clues.

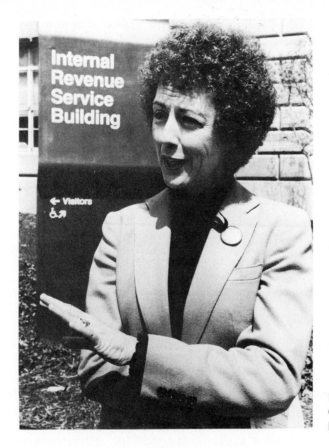

Effective speakers capitalize on fear to enhance a persuasive message.

Of course, both deductive and inductive reasoning can be false. Let us consider an observer at an athletic event who notices that all of the track stars are wearing a particular brand of running shoes. He purchases a pair for his son and is disappointed when the boy fails to finish the marathon race sponsored by a local youth organization. Just because a large number of good runners wear these shoes, it does not follow that any person wearing the same footgear will be a good runner. The deductive process in this case did not prove reliable.

An example of false induction is the case of a woman who hires a small moving company to transport her furniture to her new home in another state. As she unpacks the shipping cases, she discovers that many things have been damaged, and she angrily resolves never to trust a small company again. In reality, many small companies are just as reliable as the larger ones, but she has falsely induced from her particular experience that all small company operations will be equally poor.

When you draw conclusions or make assertions, you must be able to support them by supplying the audience with the basis for your reasoning. In other words, you must convince the audience that your arguments are based on logical thinking.

Reasoning is that process of thinking by which an individual arrives at conclusions. A detective, a scientist, a labor mediator, and a public speaker all use the reasoning process as a tool of their respective trades. The ability to reason or think in a logical way is one of the distinguishing characteristics of the human mind. It is through reason that humans learn about their surroundings and generalize about their environment. Without this ability we could neither adapt nor function successfully in this world.

PATHOS: FEELING.   A speaker may decide that *pathos,* an appeal to the emotions, will be more effective than logos, an appeal to reason. The effectiveness of emotional appeals depends on the mood of the audience, the topic and the specific purpose in creating the message.[4] Pathos is especially effective in situations in which emotions tend to override logic. Pathos includes reward appeals, fear-arousing appeals, and appeals to needs, desires, and values.

A *reward appeal* promises the listener some personal gain or profit if he or she believes or behaves in the manner suggested by the speaker. The intended reward may be either material or psychological. For example, a high school dropout who hears a speaker at a job placement center may be persuaded to attend night school to get his diploma if he is made to feel that it will better his chances for obtaining gainful employment. When the same individual attends his first class at the adult education center, he may be even more determined to finish if the instructor speaks about the increased self-confidence and sense of achievement he may expect as a result of his efforts.

The opposite of the reward appeal is the *fear-arousing appeal.* People tend to be more vulnerable to persuasion if they perceive a threat to themselves or their loved ones. An effective speaker can capitalize on a person's fear in order to enhance a persuasive message. Advertisements for home fire alarms and various safety products are examples of this approach.

The effectiveness of a fear appeal was shown in a study conducted by Watson, Pettingale, and Goldstein, three researchers who were interested in determining the effects of an antismoking film on groups of smokers versus nonsmokers.[5] Using levels of arousal and anxiety as measures for testing the persuasiveness of the film, the researchers showed subjects a videotape of a TV program on the adverse effects of smoking. Results of the study indicated that the fear appeals used (in other words, the adverse effects of smoking that were discussed) indeed increased levels of anxiety in the group of smokers. Watson and her colleagues concluded that fear appeals that address the adverse effects of smoking may alter listeners' levels of anxiety and may thereby diminish their desire to smoke.

Although fear arousing appeals are often used when constructing messages concerning health, the value of such appeals is sometimes overlooked. The following example illustrates a situation in which a fear appeal was not used and lack of persuasion resulted. In a scenery workshop for

---

[4] Ibid., 310–11.
[5] M. Watson, K. W. Pettingale, and D. Goldstein, "Effects of a Fear Appeal on Arousal, Self-Reported Anxiety, and Attitudes Toward Smoking," *Psychological Reports* 52 (1983), 139–46.

The logos, pathos, and ethos of a public-speaking situation are not only recognized but controlled by an effective speaker.

the theater department of a university, the instructor presented the ground rules for participation in the class. Along with reminders to show up on time and to clean up before leaving, the students were advised to use the power saws only if supervised, to wear safety goggles and aprons when needed, to remove their jewelry, and to tie their hair back if it was long. The teacher did not really make clear the possibilities for serious harm to his audience, and the students were only too eager to start hammering and sawing. Some weeks later, one student lost his footing on a ladder and almost dislocated his arm when the leather thong bracelet he wore around his wrist caught on a protruding nail. In this case a greater fear appeal might have spared someone a badly wrenched shoulder and a puncture wound in the palm of his hand.

While certain fear appeals are justified, others become scare tactics. People are easily persuaded when they are made to feel threatened. Residents of a small middle-class neighborhood in New York City became vehemently opposed to the building of a low-income housing project when community leaders made them fearful that the project would mean an increase in crime and a deterioration of the neighborhood. Although the arguments used were purely emotional, they aroused enough fear and opposition to delay the building for some time.

In the previous example, the fear appeal was directed at a need for safety and security. Other psychological *needs* can be targets for the persuasive speaker as well. The need to be loved, the need to be respected, and the need for self-fulfillment can all be used as means of persuading an individual to change attitudes, beliefs, or behavior.

An effective speaker can also use human *desires* as a means of persuasion. When an attractive actress advertises an automobile, the appeal is intended to be sexual. Similarly, promises that a particular soap or cologne will make a man virile or a woman enticing are definitely based on an emotional appeal to desire. Other common targets for the effective persuader are the desire to be powerful, the desire to be unique and the desire to remain youthful.

Yet another type of emotional appeal aims at our sense of **values**—the things we consider important. The individual who has two big cars, fancy clothes, and no money in the bank values material possessions over security. The parent who sacrifices a vacation each year to put a child through college values education above leisure. An effective speaker can use a person's sense of values to accomplish his or her end. In a television advertisement a young husband is seen telling his wife that he wants to buy life insurance. Feeling unnerved by the subject, the wife asks that they not discuss it. The husband responds with, "Let's talk about how much I love you, instead." This ad clearly equates love and security and emphasizes the values of the family man.

As stated earlier, a good persuasive speaker will take care not to alienate his or her audience with a badly organized message. One of our primary concerns as listeners is how the organization of a message will affect us on an emotional level. Studies have shown that a well-organized message prevents listeners from feeling frustrated or angry and consequently increases the chance for an appeal to more sympathetic emotions. The importance of this factor is relative to individual listeners, since some people need greater structure than others to make sense of a message.

ETHOS: SOURCE CREDIBILITY.   *Ethos,* or source credibility, is the way in which a speaker is perceived by the audience. According to Aristotle, speakers will be held in high esteem if they are perceived as intelligent and moral and if they demonstrate good will toward the audience. Aristotle believed that these qualities alone were enough to create attitude change. Today we tend to analyze a speaker's ethos in terms of his or her expertise and trustworthiness. Source credibility contributes much to the persuasiveness of a message when the audience has no direct experience or knowledge of the topic.[6] However, whether the audience is informed or not, the speaker must be perceived as trustworthy and knowledgeable in order to carry any weight. If the author is perceived to be informed yet dishonest or devious, the speaker's persuasibility will be undermined.

Sometimes a speaker's ethos will be established long before a particular speaking situation. For example, a Nobel Prize-winning physicist will probably be highly regarded by an audience because of prior accomplishments. His or her message would probably be more persuasive than that

---

[6] W. Chenghuan and D. R. Shaffer, "Susceptibility to Persuasive Appeals as a Function of Source Credibility and Prior Experience with the Attitude Object," *Journal of Personality and Social Psychology* 52, no. 4 (1987), 677–88.

Credibility is a function of both expertise and trustworthiness.

of a local high school science teacher, even if they presented identical messages.

When speakers lack ethos, however, it is harder for them to persuade. Let us look at the following situation: A college president, distrusted by the student body because he or she overreacted and called in the police to deal with a nonviolent protest, convened a conference of the student government to persuade students not to discuss the protest incident with the media. The president's ethos at this time was very low, and the students were particularly resistant to this persuasive attempt.

In many situations, however, a speaker is unknown to the audience and approaches the situation without a reputation of any kind. In this case the speaker must *establish* ethos, or credibility, so that the audience will perceive him or her as knowledgeable and trustworthy.

One factor that is influential in establishing ethos is organization. Aside from affecting comprehension, the organization of a speech affects speaker credibility. Studies in this area have shown that a speaker who is well organized in his or her presentation will be regarded as a more credible source than a speaker who is disorganized. Interestingly, however, an audience's perception of source credibility can change in midstream, as demonstrated by pre- and post-attitude tests. For example, the use of visual aids in organized messages tends to increase source credibility of a speaker, as evaluated by attitude tests given before and after the speaker's presentation.

The following is a partial list of factors related to source credibility.[7]

[7] Adapted from R. N. Bostrom, "The Components of Credibility," in *Persuasion* (Englewood Cliffs, N.J.: Prentice Hall, 1983), 71–74.

1. *Qualification/expertness*: This component of credibility operates when listeners are convinced that a source has enough training, ability and experience to merit belief. For example, a nuclear physicist who presents a lecture on radioactivity would be rated higher on this dimension of credibility than would a high school student reading a report to a physics class.

2. *Safety/trustworthiness*: This factor operates when a source is believed to be telling the truth and not presenting falsehoods to the listeners. For example, someone who makes money selling video- and audio-tapes for real estate sales would be rated as less credible and persuasive on this dimension than would a realtor and friend of the family who is talking with you about real estate.

3. *Compliance/dynamism*: Sources who have either real or implicit power in a relationship often are more believable and persuasive than those who do not have power.

4. *Normative/identification*: Finally, credibility arises when a source is identified with a particular group that is important to the listener. To illustrate, Tommy is a chapter member of a local conservation club. When he discovers that James Kingry, president of the national organization, is to be a guest lecturer in one of his classes, Tommy will probably perceive that Dr. Kingry is a more credible source than his classmates will, even though Dr. Kingry is speaking on a topic unrelated to conservation or ecology.

Contemporary Approaches

Clearly, Aristotle had much to offer the student of communication. More specifically, he was perhaps the first person to articulate three primary ways in which an individual might be persuasive. Based solely on the value of his approach, several twentieth-century communication scholars have argued that nothing "new" has been written on the subject since Aristotle's time.

Although Aristotle indeed made substantial headway for communication students in the twentieth century, several, more recent theories of persuasion have contributed to our understanding of the overall process, as well. These theories include social judgment theory, balance, and cognitive dissonance theories (two consistency theories), and Milton Rokeach's theory concerning beliefs, attitudes, and values. We now turn to a more complete discussion of each.

SOCIAL JUDGMENT THEORY.   Social Judgment Theory is primarily associated with the work of Sherif and his associates.[8,9] Basing his work on experiments in the area of psychophysics, Sherif used information about how people

---

[8] M. Sherif, *Social Interaction: Process and Products* (Chicago: Aldine, 1967).
[9] M. Sherif and C. I. Hovland, *Social Judgment* (New Haven, Conn.: Yale University Press, 1961).

judge physical objects (such as weight and distance) to understand the ways in which people make judgments about social objects (such as differences in one's own and others' attitudes). As a result of his comparisons of the physical and social world, Sherif developed four important concepts which could explain social judgments. These concepts included latitudes of acceptance, rejection, and noncommitment, and the notion of ego-involvement as it affects judgments.

According to Sherif, people make judgments about objects or persons based on "anchors," or reference points. For example, if you were to hold in one hand a jar of peanut butter and in the other, a jar of jelly and two pieces of bread, you would judge which of the two was the heavier based on how heavy one of the objects was (the peanut butter, for example) in relation to the other (in other words, the jar of jelly and the bread). In this instance, the jelly and the bread would serve as an anchor point for your judgment concerning which was the heavier object.

Much as we make judgments concerning physical objects in the way just described, Sherif argues that we make social judgments in a similar fashion. For example, if a visiting speaker at your university were to deliver a message supporting increased government spending, your attitude about the topic at that moment would serve as an anchor for determining your response to the speaker and her message. If the speaker's attitude is similar to yours, her message would fall within a ***latitude of acceptance***, or within a range of messages that you would define as acceptable (and hence believable). In contrast, if her discussion revealed attitudes or beliefs dissimilar to yours, her message would fall within your ***latitude of rejection,*** or within a range of messages that you would define as unacceptable. In this instance, for you, the speaker would probably be less persuasive. Finally, if the speaker's message revealed an attitude about which you felt neutral, her message would fall within your ***latitude of noncommitment.*** In other words, the speaker's message would fall within a range of messages about which you feel neutral. As a result, she would probably persuade you in neither direction.

Another important concept in social judgment theory is that of ***ego-involvement,*** or the degree to which a given issue is important to you. Although Sherif's "latitude" concepts do explain persuasion to some extent, Sherif and his colleagues further argue that level of ego-involvement will affect persuasibility. In other words, the more important an issue is to you, the less likely you are to be persuasible about it.

To illustrate the importance of ego-involvement in persuasion, think of some issue about which you feel very strongly. It may be an issue like abortion, nuclear waste, "Star Wars" defense, or legalization of marijuana. When someone speaks on one of these topics (or another important issue) to you, how easily are you persuaded in the opposite direction? According to Sherif, you probably would not be easily persuaded. Sherif would argue that your ego-involvement in this instance would serve to decrease your ability to be persuaded. As a result, a speaker who talks about one of these issues will find himself or herself less able to to persuade you. Should you become less ego-involved, however, the job would become much easier.

> The ability, Phaedrus, to become a finished performer is probably . . . like everything else: If it is in your nature to be a speaker, an eloquent speaker you will be if you also acquire knowledge and practice.
>
> —Plato

To this point, we have described social judgment theory from the viewpoint of the listener. However, how can you as a *speaker* take this information into account as you prepare a persuasive message? Perhaps the most practical way in which you might utilize this theory is to first take into account Sherif's description of the effects of ego-involvement. You may decide that the most effective way to construct a persuasive message is to find ways to strengthen or weaken the audience's involvement, depending on whether your position is viewed as favorable or unfavorable. If you are giving a speech on a favorable topic, strengthening their ego-involvement can help you to strengthen beliefs as well. However, you will want to decrease their ego-involvement if the audience is unfavorably disposed.

A second way in which social judgment theory can guide you in constructing effective persuasive messages lies in its concepts of latitudes of acceptance and rejection. If your audience's reference points or anchors are far from yours, attempting to illustrate similarities between you and the audience might help to reduce the distance. If their anchor point lies closer to yours, persuasion will be an easier task.

COGNITIVE CONSISTENCY THEORIES.   In Chapter 1 we learned that attitudes are the tendency to respond positively or negatively to people, objects, or ideas. When our purpose is to persuade, we want to alter a person's way of thinking or change his or her behavior. Consistency theories help speakers examine methods people use to cope with arguments and ideas that are consistent or inconsistent with their attitudes.

The first of these theories, **balance theory,** originated by Fritz Heider, is based on positive and negative evaluations of all attitude objects, including persons, things, and ideas.[10] The relationship between our positive and negative evaluations determines whether we are in a state of balance or imbalance. A person is in a state of balance if one of three conditions exists:

1. Two positively evaluated objects are positively related. For example, if your favorite professor likes your favorite poet, there is a positive connection between two positively related objects (which in this case are the professor and the poet).
2. Two negatively evaluated objects are positively related. For example, you find out that two people whom you dislike are getting married to each other. A balanced state exists here since you are negatively disposed toward both people, who are obviously positively disposed

---

[10] F. Heider, "Attitudes and Cognitive Organization," *Journal of Psychology* 21 (January 1946), 107–12.

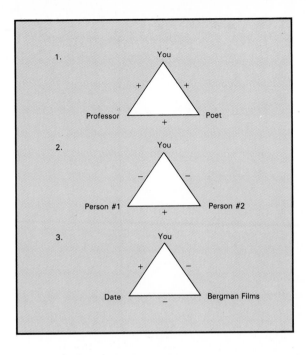

'RE 10–1
Balance

toward one another. You probably will say to yourself, "Good, they deserve each other!"

3. A positively evaluated object dislikes a negatively evaluated object. For example, you find out that the person you are dating dislikes Bergman films as much as you do. In this case, the positively evaluated object, your date, dislikes the negatively evaluated object, the Bergman films.

When the mind is in a state of balance, there is no need for attitude change to occur. If a person is in a state of imbalance, however, he or she may be psychologically uncomfortable and desirous of change.

A state of imbalance may occur in the following situations:

1. When two positively evaluated objects are negatively connected. For example, suppose that favorite professor of yours thought that your beloved poet wrote nothing but drivel. Your respect and admiration for the professor would be in conflict with your respect and admiration for the poet. This situation would tend to make you feel psychologically uncomfortable.

2. When two negatively evaluated objects are negatively related. Suppose the two people you disliked so much loathed each other as well. The fact that you shared an opinion with these people would cause imbalance.

3. When a positively evaluated object and a negatively evaluated object are positively related. For example, suppose that your date really enjoyed the Bergman films you disliked so intensely. The state of

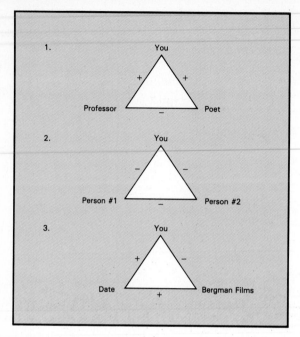

FIGURE 10–2
Imbalance

imbalance would be created by the fact that your date (positively evaluated object) differed with you concerning the Bergman films (negatively evaluated object).

The effective persuader tries to create a state of imbalance in the listener so that persuasion can take place more readily. The imbalance created in the preceding situations might result in the following:

1. It might allow the professor to persuade you that the poet wrote trash.
2. It might lessen or increase your distaste for one of the previously mentioned individuals. You might conclude, "She hates him as much as I do; perhaps she's not so bad after all," or "If he hates her (and heaven knows he's no prize), she must be even worse than I thought."
3. It might allow your date to persuade you to go to the film with him or her.

In public speaking situations, speakers can create imbalance by building their own credibility and then speaking in opposition to audience beliefs. Ideally, the audience would then resolve the imbalance by changing its attitudes.

Using Fritz Heider's balance theory as a basis, Leon Festinger proposed a later theory known as ***cognitive dissonance***.[11] According to Festinger,

---

[11] L. Festinger, *A Theory of Cognitive Dissonance* (Stanford, Calif.: Stanford University Press, 1963).

cognitive dissonance is a form of imbalance between pieces of knowledge and/or feelings. Your knowledge, beliefs and feelings about yourself and your environment may be either in harmony with each other or out of harmony. A person who finds smoking pleasurable must also deal with the information that smoking is dangerous to health. There is an imbalance, or dissonance, between the pleasure felt and the fear-provoking information. To reduce the dissonance, the individual can stop smoking or refuse to believe the information that relates smoking to lung cancer.

No one likes to feel psychologically uncomfortable with his feelings or attitudes. Think about situations in which you have experienced a certain amount of cognitive dissonance. How did you go about resolving the conflict? Cognitive dissonance theory teaches that the public speaker who creates imbalance in audience members risks that they will resolve the inconsistency in ways other than those intended and proposed by the speaker.

For example, a young woman speaking at a health club is trying to persuade her audience to become vegetarians. She cites the youthful appearances of various swamis and the peace of mind of numerous gurus. She extols the healthful qualities of the vegetarian diet and points out the bad effects of eating meat. Finally, she appeals to her listeners on the grounds that it is wrong to kill animals for food. All of her listeners want to be youthful-looking and healthy and certainly would enjoy peace of mind. None of them likes to picture the slaughter of animals; however, their food habits and tastes are long established. They may find themselves uneasy and decide, "Oh well, that's all right for her; she's young and healthy anyway. Besides, I'm a working mother. I don't have the time to fool with all the preparation. I just joined this club to get a little exercise." In order to ease the tension created between the argument for a new way of eating and the desire to go on enjoying their steaks and hamburgers, they dismiss her presentation as not applicable to themselves.

ROKEACH: ON BELIEFS, ATTITUDES, AND VALUES.   Perhaps one of the most comprehensive theories of persuasion and attitude change is that of Rokeach.[12,13] Focusing on the relationships among beliefs, attitudes, and values, Rokeach has developed an extensive explanation of human behavior.[14] Although his theory has often been considered a consistency theory, its breadth goes beyond the consistency theories presented to this point. It will therefore be presented as a theory in its own right.

According to Rokeach, each of us has an elaborate system of beliefs, attitudes, and values. This system is best represented as a complex organization (or system) of beliefs. These beliefs, in turn, act as guides for our everyday behavior.

---

[12] M. Rokeach, *Beliefs, Attitudes and Values: A Theory of Organization and Change* (San Francisco: Jossey-Bass, Inc., 1969).
[13] Ibid., *The Nature of Human Values* (New York: Free Press, 1973).
[14] Portions of this discussion are adapted from S. W. Littlejohn, in *Theories of Human Communication* (Belmont, Calif.: Wadsworth Publishing Company, 1989. 3d ed.), 90–94.

Perhaps the best way to define **beliefs** is to conceive of them as the thousands of statements or inferences we make every day about ourselves and the world around us. These statements may be either general or highly specific and are arranged in terms of their centrality or importance to us. At the center of our belief systems lie firmly grounded, unchangeable beliefs. At the periphery, unimportant, changeable beliefs are said to reside. Examples of the former might include our beliefs that the sun will rise tomorrow and that time is a commodity. Less important beliefs might be that it is better for one to take the stairs rather than the elevator, and that wearing a hat while it's raining is better than carrying an umbrella.

Clustered around beliefs are **attitudes,** which result from our beliefs. Attitudes usually focus on objects or situations, and guide our behavior during a given event. To illustrate, think of the last time you went to a friend's house for dinner, only to find that your host or hostess was serving something that you definitely did not like to eat. According to Rokeach, you probably tried to eat the food that was served. Your behavior arose because your attitude about the situation (dinner with a friend) was more important than your attitude about the object (the food). As a result, you probably attempted to "grin and bear it." Thus, your beliefs about the "right thing to do" and your consequent attitudes served as a guide for your behavior.

Although beliefs and attitudes are important in the overall system, Rokeach believes that values are perhaps the most important of the three elements. His reasoning is that values form the very foundation of all human behavior. Thus, it is important to understand his concept of human values.

According to Rokeach, **values** are the core of our belief system. They are very specific types of beliefs that (1) act as guides for daily behavior and (2) represent the ultimate aims in life toward which we work. The former of these beliefs are termed *instrumental values*; the latter beliefs are labeled *terminal values*. Examples of instrumental values include the following: to be ambitious, broadminded, logical, loving, or responsible. Terminal beliefs might include beliefs in the importance of having a comfortable life, an exciting life, a sense of accomplishment, a peaceful world, equality for all, freedom, happiness, mature love, inner harmony, pleasure, or self-respect. These values reside at the center of our belief systems; they guide our everyday lives and result in our behavior.

At this point you may be asking yourself, "But what does all of this have to do with persuasion?" As we stated in an earlier section, Rokeach is generally considered to be a consistency theorist. As such, he is interested in *consistency* in human behavior. Rokeach's greatest contributions to consistency theory may be (1) a description of a much more complex human system than those of Heider and Festinger, (2) an explanation of human behavior that reflects a realization of the complexity of humans, and (3) his theory's predictive value. More specifically, Rokeach's theory allows us to predict and explain behavior as it relates to the persuasibility of listeners—and to understand exactly how complicated persuasion is. For these reasons, his theory truly belongs in a discussion of persuasion.

PERSUASIVE TECHNIQUES

We have thus far discussed the theories of persuasion. You may now be wondering about specific techniques that can be used in delivering persuasive messages. Indeed, using at least one of six techniques may help you construct an effective speech. These techniques include the uses of one-sided versus two-sided arguments, evidence, forewarnings, humor, primacy, and recency effects, and effective conclusions. Each of these techniques will be discussed in the following pages.

ONE-SIDED VERSUS TWO-SIDED ARGUMENTS.   When presenting a speech to persuade, a speaker must decide whether to present both sides of an issue or argument or only the side he or she is supporting. The effectiveness of either a *one-sided* or a *two-sided presentation* is determined by several factors.

In general, a two-sided argument is more effective when the audience is opposed to the speaker's point of view, when it is well educated, and when it will be exposed to opposing arguments in the future. On the other hand, the one-sided argument is more effective if the audience is predisposed to the speaker's position. For example, the woman who is in favor of abortion does not need to hear a counterargument in order to strengthen her belief. One-sided arguments also tend to be more effective if the audience is less well educated and if it will not be confronted with later attempts at persuasion.

The effective speaker in a two-sided approach can present both sides of an issue and pick apart the opposing argument in order to strengthen his or her own position. For example, a prosecuting attorney can repeat arguments put forth by the defendant and then proceed to show that these arguments are weak, inappropriate, or false.

USE OF EVIDENCE.   While you might expect that the use of evidence could only enhance a persuasive message, studies in this area have come up with inconsistent and contradictory findings. While some researchers have concluded that the use of evidence is advantageous, others have shown it to be of little significance. In general, the persuasive communicator must assess the subject and audience before relying on evidence to make the speech effective.

For example, an efficiency expert who wants to persuade a group of office managers to use a new type of computer would be wise to include statistical data as evidence. The subject of efficiency is technical and the audience is used to problem solving based on facts and figures. The listeners will be intent on hearing accurate information before allowing themselves to be persuaded.

If speakers have low credibility with their audience, the use of evidence may do little to enhance their position. The audience may "tune out" the facts and figures, thinking them to be as ill founded and unreliable as the speakers themselves. On the other hand, speakers before audiences that perceive them as highly credible need not include evidence in their presentations. The audiences will accept their messages at face value.

When the speaker is perceived by the listener to have authority or economic power over others, the use of evidence will be superfluous. The promise of reward for those who agree and punishment for those who do not will be enough. Similarly, when listeners hold the speaker in a position of respect, they may allow themselves to be persuaded without hearing much hard evidence, in order to win the speaker's approval.

FOREWARNING.   Does foreknowledge of a speaker's intent have any effect on the persuasion process? According to Hiromi Fukada, a Japanese expert in the area of persuasion, prior knowledge of a speaker's intent when he or she plans to present a fear-arousing message reduces the effect of that message by stimulating anticipatory counterarguments.[15] In other words, when an audience is forewarned of a speaker's intent to use fear-arousing appeals, audience members will generate arguments that are counter to that of the speaker during the actual presentation and will remain more resistant than audiences not forewarned throughout the message.

Of course, a speaker's intent is often well established long before he or she begins the presentation. For example, when a number of tenants refused to pay a rent increase, the landlord went before the tenant's organization. The landlord's intent was perfectly clear. The audience knew he was there to convince them that they should pay the rent increase and that the increase would mean better service. In a case like this, where the purpose is no secret, effective speakers will reveal their intent in the introduction and give a preview of what they are going to say. It thus appears that they are trying to be straight with the audience instead of trying to manipulate them.

HUMOR.   Another variable that the persuasive speaker should consider is the use of humor. Once again, studies have provided contradictory findings as to whether the use of humor enhances the persuasive attempt or detracts from it. Humor can loosen up a tense atmosphere, emphasize certain key points and entertain the audience. Yet how much humor to interject, or whether to use it at all, becomes a problem for the persuasive speaker.

Some studies have shown that humor lowers the speaker's credibility. On the other hand, a study conducted by Markiewicz found that humorous sources were considered more trustworthy than serious ones.[16] Perhaps the effect of humor on source credibility and successful persuasion depends on the listener's relation to the speaker. The data are inconclusive. According to some studies, listeners who were neutral toward or in favor of the speaker's

---

[15] H. Fukada, "Psychological Processes Mediating Persuasion-Inhibiting Effect of Forewarning in Fear-Arousing Communication," *Psychological Reports* 58 (1986), 87–90.

[16] D. Markiewicz, *The Effects of Humor on Persuasion* (Doctoral dissertation, Ohio State University, 1972).

position were equally persuaded by serious or humorous messages. Other studies have shown that humor distracts a negative audience from its preconceived ideas and increases the possibility of attitude change.[17]

Based on the contradictory findings of various studies in this area, we can only advise that the persuasive speaker proceed with caution when using humor. The effective persuader must remember that there are various forms of humor and should evaluate the message and the audience's position before deciding which type and how much humor he or she will use.

PRIMACY AND RECENCY.   An important element in organizing your message so that it will have the greatest impact is to determine the placement of various arguments and key points. There are two effects that you should consider in this organization: primacy and recency. In some cases arguments presented first in the speech tend to have the greatest effect in creating attitude change. This is an example of ***primacy*** organization. Sometimes, though, strong arguments presented near the end of a speech seem to be more persuasive. When arguments are presented in this order, a ***recency*** effect occurs.

To say that one pattern of organization is always more effective than another is incorrect, since existing information is contradictory. It is known, however, that certain factors may influence the effectiveness of placing an argument first or last. These variables include the nature of the message, audience position relative to that of the speaker, the interval between arguments, and so forth. The effect of primacy-recency on the organization of arguments within one message and on the order of two opposing messages has been studied.

Although research has not provided any firm rules for the order of presentation of ideas, some general guidelines have emerged. It is important to remember, however, that these are not conclusive or final.

1. With a one-sided persuasive message, building to a climax of strong material at the end of the speech produces a greater effect upon the audience than an anticlimactic arrangement.

2. When presenting a two-sided (pro and con) argument, it is wise to present the first half in a climax order and the second half as an anticlimax. In other words, build to your strongest supporting material and then lead on from strong opposing evidence to weak. The audience, as a result, will evaluate the first half of your presentation more positively than the second.

3. In a one-sided persuasive speech, it is best to underscore weak arguments with strong ones. If a strong argument is followed by several feeble ones, the total impact is lessened.

4. Weak arguments have more effect at the beginning or end of a speech.

---

[17] R. L. Applbaum and K. W. Anatol, *Strategies for Persuasive Communication* (Columbus, Ohio: Charles E. Merrill, 1974), 104.

When contained in the body, they are likely to be overshadowed by the surrounding material.

5. Strong messages presented in a set or in proximity to one another will result in greater audience retention of material. A group of weak arguments (unless they lead up to a more forceful message) will not be particularly effective.

6. In a two-sided presentation, it is best to place the pro, or supporting arguments, before the con, or opposing view.[18]

THE CONCLUSION.   Conclusions summarize and reinforce the speaker's point of view. Although any speech, regardless of purpose, should have a conclusion, it is particularly important in a persuasive speech. Comparisons between a speech in which the conclusion is left to the audience and one in which it is stated show that an explicit conclusion has a greater persuasive effect. This finding emerged in a study by Weiss and Steenbock in which two groups of college students were asked to read literature supporting the need for a particular course of study that most of the student body opposed. One group was given a statement with a concluding paragraph. The second was given the identical literature without the conclusion. Student attitudes toward the course were evaluated before and after reading the literature. Measured against a control group that was not given any literature about the course, results showed that the group given the concluding paragraph showed greater attitude change than did the other groups.[19] Therefore, the effective speaker uses the conclusion as a means of enhancing a message.

PERSUASIVE SITUATIONS

Persuasive communication is widespread. One of the most obvious settings in which persuasion occurs is in the courtroom. Here the court must decide whether there is enough evidence to warrant a trial, or a jury must decide upon the guilt or innocence of the accused. The prosecuting attorney may use a logical form of persuasion to convince the jury of the defendant's guilt: "The culprit was also described by several witnesses as a middle-aged man wearing unusually large sunglasses and a bright green athletic jacket. The defendant was arrested several blocks from the scene of the crime wearing such a jacket. The sunglasses were found in a trashcan in a nearby parking lot. From the color of his jacket and the fact that the sunglasses were found near the scene, it naturally follows that he is the man responsible for the burglary."

A defending attorney may appeal to the emotions of the jury. "The defendant was wearing a green athletic jacket, but he was on his way to

[18] A. J. Clark, "An Exploratory Study of Order Effect in Persuasive Communication," *Southern Speech Communication Journal* 39 (1974), 322–32.

[19] W. Weiss and S. Steenbock, "The Influence on Communication Effectiveness of Explicitly Urging Action and Policy Consequences," *Journal of Experimental Social Psychology* 1 (1965), 396–406.

his son's Little League game at the local ball park. This is the kind of family man who is more likely to wear an American flag tie pin than a pair of gaudy sunglasses." By associating the defendant with the family, the favorite American sport, and patriotism, the defense counsel attempts to persuade the jury of his client's upright citizenship and innocence.

On a less dramatic but equally effective level, persuasion is also the basis of sales and advertising. The appliance salesman, the encyclopedia saleswoman, and so forth, all hope to gain access to your home and your pocketbook as they go from door to door. A good salesperson can be so persuasive that many states have adopted legislation that enables a person to cancel an order or void a contract within several days of the initial sale. This type of law protects the consumer who may be "talked into something" by a persuasive salesperson.

Perhaps the most effective sales pitches are the ones that appear on television and radio or in newspapers and magazines. So powerful are these media that manufacturers invest millions of dollars annually in advertising costs. So persuasive are these media that Whittle Communications, creator of *Channel One*, the controversial news and advertising program for the classroom, boasted a projected income of $152 million for fiscal year 1989.[20] While sponsors of such programming hope to entice the audience into buying their products, they also hope to expose the audience to new ideas and items. Many people go into the grocery store and buy a product that they have just heard about or seen advertised on television. Others are persuaded by their children to buy a new toy that has been bombarding the airwaves. Exposure and the power of suggestion account for much of the success of mass-media advertising.

Not all sales pitches come from manufacturers. In discussing persuasion, we must not overlook the charity drive. We tend to forget this form of selling, since the product we buy is either good will or a tax deduction. The most frequently used approach in a charity drive is the emotional appeal. While certain charity drives occur all year round, they seem to be most prevalent during holiday time, particularly around Christmas. The timing is not accidental; most people are more vulnerable and charitable at this time of year.

ENTERTAINMENT, CEREMONIAL, AND OTHER SPECIAL-OCCASION COMMUNICATION

In the beginning of this chapter we divided public communication according to purpose. We have already taken an in-depth look at speeches designed to inform and persuade. We are now ready to focus our attention on the third category, the speech to entertain and the special-occasion speech. While these two categories are often thought to be synonymous, it should be pointed out that special-occasion speeches include eulogies, farewells, and resigna-

---

[20] S. Elliott, "Whittle's Approach Riles Rivals," *USA Today* (March 8, 1989), B1.

tions, which are seldom meant to entertain. However, since many special-occasion speeches, such as introductions, acceptances, and after-dinner talks, are often intended to entertain, we will discuss them as separate but related in purpose.

Kinds of Special-Occasion Speeches

There are many different types of special-occasion and ceremonial speeches. Let us take a look at a few of the more familiar ones. A **welcoming speech** may be presented to an individual or an entire group about to join an organization or attending a particular meeting or seminar. The speaker who presents the welcoming speech should mention the group extending the welcome and should make some comment on the occasion. Perhaps you remember the dean of students presenting a welcoming speech at your freshman orientation. Similarly, when you graduate, a fellow student or member of the faculty will welcome the parents and friends of the graduates. A welcoming speech should be brief and to the point. It may be humorous in nature, depending on the situation or occasion.

Two additional special-occasion speeches are the **award presentation** and **acceptance speech.** You are probably familiar with these types of speeches from having seen televised presentations of the Oscar, Tony, and Emmy awards. It is likely that you have participated in some sort of award presentation as a presenter, recipient, or member of the audience. At some time in your life, you may have attended a high school awards assembly, a scouting club breakfast, or a church supper, where awards for superior performance were presented to deserving recipients. Whether an individual presents an award or receives one, he or she should emphasize the significance of the award. While the presentation speech focuses on the many ways in which the recipient qualifies for the award, the acceptance speech is a way of saying thank you.

The **after-dinner speech** is often, but not always, a speech to entertain; certainly, it is intended to make the audience feel relaxed and comfortable. The content of the speech depends on the nature of the banquet. A more formal occasion will warrant a more serious presentation. The after-dinner speech at a hundred-dollar-a-plate political banquet will probably be more serious than the one presented at an annual fraternity ball. The after-dinner speech should be relatively brief, since other announcements, introductions, and speeches are usually on the agenda.

In a **farewell speech,** the speaker expresses regrets about leaving a particular group or organization and offers thanks to those who are left behind. A person who retires or is joining another company, the valedictorian of the high school graduating class, the employee who has joined the ranks of management, or the man or woman going off to join the military all share a common purpose in saying goodbye and thank you to the people they are leaving.

One particular type of farewell is the **eulogy,** a ceremonial speech marking someone's death. A eulogy may be presented at the funeral service or at a later date, as a memorial. Numerous memorial services are held on

Acceptance speeches are a way to say "thank you."

January 15 to mark the birthday of the Reverend Martin Luther King, Jr., renowned civil rights leader. The eulogy is a farewell speech that praises the virtues and accomplishments of the deceased. While a eulogy is often delivered by a member of the clergy, sometimes friends, family, or colleagues make the presentation in addition to or instead of the clergy.

Although there are numerous other special-occasion speeches, the last category we will discuss is the ***impromptu speech.*** "Impromptu" refers to the manner of presentation. An impromptu speech is one that is made on the spot, without any sort of preparation. Someone who wins an unexpected award will be expected to give an impromptu acceptance speech. Someone filling in at the last minute for a scheduled speaker may be asked to give an impromptu welcoming or after-dinner speech. The most important thing to remember when delivering an impromptu speech is to stick to the topic and try to present your speech in an organized and interesting manner.

Principles of Effectiveness

In any special-occasion speech or speech to entertain, there are several principles of effectiveness that you should consider. The first of these is to use humor appropriately. Remember that not all speeches or occasions should have a humorous approach. If the occasion does call for humor, you must decide if your speech should be really funny or just mildly amusing. Humor should be used as a means of accomplishing your purpose, not of offending or distracting your audience.

Another principle is to have a central theme. This is particularly important in special-occasion speeches. The speaker should know his or her purpose and relate the entire speech to that purpose.

Finally, the speaker should avoid belaboring points and should be clear, cogent, and brief. These qualities are particularly desirable in ceremonial or special-occasion speeches.

Chances are that at some time in your life you will be asked to deliver a special-occasion speech or a speech to entertain. It might be at a community affair, at a political banquet, or at a class reunion. If you keep these principles in mind, you will increase your chances of success.

SUMMARY

The major communication goals are information exchange, persuasion, and entertainment. In the first case, the speaker must aim for audience learning and comprehension. In the second, the speaker tries to modify the attitudes, beliefs, or behavior of the listener. A speaker whose purpose is entertainment must strive to amuse or please the audience.

When presenting an informative speech, the speaker must keep in mind the factors that affect audience learning. The speaker must try to motivate the audience to listen and learn. The message must be organized, and ideas must be effectively developed. The speaker may emphasize important information by repetition or by the use of visual aids. Information exchange may take the form of audience participation.

At least four major approaches to persuasion can help us to better understand the persuasive process. The Aristotelian approach provides us with three modes of persuasion: logos, pathos, and ethos. Social judgment theory provides a description and explanation of the social judgment process. Balance and cognitive dissonance argue that if and when a psychological imbalance is created in the listener, the possibility for attitude change is increased. However, there is always the chance that the audience will not resolve such imbalance in the manner the speaker intends. Finally, Rokeach's theory allows us to distinguish among beliefs, attitudes, and values and documents the true complexity of persuasion; it gives us a more complete understanding of human complexity.

In addition to the tools these theories provide in persuasive situations, a speaker may increase the persuasive effects of his or her presentation through the use of specific speaking techniques. An appropriate use of one- and two-sided arguments, sound and sufficient evidence, or forewarning of purpose may help to change the attitude of the listener. Explicit conclusions and the proper use of humor may also be persuasive. Consideration of the primacy-recency effect, the arrangement of ideas and arguments within the speech, may also improve the potential for successful persuasion.

The final kind of public communication is the speech to entertain, whether for ceremonies or for other special occasions. The entertaining speech is intended to bring pleasure and amusement to the listener. The special-occasion speech may be a way of saying thank you, farewell, or congratulations. It may be an occasion for awarding praise or it may be a eulogy. Appropriate use of humor; a clear, concise, and well-organized presentation; and a central idea are important elements of effectiveness in any of these communication situations.

EXERCISES

GROUP EXPERIENCES

Before and After

DESCRIPTION: Most individuals need some type of motivation to listen to, and then learn, the information that is conveyed by the speaker. Without even realizing it, most of us continually provide reasons for another person to listen to us in a dyadic conversation. If you are attracted to another person, this may provide extrinsic motivation for you to listen to what he or she has to say. On the other hand, if you have been with a person over time, attraction may no longer serve as an extrinsic motivator. In cases such as these, another form of motivation would have to be developed in order to maintain interest in the conversation. This activity will help you to understand the connection between interest level and motivation.

PROCEDURE: This is a role-playing activity that is most effectively used as a demonstration technique in front of the class. There are two roles, one played by a female and the other played by a male. The team should be asked to play the following three scenes.

> *Before.* This is your first date. You are sitting in a nightclub. You are both extremely attracted to one another and excited about being together. You hang on to every word the other person says because you don't want to miss anything. Show your interest in the other person both verbally and nonverbally.
>
> *During.* You have been dating for four months. You are at the nightclub again. Your relationship is gradually shifting to where you are more interested in the music than in each other. You listen to each other on an off-and-on basis.
>
> *After.* You have been together for a long, long time. You are at the nightclub again. You have heard everything the other person has to say "a million times." Neither one of you listens to what the other person is saying. Carry on an entire conversation where you misinterpret or do not listen to what the other person is saying.

DISCUSSION: This activity demonstrates the existence of extrinsic motivation (attraction to the other person) in the "before" scene. The "during" scene demonstrates the minimal existence of extrinsic motivation, while the "after" scene demonstrates the complete absence of extrinsic motivation for listening to the other person. Logically, it can be assumed that extrinsic motivation can be replaced with intrinsic motivation, which then would increase the listening level. Can you think of a time during which you listened to another person with the absence of extrinsic or intrinsic motivation? Can you provide motivation for others to listen to you on both a physical and a psychological level? In your daily conversations, do you provide motivation for the other person(s) to listen?

The 60-Second Commercial

DESCRIPTION: Research suggests that many different variables should be considered when planning a speech for a particular audience. Some of the considerations include extrinsic and intrinsic motivation, organization, effective development of ideas, repetition, and visual presentation. This activity will provide you with the opportunity to use a variety of techniques in an attempt to persuade the audience to remember your product.

PROCEDURE: You are to design a 60-second commercial on a fictitious product or service. You will be paying a high price for 60 seconds of prime time, so the commercial should be designed with extreme care. Your purpose is to motivate your audience to remember the name of your product. Be creative in the design of your commercial.

DISCUSSION: The class period following the presentation of the commercials should be used to test which products were remembered. Take out paper and pencil and list all the products you remember. Next to each product you should identify why you remembered the product. After everyone has completed these lists, check to see which products were remembered the most. Why were some products remembered, while others were not? Consider the repetition, organization, and visual presentation of the message. Do you think it is difficult to develop a "persuasive" message?

How's Your Ethos?

DESCRIPTION: Ethos, or source credibility, refers to the way in which a speaker is perceived by the audience. Some of the findings related to source credibility include:

1. Receivers tend to accept conclusions advocated by sources perceived as competent and trustworthy.
2. A high credibility source can produce more attitude change than a low credibility source, even with highly ego-involved receivers.
3. When a receiver identifies with a source, it may enhance the source's chances of producing attitude change.
4. The receiver's attraction for a source increases as similarity of attitude between the two increases.
5. The status of the speaker can affect his or her persuasiveness.

The following activity provides you with an opportunity to see how these principles work.

PROCEDURE: Which of the above principles of source credibility does this example illustrate?

> *Sample Situation.* In an Arizona state prison, a program was presented on adapting to society after living in prison. Two speakers addressed the group of inmates. The first speaker was Dr. Sharon Stone, a noted psychologist in the area of social adjustment. The second speaker was Ron Harnick, a former inmate who had spent five years in the state prison system. The inmates showed greater interest in listening to Ron Harnick, and, consequently, his speech had a much greater impact than Dr. Stone's.

Two principles can be identified in this example. Principle 3 above suggests that when a receiver identifies with a source, it may enhance the source's chances of producing attitude change. In this case it can be observed that the inmates (receivers) identified with Harnick (source) because of the time the latter spent in the prison. Principle 4 suggests that the receiver's attraction for a source increases as attitudinal similarity between the two increases. It may be assumed that the inmates perceived Harnick to have greater attitudinal similarity with them as compared with Dr. Stone.

Now that you have a sample description, divide into dyads and write an example that will serve to illustrate each principle. You may use one

The environment can affect both the speaker and the audience.

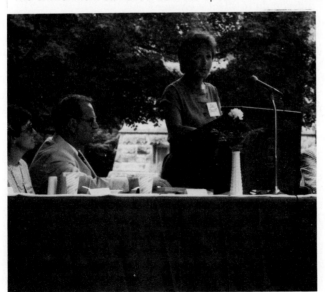

example to illustrate two principles. Each dyad should read one example to the rest of the class and ask the other students to explain the applicable principle of source credibility.

DISCUSSION: After writing and listening to various examples, can you identify other principles of source credibility? What are some of the ways in which you can be perceived as more credible? Which methods are most commonly employed by politicians to enhance their credibility?

PERSONAL EXPERIENCES

1. A state of imbalance is said to occur when (a) two positively evaluated objects are negatively connected; (b) two negatively evaluated objects are negatively related; or (c) a positively evaluated object and a negatively evaluated object are positively related. A state of imbalance is psychologically uncomfortable and usually results in an individual's desire for change. Identify a state of imbalance that you have experienced. Which principle does your experience illustrate? Did you do anything to alter the imbalance? What did you do to effect a change?

2. Obtain a copy of a transcript of a speech, or attend a speaking situation in which the speaker is clearly attempting to persuade his or her audience. Was the speaker ethical? List your criteria for a code of ethics in public speaking.

3. A common misconception about public speaking is that the ability to make speeches is instinctive and cannot be learned. Interview one or two people in your community who are considered to be effective speakers. Find out how they began public speaking. Were they ever afraid to speak in front of groups? Did they ever deliver a "bomb"?

DISCUSSION QUESTIONS

1. What are the criteria used to distinguish public communication from private communication?

2. What is an example of a persuasive speech to (a) convince, (b) stimulate, and (c) actuate?

3. Are the qualities of ethos, pathos, and logos inherent in every good speech? Why? Why not?
4. Under what circumstances would a one-sided argument be more effective than a two-sided argument?
5. What forms of motivation would be most effective to use when speaking to a group of college students?
6. In what ways do persuasive messages affect your day-to-day activities?
7. What techniques can a speaker employ to increase audience participation?
8. What are some creative ways you can think of to repeat the same information in different forms?

11

Developing and Organizing the Message

KEY CONCEPTS AND TERMS

Personal interview
Survey
Introduction
Thesis statement
Body
Conclusion
Transition
Topical pattern
Chronological pattern
Spatial pattern
Increasing levels of difficulty pattern
Chain of events pattern
Inductive pattern
Deductive pattern
Cause-and-effect pattern
Problem-solution method

Simplicity
Coordination
Subordination
Progression
Symbolization
Real example
Hypothetical example
Extended example
Illustration
Anecdote
Description
Comparison-contrast
Operational definition
Statistics
Testimony

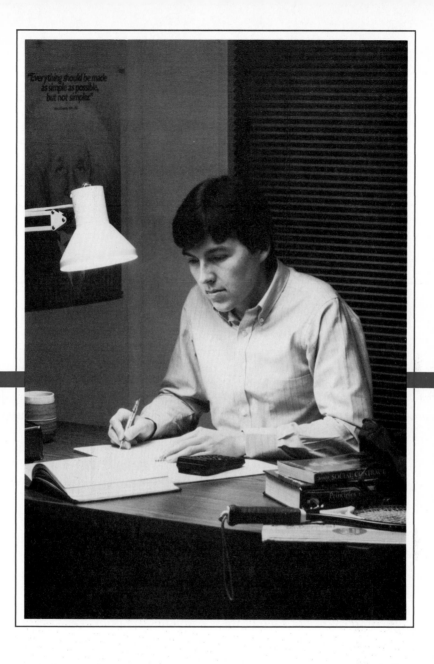

As Drew sat in his office pondering how he could best structure his presentation for the board, his eye caught a glimpse of an old photograph that had been with him for years. Framed in oak and sitting at eye level on the mantel, the photo seemed to come to life as his gaze traveled lazily toward the crackling fire. As his eyelids grew heavy, Drew found himself returning to an earlier time in his life—a time when he, Bobby Harper, and Randall Morris, the subject matter of that old photo, would camp out and tell ghost stories in the woods beside the creek. Hypnotized by the flames, Drew could almost hear the wind through the trees and the words that Bobby whispered. Bobby's voice had always trailed into a whisper when he got to the scariest parts.

As he heard the owl's hoot and the final words of Bobby's story, Drew actually experienced the "startle reflex" that he always associated with Bobby's dramatic conclusions. Jarred into reality, Drew sat upright with a start and looked suspiciously around the room. Then his eyes traveled back to the photo on the mantel, and he slowly began to smile. *"That's how I'll approach this presentation,"* Drew said to himself. "I'll create a story that'll keep 'em hanging on every word." As he reached for the pad and pencil that had now been idle for over an hour, he scribbled notes that would transform his message into a colorful story. With two hours to spare and newfound inspiration, Drew knew he had this presentation "in the bag."

All of us have probably experienced childhood memories such as Drew's—memories of sitting around a campfire telling ghost stories. Interestingly enough, it's no different when we're grown: Stories can bring to life the main point that we are making and capture the imagination of the audience. Like every good story, a public speech has an introduction and conclusion. Both also have climactic moments, color, and imagery.

In this chapter you will learn how to create more effective presentations by using many of the principles that successful storytellers use. However, public speakers, like storytellers, must be prepared. Speaking in public is a challenge that requires selecting a topic or approach that will enthrall, gathering information that will add not only substance but also color and form, and organizing the message with the rhythm and ebb and flow of a story. More than any other in the book, this chapter is a kind of handbook of do's and don'ts. It is meant to give you practical advice. The suggestions on how to choose your topic and gather source materials will provide you with the foundation for creating more effective presentations. Likewise, we hope the information on organizing and supporting the body of your speech and on preparing an effective outline will help. (Appendix B illustrates how the process works by presenting and annotating an effective speech.) Given the importance of each of these elements to public speakers and storytellers alike, we now turn to a discussion of how to select and narrow presentation topics.

SELECTING THE TOPIC

Finding a suitable topic is sometimes half the battle. In some instances there is no choice. The topic may already have been decided for the speaker. For example, a union representative may be invited by the membership to discuss pension benefits at the monthly meeting, or a veterinarian who services a rural community may be asked by the local farmers to discuss precautions against cattle diseases.

You and the Topic

When you must choose your own topic, however, certain guidelines must be considered. The first concerns you, the speaker—what you know about, what you're interested in, and what you believe in.

KNOW YOUR TOPIC.   It's always easier for people to discuss subjects they are familiar with than ones about which they know little. An art historian would probably feel quite comfortable discussing Leonardo da Vinci but ill at ease talking about the advantages of solar energy. Although a good speaker researches *any* topic, previous knowledge of a subject can make the selection process easier.

BE INTERESTED IN YOUR TOPIC.   It is also very important to select a topic in which you are interested. If you are genuinely interested in the subject you are to speak about, your enthusiasm will be communicated to your audience when you deliver your speech. Interest in your topic also increases motivation to investigate and research it thoroughly.

BELIEVE IN YOUR TOPIC.   Consider your personal values and beliefs when selecting a topic. Make sure that your beliefs and the topic you choose are compatible. This is particularly important in persuasive speaking; you could hardly expect your audience to be convinced of the need for tougher environmental laws, for instance, if you yourself were not firmly convinced. A firm belief in your topic will make the presentation more vital to you and to your audience.

NARROWING THE TOPIC

Once you have selected a topic, you must narrow it so that it is workable. Don't be like the high school student who decided to deliver his first speech ever on "the French Revolution." How narrow should your topic be? That depends upon your purpose. The thrust of a speech will vary according to whether it is intended to inform, persuade, or entertain. For example, in a well-coordinated effort, several elected city officials addressed their fellow citizens on the financial crisis in their city. The focus of each individual address was different. In a formal televised statement, the mayor, whose purpose was to inform the public of the crisis situation, focused on the current fiscal deficits and the long-range consequences of inaction. At a later press conference, a councilman outlined the kinds of legislation necessary to relieve the crisis situation. A third member of the city council was given the job of persuading the citizens who attended a town meeting to write letters or send telegrams to state and federal government officials encouraging them to pass legislation to relieve the financial crisis. Although each speech dealt with the finances of the city, the thrust of each address was determined by the speaker's purpose.

A good speaker should consider personal purposes and goals as well.

These, too, will aid you in achieving desired results and in fully informing the audiences. One way that you might begin is to make a list of objectives, ideas, opinions, and conclusions that you have drawn (keeping in mind, of course, the audience and time limits involved!). Next, ask yourself the following five questions:

1. What action should result from the speech?
2. What message must be communicated to initiate this action?
3. When should this action be taken?
4. Who should generate the action?
5. Are opinions, general concepts, or conclusions the most important to convey?[1]

Determining your central thought is a final consideration when defining and narrowing your topic. One of the most glaring speaking errors of beginners and poor speakers is lack of focus. As noted earlier, good speeches are much like other works of art—stories, musical compositions, paintings, plays, or literary works. They consist of separate elements that become unified into a whole by means of a central idea or thought.

GATHERING SOURCE MATERIALS

After selecting your topic and narrowing it, you can begin to collect the materials you need to build your speech.

Use of Sources

It is usually to your advantage to select from a wide variety of sources. The type and number of sources you use will depend on the specific purpose of your speech. When presenting an informative speech on a controversial issue, you should always secure information on at least two opposing views, especially when one source of information is biased. For example, if you were presenting a speech on "rising gasoline costs," you might find that the explanations of the shortage and the consequent increase in prices presented in an oil company publication would be quite different from the facts and arguments put forth in a consumer group pamphlet. In a situation like this, you should consult several sources in order to get the true picture. Of course, when presenting a persuasive speech, you may choose to include only those sources that support your particular point of view. Even then it is important to be aware of the opposition.

Whether you conduct an interview, read a magazine article, or watch a videotape, it is essential to take notes. Your notes should include summaries of the information and direct quotations, particularly if you plan to use

---

[1] Adapted from "Public Speaking Requires Effective Preparation." In *The CPA Journal* 54, no. 4 (1984), 77.

them in your speech. Ethical considerations and accuracy necessitate the use of a quotation in the context in which it was found. When direct quotations are not in order, summaries of information are sufficient.

You as Source

The most basic and obvious source at your disposal is yourself. Whether you realize it or not, you represent a storehouse of knowledge, experience and observations. The fact that you remember paying twenty cents for a slice of pizza when you were in junior high school may be trivial. If you are going to give an informative speech on inflation and the cost of living, however, this information could suddenly assume significance. In general, personal anecdotes, examples, experiences and observations make a speech more meaningful for the speaker and more colorful for the audience.

Interviews

You will often find that the best source of materials for a particular subject is another person or group of people. In that case you may want to gather your material by conducting an interview.

PERSONAL INTERVIEW. A *personal interview* is conducted on a one-to-one basis with a person who has information or knowledge about the topic of your speech. For example, if you were to present a speech on penal reform, you might want to interview an attorney, an inmate, a judge, and other individuals connected with the penal system. If you were presenting an informative speech on a particular diet fad, you might find it valuable to

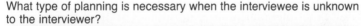
What type of planning is necessary when the interviewee is unknown to the interviewer?

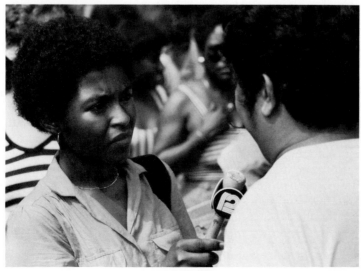

interview a doctor, a nutritionist, someone who had success with the diet, and someone who did not. Although a personal interview may provide a sizable amount of material, information or opinions obtained by this method should not be considered definitive. The impact an interview will have on your audience depends on how that particular audience judges the credibility of your source.

Regardless of the subject, a good interview requires good technique. If you choose to conduct an interview, keep certain things in mind:

1. Remember your purpose and topic and avoid getting sidetracked.
2. As an interviewer, you should try to make the person you interview feel comfortable and willing to talk. Obviously, a cooperative interviewee will make your task much easier.
3. Be prepared for the interview and have definite questions in mind.
4. Since you are trying to find out specific information or opinions, phrase your questions in such a way that they will bring clear responses.

If the topic of your speech lends itself to a personal interview and an appropriate interviewee is available, you will find this method an invaluable source of material.

SURVEY.   At times you may need to conduct a survey rather than a personal interview. A *survey* is a detailed gathering of information by questionnaire, observation, interview, and so forth. A survey enables you to gain a cross-section of information and opinions. Suppose you were giving an informative speech on the sexual mores of today's college students. You might wish to conduct a survey of as large a sample of your fellow students as possible in order to obtain some firsthand information. As in the case of the personal interview, the information and opinions obtained through a survey are not meant to be definitive. Although both sources are most useful when used informally, the validity of a survey can be judged in terms of standardization of questions and the selection of participants.

Printed Material

Printed material has long been relied on as the primary source of information for speech content. Such material includes books, magazines, journals, pamphlets, newspapers, diaries, almanacs, encyclopedias and so on. There are so many different types of printed material that it is essential to know how to locate these different sources and use them properly. Information about some subjects is almost exclusively found in printed material. For example, historical information that cannot be gained through a personal interview may be found in books or in a journal, and reports about current breakthroughs in science or medicine might be located in professional journals or magazines.

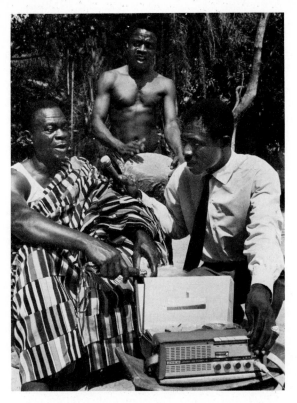

A young historian went to the Ivory
Coast to tape legends from an
Akan tribal chief.

Today, thanks to microfiche and microfilm, printed material can be stored in a minimum amount of space. Libraries are the primary storage houses for printed material, but you may find it necessary or beneficial to search out other sources. If you were doing a speech on alcoholism, you could find printed information in the vertical file of the library, or you might visit a local branch of Alcoholics Anonymous and pick up pamphlets or newsletters regarding their programs and services. Many such special interest groups, consumer organizations, churches, trade unions, and so on, publish their own small newspapers or booklets about their activities.

Electronic Media

Modern technology has provided us with additional sources of material in the form of electronic media. Films, television, cassettes, records, computerized data bases and videotapes are all valuable sources of information that can aid you in the preparation of a speech. For example, the now famous Zabruder film of the Kennedy assassination has proven to be a vital source of evidence for those who urge further investigation of the shooting. Since the advent of videotape, many events have been captured on film and are available as source material for the speaker.

PARTS OF THE SPEECH

All speeches, regardless of their purpose or length, should be composed of three basic units: the introduction, the body, and the conclusion. Each of these parts serves at least one function that is essential to the effectiveness of the speech. Although each part of the speech should flow smoothly into the next, each unit should be identifiable upon analysis of the text.

Examine the following two brief speeches, which were prepared for a training seminar for magazine salespeople. Read each presentation carefully and decide which one is more effective.

> There are many different magazines from which a person can choose. For the sports enthusiast, there are magazines like *Sports Illustrated* and *Field and Stream*. The homemaker might want to learn new recipes or tips on decorating from the *Ladies Home Journal* or *Redbook*. Those who enjoy literary magazines may turn to the *Saturday Review* or *The New Yorker*, while others may be interested in general news magazines like *Time* or *Newsweek*. These magazines vary in price and frequency of publication and are available through our subscription service.
>
> Have you ever been stuck in a doctor's office or train station without anything to keep your mind off waiting? Or maybe you were stuck inside with a cold or waiting for a delivery? Perhaps if you had an interesting magazine to read, the waiting wouldn't seem so long.
>
> There are many different and interesting magazines from which one can choose. For the sports enthusiast, there are magazines such as *Sports Illustrated* and *Field and Stream*. The homemaker might want to learn a new recipe or tips on decorating from a magazine like the *Ladies Home Journal* or *Redbook*. Those who enjoy literary magazines may be interested in reading a copy of the *Saturday Review* or *The New Yorker*, while others might be interested in a general news magazine like *Time* or *Newsweek*. These are just a few of the many magazines which can be readily purchased by subscription.
>
> The number of magazines published is quite large. One can safely say that there is a magazine for every area of interest, whether it be crafts, sports, science, health, automobiles, food, fashion, gardening, or anything else. And what makes it even better is that they are all available through subscription.

Although these two speeches contain basically the same information, the second speech is obviously more effective. It has a carefully developed introduction, body, and conclusion.

The Introduction

The **introduction** of a speech must first catch and then focus audience attention as well as preview the body of the speech. Sometimes just getting started is one of the most crucial and difficult tasks in presenting a speech.

Often a speaker has to compete with a noisy or inattentive crowd. In such cases it is even more important to capture the audience's attention with an effective introduction.

What your country is going to do
for you — ask what you can do
for your country — my fellow
citizen of the world — ask not
what America will do for you —
but rather what you can do
for freedom   Rather ask of us —
the same high standard of
sacrifice and strength of heart
and will that we need from

A speech in preparation: A portion of President John F. Kennedy's inaugural address.

In addition to the initial benefit statement mentioned at the beginning of Chapter 10, several other standard devices can serve as an effective introduction. These include the use of a startling statement (By the year 2025, the earth will run out of food), a rhetorical question (Did you ever wonder what your life would be like had you been born in another era?), statistics (Only 1,400 out of 2,000 college freshmen will earn their degree), a humorous statement (If all the world's a stage, then a lot of us get bit parts), or a famous quotation (You may fool all the people some of the time; you can even fool some of the people all the time; but you can't fool all of the people all the time). Of course, sometimes one statement produces two or more effects. For example, the statement "One out of every two marriages ends in divorce" uses statistics but may also be somewhat shocking to an audience.

THESIS STATEMENT.   The introduction of a speech should also include a *thesis statement* that presents the specific purpose of the speech. The purpose can sometimes be worked into the opening device for getting attention. For example, a museum sponsor might begin a fundraising speech with:

You don't have to go to a peep show to see some of the most beautiful nudes imaginable. Some of the world's most famous nudes can be found right here in our museum. But, unless we can find a way to raise twenty thousand dollars for maintenance costs, these nudes are going to be left out in the cold!

The opening line of this introductory paragraph begins with an unexpected or startling statement. Chances are, at least a few ears will perk up with the words "peep show." The remainder of the paragraph suggests that the museum is in financial trouble and must raise money to continue its operations. The last sentence suggests the purpose of the speech and gives some insight into what the main text will be about.

Regardless of the technique you use in your opening, be sure that the introduction is appropriate, is in good taste, and says exactly what you want it to say. You should not use a joke or anecdote unless it is appropriate to the occasion and relevant to the subject. You should avoid telling a joke or humorous story unless you feel perfectly comfortable with it. Remember, not everyone is a comedian. You should also omit irrelevant "warm up material" and clichéd beginnings such as, "A funny thing happened to me on the way . . ." Your introduction should be relatively brief and direct.

The Body

The effective introduction previews the main text of the speech and leads directly into the body. The **body** is generally the largest part of the speech and is intended to present the main points, elaborate on them, and clarify when necessary. It is also a function of the body to develop clear transitions between different ideas.

In an informative speech, the body contains the bulk of the information you wish to present. In a persuasive speech, the body contains the arguments and evidence that support the speaker's position, as well as a refutation of any counterarguments. For example, if you were trying to persuade your audience to support the abolition of capital punishment, the body of the speech would probably include moral and legal arguments along with appropriate supporting material. You might also include statistics to disprove the standard counterarguments, which contend that capital punishment is a deterrent to crime, or those that attempt to justify capital punishment on the basis of "an eye for an eye."

> Industry in art is a necessity—not a virtue—and any evidence of the same, in the production, is a blemish, not a quality; a proof, not of achievement, but of absolutely insufficient work, for work alone will efface the footsteps of work.
>
> James McNeill Whistler

The body of a persuasive speech should include a discussion of the nature, effects, and causes of the problem, issue, or controversy. A politician who is trying to change the juvenile justice system because it is too lenient

Persuasive messages generally contain moral and legal arguments.

might want to include statistics showing a high percentage of juvenile felonies, case histories of chronic juvenile offenders, and the opinions of sources who have experience in the legal system. The speaker should show why the particular problem is meaningful to the audience. The politician might try to convince the audience that it is no longer safe to go outside or that children and the elderly increasingly fall prey to juvenile criminals.

The body is the longest and most detailed part of your speech, so the arrangement of its ideas is very important. There are certain patterns of organization you can follow to help you structure the body of your speech effectively. These patterns of organization include a topical pattern, a chronological pattern, a spatial pattern, and various other patterns. Because the organization of the body is so important to effective speech making, we will discuss these structural arrangements in greater depth later in the chapter. Simply stated, however, the body of the speech should be presented in a way that is logical, coherent and easy to follow.

The Conclusion

A speech isn't over until the speaker walks away from the podium. Therefore, the **conclusion** of the speech is as important as the introduction. Although the major portion of the speech is presented in the body, it is the conclusion that can leave a lasting impression.

In general, the conclusion of an informative speech should offer a restatement of the major ideas and a summary of the overall content. Concluding a speech on what to look for in buying a car, a speaker might restate specific guidelines such as economy, safety, and size as well as summarize the ways in which these guidelines can assist the buyer. Similarly, a demonstration talk on how to make a macramé wall hanging should end with a summary of the necessary materials and specific steps involved.

The conclusion of a speech gives you an opportunity to tie up loose ends and bring the speech to a unified finish. As it is impossible for the audience to listen to and remember everything that is said, the conclusion should emphasize the main points so that the audience knows what was most important.

The conclusion of a persuasive speech may be used to arouse the audience to action. Let's examine the conclusion to the speech presented by our museum sponsor:

> In conclusion, ladies and gentlemen and patrons of the arts, it is time to assure our magnificent paintings a place inside our museum. For many years you have enjoyed the beauty of these fine paintings. Now it is time to give something in return. Take out your wallet or your checkbook and give what you can to help raise the twenty thousand dollars we need to keep our museum doors open!

This paragraph underscores the purpose of the speech and asks for some action on the part of the audience. A concluding call for action need not always be financial, of course. The president of a parents' group may end an address with a plea to parents to keep their children home from school as a protest against a cutback in school services. Or a union delegate might ask an audience to join a boycott of crops picked by nonunion workers. A political candidate might conclude a rally by asking for volunteers to distribute campaign literature. In each case the call for action would be strongest in the concluding paragraph.

Regardless of purpose, the concluding paragraph should round out the speech and bring it to a satisfying close. The final sentence should signal the end of the speech so that the audience will know that it is over. The speaker may want to close with an emphatic statement or use one of the devices mentioned in our discussion of the introduction. For example, if you want to leave the audience thinking, you might pose a rhetorical question. Or, depending upon the content of the speech, you might want to conclude with a famous quotation.

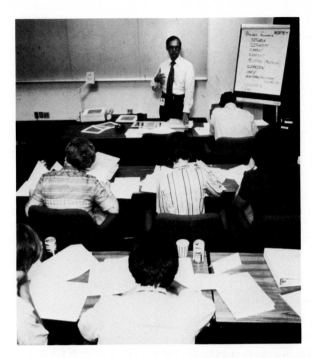

Using visual aids can help summarize key points at the conclusion of a message.

Sometimes you might want to coordinate the conclusion with the introduction by using the same type of device, or even the same statement. For instance, a community leader who opens with the quote from Abraham Lincoln that we mentioned earlier may close the speech thus: "You cannot fool all of the people all the time; and all of us here tonight know that *now* is the time to demand an end to the irresponsible actions of the City Council." Using the same quotation or same set of statistics not only reinforces a point but also lends your speech a sense of closure and balance.

Transitions

We should not overlook the use of transitions as an important aspect of speech organization. A *transition* is the bridge that allows one idea to flow smoothly into the next.

The most important transitions are those between the introduction and the body and between the body and the conclusion. However, they are also necessary between the main ideas within the body. For example, in a speech presented at a block association meeting, a neighborhood detective was discussing an increase in local crimes. One major point was that in recent years there seemed to have been a tremendous increase in auto thefts and robberies. To lead into his next point, the detective added, "But, unfortunately, the problem has not remained in the streets. Latest precinct reports show that household break-ins and burglaries in the area are up 50 percent over last year." The shift from crime on the street to crime indoors was smoothly made by a simple transitional statement.

The complexity of a transitional bridge depends upon how similar the two ideas are that are being connected. Sometimes just a few words or a simple sentence will do. For example, certain phrases, such as "in addition to," "aside from," and "in conclusion," are often used as transitional bridges.

When ideas are not closely related, you may need a more substantial transition, in other words, something that draws a connection between the two ideas or parts. A woman speaking to a group of senior citizens may wish to convince them of the need for an urban renewal project and at the same time assure them of the preservation of their neighborhood. The two points may be related in this way:

> Perhaps you feel that all of these changes I have proposed will destroy the charm of our downtown area. However, along with the plans for change are many plans for the restoration of our historical sites and parks. The kind of rebuilding now proposed will be in keeping with the tastes and needs of our community.

The effective use of transitions is one way to distinguish between a good speech and a mediocre one.

ARRANGEMENT OF THE BODY OF THE SPEECH

Patterns for Informative Speeches

We have already mentioned several standard patterns of organization that can help you structure your speech and present your ideas with the greatest effectiveness. The pattern you choose will probably depend on your topic. Certain subjects are best suited to particular patterns of organization. We will now discuss some of the standard patterns most frequently used in the informative speech. It is important to remember that audiences retain more information when speeches are logical and well organized.[2]

TOPICAL PATTERN.   One of the most frequently used organizational patterns is the *topical pattern,* in which information is presented according to a specific category or classification. This type of organization is particularly useful when the subject of the speech can be divided into subparts that form a whole. For example, a speaker at a children's concert might introduce the audience to various parts of the orchestra by using a topical approach. He could discuss the strings, then the brass, then the woodwinds, and finally, the percussion instruments. Each of the major divisions could then be broken down according to the general characteristics of each group and the specific instruments within each category.

---

[2] V. Hazleton, W. R. Cupach, and J. Liska, "Message Style: An Investigation of the Perceived Characteristics of Persuasive Messages," *Journal of Social Behavior and Personality* 1, no. 4 (1986), 565–74.

CHRONOLOGICAL PATTERN.   A second standard pattern of organization is the *chronological pattern,* which follows a subject in time. The chronological pattern is particularly useful when presenting biographical or historical information or when tracing the development of an idea, institution, or movement. A speech on the development of satellite communication could be presented in a chronological pattern by tracing the events from the launch of Sputnik I on October 4, 1957, to the most recent advances in satellite technology. Or a speech on American fashion in the twentieth century could be divided into decades and could mention such eras as the "flapper" style of the 1920s, the miniskirt of the 1960s, and the "Yuppie" look of the 1980s.

A chronological speech may span centuries or days, depending on the scope of the topic. As it is virtually impossible to do justice in a relatively short speech to a topic that covers an enormous period of time, the speaker must focus on the most important information. You must also make sure that the audience is aware of the time lapse between events, especially when the events or information you are discussing have occurred at uneven intervals. For example, in presenting a biographical sketch, you might connect one event to the next with phrases such as "two years later" or "in a matter of weeks" in order to give the audience some perspective as regards the time that has passed. The use of transitional phrases is particularly important when presenting a speech according to chronology.

Remember, nobody wants to hear innumerable small details. Even in everyday conversation, an unnecessarily detailed account of an event or an experience can become very boring. Children are often guilty of this practice. For example, you may ask a child what a certain television program was about, and he will repeat an endless sequence of events. Obviously, each step is not an integral part of the story. However, the child has not learned how to decide what information is most important. A speaker must be able to determine the most important information, for he or she cannot include too many ideas, events, or details without causing the speech to become lengthy and tiresome.

SPATIAL PATTERN.   Not every subject is suited to every pattern of organization. Topics based on the location of one part in relation to others or on a geographical progression may best be presented in a *spatial* order. A speech that traces the westward expansion of America might be divided according to the extension of different geographic boundaries. (Note that the same speech might be presented using a chronological order.) A speech based on Christopher Columbus's discovery of the New World might follow his historical routes.

A spatial organization may be appropriate for certain subjects not related to geography at all. For example, an architect presenting a speech on the Pyramids might approach the topic from a spatial order, emphasizing the relationship between one part of the structure and another. A spatial organization enables the audience to visualize the individual parts as they relate to one another in terms of the whole.

PATTERN OF INCREASING DIFFICULTY.   Because one of the primary factors in evaluating the success of an informative speech is audience understanding, the speaker must strive to present the speech as clearly and logically as possible. When a topic is relatively complex, the speaker may choose to use a pattern of organization based on *increasing levels of difficulty.* This type of structure is particularly helpful when presenting an informative talk on a subject with which the audience is unfamiliar. When a plant manager explains the changes that will take place within a factory because of the pending use of robotics, the manager may want to present the information in varying degrees of difficulty. Because the comprehension of some ideas is based on understanding other ideas, a pattern of increasing difficulty helps to ease the progression. Audiences feel much more comfortable after they have mastered an idea or understood some particular bit of information. By carefully building one idea upon another, a speaker can present increasingly complex material to an audience whose confidence in its own interpretive and evaluative abilities also increases.

CHAIN-OF-EVENTS PATTERN.   As the name implies, this pattern of organization is based on the development of a series of steps, with each step depending on the previous one. For example, a local congresswoman addressing members of the Young Democratic Club in her district might use the chain-of-events method to explain the sequence of events that must occur as a bill goes from the committee stage to its actual enactment as law. Similarly, a weatherman predicting a fifty-fifty chance of a snowstorm might outline the series of weather events that must occur in succession in order for the storm to develop. The *chain-of-events* method is particularly useful when giving a demonstration speech that explains a certain procedure. For example, a salesperson demonstrating the use of a personal computer would show the customer how to operate the computer according to step-by-step directions.

Patterns for Persuasive Speeches

Various patterns of organization are particularly well suited to the persuasive speech. While these methods are not restricted to persuasive speeches, they are often used in them. Remember that the purpose of a persuasive speech is to create attitude change within the listener.

INDUCTIVE PATTERN.   The first pattern is the *inductive pattern.* This particular pattern of organization is based on the process of inductive reasoning, which we discussed in the previous chapter. In an inductive argument, you present the audience with several specific cases that serve as the basis for a generalization. The specific cases must, of course, support the generalization. Therefore, you must avoid examples that are inconsistent with or contradictory to the generalization you wish to make.

The number of specifics necessary to formulate a sound generalization will vary. Although there are mathematical calculations to determine statistical validity, you can usually rely on common sense and intuition to decide upon the minimum number of specific cases that a particular argument demands. For example, a senior citizen who condemns all teenagers as "dope fiends," based on the solitary example of a neighbor's son, lacks a sufficient number of specific examples. Therefore, the generalization is invalid. When the generalization involves a large population, a greater number of specific cases is necessary.

Certain generalizations are easier to support than others. For example, U.S. health officials who sought to end the swine flue inoculation program used an inductive argument. Citing several incidents of paralysis as a side effect of the injection, officials provided enough evidence to ban the program. The argument might have followed this pattern:

SPECIFICS: I. Specific cases of paralysis following inoculation.
              A. Cases of paralysis in Florida.
              B. Cases of paralysis in Denver.
              C. Cases of paralysis in New Jersey.
GENERALIZATION: II. The swine flu inoculation can cause paralysis.
CONCLUSION: III. Therefore, the inoculation program is potentially hazard-
              ous and should be discontinued.

Based on the occurrence of cases of paralysis following the shots, health officials decided that the inoculation could conceivably have caused paralysis and therefore concluded that the program should be discontinued. The generalization that the inoculation could cause paralysis was evolved through an inductive process based on the occurrence of scattered cases of this side effect. While some experts discounted this argument, emphasizing that the percentage of cases of paralysis was quite small relative to the number of persons receiving the shot, the program was discontinued.

DEDUCTIVE PATTERN.   The inverse of the inductive pattern is the ***deductive pattern,*** in which a speaker applies a generalization to specific cases. The generalization, if accepted by the audience, serves as the basis for an effective argument.

In a deductive pattern of organization, the speaker must draw a conclusion about a specific case based on its applicability to a previously accepted generalization. In Chapter 10 we mentioned the syllogism, which is the most common example of deductive reasoning. An effective argument can be organized in the form of a syllogism. For example, a concerned member of the community may offer the following deductive argument at a public transportation hearing:

GENERALIZATION: We are all agreed that traffic lights reduce accidents.
SPECIFIC: There seem to be a lot of accidents at the intersection of
            40th and Vine.
CONCLUSION: Therefore, a light at the intersection of 40th and Vine would
            reduce the number of accidents.

If the traffic officials agree with the citizen's general statement, they might be quite willing to accept the solution. If the general statement is not accepted by an audience, however, the deductive argument will have little effect. Generalizations based on value judgments are most difficult to validate. Therefore, a speaker must have some insight into the nature of the audience. Let us examine the following deductive argument:

GENERALIZATION:	All war is immoral.
SPECIFIC:	Vietnam was a war.
CONCLUSION:	Vietnam was immoral.

The effectiveness of this deductive argument depends on the audience's acceptance of the general statement. Undoubtedly, an audience of conscientious objectors would accept this argument. However, the same argument would probably be vehemently rejected if presented before an audience of Veterans of Foreign Wars. Therefore, in preparing a deductive argument, the speaker must be sure that the audience will agree with the general statement.

CAUSE-AND-EFFECT PATTERN.   Closely related to the inductive argument is the *cause-and-effect pattern.* In this type of presentation, the speaker establishes a relationship between two events. The speaker attempts to convince the audience that this relationship is one of cause and effect, or that a certain result is the product of a specific event. For example, at a monthly sales meeting, an assistant buyer suggests that the increase in hosiery sales is due to a new line of pantyhose. This argument could be confirmed: According to the record of sales, the new line of pantyhose contributed to an increase of 25 percent of the total volume of hosiery sales. Therefore, the new line of pantyhose (cause) produced an increase in sales (effect). However, not all cause-and-effect arguments can be mathematically determined. For example, how could you substantiate a claim that natural catastrophes such as earthquakes and floods increase as a result of our tampering with the atmosphere? Although it might be argued that these disasters have been more prevalent following milestones in space exploration, it would be impossible to draw a causal relationship between the two events.

One effect is often the result of several causes. For example, when a heretofore losing team moved into a new stadium and started to win, the cheering fans were convinced that the new stadium brought the team luck. In a case such as this, the exact cause of the team's success would be a combination of things, including perhaps the new stadium, an increase in attendance, errors on the part of the opposition, the return of an important player after an injury, and so forth.

PROBLEM-SOLUTION PATTERN.   Another useful pattern of organization for the persuasive speech is the *problem-solution method.* This approach is much the same as the pattern of organization used in group discussions (see Chapter 7). The problem-solving method, first described by John Dewey, includes the following basic steps:

1. What is the nature of the problem?
2. What are the causes?

3. What are the possible solutions?
4. Which is the best solution?
5. How can this solution be put into effect?

Remember our traffic light example? Let's examine this example according to the problem-solution pattern. The nature of the problem concerns the number of accidents at the intersection of 40th and Vine. Causes of the problem include the use of this route as an alternative to the parkway, with a subsequent increase in traffic, and the lack of any traffic signs or personnel. Possible solutions include a traffic light, a police officer to direct traffic, rerouting the traffic, and a four-way stop sign at the intersection. The best solution would be a traffic light, since a police officer would be too costly, a four-way stop sign might prove confusing, and rerouting the traffic would cause congestion on neighboring roads. The solution could best be put into effect by a decision by the Department of Traffic and the installation of the light by the same agency.

The problem-solution pattern is based on a logical, step-by-step analysis of a particular problem. Of course, the analysis of any problem requires considerable research and investigation.

PRINCIPLES OF OUTLINING

Regardless of the organization pattern you select, an outline helps you in the preparation as well as the delivery of your speech. The outline is a tool that allows the speaker to categorize information and separate main ideas from subordinate ones. For example, in a topical presentation the speaker would classify each aspect of the subject as a main division of the outline. In our previous example of an informative speech on the parts of the orchestra, the strings, brass, woodwinds and percussion would each be represented as a major category of the outline. Each category would then be subdivided into specific instruments and general characteristics. Part of such an outline would look like this:

Parts of the Orchestra
I. The Strings
    A. Types of String Instruments
        1. Violin
        2. Viola
        3. Cello
        4. Double bass
        5. Harp
    B. Characteristics of the String Instruments
        1. Sounds produced by plucking, bowing, or striking strings
        2. Many are fretted
II. The Brass

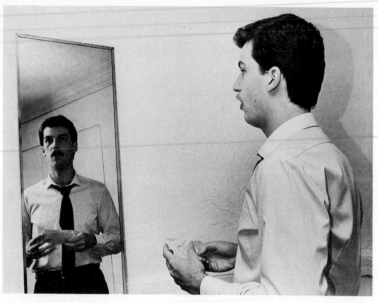

Successful speakers practice their speeches before appearing in public.

A chronological pattern of organization may be used in an outline that divides the topic by specific intervals such as decades, years, or weeks, depending on the scope of the topic. For example, a speech on American automobiles in the twentieth century might be divided into discussions of types of cars at the turn of the century, in the 1920s, in the 1930s, and so forth.

Although the outlines may vary in form, the basic principles remain the same. Some speakers prefer to use Roman numerals for each major part of the speech, using I for the introduction, II for the body, and III for the conclusion. Capital letters are then used for main ideas within the text of the speech. However, regardless of the form, you should remember that details presented in an outline get more specific with each subdivision. Look at the outline in Figure 11–1. Notice how the two major divisions (I and II) relate to the general topic of the outline (Effects of Air Pollution). As you can see, the information gets more specific with each division, and each detail relates directly to the preceding category.

All forms of outlining share certain basic principles. These principles include simplicity, coordination, subordination, progression, and symbolization.[3]

Simplicity

The outline is intended to assist, not confuse, the speaker. Therefore, you should keep the outline simple, so that each line of it represents a single

[3] G. E. Mills, *Putting a Message Together*, 2d ed. (Minneapolis: Bobbs-Merrill, 1972), 26–29.

Effects of Air Pollution

I. How Does Air Pollution Affect Health?
   A. What respiratory conditions are related to pollution?
      1. Respiratory condition X
         a. Cases of X
         b. Deaths due to X
      2. Respiratory condition Y
         a. Cases of Y
         b. Deaths due to Y
   B. What allergies are related to pollution?
      1. Allergy Q
      2. Allergy Z
II. How Does Air Pollution Affect Environment?
   A. How does air pollution affect agriculture?
      1. Effect on growth of vegetation
      2. Effect on crop yield
   B. How does air pollution affect the atmosphere?
      1. Increase in carbon dioxide level
      2. Destruction of ozone layer

FIGURE 11–1
A Sample Outline

piece of information. You should decide whether to use single words, phrases or sentences and then be consistent throughout the outline. The outline is a valuable organizational tool if it is not allowed to become too cumbersome.

Coordination

The principle of **coordination** is basic to the logical arrangement of an outline. The speaker must remember that all points within a subdivision must be related. For example, a speech on Bicentennial sights in the eastern United States might be organized spatially by specific states.

Bicentennial Sights in the Eastern United States
I. Sights in Massachusetts
   A. Concord
   B. Plymouth Rock
   C. Boston Harbor
   D. Liberty Bell

If you know your American history, you will observe that entry D is out of place, since the Liberty Bell is in Pennsylvania. Incorrect placement of information is a problem of coordination. Although the example just cited is quite obvious, the speaker may sometimes have a difficult time finding an appropriate spot for certain information. If the information is essential, it may mean reorganizing the categories to include it.

Subordination

The principle of *subordination* refers to the way a main idea is divided into subordinate points, with each specific piece of information relating directly to the preceding category. In the previous example, Concord relates directly to the larger category of Bicentennial sights in Massachusetts, which in turn relates directly to the overall topic of the speech, Bicentennial sights in the eastern United States.

Progression

It is important to arrange ideas in some sort of logical *progression.* For example, in a speech about local government, the speaker might identify the three main categories of the outline as local government in the city, in the county, and in the township. The speaker should then decide upon the order of these main categories, based on either ascending or descending order of complexity or size. The speaker should select a logical progression of ideas and remain consistent in the arrangement of major ideas and subordinate points.

Symbolization

The *symbolization* of the outline serves as a visual form of the coordination, subordination, and progression of the speech. Therefore, it is important that use of numbers and letters be consistent throughout the outline. To check the coordination of the speech, you may ask yourself, "Do subdivisions A, B, and C all relate to main point I?"

The indentation of subdivisions represents their position as subordinate points. A general rule to follow is that in breaking down a category, there should always be at least two subordinate points. If there is a capital A there should be a capital B. Similarly, if capital A is to be subdivided, there should be numbers 1 and 2. If you find this rule hard to follow, chances are you need to expand particular categories.

Last, progression is logically represented through symbolization. If your speech is based on degrees of increasing complexity, you may check that the materials presented in points I and II lead up to and provide the basis for what you will present in division III. (For more detailed outlines, see Appendix C.)

SUPPORTING MATERIAL

One of the advantages of using an outline is that it enables you to see if you have adequate supporting material. Supporting material serves a variety of functions and is essential to all speeches, whether they are to inform, persuade, or entertain.

Clarification

One of the basic functions of supporting material is to clarify an idea, opinion, or argument. Remember that in an informative speech, it is the goal of the speaker to make sure that the audience understands the message. In a persuasive speech you must be sure that the audience has a clear understanding of your position. If you want to entertain or impress an audience with a story of perilous travels in the desert, you may need to make clear the distances between watering places or the hostile nature of the surrounding peoples. Clarification is an important aspect of all speeches.

EXAMPLES.   You can clarify an idea, opinion, or concept in many ways. One way is to use an example. The example may be real, hypothetical, or extended. Examples have been given throughout this text to help you better understand particular concepts. Some of the examples have been real, others hypothetical. A *real example* refers to an event or incident that actually happened. A *hypothetical example* is based on something that could possibly occur but that did not really happen. In the previous section on the organization of persuasive speeches, we offered two examples of inductive reasoning. The swine flu inoculation example was based on real events; the pantyhose example was hypothetical. Yet both examples helped to clarify a description of the inductive pattern that otherwise might have been meaningless to the reader.

An *extended example* is one that is carried out to considerable length in order to clarify or emphasize a very important idea. Often when athletes and rock stars speak to young audiences and advise them to "say *no* to drugs," they offer examples of their own personal experiences as users and, then, extend the example to what might happen to audience members who do the same. Their extended examples are real. However, a speaker can extend a hypothetical example as well. For instance, a dietician might discuss the future health problems of a hypothetical family that is indifferent to the impact of nutrition in its members' daily lives.

ILLUSTRATIONS.   Another means of clarification is the use of *illustrations*. While examples are verbal illustrations, the speaker may sometimes find a visual aid very helpful in clarifying information. A surgeon delivering an informative speech on a new technique for open heart surgery would probably find a series of diagrams useful in her presentation. If you have ever attempted to assemble an "easily assembled" piece of furniture or equipment, you may appreciate the value of a visual aid in clarifying otherwise confusing directions.

ANECDOTES.   Speakers sometimes use an *anecdote* to clarify a particular idea or point of information. An anecdote is a brief story that relates to an important idea in the speech. It is particularly useful as an introductory device when appropriate to the overall topic of the speech. For instance, a young woman who wishes to give a humorous talk about college life may start with an anecdote about finding her mother's old raccoon coat in a trunk in the basement.

An anecdote may be real or imaginary, personal or impersonal. Although an anecdote does not offer any hard evidence, it does help clarify and emphasize your point or position. For example, a fire official delivering a speech to elementary school children on the dangers of false alarms might relate the well-known fable "The Boy Who Cried Wolf" as a way to clarify the message.

DEFINITIONS.   After analyzing your topic and audience, you might decide that a definition of terms is necessary to make sure that the audience understands your points. Since language is often ambiguous, it is important that you clarify any misunderstanding relating to definitions of words.

There are several different ways to define a word, idea, or concept. Some ideas can be defined by *description.* For example, in a speech on the kibbutzim of Israel, a speaker might want to describe this type of communal living in order to clarify audience understanding of the topic.

Sometimes a word, idea, or concept can best be defined by *comparison* or *contrast.* A definition by comparison suggests the similarity of something unknown to something with which the audience is already familiar. Someone discussing musical instruments of the Middle Age might define a lute by comparing it with a guitar. Similarly, a speaker may define a term through contrast. In the same lecture the speaker might define a clavichord as an early ancestor of the piano, pointing out the essential differences between the two.

Sometimes a speaker has to provide the audience with an *operational* definition, one that is used only for the duration of the speech. For example, the president of a large corporation, addressing stockholders on the success of the company in the previous fiscal year, has to clarify what he or she means by "success." It is possible that the president's definition does not coincide with that of the stockholders.

Support

Some material is used to support rather than to clarify. Particularly in persuasive speeches, speakers must carefully provide material that gives substance to their message and enhances their position. Using evidence in a speech supports your position. It also enhances the listeners' learning process.[4]

> The source of authority may be expert opinion, official pronouncements, religious symbols, the pomp and ceremony of institutional practice, the sayings or doings of the socially elect, or even the printed word or the tone of voice.
>
> Daniel Katz and Richard L. Schanck

---

[4] V. O'Donnell and J. Kable, "Persuasion: An Interactive-Dependency Approach" (New York: Random House, 1982), 139.

EXAMPLES.   Once again, the use of examples can be helpful. As communication specialist P. J. Wexler has argued, examples not only serve as "appeals to shared experiences" between speaker and listener, they also save them both from overgeneralization.[5]

When using examples as a form of support, however, you must be sure to use a sufficient number to confirm your ideas or opinions. A journalist reporting on corruption in a city agency should be able to come up with several examples of wrongdoing in order to demonstrate the problem. While one incident might make an important story, many examples would be needed to prove widespread corruption.

You also must give examples that are representative or typical of the position you support. If a psychiatrist advocates a certain kind of therapy for severe depression, he or she might support this position by citing several examples of cases in which this therapy was successful. If the cases described were not cases of severe depression, the examples would be inappropriate and unsupportive.

Examples used to support a position must also be representative of the total picture. When the owner of a nursing home sought to defend himself against media charges of poor conditions, he cited the case of one elderly gentleman who found the home so comfortable that he wrote the owner a thank-you note. On investigation it was found that this example was atypical and certainly not representative of what most of the patients felt. A speaker must be extremely careful when choosing examples.

STATISTICS.   Another way to support your presentation is with facts and figures. Statistics can be very valuable if used skillfully. A business executive suggesting a merger with another company could incorporate statistics into the speech to show how the merger would be profitable for the firm. A scientist promoting a particular drug would cite statistical results of different experiments.

It must be stressed that statistics have to be used effectively. In most situations the speaker should round off statistics to the nearest whole number. Remember, the audience is hearing the statistics for the first time, and the numbers must be easily interpreted. Statistics can be intimidating, so avoid overwhelming your audience with too many facts and figures. Fractions and decimals are often confusing and add little to listener understanding. Approximations such as "close to 30 percent" or "over a quarter of a million" give a general picture without burdening the listener with specific numbers. Nonetheless, the speaker must know when it is important to use exact figures. For example, a proponent of a particular bill narrowly defeated by Congress may quote the exact figures when discussing the issue at a press conference to show that there had been considerable support for the legislation.

If you use statistics, you must always make them meaningful for the listener. One way to do this is to present the statistics in the form of

---

[5] P. J. Wexler, "Explanation by Example," *Language and Communication* 2 (1982), 303–309.

Fumbling

Preparation and delivery of a speech go hand in hand. One supports the other. In a delightful passage from *Night and Day*, Virginia Woolf describes a speaker who could have benefited from closer attention to both. A disaster such as this emphasizes the need for careful planning.

His paper was carefully written out, but in spite of this precaution Mr. Rodney managed to turn over two sheets instead of one, to choose the wrong sentence where two were written together, and to discover his own handwriting suddenly illegible. When he found himself possessed of a coherent passage, he shook it at his audience almost aggressively, and then fumbled for another. After a distressing search a fresh discovery would be made, and produced in the same way, until, by means of repeated attacks, he had stirred his audience to a degree of animation quite remarkable in these gatherings. Whether they were stirred by his enthusiasm for poetry or by the contortions which a human being was going through for their benefit, it would be hard to say. At length Mr. Rodney sat down impulsively in the middle of a sentence, and, after a pause of bewilderment, the audience expressed its relief at being able to laugh aloud in a decided outburst of applause.

From Virginia Woolf, *Night and Day* (*New York: Harcourt Brace Jovanovich, A Harvest Book, 1948*), 53.

comparisons. In a speech on state aid to education, for example, a senator may tell her audience of college students that "for every dollar you spend on tuition, the state legislature spends five to educate you." In this case, the relationship between student expense and state expense is made clear by comparison.

The ethical speaker will keep in mind that statistics are often misleading and that certain statistics can be found to "prove" almost anything. The speaker and the audience should be aware that statistics do not always give an accurate representation. For example, an audience was greatly impressed when a golfer reported that he came in third in a recent tournament until they found out that there were only three participants. It is a matter of ethics to avoid such misleading information and half-truths.

Testimony

You should not overlook the value of *testimony* as supportive material. A person's testimony can often add validity to an informative or persuasive speech. Of course, the value of testimony depends on the credibility of the source. Basically, testimony can be derived from either a direct witness to an event or from an expert in a particular field. The appropriate use of testimony is determined by the nature of the subject. For example, in discussing the safety hazards in building construction, a speaker might give the testimony of several people who survived the collapse of a recently constructed hotel.

Expert testimony often proves helpful in both persuasive and informative speeches.[6] A speaker supporting the idea of a conspiracy in the Kennedy assassination might cite the testimony of ballistic experts who claimed that more than one gun was fired.

By being careful to provide support and clarification for the ideas in your speech, you can increase the chances that your audience will understand your message and be persuaded by it. Concern for your audience and the integrity of your presentation are key issues in the preparation of a speech. When an audience feels your concern, it is likely to reward you with a positive reaction to your speech and increased credibility.

It should now be evident to you that a well-prepared speech combines many skills and carefully selected elements. Take a look at the sample speech presented in Appendix B. Analysis of any effective speech will reveal the basics with which it was built.

SUMMARY

Careful planning, organization, and preparation are essential when speaking in public. Athletes train for competitive events, musicians rehearse for concerts, and artists sketch before they paint. In the same way, you must prepare yourself to go before your audience. The success of your delivery will largely depend upon how well you have organized your message.

Begin by selecting a topic that interests you or one that you have some previous knowledge of or familiarity with. Make sure, if your speech is supposed to be persuasive, that your personal convictions are in agreement with your topic.

Good speeches are focused. Decide your purpose in speaking: Will you inform, persuade, or entertain your audience? Your subject should not be too general but should serve as the unifying or central idea of your speech.

As you gather information for your speech, keep your purpose in mind. An objective discussion of a controversial issue requires presentation of opposing views. If your purpose is to persuade, you may rely upon those sources that support your view. There are a wide variety of sources of information. Draw on your own experience, personal interviews, or surveys when appropriate. Take advantage of the wide range of printed materials, films, recordings, and videotapes available.

Consider the functions of the three basic parts of your speech. The introduction serves to catch and focus audience attention. Use the standard introductory devices, statistics, rhetorical questions, famous quotes, and so forth, when appropriate. You present your main purpose and set the tone for your speech in your introduction. The body of your speech will contain the bulk of information and elaboration of your main ideas. These main ideas should be connected by smooth transitions. The conclusion should be used to leave a lasting impression on your audience and to reemphasize your main idea.

As you organize the body of the speech, decide upon a pattern of arrangement. Informative speeches may be topical, chronological, or spatial or follow the

---

[6] S. C. Bank and N. G. Doythress, "The Elements of Persuasion in Expert Testimony," *Journal of Psychiatry and Law* 10 (1982), 173–204.

patterns of increasing complexity or chain of events. Persuasive speeches may follow inductive or deductive reasoning or develop according to patterns of cause and effect or problems and solutions.

Your outline is a map—be sure to provide yourself with a workable guide for your delivery. Remember the principles of simplicity, coordination, subordination, and progression, and keep your symbolization consistent.

Supporting material is important to clarify and substantiate your ideas. Use real, hypothetical, or extended examples when appropriate. Employ illustrations or anecdotes to clarify your points. Define your terms when necessary by description or by comparison or contrast with terms familiar to the audience. You may reinforce your main ideas with the use of statistics or testimony.

The importance of good preparation cannot be overestimated. Using the methods of organization outlined in this chapter will help you in effective public speaking.

EXERCISES

GROUP EXPERIENCES

Come On Up and Introduce Yourself!

DESCRIPTION: As outlined in this chapter, the introduction to a speech serves several important functions. One of these functions is to catch and then focus audience attention. If you fail to catch your audience in your introductory comments, it is unlikely that you will get its attention later. This activity will provide you with the opportunity to write several different types of introductions to the same speech.

PROCEDURE: Select a topic for a speech. Then outline the main body of the speech. You will not have to deliver the speech itself, but you will have to deliver "introductions" to the speech. Therefore, it is important that you determine the theme and organizational structure of the speech so that you can preview the body of the speech in your introduction. Now—write three different introductions for the same speech. You may wish to review the various methods suggested in this chapter, such as the use of a startling statement, a rhetorical question, or a humorous statement. Each introduction should be no longer than sixty seconds. After hearing the introduction, your audience should (1) be motivated to listen to your speech, (2) be able to identify your central theme, and (3) have a general idea about what you will cover in the body of your speech.

Each member of the class should be asked to deliver his or her introductions to the rest of the class. The introductions should be done so that no one person will present two or three consecutive introductions. Each introduction should be evaluated by class members, based on the following three scales:

> *Scale 1*. Did the speaker motivate you to listen to the speech? (1) not at all motivated; (2) slightly motivated; (3) motivated; (4) highly motivated.
>
> *Scale 2*. With what degree of accuracy do you think you can identify the speaker's main theme? (1) not at all accurately; (2) slightly accurately; (3) accurately; (4) highly accurately.
>
> *Scale 3*. With what degree of accuracy do you think you can describe what the speaker will cover in the body of the speech? (1) not at all accurately; (2) slightly accurately; (3) accurately; (4) highly accurately.

Each speaker should carefully review all the evaluations of his or her introductions. You may wish to add the total number of points possible for each scale and then the number of points actually received on each scale.

DISCUSSION: After reviewing your point totals for each introduction and each scale, can you identify problems with a particular introduction

Poise and self-confidence are two important aspects of successful public communication.

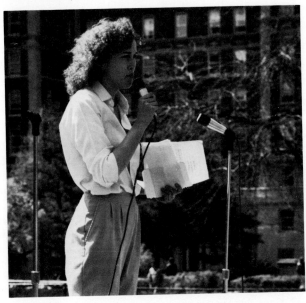

or scale? Do you need to spend more time in preparing introductions? How did your introductions compare with the others presented?

Concluding Remarks

NOTE: The procedure for this activity is the same as for the activity just described, except that *conclusions* are presented instead of *introductions*.

Patterns

DESCRIPTION: Persuasive speech patterns can easily be identified as inductive, deductive, cause-and-effect, or problem-solution. The purpose of any persuasive speech is to create attitude change in the listener; the various patterns are alternative methods for pursuing that goal. The purpose of this activity is to familiarize you with persuasive speech patterns.

PROCEDURE: Locate three speech transcripts. Analyze each speech to determine the speech pattern used. Keep in mind that a speech may have a combination of patterns. After identifying the patterns in each speech, write a short outline for each. For example, if you have identified a deductive pattern, you should point out the generalization, the specific statement, and the conclusion. Bring your analyses to class.

Divide into groups of four. Compare your analyses of the three speeches. If there are discrepancies among group members as to the patterns used in the speeches, determine the specific conflict. After 45 minutes each group should have reached an agreement on the patterns used in each speech and should report its results to the class.

DISCUSSION: Did you experience any difficulty in analyzing the speeches? Do you believe that organization in a speech is important for producing attitude change? Why? Why not?

PERSONAL EXPERIENCES

1. Start your own collection of jokes, stories, or other types of interesting introductions for speeches. Collect these from books, magazines, television, or public speakers. Your collection can be used for introductions to speeches, stories, or papers.
2. Develop a list of statements made by yourself and others that demonstrate some form of illogical reasoning. Then consider the problems that are created when illogical reasoning is used. How often do you make invalid claims?
3. Identify all the "creative" ways in which you could collect source materials for a speech. Consider, for example, cartoons, fairy tales and poems. Too often we look only in the standard places (reference books, interviews) for material. Consider the creative use of collections of information parallel to a multimedia presentation.

DISCUSSION QUESTIONS

1. What are some of the principles of outlining you should use in writing a speech?
2. What are the intended purposes of the introduction, body, and conclusion of a speech?
3. Provide an example of the following types of supporting material: illustrations, anecdotes, definitions, and examples.
4. Can a speech effectively use a combination of the spatial, chronological, and topical patterns of organization?
5. What are the factors you should consider when preparing to speak in public? (List the factors in the order in which you believe they should be considered.)

12
Speech Delivery

KEY CONCEPTS AND TERMS

Communication apprehension
Rapport
Delivery
Gesture
Vocal delivery
Phonation
Voice
Larynx
Resonance
Articulation

Pitch
Volume
Rate
Vocal quality
Style
Clarity
Appropriateness
Economy
Lively quality

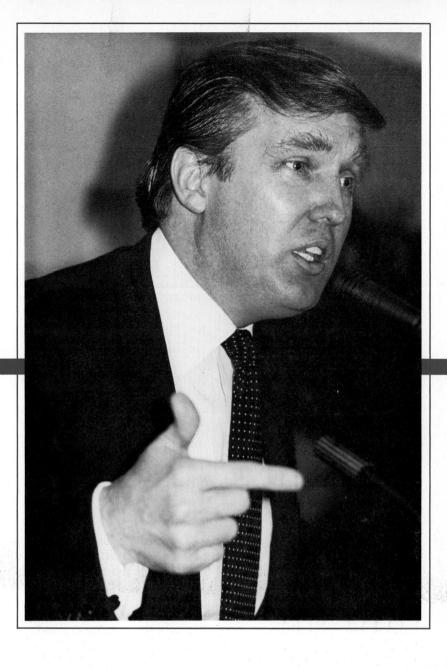

As a newcomer running for public office, Jerry knew that the success of his campaign would depend on his ability to make himself known and to garner the trust of his constituency. As his platform was basically the same as that of his opponent, Jerry felt that the presentation of his speech would be of even greater importance than the content of his message. As a result of this knowledge, and on the advice of his campaign manager, Jerry decided to videotape rehearsals of his speech and to play them back to determine specific areas in which he needed to work. After analyzing the replays, Jerry noticed that he seldom looked at the audience and nervously jingled the change in his pocket. Although he interjected bits of humor in the speech, Jerry kept a solemn expression throughout, except once or twice when he nervously laughed. His gestures seemed awkward and his voice somewhat shaky. Fortunately, through the use of video as a tool, he was able to identify his specific delivery problems and overcome them.

Throughout history, public speakers like Jerry have been keenly aware of the importance of dynamic delivery. Prophets, poets, philosophers, and storytellers have practiced through the ages to capture the minds and imaginations of their audiences. As a modern student of communication, you too must develop your own unique manner of presentation. Even the most powerful speech can be ruined by a poor delivery, whereas a mediocre speech can be improved if delivered in a dynamic way.

We have already discussed body movement, gestures, eye contact, facial expressions, and paralanguage. However, we will now look more closely at these and other related behaviors in the context of public communication. While this chapter may not help you to win an election, you will improve as a public speaker if you practice the principles outlined herein.

The importance of delivery goes beyond maintaining audience interest. Research has shown that delivery affects speaker credibility, message comprehension, and persuasiveness.[1]

A speaker's credibility can be established or destroyed during the presentation of a speech. Ethos, the audience's perception of a speaker as trustworthy and sincere, is greatly influenced by delivery. These audience perceptions are changed by nonverbal cues such as the speaker's appearance, facial expression, posture, and gestures.

However, the truly critical audience should always be aware of the difference between perception and reality. While an honest speaker may quite unconsciously project an image of sincerity and trustworthiness, a skillful speaker with the most selfish motives can sometimes create that same impression. For example, the prominent political figure who denies an accusation of wrongdoing can add to his credibility by looking directly at the audience, thereby gaining support with nonverbal communication.

Delivery also enhances message comprehension and retention. It does so primarily by eliminating many of the elements that can distract the listener from the message.[2] For example, if Jennifer presents a message without exchanging direct eye contact with her audience, she will never know whether she is getting her message across. Such feedback is vital in determining the impact of a message. Likewise, if Sammy plays with his pen or the piece of chalk he is holding, he may distract the audience from his message, thus reducing the chances for message comprehension.

---

[1] V. O'Donnell and J. Kable, *Persuasion: An Interactive-Dependency Approach* (New York: Random House, 1982), 239.
[2] Ibid., 239.

In addition to increasing message comprehension and speaker credibility, a strong delivery can add to the persuasive impact of a message. Perhaps one of the best examples of a speaker who uses delivery effectively is evangelist Billy Graham. Known for his sweeping gestures and his emotion-filled facial expressions, Graham maximizes his delivery for persuasive appeal.

COMMUNICATION APPREHENSION

If you were asked what you fear most, how would you respond? A national polling agency conducted a survey to discover what people fear most. Some of the greatest fears included accidents, death and heights, but over 40 percent of those polled listed speaking in public as their greatest fear. (Fear of death finished second at 19 percent!)[3] Maybe you agree with that 40 percent. But what characteristic of public speaking causes knees to shake, stomachs to turn, voices to tremble and palms to sweat? (Similar reactions are also associated with other communication situations, such as interviews and blind dates.)

Stage fright, or speech tension, has for years been defined as a fear of the situation. Today, however, most communication scholars believe that these physiological responses are caused by anxiety rather than fear.[4] Fear is a spontaneous response, whereas anxiety involves the anticipation of an event. Fear is usually provoked by an outside stimulus, while anxiety stems from insecurities within a person. Most people don't feel the fear of an automobile accident until after they barely miss a car that failed to stop at a red light. However, before giving a speech, going to a job interview, or meeting a fiancée's parents, many of us feel nervous because we are concerned with and unsure of the outcome. Some of us start to destroy our confidence before speaking assignments are due by telling ourselves, "I can't do this," "I know I'll forget something," "I bore people," or "Nobody is interested in what I have to say." We need to find ways to build our confidence instead of tearing it down.

Before signing up for speech classes, many of us secretly hope that we won't have to get up to speak. Sometimes we can avoid speaking in front of others, but what about the occasions when there is no way out of giving a speech? It is important to realize that what you are feeling is a normal response. It is natural to feel nervous before a presentation. In fact, if you don't feel some anxiety, it is likely that your performance will lack the energy needed to keep the speech interesting to an audience. Many coaches check players' palms and energy levels before important games. Because people perform better when there is some tension, coaches select as starting players those who are excited and up for the game. So, if you feel tension

---

[3] A. Kornblum, "Stage Fright in the Executive Suite," *Nation's Business* 72 (December 1984), 56.
[4] M. Beatty, "Communication Apprehension and General Anxiety," *Journal of Social Behavior and Personality* 1, no. 2 (1986), 209–12.

before speaking, it is likely that you will perform more effectively than if you feel no tension at all.

Now that we know that speech anxiety is a normal response, you may say, "But everyone can tell I'm nervous, and this bothers me." Well, even if you manifest nervousness, most audience members will not notice it. In fact, research reveals that speakers report higher levels of anxiety than is attributed to them by their audience, and that their level of anxiety is not accurately detected by their audience.[5] Audiences simply do not notice nervousness unless speakers call attention to themselves by saying, "I'm sorry my voice is quivering," "Excuse the paper, but my hands are shaking," or "If I forget something, it's because I'm scared." If you're still not convinced, ask speakers you feel are confident if they were nervous. You'll probably find that they were, even though you didn't notice it.

We sometimes build our anticipation to such a degree that we have too much energy before a speech. The following suggestions should help both to improve your confidence and to control speech tension.

Practice

Rehearsing a speech helps to build both speaker confidence and self-concept. If you are not prepared, you will have reason to feel tense. It is a good idea to practice by yourself and then give your speech to friends. Jimmy Calano and Jeff Salzman, founders of CareerTracking, one of America's foremost business seminar companies, write the following about the importance of rehearsal:

> From time to time as a professional you are going to run into situations where you absolutely have to come across as a cool customer: when you ask for a raise, go into a job interview, or make an important presentation, for instance. Never leave these situations to chance. Never assume you will say the right things. Even when you know, without a doubt, what you want to say, knowing it and saying it remain two different matters . . . especially when the heat is on.
>
> So say it beforehand. The best way to prepare for the really special performances of your professional life is to practice your lines until you know them by heart.[6]

If rehearsal is recommended in CareerTracking business seminars, surely it is appropriate for beginning (and experienced) public speakers! Thus, having set your goals, practicing alone and with others should help you to learn how both you and audiences will respond. An audience of friends can also give you suggestions for improvement.

---

[5] R. R. Behnke, C. R. Sawyer, and P. E. King, "The Communication of Public Speaking Anxiety," *Communication Education* 36 (1987), 139.
[6] J. Calano and J. Salzman, *CareerTracking: 28 Success Shortcuts to the Top* (New York: Simon & Schuster, 1988), 171.

Use Physical Activity

Physical involvement in your speech helps use excess energy. If your energy has no normal outlet, it will manifest itself in trembling hands, knees and voice. Using gestures and body movements helps use energy, emphasize points and maintain audience attention. Like speeches, gestures and movements should be practiced and experimented with before the final presentation. If you feel that you have too much energy before speaking, try taking a few deep breaths, using isometric exercises, or systematic relaxation.

Do Not Memorize, and Organize Well

When students try to memorize, they put themselves at a disadvantage. Speakers begin to worry about forgetting something—and usually do. If a speaker does forget, there are usually uncomfortable silences and abbreviated presentations. With proper preparation time, using a note card with a brief outline should be all that is necessary for prompting. Clear organization enables speakers to speak extemporaneously. It is much easier to remember points when they follow in a logical progression, so try to put them in sequences that build your confidence.

Get Involved with Your Topic

Confidence increases when speakers are interested and involved with their topics. Topics should be so important and interesting to the speaker that he or she wants to get the ideas across. Involvement in the topic helps focus attention on what is being said rather than on who is saying it, which decreases nervousness.

Develop a Proper Attitude

Proper attitudes go along with topic involvement. Speakers have a responsibility to be sincerely interested in what they have to say. Speakers must also remind themselves that their physical responses are normal reactions. The audience is an important factor to consider. Audiences usually want speakers to succeed, especially in classroom situations. The classroom audience is generally the most sympathetic audience speakers will ever encounter.

PRINCIPLES

Look Natural

In order to make a successful presentation, a speaker should practice certain principles of good delivery. The first principle is to look natural. If you are still or artificial, you will look uncomfortable and awkward. The audience may see this as a lack of confidence, which might greatly affect its perception of the speaker's ethos. At the other extreme, if you seem theatrical or overly dramatic, you may be perceived as false and insincere. The good speaker strives for a natural, easygoing style of presentation.

Match Delivery and Content

The delivery should be carefully coordinated with the content of the speech. Body movement and vocal expression should add to the presentation, not detract from it. Superficial gestures and inappropriate facial expressions can distract the audience's attention. To illustrate, while practicing her welcoming speech for the annual Opera Ball, Lisa attempted to coordinate a gesture with her opening sentence, "We welcome you with open arms." Rehearsing time and time again, Lisa tried to find the right moment to hold out her arms, palms up, facing the audience. Obviously uncomfortable with the gesture, Lisa was unsure about whether it should be used before, during, or after her spoken welcome. Although we might have laughed at Lisa's awkwardness, should we have been present in the room, we could have helped her by suggesting that she use natural gestures that would complement her verbal message—and avoid those gestures that would distract from what she was trying to say.

Although particular gestures are often associated with specific phrases, such as Lisa used above, it is best for us to utilize a variety of gestures and vocal expressions. A sudden change in volume, a pause in delivery, or a firm shake of the head can all be effective in punctuating a particular idea or argument. However, the speaker's various vocal expressions and body actions should support the verbal message and not contradict it.

Make It Appropriate

Another principle of good delivery concerns the choice of an appropriate style of presentation. The delivery of a speech must be considered in relation to the audience, the situation and the speaker. Chapter 9 discusses audience analysis in terms of message selection and preparation. An awareness of audience characteristics is also important in terms of delivery. For example, the tone of voice used when speaking to an audience of children is quite different from the tone of voice used when speaking to adults. Regardless of the age of the audience, the speaker should never talk down to them. Talking down is most often projected more by the delivery than by content. For instance, teachers' attitudes toward their students can sometimes be inferred from their tone of voice. Students often resent teachers who give simple instructions with overenthusiastic energy, as if to say. "Now children, today we are going to. . . ." While you may speak differently to children than to adults, you must remember that no audience, regardless of age, wants to be patronized.

A good speaker also takes into account any special disabilities that members of the audience may have. For example, if some audience members have hearing problems, the speaker should adjust his volume accordingly.

It is very important to make sure that the delivery is appropriate to the sitaution. To do this, you must first consider the occasion of the speech. For example, if you are delivering a eulogy at a funeral or memorial service, you should present your speech in a solemn manner. To do this, you should keep your volume low and the pace relatively slow. On the other hand, if you are delivering an after-dinner speech, you should seem enthusiastic and in good spirits. Lightness of tone, variation in pace and free use of gestures, plus a happy expression on your face, are appropriate here.

You should also consider the setting for the speech. Your delivery will be influenced by whether the setting is a small conference room, an auditorium, or a large outdoor amphitheater. During important political debates, the candidates and their advisors usually visit the location of the debate beforehand. This helps them use each setting more effectively in terms of acoustics and space.

Obviously, your volume must vary according to the size of the acoustics of the setting. Size, acoustics and seating arrangement also influence the basic mood or tone of your delivery. A casual, understated and highly informal presentation may not come across well in a very large auditorium. On the other hand, a strict sense of formality can alienate the audience in a small and intimate setting. The effective speaker will choose the degree of formality according to the setting. A quiet, casual talk would be effective in a classroom, where the audience is close enough to perceive subtle gestures and expressions, but the same kind of presentation would be inappropriate in a concert hall.

Nonverbal messages play a significant role in public presentations.

Improving

Don't be afraid to be natural, to let yourself show through. Don't pontificate, or talk down to your audience. Talk up to them. Don't overexplain what you want to say, but, instead, assume that your listeners have the intelligence to understand your various points as you make them. And, if you suddenly realize that you have forgotten to make a certain point, don't be afraid to interrupt yourself and say, "Oh, by the way, I forgot to mention—." This merely shows your audience that you are fallible and human and makes your audience *like* you.

As you start to speak, look around your audience and pick out the friendly faces, and talk to them. In every group there are always a few that are all smiles and eagerness for what you have to say. They are your blessed allies, and you should make use of them as such. If the sheer physical fact of an audience unnerves you, play mental tricks on yourself. Imagine, for example, that these people are all your dear, close friends, and that you are talking to them in your own living room. Then, when you have familiarized yourself with your audience, be alert for the moment when the faces become less friendly, when the fannies begin to stir uncomfortably in the chairs, or when the audience appears to be looking at its collective wristwatch. That's the moment to start winding it up. There's nothing wrong with leaving a few of your listeners wishing you'd said a little more. They'll like you for that, too.

Learn to recognize—and avoid, any personal mannerisms, facial or vocal, that you may have—nervous throatclearing, for example, or vocalized ("Uh . . . uh . . . uh . . .") pauses between sentences. Buy an inexpensive tape recorder, talk into it, and then listen to and analyze yourself. Use a mirror and study yourself. Do you grin too much, or gesticulate with your hands too much? This is particularly important in front of a television camera, where hands flying up in front of the picture frame seriously distract the viewer from you and what you are trying to say or sell. President Kennedy discovered that he had a habit of standing in front of an audience with his hands thrust in his pockets, jangling the keys and coins therein. It was his mother, Rose, who first pointed this out to him, and got him to stand with his hands hanging loosely at the sides, or resting easily on the lectern. It's all right to move about casually as you talk, to scratch your chin occasionally, to shift position slightly, to cross your legs from time to time—anything that makes you seem at ease and natural.

Talking and eloquence are not the same; to speak, and to speak well, are two things. A fool may talk, but a wise man speaks.

Ben Jonson

Delivery must be appropriate to the speaker's personal style or manner. The key here is to know your own personality and behave naturally—remembering that being a speaker does not mean being an actor. For example, Jimmy Carter was noted for his natural, easygoing style during his election campaign. He was unpretentious in his manner, and his characteristic smile helped him to establish a warm relationship with his audiences. Throughout the campaign, political observers watched him gain self-confidence and increase the effectiveness of his personal, informal style.

Regardless of the situation, when you are true to yourself you will project sincerity and honesty. Aim for a delivery that is consistent with your own personality.

Establish Rapport

If the speaker fails to develop and maintain a positive relationship with the audience throughout the presentation, the purpose of the speech will be lost. **Rapport** is almost entirely the result of delivery. For example, eye contact with the audience increases credibility and makes the audience more trusting of the speaker. A warm, conversational manner can achieve the same effect.

Rapport is also important because a good speaker-audience relationship can overshadow weak spots in the message itself. Entertainers devote much energy and talent to projecting a feeling of identification with their audiences. Bruce Springsteen, an American rock 'n' roll hero, is especially sensitive to the speaker- (singer-)audience relationship. As Clarence Clemons, a longtime friend and saxophonist in Springsteen's E Street Band, told *Newsweek* reporters, "He cares for every person in the audience." Although aware of the price of fame and the cruel isolation that rock stars often must suffer, Springsteen is unwilling to isolate himself "from the people he writes for." Instead he continues to mingle with the public whenever he can.[7]

> Speak the speech, I pray you, as I pronounced it to you, trippingly on the tongue; but if you mouth it, as many of your players do, I had as lief the town-crier spoke my lines. Nor do not saw the air too much with your hand, thus; but use all gently: for in the very torrent, tempest, and—as I may say—whirlwind of passion, you must acquire and beget a temperance, that may give it smoothness.
>
> William Shakespeare, "Hamlet"

PHYSICAL DELIVERY

The term **delivery** covers many different elements of a speaker's presentation, including physical delivery and vocal expression. The physical elements of delivery can be divided into various body movements, such as posture, gestures and facial expressions (including eye contact). Also included in the physical aspect of the presentation is the way a speaker uses accessories, such as note cards or a lectern.

---

[7] B. Barol, "He's On Fire," *Newsweek* (5 August 1985), 48–49.

Posture and Body Movements

As a speaker, you must be aware of your body as an important source of communication. In fact, the body is so expressive in communicating ideas and feelings that many of our verbal expressions are based on descriptions of body movements. For example, a person who maintains a positive attitude in times of adversity is said to keep a "stiff upper lip." Someone in great suspense or suffering extreme anxiety is said to be "sitting on the edge of his seat." These figures of speech accurately describe the body movements of people in these situations. Someone watching a Stephen King film may very well be sitting on the edge of his or her seat. Similarly, the actress who did not get the part she hoped for may be keeping a "stiff upper lip" to stop it from trembling.

Our body movements, especially posture, are closely related to our physical and emotional states. On the physical level, posture can reveal whether a person is tired, energetic, or in pain. On an emotional level, posture can reveal whether a person is tense, relaxed, depressed, or excited. Posture also tells us something about a person's self-image. People with a healthy measure of self-confidence move about easily, stand up straight and hold up their heads. Those individuals who are shy, ill at ease, or ashamed of themselves are more likely to slump, slouch and keep their heads and eyes lowered.

An audience's perception of a speaker is influenced by body movement and posture. While there are few specific rules governing this aspect of delivery, there are some simple guidelines. In order to appear poised and confident, you should stand at ease. If you are too stiff, the audience may feel uncomfortable. At the other extreme, a very relaxed posture may be perceived as too casual. A skillful speaker should appear confident but comfortable.

As a speaker, your movements, like your posture, should be natural, not forced. Although you should stand relatively still and avoid pacing, natural movements can add to your delivery. You can use body movements to energize yourself and your audience. A speaker who does not move from one space seems dull and restrained. Appropriate body movements help to free the speaker from nervousness and spark the audience's attention. Body movements can also convey meanings. A speaker who leans forward when revealing something new suggests to the audience that they are being made privy to this information. A step toward the audience suggests that the speaker is embracing them and breaking the imaginary barrier between speaker and listeners.

Gestures

In addition to movements of the whole body, you can use a variety of gestures. *Gestures* can convey many different meanings, depending upon the context. For example, the "V for victory" sign used by Winston Churchill in World War II became the peace sign of the 1960s. Some gestures convey meanings in and of themselves, while others are used as a part of the verbal message.

Traditional gestures are those movements of the hands and arms that have been associated with particular meanings. The boxer who has won a fight might clasp his hands above his head in a gesture of victory. Similarly, the modest speaker might push the palm of his hand toward the audience to still listeners' applause.

Other gestures are emphatic in nature and tend to punctuate the verbal message. When presenting a forceful argument, the speaker might pound a fist on the lectern to support the idea. Or a speaker may wave an index finger to focus the audience's attention on a particular thought. These gestures can serve to underscore the speaker's message, but should be used sparingly so that they don't lose their effectiveness.

Gestures can be descriptive in nature and work to enhance the verbal message. For example, try to describe a spiral staircase while keeping your hands behind your back. The feat is nearly impossible. Descriptive gestures are particularly effective when you ask the audience to visualize what you are saying. A simple gesture to illustrate size, quantity, shape, or distance can lend support to the speaker's description.

All gestures—traditional, emphatic and descriptive—must be used purposefully if they are to add to your delivery. Here are a few things to keep in mind when using gestures:

1. Avoid gestures that make you feel uncomfortable. Awkward or self-conscious movements detract from your delivery.
2. Be careful to coordinate your gestures with what you are saying; timing is important here.
3. A gesture should not call attention to itself apart from the spoken message.
4. Use gestures only when they will really add to your presentation; they lose their effectiveness when used to excess. Can you imagine a speaker who pounded the lectern at each and every strong point in the speech? The result would probably be more humorous than forceful.

Facial Expressions

In public speaking, as in other interpersonal exchanges, facial expressions are important to communication. A look of disappointment, a smile of delight, or a frown of disapproval can all be more powerful than a spoken message. In fact, it has been found that facial expressions have greater impact than verbal messages when the two are inconsistent.[8]

Facial expressions are important in establishing rapport with the audience, but the skillful speaker does not want to manipulate the audience by using them. An audience can usually sense when a smile is phony in much the same way a parent can often tell when a child is lying. Once again, as with all body movements, facial expressions should be natural

---

[8] A. Mehrabian, *Silent Messages*, 2nd ed. (Belmont, Calif.: Wadsworth, 1981), 76.

Gestures can convey a variety of meanings, depending on the context.

Style and context.

Consistency between words and facial expressions is the key to being perceived by an audience as genuine.

extensions of the verbal message. If you are genuine about the content of your speech, then your facial expressions will be consistent with your words.

Eye Contact

Of all the different parts of the face, the eyes are the most important in establishing the speaker-audience relationship. Good eye contact helps to establish rapport and speaker credibility. A speaker who looks at the audience appears more straightforward and honest than one who does not. In a study of speaker training in the areas of eye contact, gestures and initial and closing speaking behaviors, it was discovered that eye contact training produced the greatest effects on both improved audience ratings and speaker self-confidence.[9]

Although eye contact is important in delivery, it is impossible to look at the entire audience at one time. The effective speaker scans the audience and looks directly at individual members seated in various locations.

[9] E. L. Black and G. L. Martin, "A Component Analysis of Public Speaking Behaviors across Individuals and Behavioral Categories," *Communication Education* 29 (1980), 273–82.

An empty stare or unfocused, wandering eyes do not add to your delivery. To increase the effectiveness of eye contact, you should try to make all the members of the audience feel as if you are talking to them individually.

The Lectern and Note Cards

When speaking to an audience, it is usually more comfortable to stand behind a lectern. The key word here is stand, not *hide*. Because body movement is an essential aspect of delivery, you must be clearly visible to the audience. A speaker can use this spatial relationship by moving away from the lectern to develop rapport with the audience or by remaining behind it to preserve formality.

A lectern provides a space for your notes or outline. Of course, the use of written materials depends on the type of delivery. An impromptu speech, which by definition is without preparation, would not involve the use of notes. However, an extemporaneous speech, which is carefully prepared but not memorized, might require notes or an outline, especially if the speech is long or complicated. Of course, when a speech is to be read, the complete text must be available to the speaker.

When using note cards, you must be sure that they are written carefully; also, the number of cards should be limited to as few as possible. You should also be careful not to rustle cards or papers, especially when using a microphone.

VOCAL DELIVERY

The second major element of a speaker's presentation is the voice. *Vocal delivery* involves the mechanics of vocalization, vocal characteristics (including pitch, volume, rate and quality) and pronunciation. Inexperienced speakers often pay little attention to their vocal delivery, incorrectly believing that the voice cannot be altered in any way. Even though one's physical makeup influences vocal quality, much can be done to improve vocal delivery.

The Mechanics of Vocalization

To understand how to improve vocal delivery, it is important first to be aware of the mechanics of vocalization.[10] Voice and speech depend on phonation. In simple terms, *phonation* is the process by which air is pushed through the vocal cords, which then vibrate to produce sound. The sounds or tones produced in this way are what we call *voice*. Because air is responsible for the vibration of the vocal cords, the breathing mechanism plays a basic part in phonation.

When you exhale, air from the lungs travels up the bronchial tubes

---

[10] V. A. Anderson, *Training the Speaking Voice*, 3rd ed. (New York: Oxford University Press, 1977).

to the larynx. (See Figure 12–1). The ***larynx,*** commonly known as the ***voice box,*** contains two thin membranes, or vocal cords, which vibrate as the air passes through them. The sound waves that result from this vibration are the basic voice sound. Functioning like a valve, the vocal cords are controlled by muscles that regulate the amount of air passing through. In order to produce speech sounds, the cords move close enough together to partially block the escaping air and alter the tone produced.

The process of phonation is not complete until the sound produced in the larynx is resonated throughout the vocal chamber of the mouth, nose and throat. ***Resonance*** is responsible for both the amplification and enrichment of the voice. Without these chambers or cavities to give the sounds support and resonance, vocal quality would be quite unpleasant.

To better understand this process, place your finger on the bone of your nose and feel the vibration as you hum. The sound is resonating in the nasal cavity. When you have a cold or a stuffy nose, your voice sounds different without this additional resonance.

Articulation is the process by which voice is altered into recognizable speech sounds. These speech sounds consist of vowels and consonants, the building blocks of our speech.

The consonants and vowels are formed when sounds are modified by the articulators. These include the lips, teeth, tongue, jaw, gum ridge and palates, in addition to the nose, throat and oral cavities. Consonants are produced as the articulators interfere with the passage of sound. Each consonant is produced by a different articulator as it interferes in some way with the flow of sound. For example, the "p" sound is made by joining the lips, which block the passage of air for a moment and are then quickly released. A "t" sound is produced when the tip of the tongue is placed along

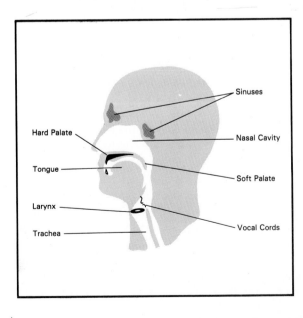

Figure 12–1
Elements of vocal delivery

the gum ridge. The articulators in each case alter the sound produced by the vibrations of the vocal cords.

Vowels are produced by altering the size and shape of the nose, throat and oral cavities. For example, contrast the shape of the mouth as you say "ah" and "oo." Unlike consonants, vowels do not require interference by the various articulators.

Poor articulation is usually the result of misuse of the articulators. For example, someone who has a lisp is not placing the tongue against the gum ridge to produce the "s" sound. Correction of this fault usually involves making a speaker aware of the error and having him or her practice the proper articulation of the sound.

Sometimes the problem is not one of carelessness or incorrect use. A person with a defective articulator will have problems producing proper speech sounds. For example, someone with an extreme overbite may have a lisp due to the improper meeting of the upper and lower teeth. With patience and practice most of these people can improve their articulation to the point where their speech fault is negligible.

Vocal Characteristics

Now that you have a basic idea of how speech is produced, we can discuss the various characteristics of the voice. Vocal delivery involves four vocal characteristics: pitch, volume, rate and quality.

PITCH.   The *pitch* of the voice refers to how high or low the voice sounds. A person's natural pitch is determined in part by the length and width of the vocal cords. Women's vocal cords are characteristically thinner and longer than men's, so women have higher-pitched voices. Each voice can produce sounds ranging in pitch from high to low. Tensing the vocal cords produces a higher pitch, while relaxing them lowers the sound. Skillful singers and speakers are able to widen their pitch range and develop pitch control by practicing appropriate voice exercises.

When you have developed control of your pitch, you can use this skill to advantage. A variation in pitch adds color and vitality to a delivery and can also be used as a means of emphasis. The most boring speakers have little pitch variety. They speak in monotones, without emphasizing important points with their voices. As you may know, it is easy to be lulled to sleep by a monotonous voice, even when the topic of discussion is interesting.

VOLUME.   The second vocal characteristic is *volume,* which means intensity or loudness. Once again, as with pitch, each of us has a volume range that allows us to project various degrees of loudness, ranging from a whisper to a scream.

A person whose voice is perfectly audible in conversation may have difficulty projecting before a large audience. Therefore, in rehearsing the delivery of a speech, you must adjust your volume to the room in which you will be speaking. Obviously, the most brilliant oration is meaningless if you cannot be heard. You should also try to overcome any distracting noise that may interfere with the transmission of the message, such as sounds from electric fans or nearby traffic.

While the most important point is simply to be heard, you can also adjust volume to add to your overall presentation. Variation in volume makes you sound more dynamic; it can also emphasize your main ideas and underscore important arguments. If you build to a crescendo, you will add impact to the verbal message in the same way a musician does when playing a melody.

RATE.   *Rate* of speech is another important vocal characteristic. If you talk too quickly, the audience may not be able to keep pace. At the other extreme, if your speaking rate is too slow, the audience may lose interest. The main concern is audience comprehension. The nature and degree of difficulty of your message help to determine a suitable rate of speech. A new or complicated message may call for a slower delivery than a subject with which the audience is familiar. An effective speaker will vary the rate of speech, pausing and slowing down to give emphasis to some material and speeding up at other points.

In addition to message comprehension, researchers have found that speech rate also affects ratings of speaker competence and social attractiveness. After listening to a sample of speech at one of five speech-rate levels, subjects in one experiment evaluated the speaker. Results of the study indicated that, for either male or female speakers, increases in speech rate were associated with more favorable competence ratings. However, the listeners perceived male speakers as most attractive when they spoke at moderate to relatively fast rates, while speech rate was unrelated to perceived attractiveness of female speakers.[11]

QUALITY.   One of the most difficult characteristics to control is vocal quality. *Vocal quality* refers to the timbre of the voice, the characteristic that distinguishes one voice from another. A resonant quality is desirable, so that the voice sounds deep and mellow. Voices that are too thin, strident, nasal, or breathy sound unpleasant and should be improved. Each of these qualities is the result of poor phonation. Understanding the vocal process and doing voice exercises can improve vocal quality, but it takes time to change something that feels natural to you.

Factors Influencing Your Voice

In addition to voice exercises, there are other factors that can influence the sound of your voice. The first of these is your physical makeup. This factor

---

[11] R. L. Street, Jr., R. M. Brady, and R. Lee, "Evaluative Responses to Communicators: The Effects of Speech Rate, Sex, and Interaction Context, *Western Journal of Speech Communication* 48 (Winter, 1984), 14–27.

involves the various parts of the vocal mechanism described under phonation—namely, the lungs, vocal cords, larynx, and resonating chambers.

Psychological factors also influence a person's voice. When you are anxious or excited, the tension may localize in the vocal cords, creating a higher pitch than normal. If you are relaxed and at ease, your voice will sound much more pleasant.

A third factor that influences voice is environment. Members of the same family often seem to have similar voices. The similarity is partially genetic and partially environmental. You pick up inflections from the people around you, including family members, peers, and members of the same ethnic group.

In addition to the influence of your immediate circle of acquaintances, your voice is also affected by regional dialects. Different regions of a country have varying speech and voice patterns that make their use of voice and language unique. A person from the South may have a "drawl" that is quite distinct from the "twang" of a Midwesterner. However, regional differences usually affect pronunciation more than voice quality.

Improving Vocalization

The best way to improve your voice is through voice exercises. You must first be able to hear your own voice and decide which aspects need improvement. Thanks to modern technology, you can listen to yourself on a tape recorder. This enables you to analyze your voice and practice a variety of exercises. You must decide, perhaps with the aid of a speech therapist or vocal coach, whether the problem concerns phonation, articulation, or pronunciation.

If the area in need of improvement is phonation, or the production of sound, then the problem may be one of force, duration, or quality. You might find that your voice often trails off at the end of a sentence, or that the volume is so low that you cannot be heard. In either case the problem is one of force.

Many people breathe incorrectly, and improper breathing can impair phonation. Some individuals lack force because they are not using their resonating chambers as efficiently as possible. Exercises to increase the use of these cavities add to a speaker's amplification.

Some people cannot speak for a long period of time without losing their voices. This can pose a serious problem for a person with many speaking engagements. Imagine the distress of politicians on the campaign trail who find their voices giving out after speaking for an extended period of time. Voice fatigue usually comes from improper use of the different parts of the vocal mechanism.

Basically, vocal sound should be supported by the partition of muscles and tendons between the chest and abdomen known as the *diaphragm*. This muscle is responsible for involuntary breathing and is one of the strongest muscles in the body. The muscles of the throat and the vocal cords are easily strained, while the diaphragm is virtually tireless. Through prescribed exercises you can learn to "support" your voice correctly and avoid hoarseness and voice loss. However, it takes time and practice to overcome the bad habits of years. As mentioned previously, problems of articulation usually stem from careless speech habits. Unless a person must compensate for a physical defect such as a harelip, poor articulation can be improved by concentrated effort and practice. We can all be inspired by individuals who are born deaf and are never able to hear the sound of words; with a great deal of perseverance, many of them have learned to articulate well enough to be understood in conversation.

An understanding of how various sounds are made will help you to improve articulation. Practice drills are good reinforcement for correcting problems of articulation, but you must make a conscious effort to carry over the correct production of speech sounds into everyday conversation as well as public-speaking situations. Faulty articulation is particularly bad for the public speaker, since an audience is easily distracted by poor speech. Mumbling and speaking carelessly affect the audience's perception of you. A speaker whose pronunciation is clear and distinct makes a more favorable impression than does someone whose speech is sloppy.

Pronunciation

Pronunciation can be important to the improvement of both speech and voice. Standards of pronunciation are often determined by geographical area or imposed by occasion or education. Americans speak the same language, but pronunciation varies according to region. While geographic regions have changed in terms of speech patterns, one can still find a difference between northern, midwestern and southern speech. In addition to the three major regions, there are numerous subdivisions. For example, New Yorkers do not sound like Bostonians, even though they are both considered northern.

Certain speakers strive for what is called "standard American speech," the type of speech exemplified by Dan Rather and other national newscasters. Although still preferred in some circles, standard American pronunciation is not a prerequisite for success. Neither John Kennedy's New England speech nor Jimmy Carter's Southern style hurt their political aspirations. The key is not regional pronunciation but careful articulation.

In addition to regional background, your pronunciation is influenced by the occasion and by your education. Certain situations, such as job interviews or press conferences, require careful pronunciation. Any person speaking before a group should pay special attention to pronunciation. If a speaker makes an error, the audience's attention may be temporarily distracted. Poor pronunciation can create a bad impression.

Education affects pronunciation in the sense that exposure to language through reading, speaking, and listening results in increased vocabulary and knowledge of the way different words are pronounced. Education includes more than formal schooling. As you read, study, travel, and speak with educated people, your vocabulary and language skills, including those related to pronunciation, improve.

There are several ways you, as a speaker, can improve pronunciation. If you are unsure of the way a word is pronounced, look it up in the dictionary.

Be particularly careful to find out the proper pronunciation of the names of people and places mentioned in your speech. If you are quoting someone or acknowledging a particular person or organization, it is important to pronounce the name correctly.

Pronunciation, articulation, and phonation have always been concerns of the public speaker. As we all rely on voice and speech for much of our communication, we should strive to improve our vocal delivery.

STYLE

We recognize that the Reverend Jesse Jackson has an effective style of oration, and we would all probably agree that Oliver North used a unique and powerful style of delivery at the Iran-contra hearings. But what is style?

In simple terms, *style* is the way an individual speaker gives ideas meaning through his or her particular brand of verbal expression and delivery. Style deals with both the wording and the delivery of the message. It includes the speaker's choice of words, the use of language, sentence structure, and the characteristics of delivery. Because style is made up of so many variables, each speaker's style is somewhat different. Some speakers have pet phrases that they include in their speeches, some are very plain-spoken, and others rely heavily on the use of metaphor or flowery language.

Style also applies to syntax, or sentence structure. A speaker may invert subject and verb to achieve a stylistic effect. For example, a disgusted sportscaster might say, "Never have I witnessed such a poor display of teamwork." Run-on or choppy sentences can also be used to achieve a stylistic effect. Although a good speaker should adhere to the rules of grammar, "poetic license" of sorts can be used to achieve a desired effect.

Our primary concern here is with the element of style that applies to a speaker's physical and vocal delivery. Of course, while every speaker develops a personal style, you should be able to adapt your style to fit the audience, occasion, topic, and purpose of your speech. Basically, your style may be formal or informal, with varying degrees in between.

Quite logically, a formal style is best suited to a formal occasion. We would expect, for example, that both a president's State of the Union address and a college valedictory speech would be formal. A casual treatment of either of these speeches would demean their importance.

The characteristics of formal style include serious and impersonal tone, correct use of grammar, sophisticated stylistic devices, and avoidance of slang. The physical and vocal delivery should be dignified and serious.

A serious tone is projected by the manner in which you present yourself and your message. Althouth you need to be solemn, you should be dignified. There is no room for flippancy in a formal presentation. To emphasize the importance of the message, you should keep an impersonal tone by avoiding the use of personal pronouns.

More often than not, the speaking engagements in which we find ourselves tend to be more casual than formal and require a less formidable style. An informal style is characterized by a light and personal tone, use of fairly simple sentence structure and vocabulary, and a bending of grammatical rules, if necessary. An informal style allows the speaker to add warmth to the presentation with informal language and humor.

Very few speaking situations are either strictly formal or strictly informal. As most fall within the two extremes, you will have to adapt your style accordingly. For example, although we might think of an after-dinner speech as being informal, the appropriate presentation would depend on the nature of the occasion as well as the audience. You should evaluate each speaking situation individually to determine the right delivery.

Characteristics of Style

Although each speaker is different, there are certain desirable characteristics that help to make any speaker's style effective. The first of these is *accuracy,* which requires a precise use of words. You may know what you want to say but have trouble getting the idea across to the audience. If an audience walks away not knowing what was said or misinterpreting the message, then you have failed in your basic purpose. As a speaker, you must choose the words that most accurately convey your message. Avoid words that are too abstract or general, as well as words that are open to many different interpretations. Words such as *good, bad,* and *nice* are really ambiguous and add little to a presentation.

Closely related to accuracy is *clarity.* The main consideration here is audience comprehension. A complicated description of a medical procedure that is perfectly clear to a surgeon may be totally confusing to an audience of lay people. Therefore, you must adapt your language and style to fit the needs of the audience.

Appropriateness is another characteristic of style. As mentioned previously, a speaker's style should fit the occasion, the audience, and the type and purpose of the speech. Each presentation should reflect consideration of all of these factors.

Another characteristic of effective style is *economy,* or the greatest efficiency of language. If you use the right words in the most efficient way, your message will be more meaningful. There is no need to use many words when a few will do. If you are concise, accuracy and clarity will be achieved as well. However, conciseness should not undermine comprehension, which sometimes makes it necessary to repeat ideas.

The final characteristic is a *lively quality* in the selection of words. Although economy is a virtue in terms of style, sometimes a speaker will use a phrase or expression that leaves a lasting impression on the audience. A poetic statement, a memorable expression, an unusual figure of speech, or a melodic phrase will jump out at the audience and capture its attention. The speaker must not overuse this quality, however, or the impact will be weakened.

An impressive style is not, of course, achieved without careful preparation and practice. Style, like good public speaking skills in general, *can* be learned, but not without the interest and effort it takes to achieve any valuable goal. If you are determined, if you strive to understand and use the communication principles suggested in this book, then more than likely you will be rewarded with the attainment of your goal: satisfying communication, the sharing of yourself and your experiences with your fellow human beings.

SUMMARY

The importance of delivery in public speaking cannot be overestimated. A speaker's delivery is the vehicle for the communication of the message. Good delivery is essential in capturing and maintaining audience attention and also affects speaker credibility, audience comprehension, and persuasive impact.

Communication apprehensiveness can affect a speaker's delivery. First believed to be fear of the speaking situation itself, apprehensiveness is currently viewed as stemming from anxiety and speaker insecurity. To overcome apprehensiveness, the speaker can do five things: (1) practice, (2) use physical activity, (3) avoid memorization and organize well, (4) get involved with the topic, and (5) develop a proper attitude.

Principles of good delivery include a natural appearance, consistency of expression and content, rapport with the listeners, and a presentation that is appropriate to the audience, the situation, and the speaker. The physical aspects of delivery include body movements, posture, gestures, facial expressions, eye contact, and the use of the lectern and note cards. An awareness and natural use of these elements can greatly enhance the verbal message.

The effective public speaker understands the vocal aspects of public speaking. Good phonation, resonance and articulation are essential to message audibility and comprehension. An awareness of pitch, volume, rate, and voice quality will enable the speaker to capture and hold the listener's ear. Vocal delivery is influenced by physical, psychological, and environmental factors. Serious students of public speaking can improve their powers of vocalization by practicing appropriate vocal exercises.

Pronunciation is another element of vocal delivery that must not be overlooked. Good pronunciation is essential to message comprehension and speaker credibility.

The style of delivery may be as important as the content of the message. The speaker may choose between varying degrees of formality. Most speakers eventually develop a unique personal style. Choice of words, use of language, and syntax are all effective stylistic elements. The speaker should aim for a style that is accurate, clear, appropriate to the occasion and setting, economical, and striking. Although this may seem a difficult task, the results will be worth the effort.

EXERCISES

GROUP EXPERIENCES

Coaching on the Sidelines

DESCRIPTION: Politicians have long been aware of the importance of public speaking. Today ghostwriters, communication consultants, and many other specialists work together to help "present" the politician to the public. This activity will give you the opportunity to act as coach or consultant to a politician.

    PROCEDURE: Divide into dyads. You and your partner have been hired to help Laura Martinez present herself to the public for the upcoming campaign. Larua is totally inexperienced in public speaking. She does not know what to do with her hands, how fast to talk, what to say, or how to say it. Needless to say, you have a big job ahead of you. Write a plan for getting Laura ready for the public. You might want to incorporate some practice speaking sessions, the use of videotape, and so forth, to prepare Laura. Share your plan with the other groups and compare the strategy plans.

    DISCUSSION: Did you forget any important steps in your plan? Can you improve a person's speaking ability? Can you create "charisma" in a person? How can delivery affect the credibility of a person?

Timing

    DESCRIPTION: A good delivery is absolutely essential for a successful presentation, along with voice, gestures and body stance: They all play an important role in a public speaking situation. A good delivery should be carefully coordinated with the content of the speech. If the gestures and facial expressions do not come at the right time, they will distract from the speech itself. This activity gives you an opportunity to see the effects on an audience of the timing of facial expressions and gestures.

    PROCEDURE: If you have a theatrical flair or a dramatic side to your personality, then this is the activity for you. Write a three-minute speech designed to sell a product of your choice. Practice the delivery of the speech several times until you have completely *uncoordinated* your gestures and facial expressions with your words. This will be difficult, because when your voice is excited, your face will have to look bored. If you state that there are three good reasons to buy your product, you may want to use a hand gesture *after* you finish saying this. In whatever way possible, by making the timing wrong, your "presentation" should look like a comedy routine. Try it out by presenting it before a class or a group of people.

    DISCUSSION: What were the reactions to your poorly timed talk? Did the audience remember what you had to say or the way you said it? Did you feel self-conscious or overdramatic? Whatever effect you created, chances are good that the lack of timing did hurt the impact of your speech. Next time you give a speech, be natural, and you will see that the facial expressions, gestures and content of the speech will complement one another.

VOICE LESSONS

    DESCRIPTION: A speaker's vocal delivery involves four things: pitch, volume, rate, and quality. By studying and practicing each quality, you can improve your speaking voice. The following voice drill is designed to help you identify specific characteristics of your voice.

PROCEDURE: Divide into dyads. With the help of your partner, practice the following line: "A person whose voice is perfectly audible in conversation may have difficulty projecting before a large audience." Say the line six times for each characteristic, focusing first on pitch, then volume, then rate, then quality. For instance: With rate, the first time you should say the line very slowly, and gradually get faster, so that by the sixth time you are saying it very fast. Your partner should select which repetition (first to sixth) is the best rate for an audience, and then do the same for the other characteristics.

Pitch: Go from a very high pitch to a very low pitch.
Volume: Go from a very soft voice to a very loud voice.
Rate: Go from speaking very slowly to speaking very quickly.
Quality: Go from a very nasal quality to a deep and resonant quality.

DISCUSSION: Are you surprised by any of the selections made by your partner? Feedback is important, particularly about the voice, for we cannot hear ourselves the way others hear us. A common problem in speaking is rate. Speakers tend to think they are speaking at a slower rate than they actually are. Try to remember and practice what your partner selected as the best rate, volume, pitch, and vocal quality for you.

PERSONAL EXPERIENCES

1. Listen to a live speaker or a televised speech. Listen carefully to the vocal characteristics of the speaker (pitch, volume, rate, and quality). Is the speaker using his or her voice for maximum effectiveness? What things, if any, would you change about the speaker's voice?
2. Observe the kind of gestures you use when talking to another person. Do you use a lot of gestures? Do you make gestures in close to your body, or are they expansive? Do you feel self-conscious when you use your hands? You use gestures as a natural part of your everyday conversations; there is no reason why your gestures cannot be just as natural in a speech. Watch them. Feel comfortable with the way your hands move. If you feel comfortable, so will others.
3. Imagine that you are going to give a speech before an audience of a hundred people. In addition, you will be talking about something that excites you. Since looking forward to giving a speech is very important, what could you do to "psyche" yourself up?

DISCUSSION QUESTIONS

1. How can communication apprehensiveness be used to *enhance* your delivery of a message?
2. What are the basic factors to consider in the presentation of a speech? Is any one factor more important than the others?

3. What physical aspects of a presentation are important for a speaker to consider?
4. What things make you "unique" as a speaker? (Consider style, vocal quality, delivery, and so on).
5. What methods can you use to improve your delivery?
6. What plan would you make for yourself in order to improve your public-speaking skills?

13
Communication through the Mass Media

KEY CONCEPTS AND TERMS

Global village
Gatekeeper
Equal time rule
Fairness doctrine
Diffusion of information
Homophily

Change agent
Opinion leader
Advertising
Public relations
Demassification

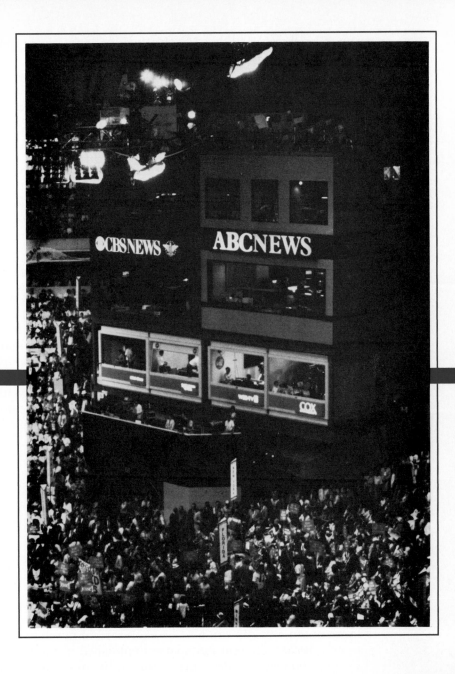

The "Preserve the Animals" fund had been in existence for almost three years without much widespread success in Dana's eyes. As the foundation director from day one of the project, Dana knew that something must be done or the foundation would fold. Closing the thick, black binder that housed the latest accounting figures, she consulted her Rolodex and then reached across the desk for her phone. Sam would know what to do. He was a whiz kid in marketing, and he had promised to help the foundation in any way that he could. As she dialed the last four digits of his office number, Dana wondered if he was still the same old Sam—as bright and witty as she had known him to be back at college.

As she waited for his assistant to buzz Sam's office, Dana quickly ran through the list of questions that she wanted to ask. How could the foundation make better use of the funds appropriated for advertising and promotion? What forms of media would be the most effective, given the foundation's limited resources? How soon could the foundation expect to benefit from any media campaign that it launched? Dotting the missed "i" in "media," Dana waited, then began a sketch of the foundation's most recent logo. At last, she heard Sam's familiar laugh and his voice on the other end of the line. Feeling her mood change instantly, she couldn't wait to get his advice.

After 45 minutes, much laughter, and, at last, the opportunity to ask her questions, Dana hung up the phone. "He really *is* the same old Sam," she said aloud, as she turned to a new page in her pad and quickly scrawled his last suggestion. Leafing back through the many ideas they had shared, Dana was surprised at the many ways that nonprofit foundations can use the media at no expense. Although she had created public-service announcements in the past, Dana had never thought of writing articles about preserving wildlife under the foundation's name. Sam had opened her eyes to a lot of possibilities, using radio, television, newspapers, and magazines in combination. "At last," Dana said to herself with a smile and a new-found inspiration, "I believe that I *can* get this foundation back on the road!"

The use of mass communication media, such as those that Dana and Sam discussed above, is the topic of this chapter. Specifically, we will focus on the characteristics, functions, and effects of these various media in an attempt to help you understand their purpose and viability as communication tools.

MASS COMMUNICATION: AN OVERVIEW

Although all forms of mass communication affect our lives, the most widely used and influential forms are newspapers, radio, TV, and film. The importance of these media can best be expressed in numbers. There are approximately 10,000 different newspapers published in the United States, not including shoppers' guides, entertainment listings, and "scandal sheets." The role of the newspaper keeps changing. At first it was entirely informative in nature; then, before the days of electronic media, it developed an important entertainment function, which disappeared after the advent of radio and TV. Yet today, because of keen competition among papers and other forms of media, newspapers once again include many features in addition to the

> The medium is the message.
> Marshall McLuhan

daily news. For example, the *New York Times* offers a weekly section devoted to the home, one to weekend entertainment, and another to life-styles.

Although many of us are children of the TV age, statistics about radio broadcasting help us realize the importance of radio both as a news medium and as an entertainment medium. There are close to 8,500 radio stations in the United States alone. Such a demand for the use of the airwaves has made it necessary to regulate the air frequencies and to use AM/FM bands in the interests of fairness and efficiency.

Interestingly enough, there are considerably fewer TV stations, with approximately 835 commercial stations and 280 educational channels. Yet the impact of TV as a medium of entertainment, information, and education is truly unparalleled.

CHARACTERISTICS OF MASS COMMUNICATION

Both print and electronic media share certain unique characteristics. Mass communication overcomes the barriers of time and space. This time phenomenon can be illustrated by *Roots,* Alex Haley's serialized drama, which traced his African ancestry through enslavement to freedom. The story was condensed into eight installments, totaling twelve TV hours. Some 130 million viewers witnessed part or all of 200 years of semifictionalized American history. Suddenly, events that had occurred many years ago became "real" once more as a result of mass communication.

The ability of mass communication to encompass vast boundaries of space is expressed by Marshall McLuhan's term *global village.* Global village suggests that the world is smaller than before because of advances in mass communication (especially the telephone, TV, and satellites). People in one part of the world can witness an event as it is taking place in another. People all over the world now share one another's joys and sorrows. For example, our enthusiasm in watching the Olympic Games as they are transmitted live to various countries throughout the world is certainly a contrast to the horrors we experienced each night on TV during the years of the Vietnam War—the first fully televised war. Advances in mass communications have made the world smaller; the distance between people and the space between countries no longer seem as great a barrier to communication. The Live-Aid concert, broadcasted around the world, represents a remarkable example of the power of mass communication. Over $70 million was raised to aid famine victims in northern Africa.

Delayed Feedback

By definition, mass communication suggests a widespread audience separated from a source by a great distance. Therefore, a receiver's feedback or response to a message is most often limited and delayed. For example, a person watching a charity telethon may be moved to respond immediately by calling in a pledge. Yet the sheer mechanics of the situation create a certain delay in feedback. There are varying degrees of delayed feedback,

The beginnings of a new medium of mass communication: A television set on display at the 1939 New York World's Fair.

ranging from a few minutes, as in the above situation, to several weeks or even months. Consumers responding to a TV commercial for a particular brand of deodorant may not purchase the product until their current supply runs out, which may be days or even weeks later. Consumers may not even realize that they are responding to a mass communication messsage. The fact that the source is inaccessible and that a medium is needed to transmit the response are major reasons for the delay in feedback. For example, if listeners are outraged by a remark heard on TV or radio, the best they can do is call the station. Yet even this action takes a certain amount of time and cannot represent total listener reaction, particularly in terms of nonverbal feedback.

> The new source of power is not money in the hands of a few but information in the hands of many.
>
> John Naisbitt, *Megatrends*

Gatekeeping

As one might expect, the enormous scope of mass communication requires some control in the selection and editing of the messages that are constantly transmitted to the mass audience. The term **gatekeeper,** originally used by Austrian psychologist Kurt Lewin to identify the people or organizations who control news items in the communications channel, has now come to mean any individual or organization that influences a mass communication message.[1] There are gatekeepers within the mass communication industry itself; within the government; and within big business. Each group sets certain standards and limitations that serve as guidelines for both content and delivery of a mass communication message.

INDUSTRY GATEKEEPING.   To understand the concept of gatekeeping, we need to examine the news media. Every major paper and station is flooded with news stories fed to them by the major wire services, organizations that send news stories and features by direct telegraph to subscribing newspapers and TV and radio stations. Obviously, the news media cannot relay all of this information. Since neither time nor space allows for the printing or broadcasting of each and every news event, media personnel at various levels must determine which items they consider the most newsworthy. In effect, the information that is fed to the various news media goes through a filtering process. Stories that appear on the front page in a Midwest daily may be put on the back page of a New York newspaper, if printed at all. Yet you need not make comparisons across state lines to see that news selection and editing are very subjective. Examine two papers published in the same city and compare headline stories and the location of various news items. Sometimes a story that appears in the first few pages of one paper is entirely omitted in another. Writers, editors, publishers, and other media personnel determine length and placement of the news copy. While some stories must be included, they are often condensed or distorted. For example, an involved story about suspected corruption at the state or local level may be published as fact by news services in a different state or locality because they don't have the time or space to devote to a story that does not entirely influence their readers or viewers. This, then, is industry gatekeeping.

GOVERNMENT GATEKEEPING.   In addition to a filtering system that controls message selection, agencies such as the Federal Communications Commission (FCC) and the courts also influence media content. In their roles as gatekeepers, the FCC and the courts must protect the interests of the public. To ensure proper use of the public airwaves, the FCC issues a license before a station may broadcast. A license is granted for a period of three years, after which time the station's performance is evaluated. A review of the station must show that the station has abided by the rules and regulations set forth by the FCC and that it has offered a public service. You may have noticed that sometimes when a TV or radio station's license is up for renewal, the station will invite letters from the audience to comment on how it has served the public interest. A station that has not been granted a license or that has had its license taken away may no longer broadcast.

Two important FCC controls are the equal time rule and the fairness doctrine. The *equal time rule* applies to candidates for political office. It says that a station must give all candidates the same amount of time under

---

[1] K. Lewin, "Frontiers in Group Dynamics," *Human Relations* 1 (1947), 5–41.

the same terms. Thus, if one candidate is interviewed by a station, other candidates must be given the same coverage. If a candidate buys air time to advertise his or her candidacy, other candidates must be given the same option, even if it means that the station has to preempt regular programming.

When the Kennedy-Nixon debates were broadcast in 1960, Congress suspended the equal time rule so that stations would not be overwhelmed by requests to put many minor candidates on the air. Yet, in 1976 the FCC handled the Carter-Ford debates in a completely different way. Stations can bypass the equal time rule if coverage of a candidate is considered a newsworthy event. Therefore, the FCC concluded that the presidential debates sponsored by the League of Women Voters were a newsworthy event that should be reported, thereby getting around the equal time rule.

Unlike the equal time rule, which involves people, the fairness doctrine mainly involves issues. The **fairness doctrine** states that all stations must provide some time to discuss controversial issues and that each station must encourage opposing viewpoints. Therefore, if a station offers an editorial opposing school busing, it must ask for and air the views of a spokesperson in favor of the issue. Or, if in the course of a commentary a speaker denounces a particular person or organization, that individual or group must have the right to respond.

While all government attempts to control mass communication can be interpreted as infringements of constitutional rights, guidelines used to determine whether something is obscene or pornographic are particularly controversial. Although periodically revised, court rulings that define obscenity and pornography are characteristically vague. Decisions about obscenity are now left up to the individual community, which must decide if the material in question has any "redeeming social value," or—if taken as a whole—the material "appeals to prurient interest."

ECONOMIC GATEKEEPING.   Advertisers are the primary financial support for mass media and thus control media industries to some extent. The broadcast media sell time, while the print media sell space. Because media buying is expensive, advertisers want some control over the content of anything they sponsor.

To illustrate the influence of a TV network sponsor, we can point out that during the McCarthy era in the early 1950s, a sponsor could dictate who could or could not work either on camera or behind the scenes of a program. Some sponsors were known to blacklist anyone suspected of being sympathetic to the Communist party.

The influence of advertisers goes beyond politics and has sometimes been known to dictate taste. Because the sponsor wants to capture a large audience to ensure the greatest exposure for the product, advertisers have been known to attempt to control content so that programming will appeal to the largest audience possible.

A sponsor's influence can sometimes work to the audience's advantage. For example, a sponsor might pressure the network to curb the amount of sex or violence in a program it sponsors.

MASS COMMUNICATION MEDIA

Now, more than at any time in history, we are a media society. No day goes by without our feeling the effects of mass communication. "That's not true," you say. "I don't watch TV every day!" Maybe not, but did you wake up to news on the radio, read a paper over breakfast, play a compact disc, read a billboard, go to the movies, read a book, or get a magazine at the newsstand? We employ mass communication daily by using it to inform us of world events, to help escape into another realm, or to plan our weekends based on weather reports.

We have already examined the characteristics of mass communication. We will now look at four of the most important forms of mass communication: film, recording, radio, and television.

Film

From its beginning as a method of recording history, film has developed into a major form of recreation and entertainment. Film has been around longer than any other electronic medium, and it stays alive because it is the most creative and artistic of all media. The "film experience" (1) is of high technical quality (visually and aurally), (2) stimulates involvement, (3) provides a comfortable environment (food, seating, no interruptions, and so on), and (4) is the most realistic of all mass media forms.[2] Trends have included the 1920s era of Charlie Chaplin silent films; the 1930s musicals with Fred Astaire and Ginger Rogers; the patriotic films featuring Humphrey Bogart in the 1940s; the 3-D and youth-oriented themes of the 1950s; the experience/involvement films such as *Psycho*, *The Sound of Music*, and the Beatles' movies of the 1960s; and the disaster films such as *The Poseidon Adventure*, *Jaws*, and *The Towering Inferno* of the 1970s. The 1970s gave us films of social comment such as *One Flew Over the Cuckoo's Nest*, *All the President's Men*, and *Coming Home;* while the late 1970s and early 1980s often gave us movies focused on music, such as *Saturday Night Fever*, *The Buddy Holly Story*, *The Rose*, and *A Star Is Born*. Recent films have also revealed an enchantment with and curiosity about space exploration and travel, particularly films such as *Star Wars*, *E. T.*, *Close Encounters of the Third Kind*, *Cocoon* (Parts I and II), and *My Stepmother Is an Alien*. What's next? Although no one knows what next season will provide, we do know that there will be something for everyone, because film readily adapts to the events and needs of the times.

Recording

Is there a special song that reminds you of the first time you fell in love? Do you play a certain album when you're lonely and want to think? Can some music make you wiggle your toes or hop in the car? Music is everywhere

[2] E. J. Whetmore, *Mediamerica*, 2nd ed. (Belmont, Calif.: Wadsworth, 1982).

in our society, from Muzak in doctors' offices to country and western or punk rock in the local nightclub. Just as we remember songs from different periods in our lives, we also remember different decades by the music that was popular at the time. The Big Band and swing era of the 1940s gave birth to the first recording hero, Frank Sinatra. The Comets arrived in 1955 with "Rock Around the Clock," and Elvis gave birth to rock 'n' roll in the late 1950s. The early 1960s were best known for the Beatles and later for songs of social discontent and alienation. The 1970s were a decade of no real trend, with gentler rock, hard rock, disco, punk rock, new wave music, and the rise of country and western music. More recently, during the 1980s, the trend has been toward music that raises our social consciousness—for example, about famine (Michael Jackson and Quincy Jones, "We Are the World"), child abuse (Suzanne Vega, "Luca"), and the plight of AIDS victims (Dionne Warwick, Elton John, and others, "Friends"), moral responsibility (U-2, "The Joshua Tree"), and life-styles (Tracy Chapman, "Fast Car"). The Band-Aid, Live-Aid, and Farm-Aid concerts represent a few of the efforts of musicians in this decade to step out and help their fellow humans.

The recording industry has music for all ages and tastes. Because record buying is dominated by people under 30, recorded music is generally thought of as a youth medium. Eight out of every ten singles are bought by people under 25, and two-thirds of all albums are bought by those under 30. Many try to make it big in recording, but hopes are often shattered. To break even, a single must sell 25,000 copies, and an album must sell 85,000.[3]

Radio

Driving to class or to work, or driving out of town, many of us turn the radio dial, looking for a favorite station. It is usually fairly easy to find a station to meet our needs since there are approximately 4,750 AM stations and 3,600 FM stations playing all types of music. Although it has not always been so convenient, radio has been popular for over 50 years. During the 1930s and 1940s, radio was the television of today, with situation comedies, musicals, political addresses, and game shows. The late 1940s were a time of great change because of the development of television. Sponsors were quickly changing over to the visual medium. To save radio, a deejay format was introduced in 1951. With the deejay format, stations began to design programs for specific audiences; today we have everything from all-music to all-talk radio.

The success of radio is often attributed to its mobility. Portable transistors allow us to carry radios in our pockets and bring them anywhere, from beaches to offices. Radio is also the most reliable form of communication because it can use batteries instead of electricity. Further, radio is beneficial to advertising. Many small organizations that cannot afford the expense of TV can still get inexpensive publicity through radio.

---

[3] H. Bohn and D. F. Unguvait, *Mass Media II*, 3rd ed. (New York: Longman, 1982.).

Television

You are a member of the television generation. Men, women, and children find it easier to identify with television personalities such as Bill Cosby, Roseanne Barr, Oprah Winfrey, or Judd Hirsch than with members of the President's cabinet or former schoolteachers. Television is the most powerful and influential mass medium. In 1941, only 5,000 to 10,000 homes had television; today, however, 98 percent of all homes in America have at least one TV.

Unlike film, recording, and radio, which now cater to specialized audiences, television designs programs to please every viewer. Cartoons, documentaries, soap operas, variety shows, game shows, adventure series, sports spectaculars, movies, news, educational programs, and family shows try to meet the needs of all viewers. Some people watch TV to satisfy social needs by receiving information from news shows, fireside chats, or *Meet the Press*. Others live vicariously through programs such as *International Outdoorsman* or *National Geographic: On Assignment*. People escape into other worlds and live fantasies by loving and hating men and women on soap operas such as *General Hospital* or *Days of Our Lives*. Still others reinforce their sense of values by watching shows such as *Beauty and the Beast* and *The Equalizer*, in which good always triumphs over evil. The variety and flexibility of television make it America's most popular form of entertainment.

> The average viewer of a given program reflects, to a large extent, the values of that program.
>
> Larry Tritten

FUNCTIONS OF MASS COMMUNICATION

In Chapter 10 we identified the purpose of public speaking: to inform, to entertain, and to persuade. Basically, these three purposes also describe the primary functions of mass media.

To Inform

Although there is considerable overlap among these three areas, one can say that the dissemination of information belongs primarily to the news media, both electronic and print. Yet the news media have come a long way from just "telling it like it is." Local news shows throughout the country have expanded their formats to include human-interest stories as well as news features. Even the coverage of the news has changed dramatically. Instead of merely reporting events, reporters and broadcast journalists have become news analysts who discuss the implications of important news stories.

GOOD NEWS VERSUS BAD NEWS.   Today the broadcasting of news events is so immediate that the impact of a story "hot off the press" (or hot off the wires) can have a jolting effect. On certain days we may turn on the radio news report and hear nothing but bad news. A war, a famine, a plane crash, a murder can all be news events on any given day. The immediate reporting of these unfortunate events is bound to have an effect on listeners.

In fact, several studies have been conducted to test the effects of good news versus bad news on people's feelings and perceptions about the media reporting the news. In one such study, subjects exposed to newspapers that were "heavy" on bad news rated the newspapers more negatively than newspapers reporting greater amounts of good news. Additionally, the newspaper's image as a "community watchdog" was rated higher for the "good news" issue than those reporting higher numbers of fraud and malfeasance cases.[4]

Some individuals have a preference for receiving their news from newspapers, while others rely on TV or radio. Even within each medium, people usually select a particular newspaper or a particular channel for a report of the daily news. However, it has been found that TV news programs are less effective in influencing viewers on political issues than are newspapers. Specifically, reading a newspaper, in contrast to watching television, increases individuals' abilities to discriminate between candidates in an election.[5] These findings may best be explained by the format of the TV news program, which gives brief coverage of many stories each evening. Therefore, viewers are not exposed to in-depth coverage that might affect their voting habits. Since most stories are given limited coverage, a viewer may walk away from a TV news program not knowing which stories are most significant. Newspapers and other print media suggest the significance of various stories by the space allotted to each story, its location in the paper, its layout and the boldness of its headline. However, a story of great visual appeal or catastrophic dimension will probably have greater effect when seen on television.

PUBLIC BROADCASTING SERVICE.   We cannot talk about the information media without mentioning educational television or the Public Broadcasting Service, a nonprofit organization that attempts to emphasize the educational and enlightening aspects of television. Unlike commercial networks, which sell air time to sponsors, educational stations buy programs from the PBS network with money obtained from donations, federal funds, and commercial grants. You might notice that at the beginning or end of a program on PBS, the source of funding for the program is announced: "This program was made possible by a grant from. . . ." This type of sponsorship, which eliminates the need for advertisers, represents one of the most striking differences between commercial and public broadcasting.

Unlike commercial networks, PBS has attempted to realize the educa-

---

[4] J. B. Haskins and M. M. Miller, "The Effect of Bad News and Good News on a Newspaper's Image," *Journalism Quarterly* 61, no. 1 (1984), 3–13, 65.
[5] J. Wagner, "Media Do Make a Difference: The Differential Impact of Mass Media in the 1976 Presidential Race," *American Journal of Political Science* 27, no. 3 (1983), 407–30.

tional values of television. Many of its programs are instructional in nature, the most widely known being *Sesame Street*, a program for preschool children.

PBS also provides a forum for many experimental and innovative programs that would be too risky for commercial sponsors. PBS does not aim its entire schedule of programs at a "mass audience"; instead, it offers programs that appeal to a limited audience, a practice that would be impossible for a commercial network. Unfortunately, the artistic principles and practices that make PBS unique also create difficulties. Aside from obvious financial difficulties, PBS stations are sometimes uncertain as to just what their educational function should be.

DIFFUSION OF INFORMATION.   *Diffusion* of information refers to the way the public learns about news events, products, changes in policy, ideas, philosophies, and so forth. We might guess that most of our information comes from the mass media. However, studies have shown that although the mass media are particularly effective in informing the public of major news stories and events that have just occurred, they are much less effective when information has less news value or concerns something new about an event or idea that is already known. While many people learn about a famine or an earthquake through the media, information concerning a change in library hours or a change in traffic regulations must be diffused in a different manner. A much-cited study by Greenberg showed that 50 percent of his sample said that they had learned about the Kennedy assassination from another person.[6]

The diffusion of information from one individual to another is based on the principle of *homophily*, which is the degree to which two interacting individuals are similar in characteristics such as beliefs, values, education, social level, and so on. Diffusion of information occurs most often when a source and a receiver are alike. A student is more likely to acquire information from another student, a construction worker from another construction worker, and so on.

The diffusion of information can be analyzed in terms of change agents and opinion leaders. A *change agent* is someone who is responsible for making policy and creating change. By the nature of their position, change agents are usually not homophilous with the people to whom they must disseminate information. The change agent generally interacts with an *opinion leader*, who is more homophilous with the general public and disseminates information to them. Opinion leaders are usually respected by their peers and have considerable influence in forming and changing attitudes within their spheres of influence.

Mass communication has certainly aided the diffusion of information. Opinion leaders rely on the mass media for reports of certain news events, which they in turn disseminate to the general public. For example, when the controversy regarding the building of a new nuclear power plant in

[6] B. S. Greenberg, "Diffusion of News about the Kennedy Assassination," *Public Opinion Quarterly* 28 (Summer 1964), 225–32.

Louisiana began, protest leaders relied heavily on the media for information. As new developments arose, protest leaders would report and analyze important events for their followers. Because of mass media as well as telephones and telegraphs, the process through which information is diffused has been greatly speeded up.

To Entertain

The most common function of mass communication is entertainment. Although radio, TV, and films function as information media, entertainment provides the primary source of their revenues.

Entertainment covers many different things. For example, entertainment sections in newspapers include comics, horoscopes, and advice columns, as well as crossword puzzles and other word games. In television, entertainment includes MTV, game shows, situation comedies, soap operas, movies, drama, variety shows and sports events. Radio entertainment today consists primarily of music, although radio plays, talk shows and comedy routines make a major contribution. When we talk about film, we are talking mainly about an entertainment medium, with the possible exception of documentaries. What do all these forms have in common? By nature, an entertainment

Talk shows help distract us from the stresses of everyday life.

medium is one that provides the consumer with some sort of escape or diversion from the realities and anxieties of daily living.

To Persuade

Another function of the mass media is persuasion, as presented by advertising for products, political candidates, service organizations, charities, businesses and so forth. Both electronic and print media have great persuasive potential, but, depending on the nature of the message, a full-page ad in a major newspaper can sometimes have greater impact than a minute of air time. There are media specialists who analyze where and how messages should be placed to have the greatest influence. For example, one study found that newspaper and magazine readership (in that order) were more positively related to voting participation than television viewing. Additionally, heavy television viewers were found to be less likely to vote than other individuals.[7]

ADVERTISING

Each day our dreams, fears, desires, and concerns are analyzed by advertisers anxious to sell products. *Advertising's* chief purpose is to persuade people to buy, and to continue to buy, certain products. Radio and TV advertisements are geared to the particular audiences that will be tuned in. During a weekday afternoon, soap operas that attract millions of women are interrupted with commercials featuring laundry, cleansing, beauty, and feminine hygiene products. Through demographic analysis, companies have found out about the types of people in viewing audiences and what products they would be most interested in buying.

Many of you can easily recall certain advertising slogans or commercials. These advertising messages must do more than keep attention to be successful. No matter how interesting a radio or TV spot may be, if it fails to influence consumer buying habits, it fails. Advertising has been widely accepted in the print media, but many people view broadcast advertising as an invasion of privacy. They resent their lack of control over the type and length of commercials. For this reason, many TV viewers are turning to cable television or remote-control devices to turn off advertising. Consumers can have a voice in methods of advertising. Because of consumer complaints about exaggerated claims, broadcast regulations now govern the content of advertisements.

One medium can be more successful than another for certain products. Radio is most effective in announcing items such as dry-cleaning specials, food discounts, and clothing sales, where the visual appeal is not as important as the information. TV is highly successful where both visual and verbal

---

[7] R. T. Rust, M Bajaj, and G. Haley, "Efficient and Inefficient Media for Political Campaign Advertising," *Journal of Advertising* 13, no. 3 (1984), 45–49.

content is important. Seeing how a drop of super glue suspends a 500-pound weight is more effective than just hearing about it.

Advertisers and politicians depend heavily on mass media. How else would sponsors promote new products, or candidates introduce themselves to the general public? Very often, however, consumers are unaware of the widespread influence of the mass media. A consumer may buy a product without realizing that the seed for that purchase was planted by a TV commercial or newspaper ad.

PUBLIC RELATIONS

While a fine line is drawn between advertising and public relations, advertising is generally concerned with selling a product, and public relations with selling an image. *Public relations* is a more subtle form of advertising, which is designed to influence attitudes and beliefs. McDonald's is interested in selling its food products, but it also tries to gain recognition by giving contributions to charity, sponsoring restaurant tours for children, and writing articles about employee satisfaction.

Corporations are not the only organizations interested in public relations. Nonprofit groups, governmental agencies, churches, and universities are all involved with publicity campaigns. These organizations use public relations agents and agencies to get specific information to the public via the news media. One of the goals of public relations is to utilize space free of charge. Television news coverage of a political candidate participating in a national walk-a-thon is probably more influential in projecting a favorable image than a 30-second, $50,000, prime-time TV spot.

Although many people resent the persuasive impact of advertising and public relations, we must also realize that this influence can sometimes be constructive. Self-help groups such as Alcoholics Anonymous and different social service agencies use the media to help make people aware of the groups' existence as well as to persuade those in need to seek out their help.

EFFECTS OF MASS MEDIA

Considerable controversy exists about whether mass media serve to reinforce or change preexisting ideas. This question has been studied in the context of both political campaigns and commercial advertising. In the 1940s and 1950s, studies by Bernard Perelson and Paul Lazarsfeld contradicted the long-held theory that people's voting habits were easily swayed by persuasive messages in the media. According to their studies, voting behavior is most influenced by family and acquaintances, and voters select those political messages that reinforce preexisting beliefs. Yet studies in the 1960s, 1970s, and 1980s found that a voter may sometimes completely change his or her vote as a result of a political message. Thus far the results of studies dealing with advertising are inconclusive. The question remains as to whether people

The Nature of the Medium

In accepting an honorary degree from the University of Notre Dame a few years ago, General David Sarnoff made this statement: "We are too prone to make technological instruments the scapegoats for the sins of those who wield them. The products of modern science are not in themselves good or bad, it is the way they are used that determines their values." This is the voice of the current somnambulism. Suppose we were to say, "Apple pie is in itself neither good nor bad; it is the way it is used that determines its value." Or, "The smallpox virus is in itself neither good nor bad; it is the way it is used that determines its value." Again, "Firearms are in themselves neither good nor bad; it is the way they are used that determines their value." That is, if the slugs reach the right people firearms are good. If the TV tube fires the right ammunition at the right people it is good. I am not being perverse. There is simply nothing in the Sarnoff statement that will bear scrutiny, for it ignores the nature of the medium, of any and all media, in the true Narcissus style of one hypnotized by the amputation and extension of his own being in a new technical form. General Sarnoff went on to explain his attitude to the technology of print, saying that it was true that print caused much trash to circulate, but it had also disseminated the Bible and the thoughts of seers and philosophers. It has never occurred to General Sarnoff that any technology could do anything but add itself on to what we already are.

From Marshall McLuhan, *Understanding Media: The Extension of Man* (New York: McGraw-Hill, 1964).

are capable of withstanding ad campaigns or are manipulated by media sponsors.

Children and TV

There has been considerable investigation of the effect of TV on children. Not all findings are consistent. Some theories suggest that television provides vicarious reinforcement; that is, imaginary participation in an activity that is rewarding for the characters on the screen will reinforce this same type of behavior in a real-life situation. This does not imply a negative or positive value. Yet, when the activity is violent, or when youngsters cannot separate themselves from fantasy, this effect can be harmful. To support this claim, Sparks investigated developmental differences in children's reports of fear that are induced by mass-media programming. Results of his study revealed that younger children (ages five through seven) tend to report fright from programs that depict "impossible content" (that is, present grotesque, ugly figures or portray physical transformations of the main character), whereas older children (ages eight through eleven) report fright from programs that portray "possible events" or contain violent content.[8]

Another criticism of television is that it stifles a child's creativity. To prove this claim, a research team from the University of Southern California exposed 250 intellectually gifted elementary school students to three

---

[8] G. G. Sparks, "Developmental Differences in Children's Reports of Fear Induced by the Mass Media," *Child Study Journal* 16, no. 1 (1986), 55.

weeks of intensive television viewing. Based on pre-test and post-test evalua-tions, the study found that the children showed a "marked drop in all forms of creative abilities except verbal skills."[9] This study provided empirical data on an effect that many elementary school teachers have been observing for some time.

Because children watch television for a number of reasons, ranging from entertainment to loneliness, they unknowingly become involved in a process of "observational learning"; that is, they learn certain things simply by watching the behavior of TV characters. The amount of observational learning that takes place depends upon several factors, which include the following:

1. The age of the child (two-year-olds are more prone than teens to imitate behavior, given that they are unable to see a relationship between behavior and motives).
2. A belief that behaving in the way presented on television will be rewarded.
3. The degree to which a child identifies with a television character.
4. The degree to which a child rehearses a given behavior by daydream-ing about it or using it in make-believe play.[10]

Children learn many things through observation, including skills, values, norms, roles, and sex stereotypes. What a child learns can be either positive or negative, depending on content.

Another important effect of TV is that it oftens replaces parental influence and supplies role models for children and adolescents who have inadequate ones at home. The TV set can become a substitute parent, baby-sitter, and a replacement for family interaction. This effect is not unusually in the individual's best interest.

TV VIOLENCE. We cannot discuss TV and children without emphasizing the effects of TV violence. Once again, not all findings agree. However, an extensive body of literature demonstrates that exposure to television violence indeed contributes to increased levels of aggression among the young.[11] In one such study, the researcher was interested in the effects of realistic TV violence versus fictional violence on aggression in children. To test the effects of violence, he presented to preadolescents a six-minute newscast which featured a fight scene as one story, and to a different group of children the identical fight scene as a part of a movie preview promotion. Both the fantasy and reality fight segments produced higher scores on a hypothetical situa-tional aggression test than were obtained in the control group, which com-pleted the test without having viewed either film segment. Alarmingly, Atkin

[9] "What TV Does to Kids," *Newsweek*, 21 February 1977, 63–70.
[10] D. Pearl, "Violence and Aggression," *Society*, 21 (1984), 17–22.
[11] For example, see L. R. Huesmann and N. M. Malamuth, "Media Violence and Antisocial Behavior: An Overview," *Journal of Social Issues* 42, no. 3 (1986), 1–6.

also found that scores were higher on the aggression measure completed by children who viewed the news version than by children who viewed the fantasy segment of the fight scene.[12]

It is interesting to note how TV violence, in addition to producing aggressive behavior, affects our reactions to violence in real life. It is sometimes said that exposure to very violent scenes makes viewers more sensitive to the painful consequences of violent actions. Yet there seems to be more support for the notion that TV violence "desensitizes" its audience to violence in real-life situations. According to this view, the audience becomes apathetic toward or accepting of violent acts in society.[13]

The movie industry has also been faced with pressure concerning violence in films. The rating system imposed by the movie industry in the late 1960s was an attempt to deal with this matter, although both sex and violence determine the rating. While the rating system does not alter the content of a film, it does serve to keep children from seeing certain films and warns other viewers of what to expect. This same function is served by the disclaimers that precede certain TV programs.

TELEVISION COMMERCIALS.   The effect of television advertising on children is another area of concern. Especially on Saturday mornings, children are bombarded by enticing cereal, candy, toy, and game commercials. In a 36-minute time period, at least six minutes are devoted to advertising. Like the advertising designed for adults, children's advertising encourages youngsters to persuade their parents to buy and use certain products. The commercials often offer rewards and prizes, such as iron-on decals and toys inside the box.

Parents display mixed emotions about children's television advertising. Faced with endless demands for certain products and specific brand names, they often feel at the mercy of televised commercials that have influenced their children. However, a study of Galst suggests that parents may have the resources to fight back—and to influence their children's preferences for snacks. In Galst's study, three- to six-year-old children were exposed over a four-week period to cartoons, with interjected commercials for food products with added sugar or commercials for food products with no added sugar. Additionally, pronutritional public service announcements (PSAs) were included in the segments, with or without additional adult comments to the children about the product portrayed. Following each televised segment, the children were allowed to select a snack from a snack table which included all advertised products to which the children had been exposed, as well as similar product types (such as additional candies and fruits). The form of intervention that was found to be most effective in reducing the selection of snacks with added sugar was exposure to commercials for food products without added sugar and pronutritional PSAs with accompany-

---

[12] C. Atkin, "Effects of Realistic TV Violence vs. Fictional Violence on Aggression, *Journalism Quarterly* 60, no 4 (1983), 615–21.
[13] B. G. Rule and T. J. Ferguson, "The Effects of Media Violence on Attitudes, Emotions, and Cognitions," *Journal of Social Issues* 42, no. 3 (1986), 29–50.

ing positive evaluative comments by an adult.[14] Indeed, it seems that parents *can* fight back—but parental monitoring of television viewing is the key.

> I am entirely persuaded that the American public is more reasonable, restrained and mature than most of the broadcast industry's planners believe. Their fear of controversy is not warranted by the evidence.
>
> Edward R. Murrow

Political Campaigns

Although we have already touched on mass communication and politics, we should review some of the research designed to test the effects of mass media on political campaigns. Some people believe that mass communication is the key to political victory. Certain political observers even suggest that Michael Dukakis lost the 1988 Presidential debates *and* the election because he was not as "telegenic" as his opponent (that is, he did not come over on television as well as George Bush).

A survey was conducted by Sharyne Merritt, a marketing expert from California State Polytechnic Institute, to examine the effect of negative political advertising, or advertising which seeks to degrade perceptions of an opponent. Results of her study indicated that negative political advertising (so often used in campaigns) actually evokes negative emotions toward both the targeted opponent and the sponsor.[15] Thus, negative advertising seems to yield no fruitful results. These findings should be especially salient to minority party candidates who, coming from a position of less strength, often use negative advertising as a campaign strategy.

Television, if used effectively, can aid a political campaign. As previously noted, however, candidates must be selective in choosing their strategies and media. In order to use the television medium most effectively, candidates apparently have to purchase television spots to introduce themselves and their ideas. Although televised news coverage is free and spot commercials are expensive, the commercials have a much greater impact. Whether or not this exposure reinforces or changes viewers' voting habits is still inconclusive. In terms of exposure and information, however, the advertising spots have a much greater effect than television news coverage.

Of all forms of media, television is the most expensive and therefore must be used most efficiently. Advertising agencies may plan a media campaign for a political candidate in much the same way that they promote a new product. In fact, books such as *The Selling of the President*, by Joe McGinniss, have explored this similarity.

---

[14] J. P. Galst, "Television Food Commercials and Pronutritional Public Service Announcements as Determinants of Young Children's Snack Choices," *Child Development* 51 (1980), 935–38.
[15] S. Merritt, "Negative Political Advertising: Some Empirical Findings," *Journal of Advertising* 13, no. 3 (1984), 27–38.

Mass media reflect society's attitudes and shape our lives.

Sex Stereotyping

The mass media have usually reflected society's attitudes toward sex roles, so, until recently, little effort was made to contradict sex stereotypes. Women were portrayed as passive, while men were usually shown as aggressive and powerful. If you were to look at the TV programs of earlier decades, you might think that every woman in the country was a hard-working housewife who wanted only to stay home and care for husband and children. Occasionally, a spitfire like Lucille Ball, Gale Storm, or Ann Sothern would show that women could have spunk, although their exploits always involved scheming and inevitably backfired. During the early days of TV, there were proportionately fewer women on TV than men, and seldom did you see them on a news program. In the print media, women's magazines catered to the housewife and mother, assuming that this was the only possible female audience.

While things have certainly not changed entirely, we have begun to see a shift. We now have TV situation comedies about single women (*Murphy Brown*) and widows (*Golden Girls*). We see these women as the family bread-winners, sometimes competing professionally with men. A look at both local and network news shows reveals an increase in female newscasters, many of whom are in key spots.

The increasing number of women in today's work force has brought about changes in the mass media. For example, today there are magazines published just for the working woman; and more and more the various news and entertainment media are covering stories relevant to women as well as men.

Shaping of Events

The mass media are so important in our lives that they often have an effect on the shaping of the events they cover. Sometimes events are planned with an eye toward media coverage. The Super Bowl is a perfect example of a spectacular event that grew out of the media. On a smaller scale, basketball and football games that are broadcast live allow time out for a word from the sponsor.

There are numerous examples that show how media can shape events. A politician may delay a press conference until a broken TV camera is repaired, or a track star may be asked to repeat a final lap so that his of her action can be recorded on film.

The media sometimes overstep their bounds in shaping events. A major network was once accused of contributing money to invasionary forces in Haiti in return for the right to film the takeover. Although the event never came off, the thought that it might have succeeded is rather frightening.[16]

Effects on Government

Related to media influence in shaping events is the effect of mass media on government. In a society where there is free speech and free press, the media serve as watchdogs over the government. For instance, exposing the Watergate affair was the work of two reporters for the *Washington Post*. After the Watergate scandal was uncovered, TV aired the Congressional hearings, which affected public opinion and ultimately the Nixon administration, ending in the President's resignation. In addition to the watchdog effect, the media also serve the government by disseminating information to the public.

---

[16] D. R. Pember, *Mass Media in America*, 3rd ed. (Chicago: Science Research Associates, 1983), 36.

APPEARING ON RADIO AND TELEVISION

Let's now turn our attention behind the scenes and look at the organization of a broadcasting station. Because the broadcasting industry is dependent upon performers, we will conclude this section with some discussion about performing on radio and television.

About the Station

Jobs at a broadcasting station range from artistic to financial positions. While the organization of each individual station may vary, certain similarities do exist. Basically, the organization of all stations can be broken down into three major areas: management, sales and production.

Because broadcasting is a multimillion dollar industry, the management area is of great importance. Management must assume the financial functions of accounting and bookkeeping as well as major responsibilities related to keeping the station in operation. Depending on the size of the station, distinctions may be made between general administrative functions and business management.

Because commercial broadcasting depends on selling air time to sponsors, the sales department of any station serves as its financial life-support system. Again, depending on size and volume of sales, some stations separate this department into two sections: one to deal with local sales and one to deal with national sales.

The production end of the broadcasting industry includes a variety of functions, some operational, others creative. One of the most important aspects of production is the programming department, which deals with the selection of programs and the scheduling of air time. Large stations tend to divide this department into major areas such as sports, arts, community affairs, and so on. Other production responsibilities include coordinating all operations and overseeing artistic considerations.

When you think of how complex the broadcasting industry has become, with many stations providing programming 24 hours a day, you can see the need for a highly specialized pattern or organization to ensure the smooth operation of the station.

Inside a Television Studio

A look inside a television studio reveals an array of cameras, monitors, and lights. The amount of equipment and sophistication of the video system is determined by the size and productivity of the station. Local stations have modest setups in comparison to the large studios of network-affiliated stations.

The first visit to a TV studio can be both fascinating and disillusioning. While the activity in the studio is very exciting, the discovery that so much of television is illusion may be disappointing. For example, you may find

The camera operator coordinates the video and audio components of a production.

that the backdrop for a TV talk show, which looks so glamorous on the air, is really very ordinary. Or a set that is supposed to be the large and luxurious living room of your favorite soap opera character may turn out to be a closet-sized piece of cardboard. Even the most basic television lighting and camera work can create many illusions, not to mention those reated by the more sophisticated special-effects equipment.

A studio is divided into two areas: the main studio, where the camera work is done, and the control room, where the master console is located. The technicians who work this console are able to control the picture that viewers see at home. The individuals who monitor the video console can produce a composite picture by mixing images from two or more different cameras; they can dissolve from one shot to another; and, when the equipment is sophisticated enough, they can even create split-screen or superimposed images. For example, during a television debate the console may create a split-screen effect so that both opponents can be seen at the same time.

A study of the television studio is not complete without a look at the people who work in it. The producer organizes a show, coordinates schedules, and supervises the overall production. Among his or her other responsibilities are the overseeing of financial matters, promotion, and the technical aspects of the production. It is the producer's job to see that a production runs smoothly.

While the producer is concerned with the production as a whole, the director is in charge of the creative aspects of the production. A good theater director is not necessarily a good television director, or vice versa. A good television director must make the most of the creative elements of television—for instance, the director must realize the sensitivity of the camera in picking up nuances and be sure that the camera captures the intended effect.

The producer and the director are powerless without the aid of other people whose jobs are also behind the scenes. The floor manager is an intermediary between the director and the actors. It is he or she who cues the actors, tells them where to stand, where to sit, where to cross the floor and so on.

Camera operators are a necessity, as is the technical director. The latter is in charge of the control console, at which he or she coordinates the video and audio mechanisms.

The next time you watch your favorite television show, think about all the people and equipment that make it possible. Even the simplest news show requires sophisticated equipment and highly trained personnel.

Performing on Radio and Television

One of the most basic parts of the broadcasting industry is the "talent," the term used to describe the men and women who perform on radio and television. Usually thought of as having the glamorous jobs in the industry, the "talent" includes newscasters, sports announcers, actresses, actors, disc jockeys, and game show hosts, to name just a few.

Talent may also include amateurs who are invited to participate in local programs. In fact, you may one day be invited to discuss a school project or community event at a local broadcasting station. When you accept such an invitation, you should prepare for a communication environment that is different from any you have every experienced. Understanding the conditions placed on professional performers will help you to be a better communicator.

Regardless of their particular roles, performers must adapt to the medium in which they are working. For example, when working on radio or television, a performer must get used to working without feedback, since

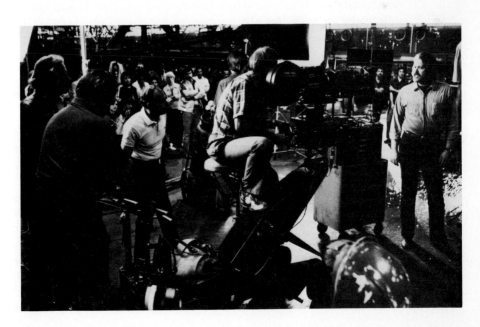

most often there is no audience present. Therefore, an individual must develop a sixth sense to determine the effect his or her material or delivery is having on the audience at home.

Other adjustments that a radio or television performer must make concern the limitations imposed by the audio and video equipment. On the air a radio performer must speak into the microphone; the TV performer must not only be near enough to the microphone but must also be in camera view. Therefore, natural movements and expressions must sometimes be consciously curtailed.

In addition, both radio and television performers must contend with numerous technical cues as well as technical distractions. The smoothness of a performance is determined by how well a performer maintains his or her concentration. Of course, working on a tape that will be aired at a later time allows for retakes and editing, two luxuries that are not part of a live broadcast.

While there are certain similarities between performing on radio and television, there are also considerable differences. The radio performer's most important tool is her or her voice. Think about different radio personalities you have heard. What is it that you like or dislike about their voice quality or style? Many of the characteristics that we discussed in our chapter on delivery play an important part in radio performance. Rate, emphasis, vocal expression, pronunciation, and articulation are all areas that need much practice if you are interested in pursuing a career in broadcasting.

Performing on television adds many new dimensions to the list of "things to do" before going on the air. While a radio performer can hide behind a microphone, the television performer is under close scrutiny. Clothing, personal appearance, and body movements are extremely important. You may have noticed that when a station is breaking in a new sportscaster or newsperson, it takes a while before the person feels and looks comfortable before the camera. An unseasoned performer might very well feel self-conscious and uneasy when first appearing on television. Again, performers must learn to use the medium and make it work for them.

THE FUTURE OF MASS COMMUNICATION

Unlike other forms of communication, the development of mass communication has depended on advances in technology. The first major contribution to this development was the invention of the printing press, which led to the print media. For hundreds of years print was the only form of mass communication. Radio, television, and film did not become realities until the twentieth century. Because the electronic media have such a powerful impact on our daily lives, it is almost impossible to imagine what our lives would be like without them.

Yet many advances in mass communication have occurred in just the last few decades. Words such as *DAT* (digital audio tape/technology), *CD* (compact disk), and *satellite* are now part of almost everyone's vocabulary, although they were developed only recently. The development of mass communication has certainly not stopped; we can expect that as our technology becomes even more sophisticated, there will continue to be additions to the realm of mass communication.

The Concept of Demassification

One way to view recent advances such as the introduction of satellite communication is through the concept of *demassification.* This term, coined by futurist Alvin Toffler, is closely tied to the notion that the wave of the future will be the use of channels of communication targeted at highly specialized interest groups rather than at the overall masses.

Indeed, we need only look around us to see that the age of demassification is already upon us. The present nature of the print media is only one example of the many changes that have been made in the process of transmitting information. No longer are the nation's major newspapers thriving as they did in earlier years. In the fast-paced world of high technology, particularly in the mass media, the oldest form of mass communication is losing readership every day to a virtual avalanche of highly specialized mini-circulation weeklies, bi-weeklies, and "shoppers" that serve specific communities and towns. Likewise, the deaths of major national magazines such as *Look, Life,* and the *Saturday Evening Post* (and their replacement by virtually thousands of mini-magazines targeted at small, special-interest markets!) seem to show that, indeed, demassified media are flexing their muscles. Pilots, housewives, camera nuts, teenagers, tennis players, and women in general may purchase any number of periodicals targeted specifically at their interests. Likewise, the growing popularity of regional magazines such as New England's *Yankee,* Dallas's *D,* or *Western Farmer* seem to reflect the growing interests of an increasingly demassified audience.[17]

The print medium, however, is not the only medium that is courting the demassified audience. Television and radio are becoming more highly specialized. The late 1970s and early 1980s witnessed the emergence in radio of all-news radio stations aimed at the educated middle class; hard rock, soft rock, religious rock, and punk rock stations, each aimed at a different sector of the youth audience; classical music stations targeting upper-income adults; and foreign language stations targeting the many ethnic groups which are part of our society.

The nature of television viewing has also changed in this direction during the 1970s and the 1980s. Think for a moment of the variety of options that we have: sports networks; all-news networks; cable systems; news, weather and sports information services; and the emergence of systems such as Columbus, Ohio's QUBE—a two-way cable system that allows viewing audiences to send as well as receive information.[18]

Last, and perhaps one of the greatest contributors to the age of demassified media, is the current information explosion and technological advances

[17] A. Toffler, *The New Wave* (New York: Bantam Books, 1981), 158–60.
[18] Ibid., 163.

Computers make today's possibilities tomorrow's realities.

in the computer world. Not only do computers facilitate the flow of information in the fast-paced interactions of corporations, but the computer has also made possible feats such as teleconferencing, the transmission of information through TELEX, "computer conferencing," and FAX. Computer conferencing allows two or more people to communicate through computer terminals in their offices or homes. An example of such a use of conferencing is the existence of the Electronic Information Exchange Service, which allows scientists, planners, and educators in several countries to conduct discussions about energy, economics, politics, or space satellites with one another through the use of teleprinters and video screens; they can use the system across varying time zones and at whatever time of the day or night they choose to work.[19]

As you can see, the shape of mass communication is rapidly changing. The possibilities are limitless, as the science fiction of today becomes the reality of tomorrow.

---

[19] Ibid., 252–53.

SUMMARY

Mass communication can be defined as the spreading of a message to an extended, mixed audience, using rapid means of reproduction and distribution, at a low unit cost to the consumer.

The most outstanding characteristic of mass communication is its dependence on an intermediary channel to transmit a message from the initial source to a diverse audience. In addition, the sender-receiver relationship of the mass communication process suggests an element of delayed and limited feedback.

The scope of mass communication is enormous, overcoming the barriers of time and space. Because of this, regulation and direction are necessary. This control, known as gatekeeping, comes from the different media, the government, and various economic interests.

Mass communication media have continued influences on their audiences. Four forms of electronic media are film, recording, radio, and television. Each has been developed to meet the changing needs of our society.

Mass communication serves a number of functions. It can be used to inform, to persuade, and to entertain. The informative function of mass communication is primarily concerned with the news media. Newspapers and radio are still important forms of news media, and under some circumstances they are even more effective than TV in fulfilling this function.

The entertainment function of mass communication is quite diversified. Comics in newspapers or a quiz show on TV both entertain an audience. TV and film are primarily entertainment media.

The persuasive influence of the media is recognized in advertising for political candidates, service organizations, charities, and manufacturers. The relative persuasiveness of one medium over another depends upon the nature of the message as well as the individual medium.

While there has been considerable research on the effects of the mass media, many of the findings are inconclusive. Educators, psychologists, and sociologists are among those interested in the effects of mass media. Some of the areas they have explored include the effects of the media in terms of violence, politics, and government.

We also looked at the operations that go on behind the scenes at a broadcasting station, including station organization and management. We then commented on performing on radio and television. We can only guess where the advances of the future will lead us, as our discussion of demassification made clear: Where we go from here is limited only by the boundaries of imagination.

EXERCISES

GROUP EXPERIENCES

Delayed Feedback

DESCRIPTION: Mass communication, by definition, suggests a widespread audience separated from a source by a considerable distance. As a result, a receiver's feedback or response to a message is usually limited and delayed. There are varying degrees of delayed feedback, ranging anywhere from a few minutes to several weeks or months. For example, a television commercial urging a customer to purchase a particular brand of detergent may have a delayed response of several weeks until the consumer runs out of his or her current brand of detergent. This activity will give you the opportunity to identify various degrees of delayed feedback.

PROCEDURE: Television and radio both operate on the premise that a receiver's feedback or response to a message is both limited and delayed. For this activity you are to identify two examples from radio or television of (1) immediate, (2) delayed, and (3) long-term feedback. For the purpose of this activity, we will define immediate feedback as a response that occurs with a 30-minute period; delayed feedback includes responses up to two weeks; long-term feedback involves responses that require more than two weeks.

DISCUSSION: What are the effects of the varying degrees of delayed feedback on the receiver? Have you ever considered writing to a television show for a specific purpose and later decided that it would take too long to get an answer? Do you think that the nature of television and radio feedback reduces the number of written responses from viewers? How do television and radio stations attempt to accurately assess the feedback of receivers? Are you aware of the various degrees of delayed feedback with which you respond to mass media?

Industry Gatekeeping

DESCRIPTION: Every major newspaper and television station receives numerous stories fed to them buy the wire services. However, neither time nor space allows for the printing or broadcasting of each and every news event. Media personnel at various levels determine which items they consider the most newsworthy. This activity will give you the opportunity to select the stories you and a team of experts consider to be the most newsworthy.

PROCEDURE: Divide into groups of four. You and your three group members will be industry gatekeepers. As a team, it is your responsibility to report the best news in the limited amount of air time available.

Each class member is responsible for bringing six news stories to class; two national stories, two state stories, and two local stories. From the pool of news items, each group should be given eight national, eight state, and eight local stories selected at random.

Each group is given 30 minutes to prepare a five-minute television newscast. During this preparation period group members should select the stories they feel are newsworthy. All group members should be involved in the broadcast. All newscasts should be evaluated by class members on a scale of poor, fair, average, good, or very good.

DISCUSSION: What variables contributed to a successful or unsuccessful newscast? What criteria did your group develop for the selection of news items? Do you consider the task of gatekeeping a difficult one? After listening to other newscasts, what criteria would you develop now for selecting items that are newsworthy?

The Big Debate

DESCRIPTION: One of the most compelling questions with regard to television is the effect of television on children and adolescents. Although there has been considerable research on the effects of television, findings are inconsistent. Some of the criticisms of television are that it stifles creativity, promotes violence, and has a negative effect on social morality. This activity will give you a chance to view both sides of the controversy.

PROCEDURE: All class members should research the effects of television on children and adolescents. Half the class should be instructed to find evidence to support the continuation of television programs, while the remaining half should find evidence of the negative effects of television. After the research has been collected, four class members should be selected to participate in a debate. One team (two members) will represent the position that television produces negative effects on children and adolescents (the negative position). The second team, also consisting of two members, will represent a major network (the affirmative position). The following format should be used for the debate:

Affirmative Speaker 1:	5 minutes
Negative Speaker 1:	5 minutes
Affirmative Speaker 2:	5 minutes
Negative Speaker 2:	5 minutes
Negative Speaker 1:	2 minutes
Affirmative Speaker 1:	2 minutes
Negative Speaker 2:	2 minutes
Affirmative Speaker 2:	2 minutes

Following the debate, the class members should reevaluate their positions on the topic.

DISCUSSION: What is your opinion on the effects of television on children and adolescents? Can you support your position with research findings? Can you identify any of the effects television has had on you? Can the effects of television be controlled or directed? How?

PERSONAL EXPERIENCES

1. For a period of one week, watch a late-night movie every night. Try to watch a combination of romantic, humorous, violent, and horror shows. Then keep a TV dream diary in which you record in detail all the dreams that you have. It would be best to record your dreams first thing in the morning, before you do anything else. What relationship, if any, do your dreams have to the television shows that you viewed?
2. How are you influenced during presidential campaigns? List the various ways in which you receive information about the candidates. How many

of those sources involve some form of mass communication, such as televised debates, radio, or newspapers? How has mass media changed national elections?

3. How does television reinforce or alter sex stereotypes? Select six different television serials and identify whether or not they reinforce sex stereotypes. Identify the methods by which programs characterize males and females according to sex stereotypes. Are there programs that attempt to change or even revise sex stereotypes?

DISCUSSION QUESTIONS

1. How do mass media differ from other communication systems (intrapersonal, interpersonal, and group communication)?
2. What are the positive and negative effects of television on its viewers?
3. What do you envision for the future of mass media? Describe the advances in technology that you feel will take place in the next 30 years. For instance, do you anticipate three-dimensional television in every home?
4. How does mass communication overcome the barriers of time and space?
5. Identify the television shows that are used primarily to (a) inform, (b) persuade, and (c) entertain. Are the most successful shows a combination of all three purposes?

A

Preparing for a Job Search

Anyone who has looked for a job knows that the interview is the most important step in the job-hunting process. If you do not perform well in a job interview, chances are you won't get the position, no matter how well qualified you are. Likewise, if you as the job interviewer do not know the correct skills, you may discourage qualified applicants or simply choose the wrong person for the job. Yet few executives and supervisors make an effort to learn specialized interviewing skills; they underestimate the importance of these interactions. Instead, they handle interviews with little advance planning, relying only on experience and improvisation. An understanding of the interviewer responsibilities should give you insights into how to prepare for your first interview.

Responsibilities of the Interviewer

Even though you may never be a personnel recruiter, there will be times when you will be responsible for conducting interviews. There are formal rules for interview situations. James Black, for example, offers a checklist of principles on sound interviewing practices.[1] Black first suggests that as an interviewer, you prepare yourself for the task of gathering a lot of information in a limited period of time. Because the interview is so short, you must

---

[1] J. Black, *How to Get Results from Interviewing* (New York: McGraw-Hill, 1970), 1.

decide in advance how much time you wish to devote to each area of discussion. Preparation also includes studying the data already received about the interviewee so that no time is wasted in asking unnecessary questions.

Second, you must define your objectives and follow an organized plan to achieve them. A directionless interview is inefficient and will probably annoy the interviewee, giving him or her a poor impression of the company. Thus, the reason for the interview and the information to be obtained from it must be clear in the minds of both you and the person being interviewed.

Third, the environment of the interview must be considered. Positive communication often depends on comfortable surroundings. The room should be well lit and quiet. To ensure good eye contact and attentiveness, the two participants should always sit facing each other. The accommodations should be relaxed, pleasant and above all, private. Taking telephone calls in the middle of an interview is rude and wastes valuable time.

Fourth, as the interview opens, it is up to you as the interviewer to break the ice—to make the other person feel at ease. Perhaps a question about an outside interest or about the person's family can serve this function. When interviewing, you should use words and phrases that the interviewee can understand. Trying to impress someone with your high-powered vocabulary will only block communication. Since you would like a productive interview, you must be able to develop a friendly relationship quickly, and, even more important, you must create a feeling of trust and confidence. The only way to do this is to be genuinely open and receptive rather than distant, authoritative, or condescending. These positive attitudes show the interviewee that you are sincerely interested in what he or she has to say.

Fifth, as the interviewer, you should decide the nature of the questions that will give you the necessary information. These questions should evoke more than a simple "yes" or "no," which would force you to do all of the talking. Also, the conversation must be free and open, and not become a cat-and-mouse game in which you try to trap the person with trick questions. In this situation you will lose the trust of the person you are interviewing, who will then reveal as little information as possible.

Sixth, you must listen attentively and intelligently. If your eyes wander or if you are constantly glancing at papers on the desk when you interview, the people you interview will feel uneasy. They will either speed up their answers or break off before they finish all that they have to say. On the other hand, if you show interest and attention, they will speak openly and freely and may even give more information than expected. Empathy is also important when listening. You should try to put yourself in the place of the person being interviewed and understand the real meaning behind the spoken words.

Seventh, interviewees should not be rushed into careless answers at the end because you must hurry them out. The interview should end gracefully and naturally. The interviewee will know it is coming to an end by the type of questions being asked and by the way you use your voice.

Eighth, at the end of the interview, interviewees must be told what to expect in the future: when they will find out whether they got the job, or what action will be taken to handle the matters that were discussed.

Finally, when the interviewee leaves, the interviewer's work must be completed. While the interview is fresh in your mind, you should make notes and evaluate the information you received. This evaluation should be as objective as possible. As the interviewer, you must put aside your own prejudices and must not distort the facts. Therefore, you must possess sound judgment, emotional stability, and the ability to make objective decisions.

Responsibilities of the Interviewee

Now that you are familiar with some of the tasks facing the interviewer, it's time to look at your responsiblities as an interviewee. You may think that all you'll need to do is to answer a few questions, but these questions will probably be the most difficult you've ever encountered, especially if you haven't prepared for the interview in advance. Job hunting is hard work, and sometimes even your preparation might seem difficult. The next few sections provide guidelines and principles to follow while preparing for your first interview.

SELF EVALUATION.   Do you know who you are? We all think we know ourselves pretty well, but during the next few minutes you may begin discovering parts of yourself that you never knew existed. The first step in preparing for your job search is to conduct a personal inventory. Most interviewees think they know the type of job they're looking for, where they'd like to work, the type of people they would enjoy working with, and so on, but campus recruiters find that students often fail to evaluate their personal and professional goals. Figures A–1 and A–2 give guidelines for you to follow when conducting personal and job inventories.

FIGURE A–1   Analyzing Your Personality Strengths

Listed are fifty characteristics that many employers consider positive and important. They are qualities that anyone *could* have, but not everyone *does* have. Rate yourself from "1" to "5" on each factor. Note that this list is not comprehensive; include other traits under number 51.*

	(Poor)		(Average)		(Excellent)
	1	2	3	4	5
1. Honest	( )	( )	( )	( )	( )
2. Dependable	( )	( )	( )	( )	( )
3. Motivated	( )	( )	( )	( )	( )
4. Assertive	( )	( )	( )	( )	( )
5. Outgoing	( )	( )	( )	( )	( )
6. Persistent	( )	( )	( )	( )	( )
7. Conscientious	( )	( )	( )	( )	( )
8. Ambitious	( )	( )	( )	( )	( )
9. Punctual	( )	( )	( )	( )	( )
10. Creative	( )	( )	( )	( )	( )

* Beside any characteristic that you have rated as 4 or 5, describe an instance from your experience when you exhibited this quality. For example, "I showed dependability last summer when I . . . ."

FIGURE A–1 *(Continued)*

	(Poor)		(Average)		(Excellent)
	1	2	3	4	5
11. Intelligent	( )	( )	( )	( )	( )
12. Mature	( )	( )	( )	( )	( )
13. Emotionally stable	( )	( )	( )	( )	( )
14. Enthusiastic	( )	( )	( )	( )	( )
15. Flexible	( )	( )	( )	( )	( )
16. Realistic	( )	( )	( )	( )	( )
17. Responsible	( )	( )	( )	( )	( )
18. Serious	( )	( )	( )	( )	( )
19. Pleasant	( )	( )	( )	( )	( )
20. Sincere	( )	( )	( )	( )	( )
21. Analytical	( )	( )	( )	( )	( )
22. Organized	( )	( )	( )	( )	( )
23. Appearance	( )	( )	( )	( )	( )
24. Able to get along with co-workers	( )	( )	( )	( )	( )
25. Able to get along with supervisors	( )	( )	( )	( )	( )
26. Oral communication skills	( )	( )	( )	( )	( )
27. Written communication skills	( )	( )	( )	( )	( )
28. References	( )	( )	( )	( )	( )
29. School attendance	( )	( )	( )	( )	( )
30. Job attendance	( )	( )	( )	( )	( )
31. Willing to work long hours	( )	( )	( )	( )	( )
32. Willing to work evenings and weekends	( )	( )	( )	( )	( )
33. Willing to relocate	( )	( )	( )	( )	( )
34. Willing to travel	( )	( )	( )	( )	( )
35. Willing to commute a long distance	( )	( )	( )	( )	( )
36. Willing to start at the bottom and advance according to own merit	( )	( )	( )	( )	( )
37. Able to accept criticism	( )	( )	( )	( )	( )
38. Able to motivate others	( )	( )	( )	( )	( )
39. Able to follow through on something until it is done	( )	( )	( )	( )	( )
40. Able to make good use of time	( )	( )	( )	( )	( )
41. Goal- (or achievement-) oriented	( )	( )	( )	( )	( )
42. Show initiative	( )	( )	( )	( )	( )
43. Healthy	( )	( )	( )	( )	( )
44. Able to follow directions	( )	( )	( )	( )	( )
45. Detail-oriented	( )	( )	( )	( )	( )
46. Able to learn quickly	( )	( )	( )	( )	( )
47. Desire to work hard	( )	( )	( )	( )	( )
48. Moral standards	( )	( )	( )	( )	( )
49. Poised	( )	( )	( )	( )	( )
50. Growth potential	( )	( )	( )	( )	( )
51. Others	( )	( )	( )	( )	( )

Before you find a satisfactory position, you will need to evaluate your qualifications, preferences, knowledge, training and experience. Don't just look at your strengths; also look at areas where you need improvement. A favorite question that recruiters ask applicants is, "Now that we have talked about some of your strong points, tell me some areas you feel weak

FIGURE A–2 Analyzing Factors of Importance to You in Jobs and Companies

Listed are factors that many people value in jobs and organizations. Rank the factors from "1" to "3" in terms of their importance to you. Put an asterisk beside the five most important factors.

1—Not Important	2—Average Importance	3—Very Important

	1	2	3
1. Challenge	( )	( )	( )
2. Responsibility	( )	( )	( )
3. Stability of company	( )	( )	( )
4. Security of job within company	( )	( )	( )
5. Size of company	( )	( )	( )
6. Training program	( )	( )	( )
7. Initial job duties	( )	( )	( )
8. Advancement opportunities	( )	( )	( )
9. Amount of contact with co-workers	( )	( )	( )
10. Amount of contact with the public	( )	( )	( )
11. Starting salary	( )	( )	( )
12. Financial rewards "down the road"	( )	( )	( )
13. Degree of independence	( )	( )	( )
14. Opportunity to show initiative	( )	( )	( )
15. Degree of employee involvement in decision making	( )	( )	( )
16. Opportunity to be creative	( )	( )	( )
17. Type of industry	( )	( )	( )
18. Company's reputation in the industry	( )	( )	( )
19. Prestige of job within the company	( )	( )	( )
20. Degree of results seen from job	( )	( )	( )
21. Variety of duties	( )	( )	( )
22. What the boss is like	( )	( )	( )
23. What the co-workers are like	( )	( )	( )

From *Interviewing . . . A Job in Itself*. Copyright Lois Einhorn and The Career Center, Bloomington, Ind., 1977, 3–6.

in, and tell me what you are doing to overcome these weaknesses." That's a tough question, and unless you've prepared before the interview, you may have difficulty answering it effectively.

John, an English major, wants to work in a consulting firm developing written communication training programs for business and industry. After John makes a list of his skills and training, he realizes that he's never taken business courses. John can overcome this potential job-hunting weakness by taking appropriate business courses and/or by getting a part-time job in business.

The evaluation form in Figure A–3 is excerpted from *Jobs '77* By William N. Yeomans. It is designed to help you evaluate your job marketability. By now you should have thought about who you are, what you have done, and what talents, skills, and interests you possess. With all this firmly in mind, complete this questionnaire. The scoring has not been scientifically tested, but it does view applicants in the same way organizations evaluate potential employees.

FIGURE A–3 Job Marketability Evaluation Form

Scholastic Standing	Score
Phi Beta Kappa; top 10% of class	6
Top 25% of class	4
Top 50% of class	2
Lower 50% of class	0

Academic Rating of Your College	
Very high; Ivy League caliber	6
Good, well-respected academically	4
Not known for academic excellence	1
Barely accredited or not accredited	0

Work Experience	
Full-time work in your major field	6
Summer or part-time work in your major	4
Work in unrelated field	2
No work experience	0

College Expenses Earned Yourself	
75–100%	6
50–75%	4
25–50%	1
Under 25%	0

Campus Activities	
Major elected offices; many activities	4
Minor elected offices; some activities	2
No elected offices but some activities	1
No elected offices and no activities	0

Appearance	
All-American handsome or beautiful	4
Good-looking	3
Nice, but forgettable	1
Weird-looking	0

Personality	
Popularity plus. Well-liked; meet people easily	4
Pretty well-liked; meet people easily most of the time	3
Some friends; not too great at meeting people	1
Zero personality	0

FIGURE A–3   (*Continued*)

Height (If Weight is Proportionate)	Score
5'10" to 6'4" for men	3
5' to 6' for women	3
4'1" or under; 6' or over, or overweight, for women	0
Under 5'10", over 6'4", or overweight, for men	0

Bearing (Voice, Posture, Eye Contact)	
Commanding, immediately impressive	3
Mostly impressive	2
Not too impressive	0
A laugh	0

Total Score _____

Results

35–42   Outstanding! You should be able to pick and choose a suitable position. However, people rarely score this high, so evaluate yourself again to be sure.

20–34   Excellent prospect. You should have several job possibilities without much trouble.

8–19   Average candidate. Job opportunities will depend on the economy and labor market. Need to try to develop some different areas to increase your chances.

0–7   Not so good. You will probably have difficulty in getting a desirable job. Need to think of ways to improve your score, or you may have evaluated yourself too severely.

You may already know the type of positions for which you'd like to apply, but you may now know what's available to someone with your major, background, and skills. You may have chosen a major because the prospects for earnings looked good, the courses were easy, your parents suggested it, or it was something you'd always wanted to do. After getting your degree, and maybe after getting a job, you realize that you won't be challenged or happy working in this area for an extended period of time. Some people, for example, major in elementary education, get a job, and realize that children drive them crazy. Others get preprofessional degrees and then are not accepted into medical school, law school, or graduate school. What then? An inventory of your job preferences can help you look for positions to meet your needs. For additional help go to your campus career planning office or to professional personnel agencies, study self-help manuals, or take a course on career planning. Laird Durham's book *100 Careers: How to Pick the One that's Best for You* is very useful. It is hoped that the exercises and examples in this section have given you greater insight into what your strengths, weaknesses, training, preferences and other qualifications are so that you'll know what you have to offer during a job search.

WRITTEN PREPARATION.   You have now evaluated your assets and liabilities and know what you can expect from an organization. With your job objectives clearly in mind, you need to find a way to get an interview. The most widely used method of introducing yourself to an organization is through a letter of introduction and a *résumé*. Although cover letters and résumés are the most commonly used method of getting an interview, many have the opposite or no effect. Abbott P. Smith, a professional recruiting and placement specialist gives 12 basic guidelines to help you ensure that your next résumé is not your obituary.[2]

1. Do some soul searching before you begin (conduct a personal and job inventory).
2. Write your objective (what do you want to do?).
3. Sell yourself (tell what you have done and what you can do).
4. Be brief and nonrepetitive (aim for a one-page résumé).
5. Write it yourself (steer away from professional résumé-writing services).
6. List the jobs you have held (include job titles and dates).
7. Forget the references (applicants list references that will give positive comments).
8. List personal information first (name, address, phone number, etc.).
9. Don't elaborate on personal information (keep it brief).
10. Make it neat (this may be the time to invest in a professional typist).
11. Write a neat, short, personal cover letter (give reason for writing and what you know about the organization).
12. Put yourself into your résumé (find a way to stand out from the other candidates).

Résumé formats and what is included in résumés differ considerably. (Table A–1 lists résumé terms in order of importance.)[3] Figure A–4 provides an example of a résumé. You may be able to apply for several types of positions. If you do, you may need to write different résumés directing the content of each to a particular position. Applicants looking for a position in education usually use an academic vita, which has a different format. Some valuable source books to help with your preparation include *What Color Is Your Parachute?* by Richard Bolles; and *How to Find a Job*, by Darold Larson. Just as the résumé is important, so too is your cover letter.

---

[2] A. P. Smith, "How to Make Sure Your Next Resume Isn't an Obituary," *Training* (May 1977), 63–66.
[3] H. S. Field and W. H. Holley, "Résumé Preparation: An Empirical Study of Personnel Managers' Perceptions," *The Vocational Guidance Quarterly* (March 1976), 234.

TABLE A–1   205 Personnel Managers' Ratings of Importance of Items in Résumé

Rank	Important Items	Rank	Unimportant Items
1	Current address	26	Class standing
2	Past work experience	27	Sources for financing college studies
3	Major in college	28	References
4	Job objectives and goals	29	Percent of money earned for college
5	Date of availability for employment	30	Computer programming skills
6	Career objectives	31	Birthday and birthplace
7	Permanent address	32	Membership in honorary societies
8	Tenure on previous job	33	Membership in college social organizations
9	Colleges and universities attended		
10	Specific physical limitations	34	Offices held in social organizations
11	Job location requirements	35	Student body offices held
12	Overall health status	36	Hobbies
13	Salary requirements	37	Foreign language skills
14	Travel limitations	38	Marital status
15	Minor in college	39	Complete college transcript
16	Grades in college major	40	Height and weight
17	Military experience	41	Number of children
18	Years in which degrees were awarded	42	Typing skills
19	Overall grade point average	43	Spouse's occupation
20	Membership in professional organizations	44	Spouse's educational level
21	Awards and scholarships received	45	Sex
22	Grades in college minor	46	Photograph
23	Offices held in professional organizations	47	Complete high school transcript
		48	Personal data on parents
24	Statistical or mathematical skills	49	Race
25	Spouse's willingness to relocate	50	Religious preference

Field and Holley found that personnel managers consider five items important in a cover letter.[4]

1. The position the applicant is seeking
2. The applicant's job objective
3. The applicant's career objectives
4. The applicant's reason for seeking employment
5. The indication that the applicant knows something about the organization

Because you are trying to get an interview with the personnel director, it is also advisable to request an interview in the cover letter and to refer to your enclosed résumé.

FINDING JOB POSSIBILITIES.   The interview is the most important step in the hiring process. Some of you may have a job waiting for you, but most of you must find a way to get an employment interview. Four major

---

[4] Ibid, 229–37.

FIGURE A–4

CLARK PAGER

Permanent Address	*Temporary Address*
134 Maytime Drive	2417 Broadway Street
Jericho, New York	New Orleans, Louisiana 70125
Telephone: (516) 822-8239	Telephone: (504) 861-0041

Job Objective

Full-time summer position working with law firm concerned with athletic arbitration.

Education

1983 to present B.A., 1987, Tulane University, New Orleans, Louisiana 70118
Advisor: Dr. Guy Peters
Major: Public Policy
Minor: Business
G.P.A. 3.2 out of 4.0

1974–1983 Jericho High School, Jericho, New York 11753.
Major: College Preparatory

Work Experience

summer 1983 to present Banquet waiter at the New Orleans Hotel to cover living expenses.

summer 1982 Courier and office clerk for Blau and Kramer Corporate Law Firm. Responsible for personal delivery of documents to the Security and Exchange Commission in Washington, D.C. Also responsible for updating lawbooks.

summer 1981 Counselor and tennis instructor at Brant Lake Camp, Brant Lake, New York. Responsible for organizing, assisting, and instructing camp activities.

summer 1980 Courier and office clerk for Blau Kramer Corporate Law Firm.

Extracurricular Activities

Responsible for organizing and running intramural sports for the College of Arts and Sciences.

Sports reporter for WTUL-FM, student-run radio station. Assemble and report the latest news concerning local, state, national, and world sports on a weekly basis.

special interests: Sports, theatre arts, and travel.

References

Letters of recommendation and official transcripts will be furnished upon request.

methods of securing a job interview include (1) answering want ads, (2) taking advantage of college placement centers, (3) visiting employment agencies and (4) making cold calls.[5]

Want ads are the least popular form of organizational recruiting because they often expose employers to militants (EEOC), cost a lot of money and release competitive information to other companies. Some companies use blind newspaper ads with only box numbers to give themselves greater flexibility. Because of the anonymous nature of a blind ad, the employer is not forced to answer inquiries, leak information to competitors, or conform to governmental equal employment opportunity guidelines. Although blind ads have advantages, they get fewer responses than labeled ads.

When reading want ads, you must learn to understand advertising tactics. Recruiters advertise for the maximum qualifications they can get, with inflated requirements that are not absolute. Of course, some positions will require special expertise. A nurse shouldn't apply for a physician's position, and a brick mason shouldn't apply for an electrician's position. When answering an ad, you will either be offered the job, rejected, or offered a position not listed in the advertisement.

Newspaper ads usually ask you to send a résumé. If possible, you should avoid using the mail or telephone and try to answer the ad in person. We discussed immediacy earlier in this chapter and explained the importance of face-to-face communication when trying to get positive action. It's a lot easier for recruiters to throw a résumé in the trash if they've never met you personally.

The simplest way to get an interview is through your campus placement center. All you have to do is sign up; yet even with this easy procedure, many students fail to take advantage of placement center opportunities. Some think that their grade point average is too low, that only small companies recruit on college campuses, that companies look only for business majors, or that a lot of extracurricular activities are required. Students need to reevaluate the placement center interviewing option because it offers opportunities to students with a variety of backgrounds, experiences and education.

It may help to familiarize yourself with how the placement center works. Placement offices usually have orientation meetings at the beginning of each quarter or semester, giving essential procedural information. The placement center provides forms and starts personal files for interested students (including alumni). Files include standard data sheets, résumés, letters of recommendation and interviewing histories. Some centers also provide interview workshops, career counseling, career libraries and employer information. Centers use open sign-up systems (first come, first served), staff sign-up systems (counselors place students), or card systems (batches of high- and low-priority cards are given for company preferences). No matter which system is used on your campus, you should go through your placement center to get valuable interviewing experience.

---

[5] K. W. Stanat, with P. Reardon, *Job Hunting Secrets and Tactics* (Milwaukee, Wis.: Westwind Press, 1977).

You may now be wondering what happens after you've signed up for an interview. When your day arrives, company recruiters are given placement center data sheets and a list of interviewee names with time slots. Your interview begins before you meet the recruiter, as he or she examines your placement file. Next, the recruiter enters the lobby or waiting area and calls your name. Introductions are made, handshakes are exchanged, and then you are led into a small room or partitioned area. The interview area usually consists of two chairs, with one placed behind a desk for the interviewer. Most campus interviews last from 15 to 20 minutes. At the end of the interview, recruiters usually tell you when you should be hearing from the company. Finally, after you leave, the recruiter quickly jots down impressions before moving on to the next interviewee. This can be a grueling process for both the recruiter and you; but again, you should get as much interviewing experience as possible.

A third method of getting an interview is through an employment agency. Employment agencies vary in size, style, cost, and purpose. Some agencies may have only one or two people placing applicants, while others have divisions for sales, management, engineering, professional, or technical positions. Agencies may treat you very professionally, with preinterview testing and counseling, or they may send you to an interview without preparation. Employment agencies stay in business through the fees they collect from either or both the employer and the interviewee. You may pay 10 to 20 percent of your first year's salary, or the company may pay all fees. As often as possible it is best to interview with fee-paid organizations. Some professional search agencies charge 20 percent and higher but guarantee job satisfaction, testing and training, and résumé-writing services. The purposes of employment agencies also differ. Agencies fill temporary vacancies, place technical or specialty personnel, find executives, or say they can place anyone.

Advantages of using employment agencies include their efficiency, saving time by having others do the searching for you and confidentiality. One of the best methods of selecting an employment agency is to look at the classified section of your Sunday newspaper to see which agencies do the most advertising. Then scout several agencies and select two or three that seem most suited to your needs. Tell the agencies that you have registered with other agencies to let them know they have competition. As an interviewee, you must be prepared for critical analysis from agency counselors. They want to increase your job marketability and will sometimes get tough to help you perform more effectively during appointment interviews.

The final way to get an interview is by making cold calls. You can either send a résumé, or phone, or go in person. As mentioned earlier, it is best to go in person, yet this is probably the most difficult and ego-deflating situation of all. Having a job places you in a better bargaining position, but whether you have a job or not, you have to be persistent and make use of special cold-call tactics.

The best time to show up is about 10 A.M. or 3 P.M., because these are the least hectic times in organizations. When making plans, also try to go on Tuesday, Wednesday, or Thursday rather than Monday or Friday.

The beginning of the week is busy, and at the end of the week you'll find that the important people may be away. It is best to apply before November 15 and after January 1 because of holidays and fiscal years. If you want to make one friend before seeing a personnel director, it should be the company receptionist. Receptionists have the power to help or hurt your chances of getting an interview. However, even though you want to make friends with receptionists, don't give them your résumé. After you turn over your résumé, you lose bargaining power and may never get a chance to talk to the people who make hiring decisions. You'll learn tricks of the trade with experience. Just remember not to give up until you get the interviews you want.

RESEARCHING THE COMPANY.   It is essential that you find out about the company before the actual interview. Just as you feel good when someone you meet knows something about you, recruiters are also flattered when you know something about what is important to them—their company. Know everything possible. The knowledge will increase your confidence and ease during the interview. However, remember too that timing is important. Don't interject some obscure company fact at inappropriate times.

The best place to begin is at your placement office. It usually has company literature, annual reports, brochures, and fliers. If not, write or phone the organization and ask someone there to send you the information. Next, try to talk with people who work in the organization. They'll give you greater insights than any written material could provide. Finally, local libraries usually have information in business periodicals, newspapers, stock market reports, and so on. The questions you will want to answer depend on the type of organization you are investigating. In applying for a teaching position, you'd want to know the number of schools in the district; for a manufacturing firm, you'd be interested in plant locations and competition; and for a bank, you'd probably like to know if it was nationally or state chartered and how many branches it had. Remember, the answers to the questions are intended to help you. Now that you have examined the responsibilities of interviewers and interviewees, you should be ready to think about your first interview. Your confidence should be high because you have evaluated yourself; completed a formal résumé, found the job openings, researched the company and gotten an interview.

THE INTERVIEW

When you are being interviewed, your chief responsibility is to yourself. During an employment interview, you owe it to yourself to obtain as much information as you can, so that should you be offered the job, you can make an intelligent decision. Make sure you understand the requirements of the job (just what it is you will be expected to do). If you don't understand something, ask questions until you do. State your qualifications in a positive way, and don't be afraid to mention potential weaknesses in your background (but try to balance them with strengths). The most important thing to do during any kind of interview is to communicate—listen, speak, question, respond, and understand.

The employment interview incorporates everything we've discussed about communication, and more. After your first interview you will know additional areas that you'll need to prepare for the next time. One area that needs no further preparation is that of honesty. There is misconception that you should say anything to get the job. However, this doesn't pay off. One young man decided to alter his grade point average on his résumé. Instead of putting down his cumulative average, he listed the average in his major course work, which was considerably higher. He interviewed with his placement center and was offered a job in a major duplicating corporation. After he accepted the position and had started training, the company sent for his college transcripts. The personnel director noticed the discrepancy between the grade point averages and called him in to ask him about it. After he told the director what he had done, he was fired for dishonesty.

Lying may not get you fired, but it could cause even more serious problems. New interviewees often fall into the trap of trying to please the interviewer with all their answers. If they are asked if they'd mind traveling, some say no even if they do; or they may say they enjoy working with people, when in actuality they would rather work by themselves or with machines. You may get a job, but your dishonesty will only hurt you. Too many people are miserable in positions they should never have accepted or applied for. When you see that you would be dissatisfied in a position you're applying for, acknowledge it to the recruiter. There may be another position that you'd be better suited for, or the recruiter can keep you in mind if something does become available.

We have already mentioned a few questions that are used during employment interviews. The following list of frequently asked questions should help prepare you further for your first interview. Questions are designed to serve as indicators of your personal background; human relations skills; work background; accident, safety, and health histories; education and training; and personal objectives.

1. What do you see yourself doing in five, ten, fifteen years?
2. How have childhood experiences influenced you?
3. How would your closest friend describe you?
4. Why did you decide to go to your college or university?
5. If you could change anything about your education, what would it be?
6. Do you work well under pressure? (give some examples)
7. Would you rather be a leader or a follower?
8. What motivates you to give the most effort?
9. Are your grades a good indicator of your academic achievement? (explain)

10. Do you have plans for continued study? (explain)
11. How do you evaluate success?
12. Who is the person you admire most? (why?)
13. If you could have an ideal job, what would it be like?
14. Why should I hire you over other candidates?
15. Do you work better alone or with supervision? (explain)
16. Why are you interested in working for our company?
17. What have you learned from your mistakes?
18. What are you looking for in a job?
19. Are you a leader? (explain)
20. What qualities should an effective manager have?
21. How do you accept criticism? (explain)
22. Tell me about yourself.
23. What work experience helps qualify you for this position?
24. How do you spend your free time?
25. What qualities do you think I should be looking for in this position?

The ability to answer these and other questions should give you a good edge over unprepared candidates. Questions you will be asked are important, but you should also be giving some consideration to questions you should ask the interviewer. Toward the end of an employment interview, the interviewer usually asks if you have any questions. A few sample questions follow.

1. What type of training program do you have, and how long will it last?
2. What is the advancement potential in your organization?
3. Does your company help pay for employees to continue their education?
4. Will I have to relocate?
5. How are your employees evaluated?
6. What opportunities do you see for a person with my background?
7. What have been your most rewarding experiences with the company?
8. What is the employee turnover rate?
9. Does the company pay for moving expenses?
10. What weaknesses do you see that I should try to improve?

Job interviews do not consist solely of questions and answers. Several factors work together to make your interview a success or failure. The following list of do's and don'ts should serve as a useful reminder before your interview. Making sure that you do all the do's will not necessarily land you a job, but doing one don't could cause you not to be hired.

Some Do's and Don'ts in Successful Interviewing[6]

Do	Don't
Act natural	Criticize yourself
Be prompt, neat, courteous	Be Late
Prepare self and job analysis inventories	Present an extreme appearance
Ask relevant questions	Become impatient
Allow the employer to express himself/ herself	Become emotional
Make yourself understood	Oversell your case
Listen to the other person	Draw out the interview
Present informative credentials	Make elaborate promises
Think of your potential service to the employer	Come unprepared
Act positively	Try to be funny
	Linger over what the company will do for you (e.g., benefits, salary, promotion)
	Unduly emphasize starting salary

In this section we have covered the three Ps of interviewing: preparation, presentation, and postanalysis. The preparation phase involves four steps: (1) self-inventory; (2) occupation inquiry; (3) preparation of letter of introduction and résumé; (4) putting it all together. The interview presentation itself has four stages: introduction, background, matching, and closing. The postanalysis calls for follow-up and reevaluation of your performance. The important thing to remember about this process is that no two interview situations will be exactly the same. The most you can do is understand the overall process, prepare for that process, and go in with a positive and professional attitude, thinking, "I have something to offer you."

AFTER THE INTERVIEW

Before breathing a sigh of relief, remember that your job search is not over yet. It is not complete until you've secured the position that you've applied for. After each interview applicants can follow three simple steps to increase their chances of getting hired.

Immediately after leaving the interview, write down your recruiter's name, title, and address. Forgetting your interviewer's name could be detrimental to you later, when a secretary calls to set up a second interview and asks if you were interviewed by Mr. Barton, Ms. Kendall, or Mr. Barfield. The recruiter is now a personal contact with the organization, and all additional correspondence should be directed to him or her. You may be asked to send in letters of recommendation, transcripts, or job applications at later times, so be prepared.

After making sure that you remember your interviewer's name, find time to evaluate your interview participation by reconstructing the interview

---

[6] Reprinted from *Planning Your Future* by permission of the College Placement Council, the copyright holder. In R. A. Vogel and W. D. Brooks, *Business Communication* (Menlo Park, Calif.: Cummings, 1977), 42–43.

situation. Do you think the outcome will be positive or negative? What impressions did you make? Why? After self-analysis you may remember biting your fingernails, interrupting the recruiter, looking at your watch, answering the wrong question, or using profanity. There is a tendency for us to focus on our mistakes rather than to look at the total process. Try to force yourself to remember areas of outstanding performance as well as areas that need improvement, so that your next interview will be more successful.

One last way to leave a favorable impression with a recruiter is to write a letter of appreciation. These letters usually thank the recruiter for his or her time and for the opportunity to meet, and express interest in the organization. You want the recruiter to remember you; even if a company doesn't have a position at the present time, it will be more likely to think of you in the future if you keep in touch. By following these three post interview guidelines, you should increase your chances of success.

B

Children's Television Viewing, the Parent's Role

Elton H. Rule, President, American Broadcasting Companies, Inc.

Introduction

getting attention

I am here today in three capacities. The first is as a native Californian—this has been my home for most of my life, and I only regret that my job requires me to be away from the Golden State most of the time. I have been here, though, for most of the last month, enjoying the sun and the ocean, my friends and my family—including the newest addition, my four-year-old grandson.

establishing ethos

I mention him—his name is Patrick Elton Dunne—because being here in California and seeing him has reminded me again of what a wonderful place this is to raise children, and also because my second capacity today is that of a parent—a person who has children, and now a grandchild as well, and who thinks often of the many large and small influences that shape our children into adults.

My third capacity today is that of a broadcaster, which I have been most of my adult life—a person who has some responsibility for one of those influences, the television set in the living room. It is only in the last few years that most of us, parents and broadcasters alike, have realized just how sizable a role television plays in the lives of our children. The realization has been a sobering one. We have spent a great deal of effort trying to discover just what it is that our children get from their television watching—and when we haven't liked the answers, trying to improve the situation. We have asked what the proper role of television ought to be in the growth of our children and where the responsibility for it lies. In the next few minutes, I would like to offer a few of my own conclusions on this subject.

Body

Let me begin by admitting one of my own personal prejudices. We have all heard a great deal about what's wrong with the younger generation: that they are alienated, apathetic, illiterate, promiscuous—and so forth. No doubt there are a good many children who do have those and other problems. But my own feeling is that, by and large, today's youngsters are turning out very well. At six and at 16, they are often surprisingly mature and interesting people—people who know more about their world, and themselves, than I would have expected.

If there's any truth to this impression, I also believe that the presence of television may have been one positive contributor. Television is, after all, a window on the world wider than any previous generation has ever known—one that offers an incredible exposure to people, places, and events that were once only topics in textbooks. And television is an effective communicator—from one recent study in Michigan State Unviersity, we know that there is a distinct correlation between how much television young children watch, and how much they know about current events and discuss these events with their parents. More than that, television can aid personal, emotional development; in entertainment as well as informational programs, children can gain insights into how other people live, how they relate to each other and especially how they deal with problems common to us all.

That's not to say television cannot cause problems for children. It can. This has been brought home to us very forcefully by parents of all descriptions since television began to assume a greater role in their home lives. Beginning about five years ago, our industry—and ABC in particular—embarked on an intense and still-continuing search for ways to improve its programs as they relate to younger viewers.

This effort has involved not only those in the industry, but a broad spectrum of educators and child psychiatrists, not to mention a great many parents and children. It has brought to the screen programs altogether new to the medium—from Saturday morning news programs for children to original weekday afternoon dramatic specials both for and about children. It has brought a new policy, called "family viewing," to evening television; it provides for early-evening programs which are suitable for viewing by the entire family. And it has completely changed the face of the weekend programs made specifically for children.

One major area of concern has been the portrayal of violence (or the threat of violence) in these programs. Early on, we at ABC pledged ourselves to eliminate gratuitous acts of violence from our programs, and as a result of similar actions throughout the industry, the overall amount of violence has been declining on television. To eliminate all acts of violence would be to deny reality, however, so we needed also to learn to ensure that what violence remained had constructive value. We knew relatively little about how to do this at the beginning, so we spent $1 million on two five-year research projects by three distinguished experts in the area.

That phase of their work is not completed, and from their findings we have been able to develop some workable guidelines for the producers of our programs and for our own editors. Let me cite some examples: The presentation of violence should exclude details which could be imitated by a viewer; it should be used clearly as a dramatic example of what should not be done; and the negative consequences of such violence should be demonstrated. There is much more to be done in this area, and our research is continuing, but I think we are definitely moving in the right direction.

In addition to the question of violence, we were concerned about the ideas young viewers were getting from the programs they watched. Recently, one of our consultants, Dr. William Hooks of the Bank Street College of Education, made a list of some of the qualities we would like to shine through our programs. It is keyed to the word "respect," and I would like to repeat it here:

respect for the individual;
respect for differences;
respect for religious beliefs and ethnic qualities;
respect for all animal life and for the environment;
respect for private and public property;
respect for moral values;
respect for the feelings and sensitivities of others;
and, not least, respect for oneself.

We hope all the programs our young viewers see can live up to this principle of respect. We take very seriously our responsibility for our younger viewers.

But let me emphasize that ours is only a part of the overall responsibility for the effect that television has on our children. We in the television industry can control our programs and what happens to them right up to the point where they enter the home. But in the living room or the family room, control can be exercised only by parents. The most constructive use of television for children can come about only through the sharing of responsibility by broadcaster and parent.

Recently, the Roper Organization asked a national sample of parents with children under the age of 16 what sorts of rules they had for their children. As you'd expect, a sizable majority had strict rules about what their children ate, what time they went to bed on weeknights, when they did their homework (if they had homework), and knowing where they went when they left the house.

statistics)

assertion)

But the Roper people also asked parents what sorts of rules they had about television viewing. And they found that only about two-fifths had rules about what programs their children were allowed to watch. Less than a third of those with children under the age of 12 have rules about letting children watch television after 9 P.M. in the evening. And those who do have such rules based them on the lateness of the hour, not on the kinds of programs which are on at that hour. We know, too, from other research, that most parents are not present when their children do the greatest part of their viewing.

What this appears to mean is that parents who take active charge of most of the elements of their children's upbringing allow a kind of anarchy to prevail where television viewing is concerned. To me, this is a cause for real concern. Children are unique creatures, with their own personal areas of knowledge and ignorance, their own needs and fears and insecurities. No television program, no matter how sensitively it is designed, can be guaranteed to affect all children in the same way.

support & clarification testimony anecdote

A given television program may inform a child—or it may confuse him. It may delight a child—or it may disturb him. The difference is the degree of his parent's involvement. Eda LeShan, a noted expert in the field of child psychology, tells the story of a mother whose marriage was collapsing. She thought she and her husband had shielded their problems from their 11-year-old son, until the day she and her son watched an ABC Afterschool Special dealing with divorce.

The mother reported that "as the program went on, Andy kept inching closer and closer to me. I put my arm around him and suddenly realized his whole body was trembling. It was a terrible shock. I realized that he had known all along what was going on, was terrified, and that my husband and I should have discussed it with him a long time before. That program kicked off the most honest and important conversation I'd ever had with my child." We can all wonder what effect the program would have had on the child if his mother hadn't been there.

note transition support

That's an extreme example, but a revealing one. Let me offer a different one, from a study conducted at the University of Texas not long ago. An episode of a television program was shown in which playing hooky was involved. With one group of preschoolers, a teacher commented during the show that "that boy is in trouble. He did not go to school when he was supposed to. He was playing hooky, and that is bad." The other group didn't get that comment. Before and after the show, both groups were asked whether they thought playing hooky was all right. For the boys, the percentage of those who thought playing hooky was a bad idea increased 75 percent among those who heard the teacher's comment; it decreased among those who didn't. For the girls, the number improved 120 percent among those who heard the comment, and 80 percent among those who didn't.

statistics

assertion

Based on observations of this sort, the Texas study concluded that "parents are the single most important contributor to a child's development. Furthermore, while most parents believe they are in hopeless conflict with the ever-present television, the project's results indicate parents can directly and easily moderate the influence of television. The results indicate that

assertion
testimony

parents should not let the television become a surrogate parent. Instead, parents should watch television with their child and talk about the programs."

Problem

Eda LeShan put the same thought very succinctly: "No [television] program can seriously damage a child in any way if a concerned and loving adult shares the experience and uses it as an opportunity to talk about feelings."

Solution

ethos

So much for the problem. How is it to be solved? To begin with, I do not believe that parents are thoughtless, selfish creatures who have abandoned their children to the television set—any more than I believe that television is a vicious electronic monster programmed to corrupt the youth of America. I do think, though, that there are a good many parents who are still learning how to cope with the presence of the television set in their home, who—not knowing quite what to do about it—do nothing at all about it.

testimony

For that reason, we have tried to draw together from our outside consultants—people like Dr. Melvin Heller, an eminent child psychiatrist at Temple University, and the people at the Bank Street College of Education—a few suggestions for parents to help them deal with their children and their television set. They may sound a little obvious, but they can make a difference.

solutions
assertions

First suggestion: Know what your children watch. See the programs for yourself, and read about them as well. Not every program is suitable for every child of every age, especially late at night when we offer programs designed for more mature audiences. All the television networks provide advisory notices when the subject matter of a program may be unsuitable for younger viewers, but the final decision must rest with the parents, who know their children best. It is imperative that parents make those decisions actively, not by default. And it's useful, too, if children know the standards by which their parents select programs for viewing.

clarification

Second suggestion: Watch television with your children. No, this does not mean watch every program with your children; there's absolutely no harm in their watching television while you snatch an extra hour's sleep on Saturday morning. But do try to watch some of the things your children watch, in the morning and the afternoon as well as the evening. That is the only way to know how they react, as well as what they are reacting to.

clarification

Third suggestion: Comment on the things you see with your children. When you read stories to your children at bedtime, you probably comment on the things you are reading. Even the smallest remarks, such as "gee, that was scary, wasn't it?" can make a difference in the effect an episode has on your children.

clarification

Fourth Suggestion: Use your family television viewing as a basis for conversations. Many families find serious discussion difficult during their children's growing-up years; communication about personal feelings and *clarification*

experiences is sometimes almost nonexistent. But those feelings can often be unlocked and those experiences shared, if parents will use similar situations seen on television to initiate dialogue with their children. And there are also a number of educators who have devised games and other techniques by which parents can use television to further their children's education.

ethos

And, finally, a fifth suggestion which does not come from our consultants, but from me: Let us know what you think of the programs you watch with your children. It is an unfortunate truth that exceptional programs, for children as well as for adults, cost more than routine programs. We do not begrudge the cost of exceptional programs for children, any more than we begrudge the cost of covering a presidential election or the Olympic Games, but we need to know when our efforts succeed.

Conclusion

repetition of main points

Whether a child watches five hours of television a week, or 25, his viewing is an important part of his life. Knowing that imposes an awesome responsibility on all of us in the television industry, and we have committed ourselves in the strongest possible terms to live up to that responsibility. But the quality of our efforts can only be as good as the use to which they are put in the home. For parents who pay little or no attention to their children's television viewing, television is no more than an electronic babysitter, an informative and entertaining gadget whose value will vary from child to child in unpredictable—and sometimes undesirable—fashion. This we must try to avoid.

problem

solution

On the other hand, for parents who grasp firmly their share of the responsibility, who actively involve themselves in their children's viewing experience, television can be—and will be—a significant and constructive contributor to the growth of the generation of young people that will take over where we, their parents, leave off. That is the goal all of us should work toward. At ABC, we are doing everything we can to reach that goal, and we hope all of you will share this responsibility with us.[1]

---

[1] From *Vital Speeches* 43, 1 (15 October 1976), 24–26. Speech was delivered before the Rotary Club of Los Angeles, Los Angeles, California, 3 September 1976.

C

*Sample Student Outlines**

I. Introduction
   A. "Outside, the London nightlife is just beginning. Trafalgar Square is crammed with curious tourists, St. Martin's Lane bustling with anxious theatregoers. Inside, a lone woman makes a fateful decision. Is this what I've become? A thief? A scavenger? Heaven help me, I'm reduced to stealing food to live. Is this my curse for becoming the Spiderwoman?"
   B. Comic books are a part of every kid's and many adults' lives.
   C. Comic books are a part of the media in the United States.
      1. As a medium, comic books reflect some of society's attitudes and values.
      2. Three comic books, Red Sonja, Ms. Marvel, and Spiderwoman, reflect our notions about women.
II. Body
   A. The three comics are published by Marvel Comics, but each has its own history.

---

* These outlines were prepared by Debbie Smith of Southwest Texas State University and are reproduced with her permission.

      1. Red Sonja first appeared in 1975.
        a. The origin of Red Sonja is unclear.
        b. Red Sonja lives in the "Hyporian Age" in the distant past.
      2. Ms. Marvel was presented in January 1977.
        a. Ms. Marvel has amnesia and does not know her origins.
        b. Ms. Marvel is a superhero in the tradition of Superman.
      3. Spiderwoman is the newest of the female superheroes, with her first issue appearing in April 1978.
        a. Jessica Drew (Spiderwoman) is half-spider, half-woman from another world.
        b. Spiderwoman is attempting to learn to live on Earth.
   B. Violence is an aspect of all three comics, but each deals with violence in a different way.
      1. Red Sonja is a graphically violent comic book.
        a. The only weapons Red Sonja uses are her blade and sword.
        b. Red Sonja kills for self-preservation and pay.
      2. Ms. Marvel fights violence in true superhero tradition.
        a. The violence in the comic is beyond the comprehension of mortal man.
        b. Ms. Marvel involves fantasy violence where no one is killed or seriously injured since they are super villains.
      3. Spiderwoman uses violence only for justifiable reasons.
        a. Spiderwoman fights for the good of society.
        b. In the first issue, she does not use her full power even against a criminal.
   C. Each of the three comics makes a statement about women.
      1. Red Sonja is considered the "she-devil with a sword."
        a. The comic does not deal with women's rights specifically since it is set in the distant past.
        b. Red Sonja fights her battles alone.
      2. It is obvious from the title Ms. Marvel that this comic has been influenced by the women's movement.
        a. Ms. Marvel's slogan is, "This female fights back."
        b. Carol Danvers (Ms. Marvel's alter identity) is the editor of a feminist magazine.
      3. Spiderwoman is learning how to deal with her identity while living on earth.
        a. The comic says, "To know her is to fear her."
        b. Spiderwoman is searching for her own identity.
III. Conclusion
   A. The comics present strong, independent women.
   B. Solo female superheroes, while not very real, do suggest a growing awareness of women.
   C. But perhaps the comics say it best: "Like the Valkyre guards of Valhalla, she sweeps across the face of the earth, arms as widespread as an eagle's wings, eyes burning, jaw set, every

sinew throbbing with battle anticipation . . . her name is her own, but for want of something better we may call her Marvel, Ms. MARVEL, and because of her the world may never be the same."

I. Introduction
   A. A New York couple—Hans Kabel, seventy-eight, and his wife Emma, seventy-six—were assaulted twice in less than two months.
   B. The older people in our cities are viewed as victims or potential victims of criminals.
      1. Most are poor and unable to move.
      2. The elderly are living in fear in the cities.
II. Body
   A. Fear of a criminal attack is now the major concern of the elderly.
      1. New York City officials believe that there are thirty victims for every crime reported.
      2. Chicago demonstrates the plight of the elderly.
         a. On the South Side the elderly are faced with gangs of potential assailants on the first of the month, when Social Security checks arrive.
         b. On the West Side no one goes out after dark.
      3. Statistically, the elderly are not victimized more than any other age group, but the impact is more severe.
         a. Physical injury is greater for the elderly in an assault.
         b. Emotionally, elderly persons' lives are governed by fear of an attack.
   B. The assailants of the elderly are young juvenile criminals.
      1. The crimes are called "crib jobs" because it is like taking candy from a baby.
         a. The youngsters usually operate in teams.
         b. The elderly are young criminals' ideal victims.
      2. The rights of juveniles are so well protected that it is almost impossible for there to be repercussions.
         a. About 75 percent of the juveniles apprehended have been arrested before.
         b. Prosecutors are prevented from revealing a juvenile's arrest record.
      3. Judges do not know if they are dealing with a first offender or a longtime criminal.
      4. A juvenile who had beaten and robbed an eighty-two-year-old woman was released on a $500 bond even though he had sixty-seven previous arrests, one for murder.
      5. Violent crime against the elderly is increasing.
         a. In Seattle violent street crime has increased 18 percent.

        b. In New York two sixteen-year-olds raped a seventy-five-year-old woman.

        c. In Detroit an eighty-year-old woman was killed because she clung to her purse.

    C. Cities have started several programs to help solve the problem.

      1. Seattle engages policeman to serve as decoys.

      2. Chicago, Los Angeles, and New York have received federal funds to start self-help and victim assistance programs.

      3. San Francisco provides an escort service for the elderly.

      4. In Charleston, W. Va., elderly residents call in to the police department each day.

      5. In some cities high school students serve as escorts for the elderly.

    D. The best solution is to have more police patrolling the streets.

      1. New York City has done this in a few areas, and it has been very successful.

      2. It is the solution most often recommended by the elderly.

III. Conclusion

    A. Crimes against the elderly are significant and increasing.

    B. Solutions exist that can help solve the problem.

    C. Unfortunately there are also counterproductive solutions. The Kabels, the elderly couple mentioned at the beginning of the speech, used a counterproductive solution—dual suicide—saying they did not want to live in fear anymore.

  I. Introduction

    A. In 1960, chains and conglomerates controlled 30 percent of the nation's newspapers and 46 percent of the readership.

    B. In 1977, chains and conglomerates controlled 59 percent of the newspapers and 71 percent of the readership.

    C. There has been a growing concern about the increasing group ownership of American newspapers.

 II. Body

    A. Increasing chain ownership is not viewed as threatening by some people.

      1. Chain ownership saves newspapers.

        a. Small newspapers that are going under are bought by large chains.

        b. The chains have more money to invest in the newspapers to keep them in business.

      2. The chains are improving the quality of the newspapers they buy.

        a. The chains hire more staff for the newspapers.

        b. The chains add additional news services.

      3. Some of the leading newspapers in the country, such as the *Washington Post* and *Los Angeles Times*, are owned by conglomerates.

B. Chain ownership is perceived as destructive to the press in the United States.
   1. Chains are concerned with profits.
      a. Profits take precedence over quality.
      b. Concern with profits conflicts with serving the public interest.
   2. Competition is necessary for a good press.
      a. Without competition an inferior product can be produced without challenge.
      b. With chain ownership there is no competition.
   3. Chains do not improve the quality of the newspapers.
      a. Papers tend to stay mediocre if bought by a chain.
      b. Outstanding newspapers have never been created by chains.
C. Chain ownership threatens the free press.
   1. Chain ownership violates the intent of a strong, free press.
   2. Newspapers play a special role as sources of opinion and information that should not be controlled by a limited number of owners.

III. Conclusion
   A. Chain ownership has reached epidemic proportions.
   B. The trend is continuing at a fast rate.
   C. Something should be done to prevent domination of such an important source of public information as newspapers.

Glossary

Abstract Words used to represent feelings or thoughts that cannot be sensed directly.

Accenting Use of gestures such as nods, blinks, squints, and shrugs to help emphasize or punctuate spoken words.

Acceptance Speech A speech designed for the acceptance of an honor or award.

Accuracy Precise use of words.

Achieved Role Position in society which is earned by individual accomplishment.

Action Statement Describes what has been done, what is happening currently, or plans for the future.

Active Listening Form of listening in which the listener attempts to grasp facts and feelings and to step in and out of the shoes of the listener, and in which the listener wants to listen.

Advertising Method of persuasion concerned with influencing people to buy, or to continue to buy, a product.

Affect Display Body change that conveys internal emotional states.

After-Dinner Speech In general, a form of entertainment speech intended to make the audience feel relaxed and comfortable.

All-Channel Network Communication network in which all positions send and receive messages to and from all other positions.

Alternating Monologue Unproductive communication in which each person knows the other is speaking but does not listen openly to what is being said.

Ambiguity Language difficulty caused when one symbol (word) has several different meanings.

Ambiguous Feedback Response which gives no indication that the message has been received positively or negatively.

Analytic Stage Time when child learns that word symbols may consist of separate units and begins to experiment with their order.

Anecdote Brief story that relates to an important idea in a speech.

Animation Amount of expressiveness and interest evidenced when conversing with others.

Appraisal Interview Designed to get and

425

evaluate information about a worker's past performance and future potential.

Appreciative Listening Enjoyable, entertaining form of listening (e.g., concerts of poetry readings).

Appropriateness Use of language style that is adapted to the occasion, audience, type and purpose of the speech.

Articulation Process by which the voice is altered into recognizable speech sounds.

Ascribed Role Position in society based primarily on sex, age, kinship and other factors that are out of a person's control.

Assimilation Process of incorporating some aspect of the environment into the whole set of mental functionings in order to make sense out of what goes on around us. Also, the transformation of messages to fit personal attitudes and expectations.

Attention Screening of stimuli so that only a select few come into focus.

Attentiveness Sensitivity to others.

Attitude Learned tendency to react positively or negatively to an object or situation.

Attraction Positive attitude, movement toward, or liking between two people.

Audience Analysis The act of acquainting yourself with the audience before giving a speech.

Authoritarian Leader Individual who directs the group with goal-oriented behaviors and firm opinions about how to achieve group goals.

Avoiding Relationship disintegration stage in which one or both parties act as though the other person does not exist.

Award Presentation A speech designed for the presentation of an honor or award.

Babbling Stage Language development stage in which a baby makes all the sounds found in all languages of the world.

Balance Theory Tendency for individuals to strive for symmetry in attitudes, values, and beliefs.

Barrier Factor that causes incorrect meanings, or no meanings, to be communicated.

Belief Probability statements about the existence of things or statements about the relationships between an object and another quality or thing.

Biofeedback A form of external self-feedback used to control physiological processing.

Body Manipulator Movement originally associated with body functioning, but that has come to be used unconsciously and independently of bodily needs.

Body of a Speech Portion of the speech which elaborates and clarifies the main points for an audience.

Bonding Final stage of relationship development; usually signifies commitment through a formal contract.

Business Conference Small group within an organization which meets to disseminate information or develop solutions to current organizational problems.

Business Organization Designed to give the greatest benefits or profits to the owners.

Bypassing Situation in which people argue or reach an impasse when they are actually in agreement.

Casual Audience Small, heterogeneous group of people who gather at the same place for a short period of time.

Cause-and-Effect Pattern In a speech, a persuasive structure of organization which establishes a relationship between two events.

Centrality Degree to which group communication revolves around one person.

Chain Network Similar to the circle communication network except that the members at each end of the chain send messages to and receive messages from only one position.

Chain-of-Events Pattern Informative organizational structure based on the development of a series of steps, with each step dependent upon the previous one.

Change Agent One who is responsible for making policy and creating change.

Channel Means by which a message is communicated.

Chronological Pattern Informative pattern of organization which follows a subject through time.

Circle Network Communication network in which messages are sent to the left and right of a position, but not to other members in the group.

Circular Response Mutual feedback between speaker and audience which increases participation and strengthens the bonds between them.

Circumscribing Controlled disintegration stage with less total communication and expression of commitment.

Clarity The art of saying exactly what is meant, thus increasing audience comprehension.

Coercive Organization Uses force over members as a major means of control.

Cognitive Dissonance State of imbalance between pieces of knowledge and/or feelings that individuals try to resolve.

Cognitive Processing Storage, retrieval, sorting, and assimilation of information.

Cohesion Degree to which group members identify themselves as a team.

Commercial (Commonwealth) Organization Designed to serve public interests.

Communication Process that involves interdependent and interrelated elements working together to achieve a desired goal or outcome.

Communication Apprehension Anxiety associated with the process of communication.

Communicator Style The way one verbally and preverbally interacts to signal how literal meaning should be taken, interpreted, filtered, or understood.

Comparison-Contrast Defining a word, idea, or concept by pointing out similarities and/or differences between it and something with which the audience is already familiar.

Complementing Messages Nonverbal messages that complete or accent explanations and/or descriptions.

Complementary Relationship A relationship in which one person is more dominant and the other person is less so.

Compliance/Dynamism Factor related to source credibility that reflects the amount of real or implicit power a speaker is perceived to have.

Concerted Audience Collected group of individuals with an active purpose and mutual interest without separation of labor or strict organization of authority.

Conclusion of Speech Final portion of speech, which summarizes and reinforces the speaker's point of view.

Concrete Symbolizing objects or events that can be pointed to, touched, experienced, or felt.

Conflict Management Means by which two or more people settle disputes or conflicts.

Conformity Acceptance of a group's norms.

Connotation Meanings beyond the objective reference of a word (abstract meaning).

Constitutive Rule A rule which defines what a given act (or behavior) should "count as."

Contentiousness Argumentativeness or aggressiveness.

Context Circumstances that surround and give meaning to words and statements.

Control The dimension of interpersonal relationships which focuses on the distribution of power.

Conversational Listening Form of listening that takes place in interpersonal settings; implies the change of roles between the speaker and listener.

Coordinated Management of Meaning Theory of communication that focuses on how humans coordinate and manage meanings in everyday life.

Coordination Characteristic of organizations associated with the orderly, directed interaction of members via different communication channels.

Courteous Listening Restricted form of conversational listening; involves an obligation to listen.

Covert Stimuli External changes or actions received at the subconscious level.

Credibility Determination of whether or not a person is worthy of belief or trust.

Credibility-Centered Approach When a speaker comes to a public communication setting with the objective of demonstrating competence and trustworthiness.

Critical Listening Form of listening that involves analysis and evaluation.

Deceiving Nonverbal clues which suggest falsehood but do not reveal what information is being withheld or falsified.

Decode Act of interpreting a message.

Deductive Pattern Persuasive structure which applies a previously accepted generalization to a specific case.

Deductive Reasoning Moves from the general to the specific.

Defense Mechanism   Method of resolving anxiety produced by intrapersonal conflict.

Delivery   Physical and vocal elements of a speaker's presentation.

Demassification   Using channels of communication to reach highly specialized interest groups.

Democratic Leader   Individual who guides rather than directs the group, leaving most decision making to the group itself.

Demography   Statistical study of populations (age, sex, educational levels, etc.).

Denotation   Objective reference of a word (its factual, concrete meaning).

Description   Method of defining a word, idea, or concept.

Differentiating   Relationship state characterized by increased interpersonal distance.

Diffusion of Information   Manner in which the public learns about new events, products, and changes in policy, ideas, philosophies and so forth.

Directive Interview   Structured and planned interaction situation which is generally conducted by using a step-by-step outline or format of questions.

Discriminative Listening   Form of serious listening that emphasizes understanding and remembering.

Discussion Group   Group of three or more persons characterized by cooperation among members, face-to-face interaction, shared perceptions and verbal and nonverbal communication.

Division of Labor   Characteristic of organizations associated with departmental divisions.

Dogmatism   Personality trait characterized by a closed mind and a reluctance to accept new ideas and opinions.

Dominance   The tendency to take control in social interactions.

Downward Communication   Information messages directed to subordinates within an organization.

Dramatic Behaviors   Degree to which one dramatizes events, creating closeness with others.

Dyad   Two people in close physical contact.

Economy   Use of the right words in the most efficient manner.

Ego-Involvement   The degree to which a given message is important to you.

Emblem   Commonly recognized sign (usually a gesture) which communicates a message usually unrelated to an ongoing conversation.

Emotional Processing   Nonlogical response of an organism to a stimulus.

Emotional Self   Intrapersonal processing center associated with emotions.

Employment Interview   Situation in which employers and applicants attempt to get pertinent information before making hiring decisions.

Encode   Process of generating and creating a message to be sent to a receiver.

Ends-Justifies-Means Approach   When a speaker adopts the position that any available means of persuasion may be used as long as the result is honorable, just, or desirable.

Environmental Setting   A physical condition, such as noise or crowding, that affects listening behavior.

Equal Time Rule   Stations must give all political candidates the same amount of time under the same terms.

Esteem Needs   Human desire for dignity, achievement, competence, and status.

Ethos   Perception of the speaker by the audience (source credibility).

Eulogy   Farewell speech which marks someone's death.

Evaluating   Weighing evidence, sorting fact from opinion and determining the presence or absence of bias or prejudice in a message.

Evaluation Group   Uses information from the fact-finding group to determine the scope of a problem and the priorities in finding a solution.

Exit Interview   Situation designed to find out how an employee feels about the company, work environment, and job conditions after he or she has decided to leave the position.

Experimenting   The "do you know" period of interaction development.

Exploiter   Individual whose goal is personal gain or profit.

Extended Example   Illustration or story carried out to considerable length in order to clarify or emphasize a very important idea.

External Self-Feedback   Part of a person's

own message that is heard by the person.

External Stimuli   Stimuli that originate in the environment outside of the human body.

Extrinsic Motivation   Motivation that arises from an outside source (e.g., extra credit points).

Fact-Finding Group   Type of problem-solving group which gathers as much information as possible about a particular issue or problem.

Fairness Doctrine   All stations must provide time to discuss controversial issues and must encourage opposing viewpoints.

Farewell Speech   Expresses regret about leaving and thanks those left behind.

Fear-Arousing Appeal   Threat or scare tactic designed to persuade.

Feedback   Response to a verbal or nonverbal message by a receiver.

Feedforward   Anticipation of feedback from others.

Forewarning   Information of the speaker's intent given prior to the speech.

Formal Communication   Structured communication situation in which more attention is paid to both verbal and nonverbal messages.

Formal Communication Structures   Rules, regulations and procedures within an organization.

Formal Presentation   The most structured form of organizational communication, in which responsibility is placed on one person to create interests and motivation to listen.

Forum   Type of public discussion in which the audience actively participates in the discussion.

Functional Role   Role that aids the group in accomplishing its objectives by keeping the discussion on course.

Functional Theory of Interpersonal Communication   Theory that delineates three primary purposes of communication: linking, mentation, and regulation.

Gatekeeper   Individual or organization that controls or influences a mass communication message.

Gestalt   Viewing an object or event as ''a whole'' rather than looking at its individual components.

Gesture   Movement of the body that communicates messages to others.

Global Village   Theory that the world is smaller than before due to advances in mass communication.

Group   Any number of people with a common goal who interact with one another to accomplish the goal, recognize each other's existence, and see themselves as part of a group.

Habit   Repetitive behavior so automatic that a person is unaware of it.

Hearing   Physical act of receiving sounds.

Hierarchy of Human Needs   Five basic human drives, as described by Maslow. They include physiological, safety, love, esteem, and self-actualization needs.

Holophrastic Stage   Language development stage in which children use one word to mean a number of things or run together several words to signify one thought.

Homophily   Degree to which two interacting individuals are similar in characteristics such as beliefs, values, education, social level, and so on.

Hustler   Individual who is gifted at compromise and influences others through cleverness, wit, and charm.

Hypothetical Example   An event or incident that could possibly occur but that did not really happen.

Identification   An attempt to find security by forming a psychological bond with other persons or groups.

Illustration   Use of verbal examples or visual aids to help clarify information.

Illustrator   Body expression that accents or adds emphasis to a word or phrase, shows the direction of thought, points to an object or place, depicts spatial relationships, rhythms, or bodily actions, or demonstrates shape.

Imitative (Learned) Behavior   The belief that interaction with other human beings is necessary for language development.

Immediacy   Degree of liking or disliking for a person or task.

Impromptu Speech   Presentation made on the spot without any preparation.

Increasing Levels of Difficulty Pattern   Informative organizational structure used to present complex topics clearly and logically.

Inductive Pattern   Persuasive structure which presents several specific cases that serve as a basis for a generalization.

Inductive Reasoning   Moves from the specific to the general.

Informal Communication   Relaxed communication situations in which speakers are free to be themselves.

Informal Communication Structure   Interpersonal relations that develop among employees in addition to the formal communication structure.

Informal Network   Messages sent haphazardly within an organization (grapevine, rumor, etc.).

Initiating   Relationship development stage in which conscious and unconscious judgments are made about others.

Innateness Theory   Belief that evolution is responsible for the ability to produce and use language.

Instrumental Values   Beliefs that act as guides for daily behavior.

Insulation   Isolation of contradictory feelings and/or information.

Integrating   Relationship stage when two persons agree to meet each other's expectations.

Integration   Proposal of new alternatives and new methods of organization to resolve intragroup conflict.

Intellectual Self   Intrapersonal processing center associated with mental processes.

Intensifying   Relationship stage when steps are taken to strengthen the bond between two persons by asking for and reciprocating favors.

Intensity   Determines which stimuli individuals will attend to when bombarded by many different ones.

Intention Statement   Statement that lets others know the purposes and motives behind one's statements and actions.

Intentional Communication   Occurs when messages are sent with specific goals in mind.

Interaction   The sharing and communication of ideas and emotions with oneself or others.

Interaction with Empathy   Communication that involves deep understanding between the participants, feeling their pain and sharing their joy.

Interaction with Feedback   Communication situation in which there is give-and-take by both participants.

Interdependence   Characteristic of organizations associated with the effect of one department's performance on that of all other departments.

Interference   Any factor or barrier that negatively affects communication.

Intergroup Conflict   Interaction which often benefits a group by increasing goal-oriented activity and causing members to value their work more highly.

Intermediary   Messenger between the source and receiver.

Internal Self-Feedback   Messages picked up through bone conduction, nerve endings, or muscular movement.

Internal Stimuli   Stimuli that originate from within a human's body.

Interpersonal Communication   Informal, spontaneous, loosely organized exchange of messages between two or more people to achieve some goal.

Interpretive Statements   Statements that indicate a person's understanding of a situation.

Interview   Dyadic communication situation designed to get information for employers and applicants by asking and answering questions.

Intimacy   The degree to which two people can uniquely meet one another's needs.

Intimate Distance   Spatial zone of interaction stretching from actual contact (touching) to 18 inches.

Intragroup Conflict   Interaction which often destroys a group by reducing cohesion, decreasing productivity and causing members to discredit their achievements.

Intrapersonal Communication   The sending and receiving of messages within an individual.

Intrinsic Motivation   Motivation that arises from an internal source (e.g., desire to learn).

Introduction of a Speech   First portion of a speech, which captures the audience's attention and prepares them for the rest of the speech.

Kinesics   Study of body movement.

Labeling   Identifying an object, art, or person by name so that it may be referred to in communication.

Laissez-Faire Leader   Individual who offers the group no direction and gives advice only when the group asks for it.

Language   Communication of thoughts and emotions by means of a structured system of symbols (words).

Language Acquisition Device   Innate device in humans that helps them sort out language and understand grammatical rules.

Larynx (Voice Box)   Transforms vibrations of air to produce basic voice sounds.

Lateral (Horizontal) Communication   Information messages between peers at the same hierarchical level.

Latitude of Acceptance   The range of messages within which a given message is defined as acceptable for a receiver.

Latitude of Noncommitment   The range of messages within which a given message is defined as neutral for a receiver.

Latitude of Rejection   The range of messages within which a given message is defined as unacceptable for a receiver.

Leader   Any person who helps the group reach its goals.

Leadership   Behavior that helps the group reach its goals.

Leakage   Nonverbal behavior that implies that information is being given inadvertently.

Leveling   Minimizing or omitting information from a message.

Linking Function   The function of communication which allows a person to interact with his or her environment.

Listener   The person receiving the message.

Listener Feedback   Involves verbal and nonverbal responses to a message.

Listening   A process that involves hearing, attention, understanding, and remembering.

Lively Quality   Selection of words that leave a lasting impression.

Locus of Control   Degree to which we perceive reinforcement either as contingent upon our own efforts or actions (internal locus of control) or as a result of forces beyond our control and due to chance, fate, or some other external force (external locus of control).

Logos   Rational approach to persuasion based on logic and reasoning.

Long-Term Memory   Permanent storage of information for future reference.

Maintenance Rule   Functional role which is concerned with the feelings and emotional behavior of the group.

Manipulation   Method of dominating and controlling others, frequently through skillful use of verbal and nonverbal communications.

Manipulator   Individual who seeks control over people and events.

Mass Communication   Process by which messages are transmitted rapidly and inexpensively through some mechanical device to a large, diverse audience.

Maturity   Differential stages of personal growth and behavior patterns.

Memory   Storage of information that a person chooses to remember.

Mentation Function   The function of communication that allows humans to conceptualize, remember, plan, and evaluate.

Message   A sign or symbol which has meaning for both the sender and the receiver. The information to be communicated.

Mutual-Benefit Organization   Designed to give members the greatest benefits from participation.

Need for Love   Human need to give and receive affection, care, and concern.

Negative Feedback   Response which indicates that a receiver has misunderstood a message.

Network   Interconnected channels or lines of communication used in organizations to pass information from one person to another.

Networking   The process of developing and using contacts for information, advice, and moral support.

Non-Allness   Korzybski's law that states that a word cannot symbolize all of a thing.

Nondirective Interview   Planned interaction situation in which freedom is given to participants in terms of how they ask questions and give responses.

Non-Identity   Korzybski's law that states that a word is not the thing it represents.

Nonverbal Communication   Involves using symbols other than spoken or written words in the communication process.

Normative/Identification   Credibility factor that arises when a source is identified with a particular group that is important to the listener.

Normative Organization   Controls actions of members through compliance with social norms.

One-Down Message   A message that relinquishes control in a relationship.

One-Sided Presentation   Persuasive speech approach in which the speaker presents only the side of the issue he or she supports.

One-Up Message   A message that exerts control in a relationship.

Open (Public) Discussion   Group meeting conducted before an audience who listens and/or participates.

Openness   Willingness to establish interpersonal relationships.

Operational Definition   Defining or delineating a term by establishing the means by which it can/will be measured.

Opinion   Positive or negative reaction to or statement of an attitude.

Opinion Leader   Receiver of information from a change agent, who then disseminates it to the general public.

Oral Communication   Messages that are transmitted out loud from one person to another.

Organization   Collected group of individuals constructed and reconstructed to work for goals that could not be met by individuals acting alone.

Organizational Communication   Focuses on ways to analyze and improve managerial styles, work environments, leadership, flow of information, job satisfaction and productivity in formal organizations.

Organizational Structure   Characteristic of organizations associated with the systematic interaction of one department with another; reflected in formal rules of the organization.

Organized Audience   Group of listeners who are directed totally toward the speaker with strict labor and authority lines.

Overt Stimuli   Internal or external changes or actions received at the conscious level.

Panel   Type of open discussion in which a group of well-informed people exchange ideas before an audience.

Paralanguage   Variations in the voice which give clues about emotional states, sex, age, status, etc.

Passive Listening   The passive absorption of words or messages, with little personal involvement.

Passive (Partially Oriented) Audience   Captive listeners who have no choice but to listen to the speaker.

Pathos   Approach to persuasion which appeals to the emotions.

Personal Distance   Spatial zone of interactions from 1½ to 4 feet, used for casual interactions.

Personal Interview   Interaction conducted on a one-to-one basis with a person who has information or knowledge about the topic of your speech.

Persuasion   A deliberate attempt by one person to modify the attitudes, beliefs, or behavior of another person or group of people by transmitting a message.

Phonation   Process by which air is pushed through the vocal cords, which then vibrate to produce sound.

Physical Delivery   Various body movements that a speaker uses during a speech (gestures, eye contact, posture, etc.).

Physical Self   Self associated with internal organ functions, external movements, and body concept.

Physiological Needs   Human drive or need to satisfy the desire for food, water, shelter, and sex.

Physiological Processing Subconscious and conscious physiological responses to internal stimuli.

Pitch Highness or lowness of vocal tones.

Platform Situation in which the audience participates in the exchange of information.

Polarization Point at which the audience members recognize their role as listeners and accept someone else as a speaker.

Policymaking Group Makes changes or takes actions after the evaluation group offers its recommendations.

Positive Feedback Response which indicates that the receiver has understood a message.

Postural Adjustments Unconscious arrangement of the body to make it easier to receive stimuli.

Power Center Characteristic of organizations associated with locale of power.

Preciseness Degree of concern with accuracy, documentation and proof in informative interactions.

Prejudice Preformed judgments about a person, group, or thing.

Primacy Effect Arguments presented first in a speech tend to have persuasive effect.

Primary Group (Psyche Group) Collected group of individuals who function as a support system for its members.

Private (Closed) Discussion Group meeting held without an audience to listen or participate.

Problem-Solving Group Most often a private group which follows a logical, step-by-step procedure to find solutions to problems.

Problem-Solving Pattern/Problem-Solution Method Persuasive structure of organization based on a logical, step-by-step analysis of a particular problem.

Professional Individual whose goal is to help others reach their fullest potential, while being committed to his or her own job.

Progression Arrangement of ideas in a logical order in a speech outline.

Projection Attributing personal traits, motives, or behaviors to others.

Proxemics Study of how people react to the space around them, how they use it, and how their use of space communicates information.

Public Communication Usually a one-way process in which one person addresses a group in a lecture or public speech.

Public Distance Spatial zone of interaction from 12 to over 25 feet, used in formal addresses or lectures.

Public Relations Method of persuasion concerned with promoting an image.

Public Speaking Communication situation in which one speaker directs a message to an audience.

Qualification/Expertness Component of credibility operating when listeners perceive a source has enough training, ability, and experience to merit belief.

Quality Vocal variations such as harshness, breathiness, stridency, and smoothness of delivery.

Quality Circle A group of persons from three to ten in number who meet periodically to discuss and develop solutions to problems related to quality, productivity, or cost.

Rapport Development and maintenance of a positive relationship with an audience throughout a speech.

Rate Speed at which words are spoken.

Rationalization Attempt to justify personal failures or inadequacies.

Reaction Formation A defense mechanism by which an individual denies personally or socially unacceptable drives by reacting in the opposite direction.

Real Example An event or incident that actually happened.

Recall Reconstruction of information that has been stored.

Receiver Person who attends to the message of the communication process.

Recency Effect Arguments presented near the end of a speech tend to have persuasive effect.

Reception Process by which the body receives stimuli.

Receptor Adjustments Physical changes in sensory receptor organs to make it easier to receive stimuli.

Recognition Awareness of familiar information based on previous experience.

Reference Group   Group that gives a person a sense of identity and help in establishing personal attitudes and a value system.

Referent   Actual object as it exists in reality.

Regulative Rule   A rule which tells us how we should behave in a given situation.

Regulators   Body movements or expressions that control verbal communication.

Regulating Function   The function of communication which allows us to regulate our own and others' behaviors.

Relational Communication Theory   Theory that addresses interpersonal communication by examining the dimensions of relationships.

Remembering   Receiving and interpreting a message, and adding it to the mind's storage bank.

Repeating   Nonverbal behavior that conveys the same message as the verbal message.

Repetition   Means by which audience learning may be increased via the presentation of material in a recurring fashion.

Repression   Keeping thoughts and feelings beneath the conscious level.

Resonance   Variations in voice from a thin and quiet voice to a loud and booming voice. Also, movement of air through the mouth, nose, and throat which gives amplification and richness to the voice.

Responding   The completion of the communication process by the receiver through verbal and/or nonverbal feedback.

Résumé   Written summary of an individual's educational background, work experience, job objectives, interests, etc.

Retrieval   Bringing back into conscious awareness information which previously has been stored in the brain.

Reward Appeal   Persuasion that promises listeners personal gain or profit if they believe or behave in a desired manner.

Role   Behavior a person performs to meet the expectations of others in different social settings.

Role Shifting   Understanding one's own style of communication in order to adapt to the styles of others.

Safety Needs   Human need to feel secure, stable, and in control.

Safety/Trustworthiness   Factor related to credibility that operates when a source is believed to be telling the truth.

Selected Audience   Group of people collected together for a specific purpose.

Selective Perception   Screening out a large number of stimuli to permit an individual to attend to just a few.

Self-Actualization   Human need to reach one's fullest potential.

Self-Concept   A person's attitude about and view of the self.

Self-Disclosure   Process of revealing significant aspects of the self to others.

Self-Esteem   Enduring evaluation of the self.

Self-Feedback   Perception of a person's own nervous system via muscular movements as the person hears himself or herself speak.

Self-Fulfilling Prophecy   Positive or negative experiences which color the self-concept and create expectations that influence later behavior.

Self-Reflexiveness   Korzybski's law that states that a word can refer both to something in the real world and to itself.

Self-Serving Role   Counterproductive role which has a negative effect on a group's emotional climate as well as on its ability to reach its goal.

Semantic (Linguistic) Stereotyping   Assuming automatic relationships between linguistic styles and personal traits.

Semantics   Study of relationships between word symbols and their meanings.

Sense   Subjective feelings about a symbol (word).

Sensory Storage   Ability to hold some information for a fraction of a second after the stimulus disappears.

Series Transmission   Communication through a number of individuals who act first as receivers and then as transmitters of messages.

Serious Listening   Form of listening that calls for the structured, formal processing of information.

Service Organization   Designed to give the greatest benefits to clients.

Sex Role   Position that is ascribed, defined, and encouraged by each society's culture for males and females.

Sharpening   Magnifying some details of a message.

Short-Term Memory   Process by which data are analyzed, identified, and simplified to be conveniently stored and handled.

Simplicity   Principle that a speaker should keep the outline of a speech simple, with each line representing a single piece of information.

Situation Ethics   When a speaker takes the position that consideration must be given to the nature of each situation before determining the "best" or "most loving" thing to do.

Small Group Communication   Process involving three or more persons with a common goal and potential for interaction between members.

Social Distance   Spatial zone of interaction from 4 to 12 feet, used by people meeting for the first time or by people conducting business.

Social Facilitation   Influence of one audience member on another.

Social Judgment Theory   Theory associated with the means by which humans make judgments regarding social objects.

Social Listening   Form of listening that calls for less structured, more informal processing of information.

Social Roles   A person's duties, skills, and norms defined by ascribed and achieved roles.

Social Utility Approach   When a speaker determines which programs he or she should advocate based on perceptions of a particular group's needs.

Sort   Selection of the most relevant information from the brain's storehouse of knowledge.

Source   Initiator of the communication process.

Spatial Pattern   Informative organizational structure based on the relation of one part to others or to geographical progressions.

Speech of Acceptance (Award Presentation)   Presentation that focuses on the many ways a recipient qualifies for an award, or a method of saying thank-you.

Speech to Convince   Speech intended to get an audience to think, believe, or feel a certain way.

Speech to Entertain   Informal speech designed to bring the audience pleasure.

Speech to Inform   Designed to increase audience learning and comprehension.

Speech to Move an Audience to Action   Persuasive speech that seeks some form of action on the part of the audience.

Speech to Stimulate   Speech intended to reaffirm or strengthen preexisting beliefs or feelings.

Speech to Welcome   Presentation to a group, or to an individual, about to join an organization or attend a meeting.

Stagnating   Relationship disintegration stage in which all efforts to communicate are abandoned.

Statistic   A numerical fact or datum.

Stimuli   Elements that cause a reaction in one or more of a person's senses.

Stimulus-Response Interaction   Communication situation in which the speaker proceeds in a set manner, independent of responses made by the listener.

Style   Individual selection, organization, and use of language.

Substituting   Using nonverbal messages to take the place of words.

Substitution   Characteristic of organizations associated with role interchangeability.

Subordination   In a speech outline, subdivision of a main idea into subordinate points, each of which must be related to the preceding category.

Survey   Detailed gathering of information by questionnaire, observation, interview, etc.

Symbol   Word or nonverbal sign used to represent objects, ideas, and feelings to others.

Symbolic Process   Use of words as symbols to represent objects or concepts.

Symbolization   Visual form of coordination, subordination, and progression of a speech outline.

Symmetrical Relationship   A relationship in which partners often mirror each other's behavior.

Symposium   Form of public discussion in which a group of experts presents its views, one speaker at a time.

Task-Oriented Role   Functional role that is directly related to a group's goal.

Tempo   Rate of speech in a given amount of time.

Terminal Values   Beliefs which represent our ultimate aims in life and toward which we work.

Terminating   Final relationship disintegration stage, which may be either rapid or delayed.

Territoriality   Possessive desire or ownership reaction to the space and objects around us.

Testimony   Information derived from a direct witness to an event or from an expert in a particular field.

Thesis Statement   Sentence that presents the specific purpose of a speech.

Thinking-Speaking Time Differential   Listener's time to summarize and evaluate what has been said. (People think several times faster than others can talk.)

Threshold of Consciousness   Boundary between conscious and unconscious awareness of stimuli.

Tolerance of Ambiguity   Ability to accept poorly defined and unclear situations.

Topical Pattern   Informative organizational structure in which information is presented according to specific category or classification.

Trait   Quality that distinguishes one person from another.

Transition   Statement which smoothly connects one idea to the next.

Transmission   Process by which messages are sent from a source to a receiver.

Trust   The responsible acceptance of the control dimension in a relationship; includes both trusting and trustworthy behaviors.

Trustworthiness   Acceptance of an obligation not to exploit control in an interpersonal relationship.

Two-Sided Presentation   Persuasive speech approach in which the speaker presents both sides of an issue.

Understanding   Analyzing the meaning of perceived stimuli so that they make sense.

Unintentional Communication   Messages (usually nonverbal) that are sent without communicators being aware of them.

Unity Principle   Need that humans have to maintain a unified conceptual system.

Upward Communication   Information messages directed to superiors or those of higher status within an organization.

Utilitarian Organization   Controls members through wages, promotions, tenure, and rewards.

Vagueness   Caused by the relative meaning of words which need more precision in usage.

Values   Specific types of beliefs which form the core of our belief system.

Verbal Communication   Involves the use of symbols which have universal meanings for all involved in the communication process.

Visual Aid   Anything (other than the speaker) that is used to get a message across to an audience.

Vocal Delivery   Mechanics of vocalization, vocal characteristics, and pronunciation.

Vocal Quality   Timbre of voice, which distinguishes one voice from another.

Voice   Sounds or tones produced through phonation.

Volume   Intensity or loudness of speech sounds.

Welcoming Speech   A speech presented to a group or an individual, about to join an organization or attend a meeting or seminar.

Wheel Network   Two-way communication network with all communication directed to and from a centralized position.

Word   Structured system of symbols which when joined with other words creates language.

Written Communication   Primarily verbal messages conveyed in writing.

Y Network   Communication network in which the central position does not communicate with one of the members.

Bibliography

ABELE, A. (1986). Functions of gaze in social interaction: Communication and monitoring. *Journal of Nonverbal Behavior, 10*(2), 83–101.

ANDERSON, E. (1981). Language and success. *College English, 43*(8), 807–12.

ANDERSON, V. A. (1977). *Training the speaking voice* (3d ed.). New York: Oxford University Press.

APPLBAUM, R. L., & ANATOL, K. W. (1974). *Strategies for persuasive communication*. Columbus, Ohio: Charles E. Merrill.

ARGYLE, M., & FURNHAM, A. (1983). Sources of satisfaction and conflict in long-term relationships. *Journal of Marriage and the Family, 45*, 481–93.

ARNOLD, V. D. (1983). Harvesting your employee grapevine. *Management World, 12*(6), 25–28, 37.

ATKIN, C. (1983). Effects of realistic TV violence vs. fictional violence on aggression. *Journalism Quarterly, 60*(4), 615–21.

AYABE, H. I., FREESE, A. R., KIM, K., ARAKAKI, M., & KAMEOKA, K. Y. (1983). Feedback and locus of control. *Journal of Genetic Psychology, 143*, 141–42.

BAIRD, J. E. (1977). *The dynamics of organizational communication*. New York: Harper & Row, Pub.

BALES, R. F. (1970). *Personality and interpersonal behavior*. New York: Holt, Rinehart & Winston.

BALES, R. F., & COHEN, S. P. (1979). *SYMLOG: A system for the multiple level observation of groups*. New York: The Free Press.

BANK, S. C., & POYTHRESS, N. G. (1982). The elements of persuasion in expert testimony. *Journal of Psychiatry & Law, 10*(2), 173–204.

BARKER, L. L., & EDWARDS, R. (1980). *Intrapersonal communication*. Dubuque, Iowa: Gorsuch-Scarisbrick.

BARKER, L. L., WAHLERS, K. J., WATSON, K. W., & KIBLER, R. J. (1987). *Groups in process: An introduction to small group communication* (3d ed.). Englewood Cliffs, N.J.: Prentice-Hall.

BAROL, B. (5 August 1985).   He's on fire. *Newsweek*, 48–54.

BAXTER, L. A., & BULLIS, C. (1986).   Turning points in developing romantic relationships. *Human Communication Research*, *12*(4), 469–93.

BAXTER, A., & WARD, J. M. (November 1973).   *An exploratory investigation of diffused point arrival time and source credibility*. Paper presented at the meeting of the Western Speech Communication Association.

BEATTY, M. (1986).   Communication apprehension and general anxiety. *Journal of Social Behavior and Personality*, *1*(2), 209–12.

BEDNAR, D. A. (1982).   Relationships between communicator style and managerial performance in complex organizations: A field study. *The Journal of Business Communication*, *19*(4), 51–76.

BEHNKE, R. R., SAWYER, C. R., & KING, P. E. (1987).   The communication of public speaking anxiety. *Communication Education*, *36*, 139.

BENOY, J. W. (1982).   The credibility of physically attractive communicators: A review. *Journal of Advertising*, *11*, 15–24.

BLACK, E. L., & MARTIN, G. L. (1980).   A component analysis of public speaking behaviors across individuals and behavioral categories. *Communication Education*, *29*, 273–82.

BLACK, J. (1970).   *How to get results from interviewing*. New York: McGraw-Hill.

BLASS, T., & SCHWARCZ, P. D. (1982).   The relative importance of four determinants of attraction. *Journal of Social Psychology*, *117*, 145–46.

BODAKEN, E. M., LASHBROOK, W. B., & CHAMPAGNE, M. (1971).   Proana 5: A computerized technique for the analysis of small group interaction. *Western Speech*, *25*, 112–15.

BONN, H., & UNGUVAIT, D. F. (1982).   *Mass media II*. (3d ed.). New York: Longman.

BOOTH-BUTTERFIELD, M. (1984).   She hears . . . he hears: What they hear and why. *Personnel Journal*, *63*, 36–42.

BOSTROM, R. N. (1983).   *Persuasion*. Englewood Cliffs, N.J.: Prentice-Hall.

BRADLEY, B. E. (1988).   *Fundamentals of speech communication: The credibility of ideas* (5th ed.). Dubuque, Iowa: Wm. C. Brown.

BRILHART, J. K. (1986).   *Effective group discussion*. Dubuque, Iowa: Wm. C. Brown.

BRODER, S. N. (1982).   Liking, own disclosure, and partner disclosure in female roommates. *Journal of Social Psychology*, *117*, 303–304.

CALTABIANO, M. L., & SMITHSON, M. (1983).   Variables affecting the perception of self-disclosure appropriateness. *Journal of Social Psychology*, *120*, 119–28.

CELANO, J., & SALZMAN, J. (1988).   *Career-Tracking: 26 Success Shortcuts to the Top*. New York: Simon & Schuster.

CHENGHUAN, W., & SHAFFER, D. R. (1987).   Susceptibility to persuasive appeals as a function of source credibility and prior experience with the attitude object. *Journal of Personality and Social Psychology*, *52*(4), 677–88.

CLARK, A. J. (1974).   An exploratory study of order effect in persuasive communication. *Southern Speech Communication Journal*, *39*, 322–32.

CODY, M. J., & O'HAIR, H. D. (1983).   Nonverbal communication and deception: Differences in deception cues due to gender and communication dominance. *Communication Monographs*, *50*, 175–92.

CUMMINGS, H. W., LONG, L., & LEWIS, M. (1987).   *Managing communication in organizations: An introduction* (2nd ed). Dubuque, Iowa: Gorsuch-Scarisbrick.

DAMHORST, M. L., & PINAIRE REED, J. A. (1986).   Clothing color value and facial expression: Effects on evaluations of female job applicants. *Social Behavior and Personality*, *14*(1), 89–98.

DANCE, F. E. X., & LARSON, C. (1976).   *The functions of human communication*. New York: Holt, Rinehart & Winston.

D'APRIX, R. (1982).   The oldest (and best) way to communicate with employees. *Harvard Business Review*, *60*(5), 30–32.

DAVIS, T. R. V. (1984).   The influence of the physical environment in offices. *Academy of Management Review*, *9*(2), 271–83.

DEWEY, J. (1933).   *How we think*. Boston: Heath.

DEWINE, S., & CASBOLT, D. (1983).   Networking: External communication systems for female organizational members. *The Journal of Business Communication*, *20*(2), 57–67.

DOVIDIO, J. F., & ELLYSON, S. L. (1982).   Decoding visual dominance: Attributions of power based on relative percentages of looking while speaking and looking while listening. *Social Psychology Quarterly*, *45*(2), 106–13.

EISENBERG, E. M., & WITTEN, M. G. (1987). Reconsidering openness in organizational communication. *Academy of Management Review*, *12*(3), 418–26.

EKMAN, P. (1980). Three classes of nonverbal behavior. In W. von Raffler-Engle (ed.), *Aspects of nonverbal communication* (96). Lisse: Swets and Zeitlinger, B. V.

EKMAN, P., & FRIESEN, W. V. (1969). The repertoire of non-verbal behavior: Categories, origins, usage, and coding. *Semiotica*, *1*(1), 49–98.

EKMAN, P., & FRIESEN, W. V. (1975). *Unmasking the face*. Englewood Cliffs, N.J.: Prentice-Hall.

EKMAN, P., ROPER, G., & HAGER, J. (1980). Deliberate facial movement. *Child Development*, *51*, 886–91.

ELLIOTT, S. (8 March 1989). Whittle's approach riles rivals. *USA Today*, B1.

ELSEA, J. G. (1985). Strategies for effective presentations. *Personnel Journal*, *64*, 9, 31–32.

EPSTEIN, S. (1981). The unity principle versus the reality and pleasure principles, or the tale of the scorpion and the frog. In M. D. Lynch, A. A. Norman-Hebeisen, and K. Gergen (eds.), *Self-concept: Advances in theory and research*. Cambridge: Ballinger.

ETZIONI, A. (1967). *A comparative analysis of complex organizations*. New York: Free Press.

FARNSWORTH, T. (1983). Test your leadership skills. In J. E. Adair, The building blocks of good leadership. *International Management*, *38*, 47, 50, 55, 77.

FELDMAN, D. C. (1984). The development and enforcement of group norms. *Academy of Management Review*, *9*, 47–53.

FESTINGER, L. (1963). *A theory of cognitive dissonance*. Stanford, Calif.: Stanford University Press.

FIELD, H. S., & HOLLEY, W. H. (1976). Résumé preparation: An empirical study of personnel managers' perceptions. *The Vocational Guidance Quarterly* (March), 234.

FISHER, B. A. (1980). *Small group decision making: Communication and the group process* (2d ed.). New York: McGraw-Hill.

FORGAS, J. P. (1983). Language, goals and situations. *Journal of Language and Social Psychology*, *2*, 267–93.

FRANK, T., & RAY, D. (1979). *Basic business and professional speech*. Englewood Cliffs, N.J.: Prentice-Hall.

FUKADA, H. (1986). Psychological processes mediating persuasion-inhibiting effect of forewarning in fear-arousing communication. *Psychological Reports*, *58*, 87–90.

GALST, J. P. (1980). Television food commercials and pro-nutritional public service announcements as determinants of your children's snack choices. *Child Development*, *51*, 935–38.

GAMBLE, T. K., & GAMBLE, M. (1982). *Contacts: Communicating interpersonally*. New York: Random House.

GEIER, J. G. (1967). A trait approach to the study of leadership in small groups. *Journal of Communication*, *17*(4), 316–23.

GELLES-COLE, S. (Ed.). (1985). *Letitia Baldrige's complete guide to executive manners*. New York: Rawson Associates.

GERVASIO, A. H., PEPINSKY, H. B., & SCHWEBEL, A. I. (1983). Stylistic complexity and verb usage in assertive and passive speech. *Journal of Counseling Psychology*, *30*(4), 546–56.

GIAMMATEO, M., & GIAMMATEO, D. (1981). *Forces on leadership*. Reston, VA: National Association of Secondary School Principals.

GREENBERG, B. S. (1964). Diffusion of news about the Kennedy assassination. *Public Opinion Quarterly*, *28*, 225–32.

HAGAFORS, R., & BREHMER, B. (1983). Does having to justify one's judgments change the nature of the judgment process? *Organizational Behavior and Human Performance*, *31*, 223–32.

HALATIN, T. (1982). Upward communication. *Supervisory Management*, *27*(10), 7–10.

HAN, PYUNG. (1983). The informal organization you've got to live with. *Supervisory Management*, *28*, 25–28.

HASKINS, J. B., & MILLER, M. M. (1984). The effects of bad news and good news on a newspaper's image. *Journalism Quarterly*, *61*(1), 3–13, 65.

HAZLETON, V., CUPACH, W. R., & LISKA, J. (1986). Message style: An investigation of the perceived characteristics of persuasive messages. *Journal of Social Behavior and Personality*, *1*(4), 565–74.

HEIDER, F. (1946). Attitudes and cognitive organization. *Journal of Psychology*, *21*, 107–12.

HESS, H. (1965).   Attitude and pupil size. *Scientific American, 212*(4), 54.

HOLLINGWORTH, H. L. (1935).   *The psychology of the audience.* New York: American Book.

HUESMANN, L. R., & MALAMUTH, N. M. (1986).   Media violence and antisocial behavior: An overview. *Journal of Social Issues, 42*(3), 1–6.

HURT, T., SCOTT, M. D., & McCROSKEY, J. C. (1978).   *Communication in the classroom.* Reading, Mass.: Addison-Wesley.

JANIS, I. L. (1982).   *Victims of groupthink: A psychological study of foreign policy decisions and fiascos* (2d ed.). Boston: Houghton Mifflin.

KATZ, T. (1984 February).   Hostile audience. Proceed with caution. *Training and Development Journal, 82.*

KIPNIS, D., SCHMIDT, S., PRICE, K., & STITT, C. (1981).   Why do I like thee: Is it your performance or my orders? *Journal of Applied Psychology, 66,* 328.

KLEINKE, C. L. (1986).   Gaze and eye contact: A research review. *Psychological Bulletin, 100*(1), 78–100.

KNAPP, M. L. (1984).   *Interpersonal communication and human relationships.* Boston: Allyn & Bacon.

KOEHLER, J. W., ANATOL, K. W. E., & APPLBAUM, R. L. (1981).   *Organizational communication: Behavioral perspectives.* New York: Holt, Rinehart & Winston.

KORNBLUM, A. (December 1984).   Stage fright in the executive suite. *Nation's Business, 72,* 56.

LASS, N. J., THOMPSON, J. N., & KIMMEL, P. A. (1982).   Identification of speakers' occupations. *Perceptual and Motor Skills, 54,* 93–94.

LEWIN, K. (1947).   Frontiers in group dynamics. *Human Relations, 1,* 5–41.

LISKA, J., MECHLING, E. W., & STATHAS, S. (1981).   Differences in subjects' perceptions of gender and believability between users of deferential and nondeferential language. *Communication Quarterly, 29,* 40–48.

LITTLEJOHN, S. W. (1989).   *Theories of human communication* (3d ed.). Belmont, Calif.: Wadsworth.

LUCAS, S. E. (1983).   *The art of public speaking.* New York: Random House.

LUFT, J. (1984).   *Of human interaction.* Palo Alto, Calif.: National Press Books.

LUFT, J. (1984).   *Group processes: Introduction to group dynamics* (3d ed.). Palo Alto, Calif.: Mayfield Publishing Company.

MacLACHLAN, J. (1983–84).   Making a message memorable and persuasive. *Journal of Advertising Research, 23,*(6) 51–59.

McAFEE, L. J., FOX, R. A., & HICKS, R. A. (1982).   Attributions of male college students to variations in facial features in the line drawing of a woman's face. *Bulletin of the Psychonomic Society, 19*(3), 143–44.

McCARTNEY, K. (1984).   Effect of quality of day care environment on children's language development. *Developmental Psychology, 20*(2), 244–60.

McCLELLAND, V. (1987).   Mixed signals breed mistrust. *Personnel Journal, 66*(3), 26.

McKINNEY, M. E., GATCHEL, R. J., & PAULUS, P. B. (1983).   The effects of audience size on high and low speech-anxious subjects during an actual speaking task. *Basic & Applied Social Psychology, 4,* 73–87.

McPHEE, R. D. (1985).   Formal structure and organizational communication. In R. D. McPhee and P. K. Tompkins (eds.), *Organizational communication: Traditional themes and new directions.* Beverly Hills, Calif.: Sage.

McPHEE, R. D. (in press).   Organizational communication: A structurational exemplar. In B. Dervin, L. Grossberg, B. O'Keefe, and E. Wartella (Eds.), *Re-thinking communication: Vol. 2, Paradigm exemplars.* Beverly Hills, Calif.: Sage.

MARKIEWICZ, D. (1972).   *The effects of humor on persuasion.* Unpublished doctoral dissertation, Ohio State University, Columbus.

MASLOW, A. H. (1965).   *Eupsychian management: A journal.* Homewood, Ill.: Richard D. Irwin & Dorsey Press.

MASLOW, A. H. (1970).   *Motivation and Personality* (2d ed.). New York: Harper & Row.

MASLOW, A. H., & MINTZ, N. L. (1956).   Effects of esthetic surroundings. I. Initial effects of three esthetic conditions upon perceiving "energy" and "well-being" in faces. *Journal of Psychology, 41,* 247–54.

MEHRABIAN, A. (1981).   *Silent messages* (2d ed.). Belmont, Calif.: Wadsworth.

MERRITT, S. (1984).   Negative political advertising: Some empirical findings. *Journal of Advertising, 13*(3), 27–38.

MILLAR, F. E., & ROGERS, L. E. (1976).   A relational approach to interpersonal communication. In G. Miller (ed.), *Explorations in interpersonal communication*. Beverly Hills, Calif.: Sage.

MILLARD, R. J., & STIMPSON, D. V. (1980).   Enjoyment and productivity as a function of classroom seating location. *Perceptual Motor Skills, 50,* 439–44.

MILLER, G. R. (1978).   The current status of theory and research in interpersonal communication. *Human Communication Research, 4*(2), 164–78.

MILLS, G. E. (1972).   *Putting a message together.* Indianapolis, Ind.: Bobbs-Merrill.

MOLLOY, J. T. (1985).   *Molloy's live for success.* New York: Bantam Books.

MONTGOMERY, B. M., & NORTON, R. W. (1981).   Sex differences and similarities in communicator style. *Communication Monographs, 48*(2), 121–32.

MULAC, A., WIEMANN, J. M., WIDENMANN, S. J., & GIBSON, T. W. (1988).   Male/female language differences and effects in same-sex and mixed-sex dyads: The gender-linked language effect. *Communication Monographs, 55*(4), 315–35.

NIIT, T., & VALSINER, J. (1977).   Recognition of facial expressions: An experimental investigation of Ekman's model. *Tartu Riikliku Ulikooli Toimetised: Trudy po Psikhologii, 429,* 85–107.

O'DONNELL, V., & KABLE, J. (1982) *Persuasion: An interactive-dependency approach.* New York: Random House.

OUSPENSKY, P. D. (1974). *The psychology of man's possible evolution* (2nd ed.). New York: Vintage Books.

PARKS, M. (1977).   Relational communication: Theory and research. *Human Communication Research, 3,* 372–81.

PEARCE, W. B., & CRONEN, V. (1980).   *Communication: action and meaning.* New York: Praeger.

PEARCE, W. B., & CONKLIN, F. (1971).   Nonverbal vocalic communication and perceptions of a speaker. *Speech Monographs, 38,* 235–41.

PEARL, D. (1984).   Violence and aggression. *Society, 21,* 17–22.

PEMBER, D. R. (1983).   *Mass media in America* (3d ed.). Chicago: Science Research Associates.

PETERS, T. (1987).   *Thriving on chaos: Handbook for a management revolution.* New York: Alfred A. Knopf.

PORTER, R. E. (1976).   An overview of intercultural communication. In L. A. Samovar and R. E. Porter (eds.), *Intercultural communication: A reader.* Belmont, Calif.: Wadsworth.

PRIOR, D. W., GOODYEAR, R. K., & HOLEN, M. C. (1983).   EMG biofeedback training of Type A and Type B behavior pattern subjects. *Journal of Counseling Psychology, 30*(3), 316–22.

Public speaking requires effective preparation. (April 1984).   *The CPA Journal, 54*(4), 76–78.

ROE, K. V., MCCLURE, A., & ROE, A. (1982).   Vocal interaction at 3 months and cognitive skills at 12 years. *Developmental Psychology, 18,* 15–16.

ROKEACH, M. (1969).   *Beliefs, attitudes and values: A theory of organization and change.* San Francisco: Jossey-Bass.

ROKEACH, M. (1973).   *The nature of human values.* New York: Free Press.

ROSENFELD, L. R. (1977).   Setting the stage for learning. *Theory into Practice, 16,* 167–73.

RULE, B. G., & FERGUSON, T. J. (1986).   The effects of media violence on attitudes, emotions, and cognitions. *Journal of Social Issues, 42*(3), 29–50.

RUST, R. T., BAJAJ, M., & HALEY, G. (1984).   Efficient and inefficient media for political campaign advertising. *Journal of Advertising, 13*(3), 45–49.

SALTER, C. A., & SALTER, C. D. (1982).   Automobile color as a predictor of driving behavior. *Perceptual and Motor Skills, 55,* 383–86.

SCHEIN, V. E. (1985).   Organizational realities: The politics of change. *Training and Development Journal, 39,* 37–41.

SCHERMERHORN, J. R., JR., HUNT, J. G., & OSBORN, R. N. (1985).   *Managing organizational behavior.* New York: John Wiley.

SCHULTZ, B., & ANDERSON, J. (1984).   Training in the management of conflict: A communication theory perspective. *Small Group Behavior, 15,* 333–48.

SHERIF, M. (1967).   *Social interaction-process and products.* Chicago: Aldine.

SHERIF, M., & HOVLAND, C. I. (1961). *Social judgment.* New Haven: Yale University Press.

SIMMS, R. B. (1986). But teacher, you went right on. *Childhood Education, 62*(4), 269–71.

SMITH, A. P. (1977). How to make sure your next résumé isn't an obituary. *Training* (May), 63–66.

SPARKS, G. G. (1986). Developmental differences in children's reports of fear induced by the mass media. *Child Study Journal,* 16(1), 55.

STALEY, C. M. (1982). Sex-related differences in the style of children's language. *Journal of Psycholinguistic Research,* 11, 141–58.

STANAT, K. W., & REARDON, P. (1977). *Job hunting secrets and tactics.* Milwaukee: Westwind Press.

STEIL, L. K., BARKER, L. L., & WATSON, K. W. (1983). *Effective listening:* Key to your success. Reading, Mass.: Addison-Wesley.

STEWART, C. J., & CASH, W. B. (1983). *Interviewing: Principles and practices* (3d ed.). Dubuque: Wm. C. Brown.

STREET, R. L., JR., BRADY, R. M., & LEE, R. (1984 Winter). Evaluative responses to communicators: The effects of speech rate, sex, and interaction context. *The Western Journal of Speech Communication,* 48, 14–27.

SYPHER, B. D., & ZORN, T. E., JR. (1986). Communication-related abilities and upward mobility: A longitudinal investigation. *Human Communication Research,* 12(3), 420–31.

TAYLOR, M. S., & WALTHER, F. T. (1981). *The relationship of feedback dimensions to work attitudes and behavior: Process and practical implications.* Paper presented at the meeting of the Midwestern Academy of Management.

TOFFLER, A. (1981). *The new wave.* New York: Bantam Books.

VANLEAR, C. A., JR. (1987). The formation of social relationships: A longitudinal study of social penetration. *Human Communication Research,* 13(3), 299–322.

VERDERBER, R. F. (1987). *Communicate.* Belmont, Calif.: Wadsworth.

VOGEL, R. A., & BROOKS, W. D. (1977). *Business communication.* Menlo Park, Calif.: Cummings.

WAGNER, J. (1983). Media do make a difference: The differential impact of mass media in the 1976 Presidential race. *American Journal of Political Science, 27*(3), 407–30.

WALTHER, F., & TAYLOR, S. (1983). An active feedback program can spark performance. *Personnel Administrator,* 28, 107, 109, 111, 147, 149.

WARING, E. M., & CHASE, G. J. (1983). Marital intimacy and self-disclosure. *Journal of Clinical Psychology, 39*(2), 183–90.

WATSON, M., PETTINGALE, K. W., & GOLDSTEIN, D. (1983). Effects of a fear appeal on arousal, self-reported anxiety, and attitudes toward smoking. *Psychological Reports, 52,* 139–46.

WEISS, W., & STEENBACK, S. (1965). The influence of communication effectiveness of explicitly urging action and policy consequences. *Journal of Experimental Social Psychology, 1,* 396–406.

WELCH, M. S. (1980). *Networking: The great new way for women to get ahead.* New York: Harcourt Brace Jovanovich.

WEXLER, P. J. (1982). Explanation by example. *Language and Communication, 2*(3), 303–309.

What TV does to kids. (21 February 1977), *Newsweek,* 63–70.

WHEELESS, L. R., WHEELESS, V. E., & BAUS, R. (1984). Sexual communication, communication satisfaction, and solidarity in the developmental stages of intimate relationships. *Western Journal of Speech Communication,* 48, 217–30.

WHETMORE, E. J. (1982). *Mediamerica* (2d ed.). Belmont, Calif.: Wadsworth.

WIGGERS, M. (1982). Judgments of facial expressions of emotion predicted from facial behavior. *Journal of Nonverbal Behavior,* 7(2), 101–15.

WISEMAN, G., & BARKER, L. L. (1967). *A workbook for speech/interpersonal communication.* San Francisco: Chandler.

WOOLF, V. (1948). *Night and day.* New York: Harcourt Brace Jovanovich.

WYSE, L. (1987). *Company Manners: An insider tells how to succeed in the real world of corporate protocol and power politics.* New York: McGraw-Hill.

ZERPA, J. J., & SMELTZER, L. R. (1984). Active listening for managers. *Credit and Financial Management, 86*(2), 21, 24.

Photo Credits

Index